Most
Favored
Nation

Most Favored Nation

The Republican

Revisionists and

U.S. Tariff Policy,

1897–1912

Paul Wolman

The
University of
North Carolina
Press

Chapel Hill
& London

The paper in this book meets the guidelines for permanence
and durability of the Committee on Production Guidelines for
Book Longevity of the Council on Library Resources.

96   95   94   93   92   5   4   3   2   1

Library of Congress Cataloging-in-Publication Data
Wolman, Paul.
    Most favored nation : the Republican revisionists and
  U.S. tariff policy, 1897–1912 / by Paul Wolman.
      p. cm.
    Includes bibliographical references and index.
    ISBN 0-8078-2022-9 (cloth : alk. paper)
    1. Tariff—United States—History.   2. United States—
  Commercial policy—History.   I. Title.
HF1756.W65   1992
382'.7'0973—dc20   91-50792
                                               CIP

For my parents

Contents

Acknowledgments

The wise counsel of many people helped shape this book. Carl P. Parrini's tolerant skepticism of my work and his own reflective scholarship were important motivators. Other faculty at Northern Illinois University who offered good guidance—not always heeded—included Mary O. Furner, J. Carroll Moody, Otto H. Olsen, W. Bruce Lincoln, Margaret George, and Albert Resis.

I particularly want to thank Martin J. Sklar, now of Bucknell University, who first challenged me to engage in a criticism unafraid of its findings and whose advice, to avoid "turning differing points of view into warring schools of thought," I continue to value.

The balanced and insightful comments of Thomas J. McCormick of the University of Wisconsin and Walter LaFeber of Cornell University were of great help in focusing my attention on developing key themes in the book.

For commentary, criticism, and comradeship of the best kind, I thank James Livingston, William B. Burr, and Lawrence H. Lynn. For helping in various ways to improve the book's focus, I also wish to acknowledge Barry Rigby, Loomis Mayfield, and Steven Fine.

Of great importance to me over the past fifteen or so years have been the comments, suggestions, arguments, and exhortations of the "usual suspects"—Bill Burr, Jim Livingston, Larry Lynn, Steve Rosswurm, Keith Haynes, Richard Schneirov, Helen Callahan, Bill Nicklas, and Bob Nicklas.

For prodigious patience, steadfast friendship, and enlightened encouragement I am especially grateful to Richard D. Greenberg, Gary N. Goldsmith, Paul L. Schechter, Elisabeth A. Weston, Thomas B. Rainey, David and Jean Farkas, Frank Carr, and Jim and Helen Shirley.

The Graduate School of Northern Illinois University provided the Provost's Fellowship, which was of material assistance in the initial year of my research. I also would like to thank the staffs of the research facilities at the National Archives and at the Library of Congress, particularly Bruce Martin, for providing me with office space and that most valuable, but of course nonfungible, commodity, the stack pass, and Chuck Kelly, who facilitated access to the manuscript collections. Larry Lynn, the "Wizard of DOS," also provided indispensable technical and computer assistance.

The careful reading of the manuscript and insightful comments of the reviewers for the University of North Carolina Press were instrumental in the development of this work. I would also like to acknowledge the patient and intelligent guidance of Lewis Bateman, executive editor at the press, and the help of Ron Maner, assistant managing editor, and Brian R. MacDonald, copyeditor. I also thank proofreader Katrina Van Duyn.

Finally, for sharing his interest, insight, and wisdom, I am most grateful to my brother, Stephen Wolman. For enduring many of the difficulties and, I hope, sharing some of the satisfaction of the making of this work, I am grateful to Diane Wolman and our daughter, Rachel E. Wolman. Finally, the support of my parents, Bernice and Ted Wolman, has been of incalculable value; I suspect that this work reflects more of their influence than any of us know.

Introduction

This study explores the movement for tariff revision in the early twentieth century and examines its efforts to reshape U.S. commercial policy. The emphasis on revisionism as a "movement" emerged from the hypotheses that the tariff politics of this period are best understood as spanning more traditional groupings such as political parties and that revisionism encompassed a coherent array of business groups, policymakers, and intellectuals that had a distinctive and purposive influence on policy. In fact, although revisionism took its predominant tone from Republicans, who then dominated executive and legislative politics, it drew strength and substance from conservative, largely nonagrarian Democrats and from Progressives as well.[1]

As a group, revisionists sought to direct the United States away from high protectionism, but they did not advocate free trade. Instead, they sought substantial and systematic reduction—not elimination—of U.S. tariffs. Initially they worked to expand the number and scope of the United States' bilateral reciprocity treaties, particularly with European nations. These efforts, although instrumental in defining revisionism politically and ideologically, foundered on resistance from protectionists and on the requirement that treaties had to be ratified by a two-thirds majority of the Senate. Revisionists then regrouped, advocating a more comprehensive restructuring that would lower tariffs by simple congressional majority, without treaty making. The new structure, essentially an analog of European or unconditional most-favored-nation practice, proposed a dual-tariff system: uniform, low tariffs for all nations that cooperated with U.S. goals in foreign trade and higher, countervailing rates for those that did not. To shift tariff making away from the "political" House Ways and Means Committee, the revisionists advocated and essentially created a "scientific" tariff commission to carry out economic analyses of trends in world production and trade.

In stationing themselves between high protectionism and free trade, the revisionists contemplated neither a half measure nor a dilute version of either policy. Instead, they sought to overcome the late nineteenth-century impasse between Republican home-market protectionism and Democratic free trade. Drawing on the liberalizing tendencies of Democratic "free raw materials" and Republican "reciprocity," revisionists sought to reduce the potential, under successive partisan Congresses or administrations, for policy seesawing between high and low tariffs and for rapid making and breaking of commercial treaties that threatened commercial stability. To break the impasse in practice, revisionists sought to build a broad consensus for the Dingley Tariff's section 4 reciprocity treaties, negotiated by the Kasson Commission and offering tariff reductions of up to 20 percent to major trading partners. Passage of these treaties promised to move the United States beyond the "tropical" reciprocity of the 1880s, which largely focused on exchange of U.S. manufactures for Latin American foodstuffs and raw products, and to extend reciprocity to the manufactured goods of competing industrial nations. Hence, revisionists proposed, implicitly or explicitly, that the tariff should be considered as a suprapartisan issue, that much of U.S. industry had passed through its "infancy" and no longer needed protection for developmental purposes, and that American and European markets were interdependent.[2]

In promoting a multiple-tariff system and in pressing for a tariff commission, the revisionists also sought to harmonize U.S. tariff practices with those of the European industrial states. The arrangements revisionists envisaged—reciprocity, multiple tariffs, and commissions of businessmen and tariff experts—were characteristic of the European states vying to establish their positions in the modern market of global industrial export competition. Thus, in the broadest sense, revisionism was a movement not merely to reshape U.S. practices but also to renovate U.S. policy for competition and leadership in this environment. William McKinley, once the personification of protectionism, underlined the significance of tariff revision when he became the first post–Civil War Republican president to describe systematic tariff reduction as indispensable to the continued growth of the United States' industrial and financial system.

McKinley was not alone. Over the next decade or more, presidents Theodore Roosevelt and William H. Taft and cabinet members including Elihu Root and Philander C. Knox, although careful to placate protectionist constituencies, treated revision of the tariff as a significant aspect of their political identities. Perhaps Roosevelt embraced revisionist ideas most inclusively in his unsuccessful Bull Moose presidential bid in 1912. But candidate Taft epitomized the outlook earlier, when he announced outright during his successful 1908 campaign, "I am a tariff revisionist."

Politicians in the legislature contributed substantially to the development of revisionism. "Progressive Republicans" such as Albert J. Beveridge of Indiana, Albert B. Cummins of Iowa, and Robert M. La Follette of Wisconsin, and traditional Republicans such as Ebenezer J. Hill of Connecticut and Sereno E. Payne of New York were revisionists of varying stripe and strength, even as they continued to portray themselves as staunch protectionists.[3]

The Democrats also provided a component of the attack on traditional protectionism. Through the doctrine of "free raw materials," Democratic party ideologists David Ames Wells and Edward Atkinson promoted expanded and liberalized trade in the late nineteenth century. Many prominent intellectuals, such as university economists Frank W. Taussig, Henry Parker Willis, and James Laurence Laughlin, and political scientist Paul Reinsch also supported trade expansion through tariff reduction in the twentieth century. Former Gold Democrats such as Franklin MacVeagh, President Taft's treasury secretary, and Arthur B. Farquhar, the steel manufacturer and popular economic writer, were influential revisionists. Only toward the beginning of World War I, however, did the mainstream Democratic party abandon the revenue tariff and embrace key tenets of revisionism, such as multilateral tariff making, retaliation against foreign tariff discriminations, and creation of a tariff commission.[4]

Wellsprings of Multilateralism

Republican party interest in tariff reduction was shaped in part by the exigencies of electoral politics. Elihu Root, a corporate lawyer who occupied key Republican cabinet and legislative posts in the early twentieth century, was among the first to understand that contemporary consumer-oriented tariff reductionism, like the nineteenth-century call for a "free breakfast table," challenged his party to prove itself independent of high-tariff monopolies and special interests. In correspondence with Root regarding the 1906 elections, President Theodore Roosevelt, too, opined that if the Republicans did not take the initiative in revising the tariff, popular demands for reduction might well defeat them at the polls.[5]

The motives of politicians and policymakers in effecting tariff revision were not narrowly electoral, however. Rather, the impetus for tariff revision derived from the contemporaneous expansion of U.S. trade and empire onto a world scale. Britain, France, and other European states were already engulfing world markets and investment opportunities in the late nineteenth century and seeking to rationalize this expansion through systems of colonialism, pan-Europeanism, empire privilege, spheres of influence, and tariff assimilation. The United States was a comparative latecomer to the struggle, and U. S. policymakers, once they fully appreciated the implications of an imminent dismemberment of the global market, sought to elaborate a vision of global trade relations commensurate with and supportive of the nation's burgeoning productive power. They responded by promulgating the "open door." Although the open-door policy ostensibly aimed at forestalling the division of China into exclusive spheres of interest, it represented far more than an attempt to preserve local U.S. interests. In fact, it proposed a systematic alternative "hegemonic ideology" to systems that would regulate access to markets on imperial, political, geographic, racial, traditional, or social grounds. Instead, the open door proposed economic or market efficiency as the supreme governing principle of international exchange and implied nondiscrimination, or at least condemned unequal discrimination, in all international financial and commercial affairs. Soon, as U.S. products flooded European and "third" markets, and as the United States sought to define tariff policies for its own new colonies and dependencies, such as Cuba and the Philippines, this very substantial entry into the global commercial system raised the meaning and application of open-door principles to a new level of international concern.[6]

U.S. advocacy of the open door presented the world with a paradox. In theory, the open door was a profession of faith in a world order of more equal access, and it challenged systems of foreign commercial exclusionism. Yet in practice, the United States retained its own high protectionist domestic tariff, molded by late nineteenth-century continental expansionism and sustained by the "logrolling" system of tariff making in Congress, through which legislators catered to their own and each others' local protectionist interests. U.S. tariff rates, in fact, were often double or treble those of European states. Moreover, the United States' commercial treaty system and conditional interpretation of the most-favored-nation clause made American tariff concessions strictly bilateral, so that no two foreign countries were guaranteed the same rate on items they both exported to the United States. This policy ran athwart European unconditional most-favored-nation practice, which guaranteed uniform, multilateral most-favored-nation rates in commercial agreements. Thus, both the high tariffs and the exceptionalist style of U.S. commercial treaties subverted U.S. claims for open-door treatment, and Europeans were quick to decry American "hypocrisy."

American protectionists responded to criticisms of the high-tariff regime by pointing to the extraordinary size and value of the American home market, to dangers inherent in the rapid growth and "cheap labor" of European industry, and to the seemingly tentative character of the European tariff order, which itself was growing increasingly protectionist. Still, the sizable rate differences and the overall incompatibility of the U.S. and European systems impeded U.S. movement toward fostering a stabler international economic order in the early twentieth century. In that sense, entrenched American protectionism may be seen as having contributed to the international economic tension that led to World War I and that the post–World War II General Agreement on Tariffs and Trade (GATT) was designed to avoid. The revisionists may not have envisioned anything quite so ambitious as the GATT, but, as this study implies, they may be seen as having initiated the U.S. movement in the direction of this modern multilateral trade order.[7]

The effort to resolve the inconsistency between the immediate and often protectionist interests of individual businesses and the overall requirements of an expanding international economy thus formed a basic dynamic of the tariff controversy of the early twentieth century. Not surprisingly, then, leading manufacturers, traders, and agricultural exporters came to play an important role in the revisionist movement. Although the businessmen of this period kept a sharp eye on their own affairs, most had a clear view of the broader international context of the tariff question as it affected their markets and their sources of raw materials. Experience in the day-to-day work of international trade and customs clearances had given practical entrepreneurs unique knowledge of European tariff tendencies and real insight into the opportunities for and impediments to expansion. Moreover, as increasing numbers of U.S. manufacturers turned to foreign markets as an escape from the depression of the 1890s, and as the United States acquired tropical dependencies of its own, capitalists inhaled and assimilated the esoteric air of empire. Hence, they also tended to think not only in terms of immediate self-interest but in terms of the collective future of their nation as the world's dominant economic power. Business leaders from Andrew Carnegie to J. Ogden Armour, although differing on the nature and timing of tariff changes, shared enthusiasms for an empire of foreign markets—not only in trade and association journals but in influential national periodicals such as the *North American Review* and the *Annals of the American Academy of Political and Social Sciences*.

Revisionism and Corporate Reconstruction

Revisionists shared an opposition both to home-market protectionism and to free trade as such. But if many trade-oriented capitalists exulted in agreeing that the protectionist tariff should be reshaped to serve American expansion, they took pause in discovering how markedly they differed about *how* it should be reshaped, how quickly it should be revised, and who among domestic and foreign interests affected by the tariff should pay the price of change.

In part, of course, disputes over tariff rates reflected the often atomistic self-interests of the producers, consumers, and traders who had a vital stake in the tariff. For example, when shoemakers sought tariff reductions on foreign leathers, or when machine tool makers endorsed U.S. reductions on cotton goods tariffs because these were necessary to secure French tariff reductions on U.S. lathes and drill presses, they clearly pursued self-interest.[8]

More fundamentally, however, the alignments and repolarizations that characterized the tariff revisionist movement of the turn of the century were shaped by the contemporaneous rise of corporate capitalism. Historians have long recognized that the victory of urban capitalism over agrarian radicalism in 1896 was a precursor to a reorganization of finance and industry, marked by an intensive merger or "trust" movement. Trusts did not originate at the turn of the century, of course. They were already widespread in the 1880s and 1890s, when the largely unrestricted manipulations of market-dominant "monopolies" in sugar, oil, steel, nonferrous metals, tobacco, railroads, and finance became notorious. What was significant about the turn-of-the-century period was the emergence of *corporations* as the dominant form of trust, a phenomenon facilitated both by the Republican electoral victory and by developments in public and private law. In the merger movement of 1898 to 1904, more than eighteen hundred firms were absorbed into horizontal combinations, most creating combinations that controlled from 40 percent to more than 70 percent of their markets. The years from 1898 to 1902 comprised the majority of mergers, including the formation of United States Steel and International

Harvester. The startling economic rise of corporations is well illustrated by the fact that by 1905, manufacturing consolidations, although comprising less than 25 percent of all manufacturing establishments, controlled more than 80 percent of all capital and employed more than 70 percent of all wage earners in the sector.[9]

The emphasis here on the extensive political and economic implications of the corporation suggests that the turn-of-the-century period marked not merely a technical or structural change of economic organization but rather the *corporate reorganization* or *corporate reconstruction* of American society. As Martin J. Sklar has described it, this was the beginning of an epochal transition from the "proprietary-competitive to the corporate-administered stage of capitalism, with attendant changes in social relations, politics, government, law, thought, and foreign policy." The tariff, concomitantly, may be seen not merely as a question of which particular industries or interests would receive the benefits of new markets gained by new policies but rather of how new rates and structures would effect or contribute to a more general recrystallization of social authority.[10]

As used here, *proprietary capitalism* signifies the mode of capitalism in which individual owner-managers control the wealth and operation of a company within a generally competitive market (even if sometimes illicitly or privately subverting competition). In contrast, in *corporate capitalism*, management commonly is under the purview of specially capable "undertaking geniuses" (as an enthusiastic early procorporate economist put it), and the relationship between management and ownership is mediated in a complex fashion. Under corporate capitalism, operations are carried out on an expanded scale, one that is more bureaucratic, more vertically and horizontally integrated, and more systematized. Large issues of stocks and other obligations, as well as investment from allied banking interests, serve as driving forces of business. In the corporate phase of capitalism, competitive and production-oriented pricing gives way to the explicit or implicit cooperative price setting or price leadership of administered or oligopolistic markets.[11]

The mergers that created a corporate economy were accompanied by complementary developments in law and ideology. Comprising also academic movements in economics, statistics, history, and politics, corporate reconstruction promoted the corporation as the means by which the United States could be restructured to fulfill its potential as a mature industrial society. In supporting corporation capitalism, prominent American thinkers and business figures argued that the abuses of monopolies were only a temporary stage in the definition of the "true economic functions of the trusts." That is, they suggested that corporations, if regulated by government to prevent the rapacity and torpidity of complete monopolization, would give the fullest scope to the United States' productive powers through economies of scale and management.[12]

Among corporations' salient advantages was that they allowed organization of capital and resources on a scale impossible or unadvisable for an individual and would avert having to resort to the agency of the state itself. Thus, in the view of their proponents, corporations vitiated arguments for organizing a regime of mass production along socialist or statist lines on the grounds that corporations' size and integration would yield comparable or greater efficiency and balance of power.[13]

But corporate combinations were not merely an antidote to socialism or collectivism. In the view of their proponents, corporations were an advantageous mutation whose integration, administered pricing, and control of large segments of the market would modulate the intense and profitless competition becoming characteristic of the American economy. Corporations, they argued, were essential to check overproduction and to protect the economy and society from devastating cyclical crises such as that of the 1890s. Although procorporate thinkers recognized that consolidations threatened the ideal of widespread control of productive property, they saw this development in Social Darwinian terms—not as the negation of individual entrepreneurialism but as its consummation—as the coordinating instrumentality through which American capitalism and its "undertaking genius" could achieve its fullest expression.[14]

Of critical importance, the proponents of corporate reconstruction argued, trusts would organize the economy for effective competition against collectively organized empire, cartel-based, and statist systems in world markets. A commensurate system of corporate combinations, they argued, was the best way for the United States to assure that it could outbid, outfinance, and outbuild such competition. Using the organizational and publicity experience they had gained in the sound money movement, corporation men in banking, politics, and the executive branches of government engaged the "trust question" in public forums with vigor, as they sought to transform the ideological and institutional foundations of the proprietary-competitive system into the basis for a new corporate order.[15]

The conception of a highly administered and centralized capitalism traduced the producerist or proprietary capitalist ideal of the free market and the control of production by dispersed and autonomous owner-managers.

Some procorporate thinkers sought to downplay the revolutionary nature of corporate reorganization with regard to proprietary capitalism by promoting the widespread sale of industrial stocks, particularly as "investments for small capital." Under such a system, smaller proprietary capitalists displaced from competitive participation in the market by consolidations could retain some feeling of their status as owners. The corporation, its advocates argued, thus represented a distinctive American form of organization that permitted large-scale integrated production and administered pricing but preserved private property and aspects of traditional market competition that could stimulate efficiency and loyalty.[16]

But trusts were not the only efficient or organized producers in the years immediately following McKinley's election. Proprietary manufacturers largely shared the expansionist enthusiasms of the corporate capitalists and saw the Republican victory of 1896 as in good measure their own. By no means convinced that mergers and the formation of corporations represented the only feasible American solution to the requirements of production and marketing on a global scale, and quite aware of the imminent threat of eclipse posed by corporate capitalism, they resisted abdicating their political and ideological dominance in American society. This was especially so for northeastern and midwestern manufacturers engaged in specialized finishing operations who were enjoying the fruits of the "American invasion" of Europe. Thus, as the corporate expansion of American trade and investment continued apace, it would meet increasing attempts by proprietary capitalists to control tariff revision, the state-business infrastructure, and trade expansion to preserve proprietorship.

As this study argues, much of the driving force in the revisionist movement derived from the conflict between proprietary and corporate world views. "Independent" or proprietary entrepreneurs then dominated groups such as the National Association of Manufacturers (NAM) and most vociferously opposed the corporations such as highly integrated and capitalized United States Steel and International Harvester. Sustaining the independent voice of the individual entrepreneur vis-à-vis the corporations was "the gist of our entire contention," wrote a key figure in the controversy, Herbert Edwin Miles, a wealthy farm implement manufacturer and the chairman of the tariff committee of the NAM. By 1907, Miles was demanding on behalf of the NAM that legislators investigate tariff schedules to find out "how far they are Congressional permits to create Trusts." This was a theme—the tariff as "mother of trusts"—that had been until only a few years before the near-exclusive property of the Democrats. Yet the Republican Miles was joined in his "radical" anticorporate revisionism by many proprietary capitalists in the NAM and other manufacturing and trade organizations and by many midwestern political figures who became identified with "Insurgent Progressive" causes. Although Robert M. La Follette and Theodore Roosevelt may have received more attention in studies of progressivism, this study suggests that the political-economic and social aspects of revisionism largely antedate its political manifestations.

The root of proprietary manufacturers' grievance against corporations was that they believed that integrated corporations were using protectionist tariffs to hold domestic prices at an artificially high level. Finishing manufacturers were primary domestic consumers of corporate products, particularly steel. In the first decade of the twentieth century, the rapidly rising prices finishing manufacturers paid for raw materials and intermediate goods were crippling them at home in their competition with integrated corporations in their industry. For example, the independent agricultural implement manufacturers felt they could not compete against consolidated International Harvester, which made its own steel at a cost they estimated as $18 a ton when they—lacking the resources to corner ore supplies and capitalize steel mills—had to buy bars from U.S. Steel at $30 a ton. Moreover, corporate consolidation and its attendant rise in prices were driving a wedge between the independents and their farm clients because Harvester had preferential access to Morgan Company capital and was able to offer far better credit terms on purchases of major pieces of equipment.

Proprietary manufacturers also were irked by market-dominant combinations' use of protectionism to facilitate cut-rate exporting, or dumping. Quite simply, corporations that controlled domestic prices for a product and were protected by tariffs from foreign competition in their home market—in particular the steel industry—could sell their products abroad at prices lower than they gave to domestic consumers. Such lower prices still brought the corporation profits, and by offering foreign consumers bargain prices, the corporations captured new markets. But domestic consumers, especially those who used products such as steel to make finished manufactures, complained bitterly that such practices enabled foreign exporters of finished manufactures to "beat us all to pieces in the neutral market on Pittsburgh steel." These were the kinds of stimuli that focused attention on the tariff and that could lead ordinarily conservative Republican manufacturers to challenge corporate enterprise by seeking to lower or even destroy the tariff walls on trust-produced raw materials and intermediate goods. This action, proprietary manufacturers hoped, would force the corporations into competition with foreign competitors, reduce prices, and preserve the integrity and marketing options of nonintegrated manufacturers.[17]

Hence, whereas late nineteenth-century opposition to "trusts" had been largely the province of agrarian radicals and embattled labor defending a republican-producerist ideal, the anticorporate thrust of the early twentieth century was led by stiff-collared manufacturers who now also came to see concentrated corporate control of markets and raw materials as tools of the destruction of the proprietary enterprise system.[18]

Not all proprietary capitalists favoring tariff revision became anticorporate radicals, however, even if they were militant tariff reductionists in other respects. Intrinsic to the revisionist movement and sharing in its expansionist goals was also a proprietary-corporate "cooperationist" tendency. Wary of the threat to entrepreneurial autonomy that seemed immanent in validating the state-imposed shackling of large businesses, and particularly leery of endorsing measures so recently associated with radical Populism, the cooperationists emphasized unity among capitalists in seeking expanded markets. That is, they supported the expansionist implications of revision and the notion that tariff policy should be removed from congressional logrolling by expanded reciprocity, legislated dual tariffs, and a tariff commission, but they deplored the radical, anticorporate thrust of revisionism. Allied with the Republican administrations and with corporations such as International Harvester, cooperationists sought to shape tariff reductions and new tariff institutions in ways that would allow proprietary enterprise to participate in and profit from cooperation with, and subordination to, a system of expanding corporate capitalism. This study thus explores, within the revisionist movement, the distinctive differences between radicals and cooperationists over the form of a proposed U.S. multiple-tariff system; the extent, timing, and nature of tariff cuts; the proposed membership, executive authority, and bureaucratic locus of a tariff commission; and the economic basis, scope, and method of tariff investigations.

Even the radicals, to the extent that they recognized corporate combinations as an inevitable outgrowth of American capitalism, shared a cooperationist viewpoint. That is, insofar as the radicals sought not to destroy or supplant but to contain or regulate the market activity of corporations, their differences with their cooperationist colleagues in the revisionist movement were principally over the degree to which proprietary capitalists could preserve their independent economic power through the state and the tariff. Hence, this study seeks to clarify not only the roots of proprietary capitalists' efforts to gain equity through tariff revision but also the evolution of an ultimately dominant tendency toward consensus among Republican-oriented capitalists to shape an expansionist tariff policy in cooperation with corporate aims. Both the radical and corporate-cooperationist aspects of the largely proprietary revisionist movement, this work argues, exerted critical influence in shaping the policies that ultimately constituted a procorporate expansionist consensus.

Some of the ideas or terms of the tariff revision movement as described here may seem familiar, perhaps because they have been captured in accounts identifying progressivism that identified it with attempts to control "monopoly" and turn the tariff against the "trusts." In fact, efforts to reshape policy and institutions in the Progressive Era often are discussed under the rubric of "reform" or of a movement of "the people" against "the interests," or under the notion of "organization." The emphasis here of "revisionism" and "revisionists" is deliberate. These are more inclusive, less melioristic, and more accurate terms for an evolving social movement that encompassed conflicting conceptions of equity but that nonetheless developed organization, ideology, and coherent policy agendas.[19]

In this regard, it is important to note that the revisionists were organized in industrial and commercial associations such as the NAM. Other similar groups included the National Live Stock Association (NLSA), the National Association of Agricultural Implement and Vehicle Manufacturers (NAAIVM), and the Merchants Association of New York (MANY). These specific associations in turn formed inclusive national lobby groups such as the short-lived National Reciprocity League (NRL) and the more influential American Reciprocal Tariff League (ARTL) and National Tariff Commission Association (NTCA). Within these groups, and often through them, revisionists politicked, palavered, and pamphleteered to develop what may be seen as a creed of "reciprocity," "maximum and minimum tariffs," a "scientific" tariff commission, and a doctrine of tariffs based on comparative costs of production.

This study thus views the ideology and action of capitalists—both proprietary radicals and corporate or procorporate entrepreneurs—in a way that emphasizes their purposive efforts to reformulate the institutional dynamics and political-economic philosophy of modern capitalism. In essence, then, revisionism is seen here as a social movement of the capitalist class, as an aspect of its formation or re-formation. Inherent in both proprietary- and corporate-oriented revisionism were specific conceptions of social order that endorsed the expansion of American foreign trade and U.S. preeminence in world commerce, the need to accept and rationalize capitalist competition at an international level, and the view that control of tariff rates and tariff-making processes was instrumental in shaping society. This approach, one might add, is faithful to the revisionists' perhaps surprisingly holistic view of domestic and international politics.[20]

Because proprietary capitalists were often in the forefront of the tariff revision movement of the early twentieth century, this study tends to give them, rather than corporate capitalists, primary attention. Yet, corporate reconstruction, although not always addressed directly, moves through this narrative with a gravitational force that even when unseen perturbs the orbits of all the participants in tariff affairs.

Although the tariff question in this period is complex, the interpretive emphasis here on revisionism seeks to clarify the dynamics of change, to unify the treatment of international and domestic affairs, and to illuminate the creative roles of conflict and consensus in the development of policy.

In brief, this study treats the evolution of U.S. tariff policy under Republican administrations from 1897 to 1913 and suggests its outcome in the Democratic Wilson administration up to about 1916. The first of its three major sections, "The Tariff under McKinley and Roosevelt," traces the early twentieth-century tariff politics of a developing American empire and the responses of Europeans to an "American invasion" of goods. Chapter 1 treats the political-economic and ideological context of the tariff from the 1860s to the close of the nineteenth century. Chapter 2 traces the tariff during McKinley's tenure, concentrating on the Kasson reciprocity treaties, which contemplated expanded importation of foreign-produced manufactures. The analysis suggests that expansionist capitalists, typified by the members of the NAM and other national commercial groups, drawing on a sense of solidarity that devolved from the victories over Populism, envisioned expanded reciprocity as a necessary step in entering the world trade order. But the NAM and other supporters of expanded reciprocity, although developing a movement of significant ideological and political impetus, were unprepared for the domestic political and economic ramifications of a reciprocity with competing industrial states. Further weakened by the loss through assassination of their chief partisan, McKinley, the revisionists failed to secure passage of the Kasson treaties in the protectionist national legislature.

Chapter 3 describes the renascence of reciprocity, as a Republican-led expansionist coalition sought to revise the legislative system of tariff making, by proposing a system of maximum and minimum tariffs and drawing both agricultural exporters and industrial tariff reductionists into a reviving revisionist movement. Despite the eclipse of reciprocity and the death of McKinley, President Theodore Roosevelt determinedly pursued tariff agreements that provisionally extended concessions to secure favorable tariff treatment from Germany, as chapter 4 details. Here, groups of East Coast merchants and midwestern livestock exporters coalesced to elaborate changes in U.S. customs rules, to support a U.S. legislative dual-rate tariff administered by the executive branch, to support a commercial mission to Germany that negotiated a comprehensive reciprocity treaty, and to advance the revisionist movement by forming the ARTL.

Chapter 5 continues the discussion of the expanding movement by elucidating the origins of "radical" Republican revisionism and the proprietary critique of the integrated corporations. It also traces the involvement of H. E. Miles, the Wisconsin farm implement manufacturer who, as an officer of the NAAIVM and then of the NAM, became a chief spokesman for the proprietary view and most active proponent of a tariff commission. As chapter 6 details, Miles and the proprietary manufacturers of the NAM promoted a "scientific," nonpartisan tariff commission to regulate the market power of integrated corporations such as United States Steel. Responding to the progressing subordination, even extinction, of their system of enterprise by expanding corporations, and seeking to preserve proprietary influence in American commercial empire, they cooperated in framing legislation with senators Albert J. Beveridge and Robert M. La Follette. In addition, the study notes the NAM's efforts to join with the agricultural revisionists of the ARTL and mercantile revisionists represented by the MANY to form a National Tariff Commission Association.

The second section of this study, "The Payne-Aldrich Tariff and Revisionist Policy," treats the framing of the 1909 tariff act and attempts to clarify the development of a "cooperationist" approach that overshadowed the radical tack of some manufacturers and progressive politicians. Cooperationists, closely allied with the Republican administration, supported the expansionist implications of revision and an executive-guided tariff commission but were uneasy with its anticorporate aspects. Chapters 7 and 8, on the Payne-Aldrich Tariff itself, suggest that cooperationism was undergirded by the developing economic and social authority of corporations and by foreign and domestic market cooperation between proprietary producers and the integrated corporations; by the preference of President Taft for working with traditional legislative Republicans rather than the midwestern "Insurgents"; by the hesitation of the NAM to pursue a radical tariff platform for fear of alienating its protectionist and antilabor allies; and by the fundamental isolation of Republican radicals from potential allies among the Democrats. Despite the political acrimony generated by these conflicts, however, the Payne-Aldrich Tariff lowered rates, created a maximum-minimum structure that removed tariff negotiations a step from the legislative branch, and legitimized a bureaucratic infrastructure, the Tariff Board, to mediate relations between capitalists and the state.

The third section of the book, "Revisionism in Practice," begins with chapter 9, focusing on the Tariff Board, the limited tariff commission set up by President Taft under the provisions of the Payne-Aldrich Tariff. It examines the system of maximum and minimum rates established by the tariff law as an attempt to create an American analog of the European unconditional most-favored-nation tariff system, a closer approximation of U.S. tariffs to the open-door foreign economic policy. Chapter 10 treats the efforts of the Tariff Board and allied revisionists to define and effect a cost-of-production method of determining equitable tariff rates, undertaken in line with Taft's objectives of implementing a tariff infrastructure that served foreign-trade-oriented businesses but that was distinctly nonradical in the content or scope of its authority.

The conclusion, chapter 11, suggests that politically the Republican solution to the question of tariff reduction and expansion was unsuccessful in the pre–World War I period, resulting in only a mild reduction and temporary tariff structures such as the Tariff Board and the maximum-minimum system, and contributing to the party divisions that led to the electoral defeat of Taft and Roosevelt in 1912. Still, in giving way, it led to a Democratic single-rate lower tariff, to the contemplation and institutional-ization of measures to deal with foreign trade discrimination, and to an enduring tariff commission. As the chapter attempts to demonstrate by examining the tariff issue during the Wilson administration, the policies conceived in the Republican reconstruction of the tariff, from 1897 to 1912, were in principle continuous with the policies of subsequent admin-istrations, promoting expansion and open-door tariffs and subsuming pro-prietary enterprise within an emergent corporate order.

Most
Favored
Nation

1 The Turn toward Revision

As momentary phases of political policy, protection and expansion may be combined, but as expressions of national temper, they are incompatible. . . . We have crossed the Rubicon.—H. H. Powers, "Expansion and Protection," 1899

Between 1865 and 1900, the protective tariff and home-market ideology played an important role in American development. High post–Civil War tariffs facilitated the development of industry, especially heavy industry in the Midwest. Protectionism and the home market were dominant ideas, commanding the loyalty of most of the Republican party, most capitalists, and much of labor outside agrarian groups.

Still, low-tariff sentiment persisted among most Democrats and on a sectoral and regional basis, especially among finishing manufacturers and in the Northeast. Moreover, lower-tariff impulses would grow up on a national basis around two centers: the conception of "free raw materials" promoted by economist David Ames Wells and entrepreneur Edward Atkinson in the Democratic party and "reciprocity," as promoted by James G. Blaine in the Republican party. Although these reductionist initiatives had only slight effect on the overall high level of late nineteenth-century American duties, in different ways they sought to accommodate the requirements of an industrializing economy expanding beyond continental limits.[1]

Tariff revisionism of the early twentieth century represented a signal departure from the tariff practices and ideologies of the late nineteenth century. Yet it drew directly from post–Civil War controversies in the United States, from a forty-year legacy of intellectual ferment and commercial change in Europe, as well as from the sea changes of political economy in the 1890s.

Equipoise

The Republican party approached the twentieth century basically committed to the doctrine of the home market, the conception that the continental United States—or the North American continent, at any rate—provided sufficient scope for the expansive energies of American capitalism. America, reasoned protectionists, was a vast cornucopia of resources that was quickly developing its own substantial manufacturing power. In such circumstances, tariffs should act as a "Chinese Wall" to bar European or other foreign goods that might supplant domestic products and discourage domestic development. Home-market protectionists allowed that European nations, because of their smaller resource and productive bases, might require their own lower tariffs and freer trade. But they generally maintained that the United States had a constitutionally ordained "internal" free trade that made the country more or less equivalent to Europe as a whole—a situation that required no potentially damaging compromises with foreign powers. In a congressional speech of 1883, for example, "Czar" Thomas B. Reed proclaimed the self-sufficiency of a "great country like this with everything in it." Such were the views of a majority of congressional Republicans of the late nineteenth century, including 1890 tariff maker and future president William McKinley and House Speaker Joseph G. Cannon.[2]

Not all Republicans were strict protectionists, however. To an extent, the Republicans who were low-tariff supporters of the late nineteenth century were the same types who would become part of the revisionist movement of the twentieth century. Many northeastern and New England manufacturers, for example, favored lower tariffs on foreign raw materials, such as coal from Nova Scotia—which they had used profitably under the terms of the Elgin reciprocity treaty of 1855–66—and scrap iron and ores traveling cheaply as ballast from Europe. Low seaborne freight rates, combined with the high, unregulated rail rates of this period, could make foreign raw materials cheaper for eastern manufacturers to buy than midwestern crude products traveling overland.[3]

Much of eastern industry consisted of finishing manufacture, including textiles; chemicals; boots and shoes; articles of brass, bronze, and copper; firearms; hardware; and machine shop products. Already inclined toward low tariffs because of their particular requirements for raw materials and intermediate goods for manufacture, eastern producers also had substantial investments in plant and equipment that disposed them toward lower tariffs. By facilitating imports and holding prices down, low tariffs would damage the relatively mature eastern enterprises only minimally but would deprive newer market entries of shelter and would inhibit potential competitors from building more advanced facilities closer to domestic sources of raw materials.[4]

The port-based "old elite" of merchants and traders, centered in New York (but also in Baltimore, Philadelphia, Boston, and New Orleans), was also inclined toward lower tariffs. Foreign branch businesses, foreign markets, foreign capital, and foreign exchange facilities continued to figure importantly in the structure of merchants' activity. Concomitantly, tariff reductionism flourished in the Chamber of Commerce of the State of New York, the New York Board of Trade and Transportation, the Democratically oriented Reform Club, and later the Merchants Association of New York. In fact, it was the wealthy New York mercantile environment that partly shaped Theodore Roosevelt's views on the tariff.[5]

Home-market protectionism was most strongly associated with newer manufacturers, especially from Pennsylvania through the Midwest. Their push for higher tariffs was generated by the post–Civil War contraction of the greenbacks, which had all but obliterated the protective effects of the American tariff, resulting in increases in imports of foreign goods that drove down prices on U.S. manufactures. Adopting the views and vocabulary of economist Henry C. Carey, the "high priest" of protection, midwestern capitalists opposed further monetary contraction and championed renewed and more forceful tariff protection. Steel, oil, and other rising midwestern enterprises that would displace the East Coast manufacturers as the dominant forces in American industry represented the salient of this new protectionism. It was they who were hungry for expanded capital and credit and believed themselves most vulnerable to European competition.[6]

It was the domestic-expansionist, protectionist impulse of the midwesterners that would become dominant in the Republican party and national policy of the late nineteenth century. That is, if the North retained regional pockets of low-tariff sentiment, the general tendency of late nineteenth-century tariffs was strongly protective, with actual tariff rates on dutiable items in the 40 percent range and duties as a percentage of all goods at around 25 to 30 percent, compared with contemporary European free trade or tariff rates of 10 percent or less. This regime, it should be noted, served a distinctive developmental end by making investment in steel plants and new smelting technologies, oil refineries, and other capital-goods-intensive manufacturing more profitable.[7]

The Democrats had tried to counter the home-market strategy in the nineteenth century. Party adviser David Wells and his associate, Edward Atkinson, had argued from the 1870s onward for free trade and then for a more limited "free raw materials." Atkinson, for example, believed that America's vast resource base was an argument not for protectionism and self-sufficiency but for lower tariffs and international interdependence. America's world "dominion" in the production of iron and coal could be used to advantage, Atkinson believed, only if the United States brought in still more raw materials and challenged its manufacturing system with the stimuli of international competition and division of labor. Wells and Atkinson thus proposed tariff reductions not merely as expressions of party or sectional self-interest, although these were also factors, but as an argument for economic stability and development.

The Republicans, led by James G. Blaine, also sought to modify the high-protection regime through the policy of "reciprocity." For Blaine, this meant signing bilateral trade treaties that would lower U.S. tariffs on "tropical" and other goods that did not and could not compete seriously with American products. This strategy would preserve much of protectionism, Blaine argued, and in exchange the United States would receive access to the markets of its treaty partners, gaining "vents" for an expanding production of U.S. manufactures that could not be sold profitably at home. Not coincidentally, reciprocity was intended to preempt Democratic demands for more drastic tariff reductions. Yet although "free raw materials" and "reciprocity" challenged the logic of home-market self-sufficiency, by the late 1890s the Democrats had failed to pass an effective "free raw materials" tariff. Moreover, although the Republicans signed reciprocity treaties with several European and Latin American nations, significant U.S. concessions were strictly limited by "standpat" protectionists, by the system of congressional tariff logrolling, and by the vulnerability of treaties to cancellation by new tariff legislation. Thus, Democratic and Republican policies, despite the political and ideological ferment, remained in an "equipoise" that left U.S. high tariffs largely unmodified during the latter half of the nineteenth century.

Europe

It is useful to recall that as the United States' "high priests" were enshrining protectionism in American policy in the post–Civil War period, Europeans were conforming to the liberal, low-tariff policies epitomized by the Cobden-Chevalier Treaty of 1860 between England and France. The Cobden Treaty effectively formed a European tariff system by generalizing a free-trade or low-tariff regime among most of the nations of Europe through treaties and through the broad use of the European, or unconditional, most-favored-nation clause, which generalized the lowest rates granted to any country to all trading partners whose treaties contained such a clause. The Cobden Treaty thus allowed relatively developed Britain, and to a lesser extent France, to become hubs of a system that could draw freely on the less developed hinterlands of Eastern and Southern Europe for raw materials and foodstuffs and trade manufactures in a complementary fashion.[8]

By the late 1870s, however, the entry of a unified Germany into European commerce began to modify European liberal tariff practices. German agrarian interests began to demand broadened protection against Russian and American grain and other agricultural products. In 1878, Bismarck raised a tariff wall against agricultural imports and gave greater shelter to Germany's developing manufacturing industries.[9]

France, too, soon began to retreat from the liberal system. Under pressure from domestic textile manufacturers, France gave up the Cobden-Chevalier Treaty in 1882, and in 1892 adopted the Méline Tariff, which raised duties substantially and abandoned the treaty tariff format for a "maximum and minimum" system, in which the legislature "autonomously" set two tariff rates—a general or maximum and a minimum. The new French system represented a compromise between protection and foreign trade expansion, because it gave interest-sensitive legislators, rather than cosmopolitan diplomats, discretion over when protection would be modified in exchange for gains in export opportunities.[10]

Whereas France and England had dominated the liberal tariff period from 1860 to 1880, Germany, the rising industrial power of Europe, now sought mastery of a new, more protectionist era. Germany retained a system of "general and conventional" tariffs. Here, the legislature adopted only the general or maximum rate that then could be modified by specific "conventions"—treaties of reciprocity or most-favored-nation treatment—that German commercial diplomats negotiated with other European states. German general tariffs came to reflect the protectionism of the agrarians in raising rates on foreign foodstuffs. They also soon protected manufactures of machinery, bicycles, hardware, tools, sewing machines, boots, and shoes. Yet it is vital to note that despite the high duties of the general tariff, the

German conventional rates were less protective and sometimes even lower than previous conventional rates. As a whole, then, the new system presented both threats and inducements. By 1891, Germany was negotiating the Caprivi treaties as a means of forming a system of favorable conventional, or commercial treaty, relations with the nations of Eastern and Southern Europe. (The United States, under the Harrison administration, was also a signatory to a treaty with Germany, the Saratoga Convention, although the status of the agreement was called into question almost immediately on the accession of the second Cleveland administration and the passage of the Wilson-Gorman Tariff of 1894.)[11]

The efforts of Germany to construct a new tariff system based on a high general rate and a lower conventional rate had mixed results at first. When the German agrarians attempted to block Russian grain exports, the Russians sought to exclude German manufactures, and a tariff war ensued. Ultimately, however, the two nations negotiated a ten-year treaty that stabilized their trade. This long-term agreement was typical of German policy and was important not merely for generating international comity but for stabilizing the economic environment within Germany. That is, assured of consistent tariffs on raw materials for a definite period, German businesses could be more willing to make long-term investments in capital goods whose profitability was based on the availability of those materials.[12]

It should be noted that the wide use of the unconditional most-favored-nation clause in commercial treaties meant that most European nations could still partake in conventional rates, if not directly then through third parties because of the generally low transport costs for reexporting in Europe. Where the changes of the post-1880 period were most marked was in an intensified reliance on trade with newly emerging agricultural exporters, including Argentina, Australia, Russia, Turkey, Greece, Bulgaria, Egypt, and China. Such trade satisfied expanding European needs for raw materials and provided some outlets for manufactures to compensate for the effects of increasing European tariffs. Thus, the turn away from the Cobden system was two-faced: The higher protectionism of the new period created some intra-European tensions, but it also attempted to meet the protectionist requirements of important domestic groups and to deflect European conflicts over resources and markets to wider hinterlands.[13]

Europe's quest for wider hinterlands was reflected in efforts to extend tariffs to colonial empires in the form of imperial and colonial preferences and systems of tariff assimilation. Empires, of course, were not defined only by tariffs, but tariff considerations were vital because they reflected the internal conditions and tolerances of national economies and regulated the international exchange of resources and material goods.[14]

Here, as within Europe, the declining dominance of the Cobden Treaty order signaled a new epoch of tariff politics. Although Britain generally retained low tariffs, France, to secure its economically weaker system, surrounded its colonies with the protective French tariff wall. This was the policy of tariff assimilation, in which the Third Republic created, in the cross-cultural metaphor of one historian, its own "huge Zollverein."[15]

French policy was highly responsive to the pressures of domestic interests—manufacturers and agriculturalists who wanted outlets for goods but no competition from colonial enterprises. This impeded the development of effective reciprocal trade between France and its colonies by alienating colonial entrepreneurs from the French metropolis and creating obstacles to colonial development and external trade. Concomitantly, because of shipping advantages, more favorable foreign tariffs, and certain factors of geographical and commercial propinquity, the exports of French colonies went heavily to nations other than France, and France remained a heavy buyer from colonies other than its own. As American and other observers noted, France had not quelled inter-European trade antagonisms significantly through its tariff policies. Instead, by failing to sustain an autarkic system, the French had transferred trade antagonisms to a wider arena.[16]

For Germany, the colonial question also was linked to industrial growth and protection. Germany's colonial thrust was very rapid. But German overseas tariff policy took an opposite tack from France's assimilation policy. The Germans regarded their lately acquired and generally peripheral possessions mainly as sources of raw materials and as bargaining chips to secure German access to other nations' more lucrative colonies and to neutral markets. Germany thus sought to extend most-favored-nation relations to colonies, a policy formalized by Bismarck in agreements with Britain in the Pacific and at the Berlin Conference of 1884–85.[17]

German colonialism—like German trade expansion in Europe—was a destabilizing factor in world commerce. Although German leaders, like their French and English counterparts, saw overseas markets as vital to their domestic social and economic systems, Germany was a comparative latecomer to imperial politics. Thus, Germany opposed "preclusive" imperialism by other states and sought to make German economic presence viable within the established commercial spheres of other powers.[18]

Germany's opposition to preclusive imperialism in some ways resembled the U.S. open door, but German trade goals ran athwart of American expansionist aims and domestic protectionism, French assimilation, and British empire preference policies. Frictions were exacerbated by the fact that Germany rapidly developed a highly competitive foreign trade apparatus. German leaders encouraged the "organization"—really the concentration and cartelization—of industry for foreign trade and promoted cooperation between its major commercial banks and the Reichsbank for long-term credits. Moreover, Germany engaged in cut-rate export selling to capture markets, created domestic cartels for export trading, and developed an extensive foreign trade infrastructure. Not all such activities were uniquely German practices. In fact, many inspired imitation by European nations and the United States. But Germany's actions were challenges to British hegemony in international trade and to the aspirations of the United States to expand its activity and leadership in international commerce at the opening of the twentieth century.[19]

Crossing the Rubicon

What would begin to change America's rationale for high tariffs was the development that protectionism had helped to engender: the transformation of the United States from an economy emphasizing proprietary production and export of raw materials to one undergoing concentration of production and stressing increasing exports of manufactures. By 1896, the United States was a net exporter of manufactures, which grew from 12.48 percent of all U.S. exports in 1880 to 31.6 percent in 1900 to almost 41 percent in 1905. Much of this growth was divided between semimanufactured steel products such as rails, wire, pipes, bars, beams, plates, billets, and ingots and finished manufactures of steel such as engines, boilers, metalworking machinery, builders' hardware, and typewriters.[20]

Unquestionably, trade with Europe was the dominant feature of U.S. export activity in this period. More important, the traditional pattern of U.S. exports to Europe was changing rapidly. Only 15 percent of U.S. exports to Europe were industrial manufactures in 1895. The figure was 21 percent in 1900, 24 percent in 1905, and nearly 34 percent in 1910. During the overall period, raw materials and crude foodstuffs had declined as a percentage of U.S. exports to Europe from 62 percent to about 49 percent, and manufactured foodstuffs remained around 20 percent of the total trade. Clearly, the "American invasion" of the European commercial system represented a major shift in the pattern of international trade.[21]

The transformation of American production changed U.S. relations with Europe. The United States had conceived of itself as relatively immune from European commercial pressures because of the strength of its home market and the indispensability of its raw materials exports to Europe—chiefly cotton, wheat, copper, animal products, and petroleum. Now, the U.S. and European economies were becoming more similar, through the greater industrialization of the United States, the increasing grasp of Europe on neutral-market and colonial raw materials, and the accumulation of capital that could not be invested profitably in domestic economies. These factors threatened to disrupt the complementary relationship that the new world had held to the old—that of a supplier of raw materials and food-stuffs. Perhaps most important for the United States, European commerce constituted sometimes competing and sometimes cooperating systems of trade that now were typified by the extensive use of dual- or multiple-rate tariff systems to which the relationship of the United States as a favored nation was basically in question: the so-called general and conventional (or treaty) tariff system, as practiced by Germany; the legislated maximum-minimum system, as practiced by France; and the beginnings of empire and colonial preference schemes in British trade. It was this system, still fluid in the 1890s and early 1900s, that the United States would confront as it entered the ranks of world commercial power.[22]

A broad range of European policy intellectuals and academics had already identified tariffs as a key to the geopolitics of the new epoch. Especially noteworthy were intellectuals influenced by the historical school of German political economy—in particular, its "younger" branch. The German free-trade economist Lujo Brentano had argued as early as 1885 that the twentieth century would know only four or five world powers. His protectionist colleague, Gustav Schmoller, in 1890 endorsed Central European commercial unity as vital in an era of "neomercantilism" to prevent the "Russian, English, American, and perhaps the Chinese world empires" from reducing "all the other, smaller, states to dependence." By 1900, Brentano's free-trade associate Heinrich Dietzel had concluded that tariffs could facilitate the division of the globe into only three autarkic systems. These ideas were not mere academic woolgathering; they became widely known through the *Verein für Sozialpolitik*, a German organization that fostered relations between academic experts and the state and had a broad audience among officials, academics, and commercial journalists in Europe and the United States.[23]

French intellectuals also sought to reconceptualize the tariff in an age of empires. Jules Ferry, sometime prime minister of the Third Republic during the 1880s, argued that less-developed France was endangered by the export outflows of Germany and the United States. Hence, he fostered protectionism and an assimilationist tariff policy that would use French colonies as sources of raw materials and vents for capital and manufactured surpluses. Ferry saw colonialism as preferable to revanchism—that is, to anti-German commercial or military warfare in Europe. By the early 1890s, Paul Leroy-Beaulieu, editor of *L'Economiste Français*, had emerged as one of France's leading imperialist intellectuals. Leroy-Beaulieu, who had been influenced by the German political-economist Wilhelm Roscher, was an ardent advocate of Pan-European free trade, which he believed was necessary for Europe to compete successfully with the continental power of the United States.[24]

Europeans such as Paul Leroy-Beaulieu were keenly sensitive, and not wholly unsympathetic, to the vast expansion of American commercial and financial power. In an 1895 article entitled "Conditions for American Commercial and Financial Supremacy," published in an American journal, Leroy-Beaulieu acknowledged that if American leaders showed the resolve to shuck off "rustic" ideologies and adopt a stable gold standard—that is, to defeat William Jennings Bryan and bimetallism—"the United States can aspire to take from England, in the course of the next century, the commercial and financial supremacy heretofore enjoyed by that country."[25]

American intellectuals and businessmen also were becoming increasingly reflective about the significant expansion of U.S. trade and its implications. Emblematic of this renewal of interest was the publication of a volume edited by Senator Chauncey M. Depew of New York in which a hundred American notables commemorated "the centenary of the Jay Treaty"—that is, the principle of commercial amity with low-tariff Britain. Many of the essayists were eastern seaboard traders, clothiers and shoe, pharmaceutical, paint, jewelry, and other finished-goods manufacturers. Others were midwestern manufacturers and meatpackers, railroad executives, shipbuilders, and government officials. Their contributions pointed to the broadening geographical and political constituency of American foreign trade expansionism of the mid-1890s.[26]

The notions of expansionism and American leadership in international commercial affairs were shared—indeed, cherished—by many American leaders. The defeat of the Democrat-Populist ticket in 1896 and the U.S. victories in the Spanish-American War would dissolve some of the antagonisms between the parties of Wells and Blaine, bringing many low-tariff Gold Democrats into alliance with the Republicans. This alliance would nurture new theorizing on expansion and development that promised to supersede the old conflicts of "home-market" protection versus "tariff for revenue only" and that might transform notions of free raw materials and reciprocity into effective national trade policies and new commercial institutions through which to carry them out. Prefiguring this hoped-for synthesis was the observation of Edward Atkinson, who reassured his aged colleague David Wells that the election of 1896 and the Spanish War had served a vital "educational" purpose: "The imagination of the people is now being aroused to the merits of an Anglo-American alliance and under that impulse obstructive duties will be swept away."[27]

In January 1898, Worthington C. Ford, an associate of Wells and current chief of the Treasury Department's Bureau of Statistics, could claim to redeem the promise of Leroy-Beaulieu in an article, "Commercial Superiority of the United States." Ford Americanized European notions of American potential by harping on the "immense economic advantage" held by the United States by virtue of its natural resources, which would allow it fullest scope to trade in manufactures without the burden of maintaining colonial staple-crop production.[28]

Expansionist American intellectuals became well versed in the relevant European political-economic literature. George M. Fisk, who earned his doctorate in Munich in 1896 with a thesis on European tariff affairs, served as a diplomat in Berlin and later wrote on tariff questions at the University of Illinois. H. H. Powers of Stanford also immersed himself in European imperial thought. His 1898 essay, "The War as a Suggestion of Manifest Destiny," written from Berlin, described the dawning era as a struggle between Romance, Germanic, Slavic, and Saxon "races." Powers predicted that the Romance and Germanic cultures would lapse into desuetude. But, echoing Schmoller, he warned that "it is possible that a generation or more will see the entire world under the jurisdiction or within the 'sphere of influence' of a half a dozen powers who will continue the struggle for race supremacy with increasing definiteness and determination." Oscar Phelps Austin, a former journalist who was then with the Treasury Department's Bureau of Statistics, wrote major works on European colonialism and on tariff systems that drew on and cited the work of Leroy-Beaulieu, Schmoller, Brentano, Dietzel, and other Europeans.[29]

By August 1898, Brooks Adams, brother of Henry Adams and intellectual confrere of Theodore Roosevelt, could write that the "seat of world empire" was about to move from Western Europe to the American shore. Propelling this transatlantic crossing, Adams was convinced, was a natural law that had seen "civilization" pass westward from China and India to Assyria, Phoenicia, Greece, Rome, and eventually to France and England. Nonetheless, like Paul Leroy-Beaulieu, Adams believed that the certainty and duration of American preeminence in this sequence of dominant societies depended on the resolution of American leaders to shape appropriate policies, as well as on the responses of the Europeans. America, Adams held, would be stripped of its full imperial patrimony if its leaders failed to consolidate their control of the domestic economy and marshal its "surplus" manufactures and capital in "a contest for the possession of the only markets left open," the "prize" of East Asia. In Adams's view, efforts to preclude a rival Eurasian empire from dominating Asia from the east required an Anglo-American alliance—implying tariff reduction.[30]

Even before Adams had constructed his grand theory, Charles A. Conant was writing in a similarly cosmopolitan vein. Conant, an 1894 Gold Democratic candidate for Congress in Massachusetts endorsed by David Wells, worked as a financial journalist for New York business newspapers, gained authority as the author of a principal work on banking systems, and would become a leading financial policy adviser of the Roosevelt and Taft eras.[31]

In his early writings on economy and empire, Conant updated, expanded, and further popularized arguments for foreign economic involvement that writers such as Wells had propounded during the late 1880s and early 1890s. For Conant, "congestion of capital" was an inevitable consequence of economic and social development in Europe and the United States. Thus, falling rates of interest on capital and declining prices for goods required the United States to foster a system of investment and trade abroad that would return profits and help preserve the domestic social order. This was what Conant frankly called the "economic basis of imperialism." Even more deeply than Adams, Conant knew the work of contemporary proimperial European thinkers and, like Adams, he appealed not so much to an interest group or region as to the nation's ruling class as a whole. In this context, Conant speculated on the potentials for reconciling views favoring reciprocity and free raw materials. Conant believed, along with other influential thinkers on both sides of the Atlantic, that an Anglo-American alliance—implying U.S. tariff reductions—would best develop and preserve domestic stability and realize the potentials of American capitalism.[32]

Such global speculations, European and American, were not merely the province of intellectuals. American policymakers, such as Frederic Emory, chief of the Department of State's Bureau of Foreign Commerce, also proclaimed that the expansion of U.S. export trade had made the nation's "'international isolation' . . . a thing of the past." Emory was entranced in 1898 by "new vistas in the struggle for ascendancy among the industrial powers." By 1900, confident of American gains in the exportation of manufactures to Europe and the footholds of American influence gained in the Far East, Emory could conclude that U.S. commerce and finance had moved from the realm of potentiality to established international influence.[33]

Even at their most enthusiastic, American leaders recognized that expansion brought dangers as well as opportunities. As Emory himself put it, the United States could "no longer afford to disregard international rivalries, now that we ourselves have become a competitor in the world-wide struggle for trade." Europeans were reacting to the "American invasion" of exports with concern. The Austro-Hungarian minister of foreign affairs, for example, urged Europeans to "close ranks" against the invader who exported greatly, mostly under most-favored-nation conditions, to Europe but maintained high tariff walls of its own. German and British trade authorities issued similar warnings. Measures against American expansion included traditional proposals of increased domestic protectionism in Europe. They also included the expanded use of nontariff barriers to trade such as sanitary inspections to block U.S. agricultural exports, and tariff measures such as the tightening of assimilation by France, the promulgation of imperial preferences by British dominions, political organization for an empire preference system by Joseph Chamberlain in Britain, and preparations for a new tariff set in motion by the Reichstag in 1897.[34]

The European reaction pointed to the potential vulnerability of U.S. expansion to systematic European countermeasures. A "preclusive imperialism" by European powers could cut off American markets, as in China; Europe might raise tariff barriers in retaliation for American high tariffs and the inroads of the American export invasion; and European combinations and cartels might overpower American exporters in Europe and in the neutral markets of Latin America and Asia.[35]

Because the United States sought continued commercial relations with the European nations and a commensurately expanded American position in the emerging world order, U.S. policymakers formulated their own approach to the rise of commercial competition—the concept of the open door. The open door originated in U.S. policy toward China, where European powers threatened to create exclusive spheres of influence. In response, the United States proposed voluntary abstention from unequal discriminations in investment opportunities, land grabbing, and exclusivistic deal making. Like British nineteenth-century policy, the open door was a global conception or attempt to construct a hegemonic ideology. But unlike the British order of the mid and late nineteenth century, the open door was not a free trade conception. In principle it recognized the exigency of metropolitan and colonial tariffs and other restrictive economic practices if they were applied for developmental purposes and if they opposed uneven or excessive discrimination.[36]

Yet a key problem for U.S. policy was that American tariff practices hardly epitomized the basic tenets of the open door. As expressed by diplomats and intellectuals, the open door opposed discrimination, but the U.S. domestic tariff, the product of the logrolling legislative system, set high rates in the United States' largest and fastest growing sphere of commerce—trade with Europe. The size of the differential itself represented some threat: Whereas U.S. tariffs on dutiable items averaged around 30 percent, European minimum or conventional rates were generally around 10 percent. More damaging still, where U.S. policy compromised American rates under the system of reciprocity, it favored only noncompetitive goods (mostly "tropical" products or European specialty manufactures such as wines and works of art) and discriminated in precisely the manner the open door opposed as a general principle. That is, the European unconditional most-favored-nation clause generalized the lowest rates of all treaties to most-favored-nation signatories, creating a composite rate made up of the baseline rates of the various bilateral treaties. But the United States' conditional interpretation extended reductions only when the other nations had given benefits the United States adjudged equivalent, not necessarily identical, to those offered by the original treaty signatory. Thus, every commercial treaty the United States signed was bilateral, unique, and implicitly discriminatory.[37]

That changes in the U.S. tariff stance had to accompany the United States' expanded role in international relations was stressed by the academic economists, who generally favored low tariffs, and Gold Democratic refugees, who in the wake of 1896 regarded the Republican party as the focus of their policy efforts. They followed the course of European tariff, foreign trade, and industrial policy and considered approximation of American tariffs to those of the United States' European trading partners as a priority. For example, economist H. H. Powers argued that "as momentary phases of political policy, protection and expansion may be combined, but, as expressions of national temper, they are incompatible." Referring to the Spanish War, Powers intoned that "We have crossed the Rubicon," suggesting, perhaps, by the analogy to Caesar that the most significant challenges for imperial conquerors lay in consolidating their power at home. Powers, like Edward Atkinson, appeared to hope that U.S. leaders would use the war and the enthusiasm for expansion it had engendered as a solvent for the ingrained "prejudice" of protectionism.[38]

C. R. Miller, the editor of the traditionally low-tariff *New York Times*, argued, in a similar vein, that the principal tasks in tariff reform were "educational." Both parties must abandon the debate of protection versus revenue, with the understanding that the priorities and capacities of a new economic age and new international economic relations outmoded them and made tariff reduction necessary, possible, and desirable.[39]

The United States' need to establish a tariff policy for its new dependencies put the issue in the context of the open door into practical form. The McKinley and Roosevelt administrations favored liberalized trade with U.S. possessions. Robert P. Porter, the U.S. commissioner in Puerto Rico, favored U.S.–Puerto Rican free trade, for example. But for its own development, Puerto Rico's tariff policy toward other nations could not be as protectionist as that of the United States. To make such distinctions, however, the right of the government to establish distinctive tariff policies for its overseas dependencies had to be proved in the U.S. courts, as it was in the Insular Cases of 1901. These judgments facilitated development in the colonies but also provided a certain degree of protection for U.S. domestic interests, because competing colonial products could now be dutied by the mainland.[40]

U.S. colonial policies, as guided by the financial expertise of men such as Charles A. Conant and by the writings of political scientist (and later U.S. ambassador to China) Paul S. Reinsch, and as established by administrators such as Porter and by William Howard Taft in the Philippines, consistently followed a developmentalist tack. In practice, however, proving U.S. colonial tariff policy different from that of the European nations and consistent with the open door was more complex. Under obligation by the terms of the Treaty of Paris, the United States had to extend to Spain for ten years any special preferences shown to U.S. goods in the Philippines. In addition, until 1909, U.S. domestic interests blocked export of large quantities of Philippine tobacco and sugar to the United States. The U.S.-Cuban reciprocity treaty of 1902 solved many problems of providing effective export markets in the United States for Cuban raw products, and thus in stabilizing the island's economy, but the exclusive nature of the reciprocity arrangement led to protest from Germany, which resented the 20 percent

Cuban reductions as a violation of most-favored-nation relations and a discrimination against German exports.[41]

A further roadblock to expanded reciprocity was the protectionism of influential Republicans such as Henry Cabot Lodge, Joseph G. Cannon, and Nelson W. Aldrich. For example, Aldrich argued that the laudable growth of commerce, and the increasing wealth of his constituency, had validated the wisdom of the protectionist policies under which they had occurred. Like Aldrich, the now-dominant Republican party had established protectionism as a shibboleth. In addition, the steel industry remained staunchly protectionist even after the formation of the powerful and efficient producer, U.S. Steel, in 1901. Myriad large and small industries, supported by groups such as the American Protective Tariff League and the Home Market Club, worried about foreign competition or, seeking protection as a means of consolidating domestic markets, supported high tariffs.[42]

Among proponents of U.S. commercial expansion, a revisionist position on the tariff evolved slowly, in good part because the rapid changes in the American economy and in European industrial policies around the turn of the century made the effects of different tariff strategies problematic. Moreover, any consensus on expansion among policymakers, intellectuals, and experts still required translation into tariff policy in Congress, where protectionism was strong and a two-thirds majority in the Senate was required to pass commercial treaties. Yet, increasingly, political, manufacturing, and commercial groups came to accept H. H. Powers's assessment that America had "crossed the Rubicon" into full-scale participation in a world commercial order. The question for tariff revisionists therefore was how to organize to reshape public consciousness and the system of tariff making to comport with their own conceptions of the domestic social order and the United States' role as a world economic power.

Some answers to these questions would appear as manufacturers began to envision security from recurrent depression and more profitable production as a result of an expanded reciprocal tariff system. Such sentiment for tariff reduction and reciprocity grew rapidly among manufacturers, agricultural producers, and commercial interests—many of them newly grouped in organizations formed in the mid to late 1890s—such as the National Association of Agricultural Implement and Vehicle Manufacturers, the Merchants Association of New York, and the National Association of Manufacturers.

Part One

The Tariff
under McKinley
and Roosevelt

2 A New God

Reciprocity, 1897–1901

Why can the country not join in melting the gods of protection and free trade into one divinity, larger, fairer, and more benignant than either.—James Deering, Deering Harvester Company, speech to National Association of Manufacturers, 1901

Among groups seeking to promote reciprocity and expand American foreign trade at the turn of the century, two were particularly prominent: the National Association of Agricultural Implement and Vehicle Manufacturers (NAAIVM) and the National Association of Manufacturers (NAM), a more inclusive manufacturing organization to which many of the implement and vehicle manufacturers also belonged. The implement manufacturers provided labor, leadership, and lobbying power on behalf of reciprocity and came to constitute a spearhead of the movement both within the NAM and nationally. In part this was because the larger and more influential NAM, although tending toward reduction, still included many industries that had protectionist agendas and hence was more divided on the tariff question.

The NAAIVM and the NAM did not begin by promoting the idea of reciprocity and foreign trade expansion in the abstract. Rather, both groups concentrated on supporting reciprocity as embodied in the Dingley Tariff of 1897 and the passage by the Senate of the commercial reciprocity treaty with France that was negotiated under its provisions and signed in Washington in July 1899.

The French treaty, which included reductions of up to 20 percent on competing industrial items according to "section 4" of the Dingley Treaty, was a breakthrough in going beyond the tropical-goods reciprocity of the Blaine era and a critical test case for U.S. commercial relations with Europe as a whole. As described by Republican Congressman Albert J. Hopkins of

Illinois in early 1897, the "chief glory" of the Dingley Tariff was its extension, under section 4, of the reciprocity provisions of the 1890 McKinley Tariff to "France, Germany, Belgium, and other European countries as well as Mexico and the Central and South American states."[1]

John A. Kasson, former ambassador to Germany and Austria-Hungary, veteran of the Berlin trade negotiations of 1885, and chief of the commission that negotiated the reciprocity treaties, told the Senate Foreign Relations Committee that the concessions were "not hard to our producers" and were essential to secure U.S. entry to Europe's minimum-tariff system. Moreover, Kasson argued, "the Dingley Act . . . put high duties on goods, having in view the possibility and necessity of reducing them under the provisions of the fourth section of the act. There is no use in our concealing the fact that the reciprocity clause was a part of that tariff as much as the duties themselves and effect must be given to it." In maintaining that the high Dingley Tariff rates were made to be bargained down, Kasson was arguing in essence that they were "maximum" rates and that the section 4 rates were equivalent to a U.S. "minimum" tariff, to be negotiated just as Germany negotiated its own tariff conventions; thus, approval of the treaty rates was vital to making the U.S. tariff system analogous to and compatible with European multiple-tariff systems. Kasson's view was challenged by some protectionists, however, and it was only the political imprimatur of President McKinley, and the efforts of Brooks Adams and other intellectuals who supported the reciprocity treaties at a critical moment in the debate that helped shape the initiative into a national political campaign.[2]

Reciprocity Ascendant

At first, the implement manufacturers seemed unlikely champions of tariff revision. Begun in 1894 as a forum of implement businessmen, the NAAIVM opposed the Democratic Wilson-Gorman Tariff, which had proposed eliminating the 35 percent duty on Canadian agricultural implements. Many implement makers opposed Democratic low-tariff policies and "radical" Populism. Yet from these protectionist origins, the NAAIVM began to move rapidly toward an activist tariff reductionism, in tandem with the Republican party and with the NAM.[3]

A crucial factor in the implement makers' shift toward reductionism was their changing position vis-à-vis the raw materials and semimanufactured goods they used. By the turn of the century, the farm equipment and vehicle industry—including the early manufacturers of trucks and automobiles—was becoming hard-pressed to secure adequate, timely, and economical supplies of raw materials such as steel bars and billets, hardwoods, and leather. Because so-called trusts were coming to dominate the supply of these items, manufacturers found themselves "radicalized" and increasingly amenable to suggestions that lower tariffs meant lower prices for trust-dominated raw materials and semimanufactures. Moreover, fear of recurrent depressions and opposition to the raw materials monopolies to a degree united the smaller proprietary operations in the implements field with some of the larger manufacturers such as the Deerings and the McCormicks, who were chiefly the makers of harvesting machines.[4]

The NAAIVM's tariff stance was a sensitive matter. The nature of their business led implement makers to favor concentrated, efficient, and mechanized farming. Hence, the NAAIVM naturally tended to minimize the need for tariffs on agricultural imports, assuming that American agriculture, with the assistance of modern machinery, could easily retain its home market. Yet because the implement makers depended on small and less mechanized farmers as well—to whom they sold products as varied as cream separators, plows, farm wagons, drills, and threshers—they tended to avoid endorsing tariff reductions on competitive agricultural goods such as Argentine and Canadian wheat. Instead, they stressed the usefulness of reciprocal agreements involving foreign raw products such as Canadian timber, because wood was in increasingly scarce supply in the Midwest.[5]

Perhaps the most active member of the NAAIVM at the national level was James Deering. Born in 1859, Deering was the Northwestern- and Harvard-educated son of William Deering, founder of Deering Harvester, then the second-largest implement manufacturer, behind McCormick. With his half-brother, Charles, James Deering increasingly managed Deering company business in the 1890s. He also chaired the founding committee of the NAAIVM and later served on its Committees on National Legislation and on Foreign Relations.

Deering Harvester would become one of the major components of the new International Harvester Corporation when that corporation was formed in August 1902, with James Deering acting as a principal in the negotiations. Deering Harvester and International Harvester would develop a distinctive position within the industry as a result of corporate consolidation. Before 1902, however, economic conditions for the large Deering operation resembled those for the agricultural implement industry as a whole. Implement makers generally were among the most innovative and technologically advanced sectors of U.S. manufacturing. They also were among the most competitive internationally and had pioneered foreign markets, especially during the depression of the 1890s. During the recovery of the late 1890s, implement makers continued their competition for sales in export markets, which they viewed as vital to their profitability and as an aspect of a domestic struggle for dominance in the industry. Here, the contest was primarily between the Deerings and the McCormicks. The latter company made 15 to 20 percent of its sales as exports. Both companies regarded sustained foreign selling as vital to their survival and took the initiative in steering the NAAIVM toward tariff reduction.[6]

During the early years of the NAAIVM, the presidents of the organization most often were representatives of the medium-sized proprietary businesses rather than the owners of the larger harvester, thresher, and vehicle plants. But the executive committee and the major national committees of the organization were heavily influenced by the larger, and later corporatized, businesses. Perhaps this was partly because those in the larger businesses could afford to delegate authority in their industrial operations while they spent weeks or even months in Washington or at NAAIVM headquarters in Chicago on political assignments.[7]

The other major reductionist group at the turn of the century was the NAM. Far less unified than the NAAIVM, the NAM was also far larger, including manufacturers of implements, tools, hardware, railroad equipment, textiles, clothing, leather goods, chemicals, pharmaceuticals, and many other items. Founded in Cincinnati in 1895, the NAM at first seemed to conceive of broadened foreign trade relatively narrowly—as a tool for alleviating the depression. Yet a long-term commitment to expansionism was apparent even in the NAM's earliest lists of priorities: a Department of Commerce or Manufactures, training of diplomatic and commercial consular personnel, and hemispheric initiatives such as an interoceanic canal, an inter-American bank, and a warehouse in Venezuela to display members' lines of goods.[8]

Tariff reciprocity was on the NAM's policy agenda from the outset. But before the election of McKinley, members seemed wary of major tariff changes and reluctant to expand reciprocity beyond the boundaries established by Blaine and McKinley in the early 1890s. In supporting Blaine's "tropical" reciprocity, Republicans touted its usefulness in exacting concessions from trading partners in exchange for lower U.S. rates, in contrast to the Democratic policy of making unilateral reductions through "free raw materials." Reciprocity was a potent medicine, Republicans and NAM members of the 1890s argued, and many wanted to see it administered only in the smallest prescription possible. For example, Charles Heber Clark, NAM member and spokesman for the protectionist Philadelphia Manufacturers' Club, argued that reciprocity could be countenanced only if confined strictly to the exchange of South American raw materials for North American manufactures. Identifying with this cautious spirit in a keynote address to the NAM's founding convention, McKinley himself—then governor of Ohio but responsible, as chairman of the House Ways and Means Committee, for the reciprocity provisions of the 1890 tariff—declaimed that "We want a foreign market for our surplus products which will not surrender our markets and will not degrade our labor to hold our markets."9

Despite the timorousness of much Republican tariff reductionism and the tendency of Republicans to venerate the party shibboleths of protection and economic stability, some NAM members—particularly conservative Democrats and some eastern and midwestern Republicans united by opposition to Bryanism—were beginning to believe that the larger the dose of reciprocity, the more beneficial its effect. In their more ambitious revisionist view, reciprocity should moderate U.S. tariffs on raw materials of all sorts and sources and effectively reverse the Republican party's traditional high protectionism. Taking the tariff talk of the McKinley presidential campaign seriously, these reductionists saw reciprocity as a natural complement of the conservative, suprapartisan concept of "sound money." Thus, it was another ideal to unite Republicans and Democrats, free traders and protectionists, in a synthesis for commercial expansion.10

The new interpretation of reciprocity appeared more conspicuously within the NAM after McKinley's victory, when Theodore C. Search, of J. B. Stetson and Company of Cincinnati, became head of the group. Two months before McKinley's inauguration, and as the Ways and Means Committee was beginning to frame the Dingley Tariff, Search announced in his own inaugural address that the spirit of "sound money" should be extended to the tariff. He argued that Republicans could agree to modify protection to the level at which the tariff would produce required government revenue. Democrats, he said, could respond by abandoning the broad use of the ad valorem system, which was subject to abuse by importers who undervalued their merchandise. Probably Search was not intending literally that Republicans should endorse the Democratic idea of a "tariff for revenue only" but was trying to suggest that debates over "protection versus revenue" were outmoded. Instead, Search suggested, the tariff should be put on a "strict business basis" that would lower excessive U.S. rates so that they provided a "just protection" that equalized U.S. and foreign "wages, costs of material, interest charges," and other operating expenses. This would open foreign markets to U.S. goods and would defend American industries adequately in most cases, Search argued.[11]

In Search's view, reciprocity was an ideal instrumentality for creating a broadly based "business tariff." Reciprocity would provide outlets for expanding American production and would thus furnish a remedy for industrial depressions. It would also appease foreign nations that had been offended by the labile rates and contradictory policies that were the legacy of frequent tariff revisions and transitions in national leadership—for example, the abrogation of the McKinley reciprocity treaties of the early 1890s by the Wilson Tariff of 1894. In the afterglow of the defeat of Bryan, Search asserted, "the views of those who accept the principles of protection as well as those who are opposed to such theories never were more marked by moderation."[12]

By early 1898, the Kasson treaties were in negotiation, prosperity was resurgent, and revision seemed imminent. Search issued only one caution, urging NAM members to "display a willingness to go at least half way if hope is entertained of our coming to any practical result." NAM members, however, were divided on where that "half way" was, and on whether it was worth jeopardizing the American market to overcome the still-incompletely enforced French and European maximum tariffs. The perspectives of manufacturers interested in recouping their depression losses were probably evident here. Likewise, during the NAM's January 1899 convention, the heady events of the previous year's war with Spain overshadowed the tariff and seemed to suggest that expansion could be had at slight cost in American blood and treasure.[13]

By 1900, the tone of tariff and reciprocity discussion had altered. On the diplomatic front, the most important Kasson treaties had been signed, but they had become stalled in the Senate—particularly the French and Argentine treaties. France's exclusion of some important American manufactures from its minimum schedule was the nub of the problem. Search agonized over the possibility that Congress would reject the treaties. But he was even more disturbed by his failure to muster unequivocal support within the NAM for the Kasson treaties, now that reciprocity had come within reach.[14]

The problem was that manufacturers who had been strenuous supporters of reciprocity in 1898 had begun to have second thoughts after they were excluded from the minimum-tariff list by the French. Machine tool makers were prominent in this group. Also irked were manufacturers of pig iron and makers of boots and shoes. So were the producers of leather belting, which was vital as a part of machine transmissions in factory production of that era. The hosiery industry was miffed at the 20 percent reduction the Kasson Commission had granted French undergarments. Likewise, live-stock interests were assailing the Argentine treaty for having given away 20 percent reductions in U.S. rates on raw wool. As president of the NAM, Search admitted that he had been so pressured by different interests that he now had to reopen the question of reciprocity to the association's general meeting. Casting about for a scapegoat for this reverse, Search complained that the Kasson Commission should have negotiated more defensible trea-ties. This complaint was largely rhetorical, but it revealed that there had been little communication and understanding between the diplomats who had negotiated the trade treaties and the manufacturers themselves, a point that would become a key contention when the revision movement turned toward agitation for a tariff commission.[15]

On the floor of the NAM convention, the debate clarified the bases of both support and opposition to reciprocity as a commercial policy. Funda-mentally, it counterposed two conceptions of commercial policymaking—one exalting equity and individual self-interest as key to national well-being, the other arguing for a riskier and more dynamic expansionist approach to garnering foreign trade. This latter view, supporting the French treaty, was assertively represented by a coalition of agricultural implement manufac-turers, some machine tool exporters, and import-export groups. They argued that the potential for expanding U.S. trade with France was vast. The United States, they pointed out, had only $4 million of France's imports and could gain a much larger share—possibly as much as $20 to $30 million—under the minimum-tariff conditions the reciprocity treaty would gain for them. Arthur B. Farquhar, the political-economic writer and implement manufacturer from York, Pennsylvania, argued that on average in the treaty the United States was getting 25 percent reduction of nearly all the French schedules, whereas the French were being given only an average of 8 percent reductions of about one-third of the total American schedule, an argument Commissioner Kasson himself was making before the Senate Foreign Relations Committee. Seconding this view was William C. Barker, an upstate New York implement manufacturer and representative of the NAAIVM National Legislation Committee, which had been lobbying energetically in Washington for the French treaty. Barker invoked the analogy Kasson himself had drawn between his treaties and the European general and conventional tariff system. The Dingley rates, Barker said, were "made to bargain down." All manufacturers, he continued, would have no worse than the 1890 McKinley rates after the treaty, and only "superstition" and greed animated the treaty's opponents, principally the perfume makers and knit goods manufacturers.[16]

Protectionists of the "injured industries" were no less accusatory. Invoking Blaine's and McKinley's reciprocity of the early 1890s, they argued that Republican tariffs must harm no domestic industry. "It is a very dangerous principle for us to establish," commented Charles H. Harding, a Philadelphia member, "that for the sake of the prosperity of 51 per cent. of our members we shall minimize for a little while the injury that may be done to 49 per cent." Harding sought to limit the NAM's endorsement of the French treaty to reciprocity for noncompeting foreign goods alone, specifically excluding French cotton knit goods from reduction. But Harding's amendment lost, 66 to 47, and the original motion of support for the treaty carried. Leather goods manufacturer William McCarroll, prominent in the New York Chamber of Commerce, sought compromise. He supported the motion with the proviso that supplementary treaties should be negotiated to liberalize the terms under which American hosiery, leather, boots and shoes, and other products slighted in the current agreement were admitted to France.[17]

Thus, only in 1900, under the pressure of internal dispute and in a test of actual treaty legislation, did the NAM have to ask whether reciprocity as embodied in the Dingley Tariff could extend to competing products and, if so, how the level of potential injury to producers of those products could be assessed. As long as reciprocity meant that the United States had only to concede rates on articles that did not compete with American industrial products, it would be a panacea, satisfying everyone. But if it was true, as Commissioner Kasson had testified before the Senate Foreign Relations Committee, that treaties could not be negotiated with industrialized European nations on this basis, the notion of reciprocity as an economic cure without side effects was dispelled, and the momentum that had made reciprocity a functional part of the 1896 electoral coalition was spent. Thus it was crucial for Republicans to attempt to break this impasse by creating a more sophisticated and practical consensus for reduction.[18]

Even though the NAM had supported reciprocity in committee by a substantial margin, the consensual nature of tariff making in the House, with its logrolling and interest trading, and of treaty making in the Senate, with its requirement of a two-thirds majority for passage, allowed well-organized minorities to obstruct commercial agreements. Reciprocity advocates within the NAM thus had to convert the minorities within their own fold if partisans of reciprocity in Congress were to have a hope of convincing their colleagues of the popular demand for tariff revision.

When the controversy over the treaties resumed within the NAM in early 1901, President Search had begun an attempt to forge a stronger consensus for reciprocity. Search returned to the reciprocity camp as an outspoken advocate, raising the specter of a European retaliation against the "American invasion." He warned the assembled manufacturers that the conditions of international trade had "changed very materially during the past year and [would] be altered still further in the near future." Whereas once Americans had been tolerated as bumptious newcomers to international trade, Europeans "who formerly were amused and entertained by American aggressiveness now are alarmed by our encroachment upon the markets which they have regarded as their own." Thus, Search argued, the United States had to make the concessions implicit in its own tariff or face escalating trade discrimination by the Europeans.[19]

Search's cause was aided by James Deering, a member of the NAM as well as of the NAAIVM. In an essay read to the convention, Deering epitomized the proreciprocity argument during the push for the Kasson treaties in 1901. Acknowledging that protection had built up American industry during the nineteenth century, Deering warned that Republicans must not make of protection a "fetish," for as such, it would prevent unified action by manufacturers in response to the changing economic conditions of the twentieth century, which required an extensive foreign trade. Deering had little patience for politicians who resisted the push for foreign markets on the "parochial" grounds that reciprocity might injure some humble "crossroads manufacturer." Nor did he approve of doctrinaire free traders. What was necessary, he argued, was a synthesis: "Why can the country not join in melting the gods of protection and free trade into one divinity, larger, fairer, and more benignant than either, which shall be entitled 'The greatest good for the greatest number of American citizens.' Protection as a divinity has done its work. Complete free trade is Utopian."[20] The new god, of course, was Reciprocity.

Other, less prominent NAM members joined the effort to make reciprocity the incarnation of American commercial practice at this critical point by seeking to promote it from an antidote to depressions and Democratic tariff policies to a permanent feature of an expansionist American commercial empire. Ohio delegate James F. Taylor, a leather goods manufacturer and spokesman for the Free Hides League, argued that if the United States pretended to the commercial—as well as the financial—mantle of Britain, Americans had to assume the national responsibilities of the systematic, consistent, and liberal tariff policy that had been the hallmark of England's commercial ascendancy in the nineteenth century. Reciprocity was an important part of this process. To applause, Taylor declaimed, "We want China with open doors and every other country with open doors, but we want to close tight the doors to America. They won't let us do it and you must take a broader and grander view." At least, Taylor pleaded, the United States must accept the principle of free raw materials.[21]

Certainly Taylor, as a leather goods manufacturer, could be accused of using spread-eagle rhetoric as a guise for self-interest. Yet manufacturers viewed reciprocity in a way that was less rhetorical and more complex than immediate self-interest could account for. Representatives of the machine tool industry from Ohio and New Jersey maintained, for example, that even though machine tools had been excluded from the present French treaty, they believed in the salability of American tools in France, at least, and saw no reason to oppose the treaty on that ground. They were confident that they would derive indirect benefits from the effects of reciprocity on their fellow manufacturers, and they approved of the flexibility of commercial treaties, which meant that specific items might be renegotiated in coming years without requiring the United States to frame an entirely new tariff.[22]

The support for reciprocity among machine tool makers and other smaller capitalists appears to be rooted in their position as proprietary capitalists attempting to adjust their trade to times of economic pressures, foreign and domestic. The machine tool makers were legitimately worried about the great growth of industry in Austria-Hungary and Germany. Some who had been abroad brought home sobering impressions of industrialization in Central Europe, where production of tools, sewing machines, typewriters, and other metals manufactures was beginning to assail the export outposts American producers had established during the 1890s. "All through Germany," opined Pennsylvania cement and iron goods manufacturer Oliver Williams, "you see factories going up to manufacture this, that and the other thing." Budapest, he added, could "rival" Detroit—the 1901 NAM convention site—as an industrial city. Williams was concerned that manufacturers not only faced the increasingly competitive European industrial apparatus but growing European protectionism as well.[23]

Seizing the opportunity for tariff adjustment was important to proprietary manufacturers for domestic as well as international reasons. As Oliver Williams argued, corporate exporters and financiers such as "Mr. Morgan" would soon see the advantages of much lower tariffs to their export trade. "These people that are exporting so largely . . . are the people to do away with a good deal of the tariff, and I think many of them are willing to do it." Smaller and midsize manufacturers, he implied, must pass legislation on the tariff that reflected their own needs in foreign markets—that is, they had to get reciprocity while it would allow them to retain their competitive position in Europe and under circumstances that would forestall a wholesale elimination of American tariffs that would endanger their domestic markets.[24]

Many other speakers echoed Williams's minatory tones. Among them was chemical manufacturer F. B. Thurber, a well-known reciprocity advocate and self-proclaimed loyal protectionist. In a phrase familiar since the Cleveland era, Thurber called for a revision by "protection's friends," via reciprocity, lest tariff reform be enacted by "protection's enemies." Tool manufacturer Fred F. Smith of New Jersey called for manufacturers' solidarity in the face of a general revision that might endanger them all, "letting each manufacturer forget his own profits for the time being and all the manufacturers acting as a unit." A copper producer from Michigan scoffed at the complaint of some manufacturers that their business would be ruined by reductions as "farcical and dishonest."[25]

Thus, within the NAM by 1900–1901 can be discerned a primary thrust for reciprocity based on an expansive imperial image of U.S. commercial destiny counterposed to a protectionism yet unwilling to risk domestic markets for the foreign prize. It is especially significant to note that the expansive concern for reciprocity and revision itself was divided. Some manufacturers, large producers such as Deering, emphasized reciprocity's capacity to transcend through expansion the distinctions among capitalists or at least to prevent those distinctions from becoming divisive. That is, if capitalists would identify with the strong producers and cease protecting every "crossroads" manufacturer, they could attain a meaningful reciprocity, Deering argued. The tool and chemical makers such as Williams and Thurber, in contrast, were emphasizing the potential opposition between proprietary producers and the large, corporate interests, symbolized by "Mr. Morgan." These proprietary manufacturers suggested that expansion and reciprocity had to be regulated by smaller producers lest corporate capitalists use it against them. In this latter sense, the "producerism" of the nineteenth century, once adamantly protectionist, had acquired a revisionist cast.

A God That Failed

As the Kasson treaties languished in the Senate Foreign Relations Committee, the NAM announced a National Reciprocity Convention. The convention's call, issued on September 4, 1901, sought to rally business support for the 20 percent reduction clauses of the French treaty and thus to press the Senate to pass the treaty.[26]

Two important ideological landmarks distinguish the period of the National Reciprocity Convention. The first was the publication, as the lead piece of the August 1901 issue of the *Atlantic Monthly*, of Brooks Adams's article, "Reciprocity or the Alternative." One of the nation's premier "imperialist intellectuals" and an intimate of Vice-President Theodore Roosevelt, Adams pleaded the case for reciprocity in his characteristically far-ranging historical and geopolitical style. Recalling the commercial isolation of powerful, protectionist France under Colbert and Louis XIV, Adams foresaw a similar ostracism for the United States if it failed to adopt reciprocal trade policies. He predicted that ultimately a policy of high protection and aggressive exporting would lead the United States, as it had led France, to war and social catastrophe.[27]

Adams's thesis was more than an exercise in recondite historical parallelism. It pressed a point that all sides in the tariff debate admitted as given: the emergence of the United States in the late nineteenth century as an exporter of huge scope that could undersell Europe in agricultural products, in manufactures of iron and steel, and in "minerals as a raw material." Adams argued that the driving economic necessity of American exports, and their sheer bulk and low cost, represented a direct threat to European industrial structures. In addition, the blithe American determination to dominate investment and trade in South America and China threatened to preempt European sources of raw materials.

As most of his readers knew, Adams considered American productive dominance a result of "natural laws" of historic geopolitical development, of a sequence of rising and decaying civilizations. But to prolong the American period of dominance in this sequence, Adams believed that some form of mediation with other powers was crucial. Given the rapidly developing European imperial rivalries, the development of a workable American reciprocity policy, Adams suggested, was one of the few remaining outlets for compromise and integration. It would allow European nations to absorb some of the flood of American products by giving them compensatory access to American markets as an outlet for their own goods.[28]

Adams also was concerned about the domestic implications of U.S. foreign commercial expansion. Continuing his historical parallel, Adams described how in France of the ancien régime, traditional practices and the interests that sustained them had carried a dangerous, ponderous weight. It was Louis's and Colbert's inability to curtail aristocratic resistance to competitive imports that underlay France's ultimate failure as an empire. Colbert's preemptive attack against the Dutch in 1672 for their retaliatory exclusion of French goods thus was "the point of departure for all subsequent European history down to Waterloo." Adams rephrased his point for pedagogic reasons: "France failed in 1672, when relatively strongest, because she lacked the flexibility to shed an obsolete social system." This left the task, as all knew, to the events of 1789. Thus, the ruling interests of the United States, Adams was saying, must wean the social and industrial system from its traditional high protectionism, lest they lead the nation to economic and political ruin and cede leadership to forces that would seek more energetically to put the nation on a footing of "economic equality with [its] neighbors." Adams therefore posed not one but two alternatives to reciprocity—war and revolution.[29]

The second landmark of reciprocity was the "Buffalo Address," President McKinley's speech of September 5, 1901, at the Pan-American Exposition in Buffalo. Effectively culminating McKinley's long advocacy of reciprocity, the speech capped a national tour that had begun originally in April. On the tour, McKinley had sought to use his popularity and reelection mandate to promote reciprocity, a strategy presaged in his second inaugural address. Although the Buffalo speech sometimes echoed the traditional protectionist doxology—as in the assertion that reciprocity should not "interrupt our home production"—McKinley's underlying theme was a challenge to traditional protectionism not unlike that of Brooks Adams. Specifically, McKinley considered unrestrained protectionism a threat: "We must not repose in fancied security that we can forever sell everything and buy little or nothing." He justified departure from traditional tariff postures by hinting that the gold standard and system of corporate consolidation, the "domestic policy now firmly established" by the victories of 1896 and 1900, was at the root of the recent outburst of industrial growth and made reciprocity a "natural outgrowth" of that system. The president proclaimed that "the period of exclusiveness is past" and added the United States' "real eminence rests in the victories of peace, not those of war." An anarchist shot McKinley the following day.[30]

Despite McKinley's death, the NAM decided to go forward with the reciprocity conference it had scheduled for November 19 and 20, 1901. For the conference, the NAM sought to broaden the organizational support of reciprocity by inviting members of the New York export-import community, represented by the Merchants Association of New York, the New York Board of Trade, the New York Chamber of Commerce, and the New York–based U.S. Export Association. These groups, which included both Republicans and Democrats, had gravitated toward the tariff revisionists within the predominantly Republican and midwestern NAM. In part, this may be attributable to their common gold-standard, "sound money" views and cooperation in monetary movements. Although NAM leaders did not expect the New York merchant community to sacrifice its organizational autonomy, they hoped that the convention would allow individuals of different regions to sort out areas of common interest that could link their tariff-reduction viewpoints.[31]

The NAAIVM in particular mobilized for the convention and to promote the French treaty directly to Congress, maintaining William Barker, James Deering, and other members of its Committee on National Legislation in Washington during the summer and fall of 1901. The committee met with McKinley and later with several prominent senators. As part of the lobbying effort, the group produced and distributed to congressmen literature on the reciprocity question. Building on themes stressed by McKinley and Brooks Adams, the NAAIVM argued that reciprocity would enable America "to march on to her possible destiny as the greatest exporter of manufactured goods in the history of the world." The committee's screed highlighted the growth of exclusivistic European tariff and commercial legislation, which it regarded as in good measure a retaliation against the high levels of the Dingley Tariff. The adoption of a maximum-minimum tariff by France and the promulgation of a similar measure by Germany would harm U.S. exports because U.S. treaties with these nations were due to expire shortly. Because the maximum tariff of France was applicable only to the United States and to Portugal, it put the United States at a near-unique disadvantage in export trade among manufacturing nations. Thus, the committee argued, the United States faced the real, rather than hypothetical, unification of Europe against American manufactured exports.[32]

The committee also noted that continued export of manufactured goods was critical not only to the United States' role as an exporting power but to the stability of the domestic economy itself, which had entered a "critical stage." Whereas in the generation after the Civil War expansion of the home market under protectionist auspices was the prime consideration, "the protective system has done its great work." Now, without foreign markets "to absorb our increasing output, it is inevitable that we shall turn upon ourselves and waste in destructive competition the energy that might, with a proper outlet, give us command of the markets of the world."[33]

In their Washington work, Deering and the committee acknowledged the divisions that had arisen among manufacturers. Although few American manufacturers really opposed reciprocity, it was probably "aimless and futile" to expect unanimous approval of reciprocity by manufacturers because each wished "to have a voice in dictating what the American concessions to reciprocity should be." Hence, the committee argued, the manufacturers' "approval of some practical measure of reciprocity already accomplished is the only method by which a definite result can be obtained."[34]

In essence, the NAAIVM was arguing that Congress had to exercise the political will to legislate against the interests, as self-conceived, of the protectionist industries in the service of a larger objective. The key to future American development, the NAAIVM contended, was in signing actual trade agreements, thus moving reciprocity beyond a mere "catchword." Legislative activity was essential: "Call it what we may, whether practical reciprocity, or commercial treaties, or a maximum and minimum tariff (and all come to what we call reciprocity in the end), a way out of the difficulties that are facing us must be found, and found promptly." It was for this reason that reciprocity transcended questions of party and was a matter of "the industrial prosperity of the country."[35]

Despite the two-pronged efforts of the NAM and the NAAIVM, hopes that the manufacturers and Congress would carry reciprocity forward were not realized. The efforts to forge a cross-regional unity at the conference that would produce a strong endorsement of the French treaty were largely unsuccessful. In fact, conflicts erupted almost immediately between manufacturers who were helped or hindered by the specific terms of the treaty. The iron goods manufacturers—mainly producers of farm implements, tools, and hardware—generally favored the NAM's version of reciprocity. But they were unable to suppress or transcend the opposition of the knit goods, perfume, and jewelry manufacturers, who proclaimed themselves sacrificial victims of the French treaty and impugned the motives of the reciprocity partisans as purely self-promoting. In effect, the conference reprised the acrimony that had divided manufacturers from the beginning of the Kasson treaty process.[36]

Home-market protectionists fought all attempts at the convention to promote wider reciprocity as a Republican principle by digging in behind the most traditional definition of reciprocity. They opposed "any change in the rates . . . which will in any manner inflict the smallest injury upon any productive industry in which the people of this country are engaged." Behind this pronouncement was Charles Heber Clark, who warned against the disruption of returning prosperity that might be caused by new tariff arrangements. He criticized the French treaty as an opening wedge toward low, Wilson-type tariffs. Moreover, he emphasized the dangers of the treaty to specific industries, saying that it would be "the knife" to the knit goods industry of the Schuylkill Valley of Pennsylvania. Here, Clark was pointing out that the United States was still developing internally, even in the East, where new textile mills were springing up in the coal and iron country around Reading. Brought into direct competition with the advanced facilities of Europe by low tariffs, these relatively poorly capitalized mills would be sacrificed to the interests of big companies such as Deering's that sought to sell more goods abroad. Clark thus was turning the "tariffs spawn trusts" argument on its head by implying that it was really control of the tariff on specific products and the relation of that level to the market conditions in each industry that was most important. This was a conclusion that the smaller businessmen, even among the tariff revisionists, found hard to refute.[37]

Finally, Clark sought to demonstrate that the recent expansion of American resources and industrial wealth merely underlined the need to preserve self-sufficiency behind a high tariff wall. "I hope never to see the day," Clark said, "when this country will be in such a position in regard to the necessaries of life as England is, who cannot feed herself three months in the year out of the products of her own soil." Although foreign trade was desirable, the United States should aim first to assure its industrial independence— "the power to stand alone, if we choose to."[38]

Aggrieved by the insults to reciprocity and by the barrage of arguments against it, its partisans counterattacked. F. B. Thurber, representing the U.S. Export Association, argued, in terms reminiscent of Edward Atkinson, that as master of "the forces which now control the world, steam, electricity, and machinery," the United States was producing more than it could consume and needed world markets. Hence, he argued, a "minority" of protectionists should not be allowed to defeat a passive "majority" of reductionists. "Reciprocity affords an opportunity to reform the tariff by its friends, which, if not embraced, may result in a tidal wave of free-trade sentiment which will be disastrous to all our industries."[39]

Yet in addition to the adamant protectionists, some NAM members who were enthusiastic foreign trade expansionists retained reservations about reciprocity in its McKinley-Kasson incarnation. For example, George J. Seabury, of Seabury and Johnson, New York medicinal goods exporters, and a longtime Latin American trader, seemed to feel that reciprocity was helpful more as a balm than a tonic—that is, only if it was applied topically to Cuba, Canada, and South American nations. Manufacturers would find more danger than opportunity if they precipitously lowered tariff barriers with advanced industrial countries. Despite the apparent competitiveness of American industry, Seabury warned, only certain sectors were truly invulnerable to European competition. Other sectors would be hurt by lower European wage rates, longer work hours, and cheaper transport and finance costs. It was safer for the majority of businessmen—by implication, the smaller businessmen—to wait for the completion of an isthmian canal and the construction of an efficient merchant marine, which would enhance American competitiveness. American manufacturers, Seabury believed, "would be fatally overmatched in competing with [the Europeans] in the same lines of materials and wares under reciprocal treaties or special trade relations." Fellow New Yorkers Henry Dalley and Charles Schieren also were concerned about the ability of individual businesses to compete against Europe and were hesitant about reciprocity in its extensive sense. They wanted a reciprocity that was closer to the idea of free raw materials.[40]

The descent of the National Reciprocity Convention into recrimination apparently doomed the French treaty. Despite continuing efforts, pro-reciprocity forces could not muster votes enough to bring it to debate and a vote in the Senate, and it fell into limbo in the Foreign Relations Committee—signed by the diplomats but spurned by the legislature. Undoubtedly, too, the absence of McKinley contributed to the decline of reciprocity sentiment. Flag-draped portraits of "the martyred President" and epigraphs drawn from the Buffalo Address emblazoned on protreaty literature were not enough.

Members of the implement industry tried to keep reciprocity alive by organizing a National Reciprocity League (NRL) in April 1902. On the league's board of directors were former ambassador John A. Kasson, Arthur B. Farquhar, and James Deering. The chairman was a former NAAIVM president, H. C. Staver, a Chicago carriage builder. The NRL held a convention in Detroit in December 1902, where the featured speaker was Iowa Governor Albert B. Cummins. The league also published a magazine, *National Reciprocity*, and agitated for reciprocity with Cuba, in line with President Roosevelt's efforts. But the NRL failed to rally support among eastern groups despite financial help from the NAAIVM and the carriage builders associations.[41]

At the same time, within the agricultural implement industry, reciprocity's mainstay during the 1897–1902 period, new conflicts were taking precedence. Increasing hostility toward the Harvester Corporation was finding its way into trade publications and into the deliberations of the NAAIVM. Whereas in the first years of the twentieth century only the pro-Democratic *Implement Age* attacked trusts vociferously, between 1903 and 1905, the pages of other farm implement journals became crowded with articles and advertisements deploring the depredations of the Harvester conglomerate on independent producers and distributors of farm equipment. It was around this time that James Deering disappeared from the high councils of the NAAIVM. The McKinley-Kasson phase of commercial policymaking seemed to have ended, but no clear alternative had come to replace it.[42]

Some of the reasons for the decline of the reciprocity push were suggested in the report of Henry R. Towne, of the Merchants Association of New York delegation, to his association. Towne commented that the reciprocity partisans had been poorly prepared and insufficiently appreciative of the difficulty of overcoming protectionist interests. The chief deficit of the movement, Towne believed, was its lack of an effective principle of operation:

> Among other facts forcibly brought out by the discussion is the great complexity of the problem at issue. . . . No industry is ready to offer itself as a sacrifice for the benefit of others, and in our opinion it is useless, if not childish, to make appeals . . . to patriotism and to public spirit. . . . Any argument for Reciprocity, to justify itself and to command general approval, must provide for the distribution of any "sacrifices" it may involve with at least some show of fairness, if not with complete equality.[43]

Reciprocity's incarnation as a divinity more "benignant" than either protection or free trade appeared to have failed. In section 4 of the Dingley Tariff, Congress had provided for reductions of up to 20 percent on foreign goods that were competitive with American products, if treaty arrangements could be made and ratified. But once the treaties had been negotiated by the Kasson Commission, Congress, responding to the tenor of discussion within the foreign trade movement and to pressure from protectionists, had recoiled from full immersion in the new faith. The momentum behind the reciprocity movement appeared to have faltered as the industries "injured" by the French agreement worked to dilute the reciprocity resolutions of those who sought to promote commercial treaties.

The failure of the treaties revealed the weakness of Republican revisionism as an effective strategy, as opposed to a talking point against Democratic revisionism. The discussions of reciprocity also revealed much about the nature of Republican support for reciprocity; expansionist manufacturers, in the midst of the period of corporate consolidations, were becoming aware of possible differences between their interests and those of large exporters of the "Mr. Morgan" or "Deering" type, and to conceive of tariff reduction not only as an aid to trade expansion but as a support for nonintegrated, proprietary capitalism. Thus, whereas at the earliest points of the reciprocity agitation, manufacturers believed that it would assure a larger field for profit for all, at later points manufacturers were beginning to conceive of reciprocity and expansion in terms more specific to their own status within the productive system. This development—though made explicit in schemes such as the "Iowa idea," which proposed using the tariff against the trusts—was submerged temporarily in the defeat of the larger reciprocity movement. The differences would reemerge, however, as corporate consolidations continued.

Another factor working toward the revival of a public movement for reciprocity in the ensuing five years was the projected German tariff revision and application of Germany's maximum rates to the United States. Here appeared the fulfillment of Brooks Adams's dire warnings of the alternatives to American reciprocity. Partisans of reciprocity therefore maintained their faith, if not all their fervor. In reciprocity's eclipse, many of its proponents began to seek a means to recast revision to avoid congressional obstacles. In this effort, they turned toward the executive branch and its new chief, Theodore Roosevelt.

3 The Rebirth of Reciprocity, 1902–1905

[Roosevelt], if he could do it by ukase, would revise the tariff.—Historian James Ford Rhodes, after White House meeting with President Roosevelt, 1905

The failure in the Senate of the Kasson reciprocal trade treaties was a debacle for Republican tariff revisionists. Industrial and commercial groups that had promoted the tariff reduction treaties as integral to a new American economic order of expanded foreign trade now had to admit that the core of their program—reciprocity with Europe in competitive industrial products—had failed to gain a true consensus.

On a practical, political level, revisionists conceded that reciprocity by commercial treaty was a dim prospect, given the requirement for a two-thirds majority for approval of treaties by the Senate. Perhaps even more significant, on an ideological level, revisionists had to acknowledge not only a resurgence of home-market protectionism but new conflicts between corporate and proprietary expansionists over the shape tariff revision might take when it did occur. Such obstacles, however, neither inhibited expansionists from supporting reciprocity in principle nor stopped them from beginning an energetic search for more negotiable routes toward tariff revision.

From 1902 to 1907, reciprocity—as a theory and policy of systematically reducing and coordinating U.S. tariff rates with those of the European industrial states—was in transition. During this time, proponents of expansion and tariff reduction sought to redefine themselves as a political movement, to bypass the pitfalls that had trapped the Kasson treaties in the Senate, and to rethink revisionism as a guiding principle of American trade policy. To these ends, prorevision Republicans contemplated a variety of proposals: for a maximum-minimum tariff enacted "autonomously" by a simple legislative majority, for expanding the powers of the executive branch to interpret matters of customs administration affecting trade, and for appointing a tariff commission with investigatory and rate-setting authority.

The renewed revisionist initiatives were at first private and largely theoretical, but they involved not only business leaders but prominent administration figures. Moreover, the revision question gained urgency and publicity as European nations began to discuss and apply maximum tariff rates to U.S. exports in the wake of the failure of the Kasson initiatives. Because a new U.S. tariff bill was not on the agenda of Congress, the primary focus of revision activity in the United States was on maintaining or modifying existing commercial treaties and customs agreements, especially with Germany, whose protectionist counterlegislation was most pressing.

The Roosevelt Administration and Reciprocity

The influence of the chief executive in promoting tariff change had been underlined by the essentially contemporaneous failure of the reciprocity initiative and the death of McKinley. With revision's proponents promoting the idea of executive administration of the tariff, the president's role would become even more crucial.

Most revisionists initially saw the new president, Theodore Roosevelt, as a tariff reformer, a view that he cultivated in his messages of 1901 and 1902, echoing McKinley in describing reciprocity as a "natural line of development" for products that "no longer require all of the support once needed to establish them on a sound basis" and for those that "either because of natural or of economic causes . . . are beyond the reach of successful competition." Soon after the failure of the Kasson treaties, however, Roosevelt narrowed his agenda to defending reciprocity with Cuba and the Philippines. Revisionists began to view Roosevelt as an inconstant friend, especially as his utterances on the tariff increasingly came to echo those of his congressional allies, standpat protectionists Nelson Aldrich, Henry Cabot Lodge, and Joseph G. Cannon.[1]

Even at his most deferential, however, Roosevelt differed with the Old Guard Republican leadership on the tariff and several times toyed with the idea of pressing Congress to undertake revision. He apparently considered some sort of tariff changes in late 1904, for example, when he called

Republican Congressman James E. Watson, an Indiana member of the House Ways and Means Committee who was close to the National Association of Manufacturers (NAM), and sounded him out on the feasibility of reductions on hides, steel, and wood pulp, notions Watson had been promoting. Watson informed Roosevelt that congressional reductionists were not prepared to take immediate action on the tariff question, however. The president, after proposing tariff reduction to his congressional associates in February 1905, decided to drop the matter, although only Cannon and Platt had opposed it vigorously. Evidently Roosevelt believed that his chances for passing a moderate Republican reduction were poor. He justified inaction by professing reluctance to "tinker" with the tariff in prosperous times. Still, Roosevelt continued to give his low-tariff associates in academia and in the New York merchant community the impression that he was a reluctant protectionist, hemmed in by powerful congressional forces. Said historian James Ford Rhodes after a visit to the White House in 1905, Roosevelt, "if he could do it by ukase, would revise the tariff."[2]

The issue on which Roosevelt did show consistent opposition to tariff revision—and what may explain in part his apparently inconsistent attitude—was that of the putative linkage between tariffs and trusts. Roosevelt believed that this idea, which had originated with the Democrats, was a wild and dangerous one, and as president he shunned it and the "radical" Republican midwestern politicians such as Albert Cummins, who also called for turning tariff reduction against the trusts. Roosevelt wanted to treat the trusts' international relations cautiously because he viewed corporations and their leaders as "naturally those that will take the lead in the strife for commercial supremacy among the nations of the world." Thus, on April 4, 1903, Roosevelt told a Minneapolis audience that, "speaking broadly," the tariff issue "stands wholly apart from the question of dealing with the trusts. No change in the tariff duties can have any substantial effect in solving the so-called trust problem."[3]

In the presidential campaign of 1904, Roosevelt mobilized his administration to dissociate the party leadership from midwestern antitrust reductionism. In various forums Roosevelt argued that duties could not be lowered against trusts without destroying independent manufacturers and weakening the American economy vis-à-vis foreign combinations. Opposition to radical Republican reductionism again may have deterred Roosevelt from affiliating himself with tariff changes during this period, despite his general support for the ideas of McKinley and Brooks Adams. In 1906, Roosevelt still identified the tariff-trust argument as a dangerous one, seemingly because it linked Republican and Democratic anticorporate radicalism. Writing to Root of William Jennings Bryan, Roosevelt allowed that Bryan was "kindly and well-meaning" but a "demagogue" who had been overly impressed by Roosevelt's vehement style and had impulsively sought to outdo him through extravagant proposals such as "advocating warfare on the trusts by refusing to allow them to use the mails, by taking off the tariff on all trust-made articles, and so forth—all of which combine with exquisite nicety folly and viciousness." The implication was that Bryan would weaken America's new corporate order for personal and partisan advantage, whereas he, Roosevelt, would seek to regulate corporations without endangering the legitimate control and expansion of large property.[4]

Despite the complexities that confronted Roosevelt in the tariff issue, he could not ignore demands for revision, nor could he long maintain an intransigent standpat position. Domestic politics, and probably his own inclinations, impelled Roosevelt to contemplate tariff reduction. Whether or not prorevision Republicans were motivated by radical trust-baiting sentiments, they constituted an important and organized segment of the party, loyal to Roosevelt for his activities in regulating rail rates and food and drug practices, and on imperial projects such as the building of the Panama Canal. These Republicans, typified by the members of the NAM, but also including many merchants, small businessmen, and agricultural capitalists such as the flour mill owners and meat producers, were reluctant to give up the image that Republican leaders of the McKinley era, including Roosevelt, had cultivated—of tariff revision as a coordinate aid to foreign trade expansion. In the Massachusetts gubernatorial election of 1905, Republican revisionist Curtis Guild, Jr., narrowly defeated a Democratic revisionist-reciprocity advocate, and even Henry Cabot Lodge had endorsed a state platform that called for tariff revision. In fact, chambers of commerce across New England were advising for revision.[5]

Indiana Senator Albert J. Beveridge, an ardent Roosevelt supporter, may have helped to make the political importance of the broadening sentiment for revision clear to the president. Beveridge had been under pressure for revision in his home state since shortly after the 1904 election, and by 1906 Beveridge had become convinced that Indiana was for revision. Perhaps part of the reason was Beveridge's close personal association with David M. Parry, the president of the NAM. Beveridge wrote Roosevelt from a hotel where he had stopped on a campaign tour that the businessmen he was meeting were all for reduction—and that they were all Republicans. Roosevelt, apparently swayed, began quoting some of Beveridge's ideas within his own political circle in an attempt to moderate the views of some of the standpats in his administration, such as Treasury Secretary Leslie M. Shaw, who had campaigned in his home state of Iowa against fellow Republican Albert Cummins's Senate bid. Roosevelt himself worried over the tariff issue in the 1906 campaign. In August he confided to Root that the Republican party was locked into support for protectionism by the strong power of Speaker Cannon and other standpat Republicans, a position that might lead to Republican defeats.[6]

Within the executive branch, Secretary Root had been advising Roosevelt since just after the 1904 election that the Republicans now ought to take the initiative in revising the Dingley rates downward. Root told the president that privately manufacturers in industries such as shoes, glass, and steel had confessed that rates were considerably higher than necessary. The secretary warned that the public suspected the Republicans of sustaining protection to facilitate systematic cut-price exporting, or dumping, by big corporations. In fact, Root argued, it was an affront to domestic intermediate and final consumers if "excessive duties enable combinations of great manufacturers to exact higher prices than are reasonable in view of cost and risk of production." Moreover, if Republicans abjured revision on partisan grounds, Root said, they would appear unable to "deal with a great and vital governmental question." In that case, Root was "quite certain that the people of the country would conclude that Mr. Cleveland was right in saying . . . that it is useless to talk about the tariff being revised by the friends of protection." Thus, Root was reminding Roosevelt that the political dangers of the tariff question came not only from tariff radicals but from resurgent Gold Democrats who could claim to be better positioned to revise the tariff from a procorporate viewpoint. Root expressed his preference for a revision in 1906, endorsing a maximum-minimum tariff.[7]

William H. Taft was also an important influence toward lower tariffs within the Republican party. The former Philippine civil governor had been chided once by Roosevelt during the 1904 campaign for calling for tobacco and sugar rate reductions for Philippine products, which had brought protests from western sugar growers and Connecticut valley tobacco farmers. Roosevelt had had to reject Taft's offer to resign. In May 1906, Taft again moved toward revision. In an address to Ohio Republicans, he suggested that the decline of imports was leading to a revenue crisis that would force either tariff revision or the alteration of the internal taxation system. In Republican campaign speeches in Maine and Ohio in the fall of 1906, the secretary of war suggested that the option he favored was tariff revision, that revisionist sentiment in the party was growing, and that "there has been a change in the business conditions of the country making it wise and just to revise the schedules of the existing tariff." According to his biographer, Taft determined to keep up his public support for tariff revision from that point onward.[8]

Perhaps equally powerful motivations toward tariff changes were the great sea changes of international commercial and political-economic life of this period. Roosevelt and the Republican leadership had sought to establish the presence of the United States in international commercial and political affairs. Roosevelt oversaw, among many initiatives, the "pacification" of Cuba and the Philippines as outposts of U.S. colonial rule. He "took" Panama, promulgated the Roosevelt Corollary to the Monroe Doctrine, presided over the Russo-Japanese peace negotiations, and played the arbiter's role at Algeciras in the dispute over access to Morocco between Germany, England, and France. Roosevelt was highly aware of the delicacy and importance of commercial arrangements in European politics and of the increasing role the United States—via its expanding exports—would play in world commercial affairs. He faced many contradictory pressures on the revision issue, however.

Revisionism Resurgent

The leading force in tariff revision during the McKinley presidency had been the National Association of Manufacturers. The defeat of the Kasson treaties forced NAM leaders into a holding action, as they sought to regroup revisionist forces. Such tactics were typified by the NAM's continuing pressure for prorevision interpretations of United States commercial agreements that were still open to interpretation and negotiation, such as those with Germany, France, and Russia, and by new proposals for broader reciprocity arrangements.

The NAM's political positions in the years following the defeat of the Kasson treaties were affected significantly by the emergence of a new generation of leaders, midwesterners David M. Parry, James W. Van Cleave, and John Kirby, Jr. Parry, an Indianapolis vehicle builder who replaced Theodore C. Search as NAM president in 1902, was a Republican activist who was a close friend of expansionist Indiana Senator Albert J. Beveridge and was spoken of as a possible running mate for Roosevelt's 1904 campaign. Parry and his successors were perhaps best known for stepping up the NAM's anti-union activities. Yet all three men were also committed trade expansionists, and Parry began his tenure by announcing the NAM's continuing support for a U.S. Department of Commerce and Industries, for expanding and upgrading the consular service, for an isthmian canal and a great American merchant marine, and for reciprocity.[9]

Beginning in 1902, Parry's NAM sought to facilitate trade relations outside of the treaty format, in the context of the laws of U.S. customs administration. In the "Russian Sugar Cases," the NAM, on behalf of a New York City sugar importer, brought suit against the Board of Classification of the Board of General Appraisers, the Treasury Department agency responsible for assessing the value of imported goods and for interpreting customs and tariff regulations. The New York appraisers had ruled that Russia's remission of its own domestic excise taxes on sugar destined for export represented a bounty, or state subsidy, to the Russian sugar industry. According to section 5 of the Dingley Act, subsidies provided by a nation for exports constituted a discrimination that could subject an offender to a retaliatory American duty. The Treasury Department, under Lyman Gage, a former Gold Democrat, had removed and reinstated American "counter-discrimination" several times since 1898 as a bargaining chip in broader U.S.-Russian trade negotiations. The NAM wanted the department to drop the countervailing duties permanently and admit Russian sugar more liberally. But when the two nations failed to arrive at more definitive treaty relations, Gage reinstated the duties. The NAM appealed against American counterdiscrimination all the way to the Supreme Court, without success.[10]

The NAM's motive in pressing for a settlement on sugar is not hard to discern. Russian beet sugar itself was of minor importance to the United States, but Russia had threatened 50 to 70 percent hikes on most of its American iron and steel imports if the United States invoked penalties against its sugar exports. Such retaliation would cripple much of the American trade in metals manufactures with Russia and, concomitantly, would cause Russia to redirect its demand for metals from America to Europe. Thus, a subtext of the contention over beet sugar was the danger of wielding the stick without also offering the carrot: Obdurate escalation of protectionist sanctions ultimately would be most harmful to nations with large export interests, such as the United States. It was this, of course, that the NAM's lawsuit sought to forestall. Despite the defeat of the NAM suit, the sugar case helped make it plain to manufacturers and East Coast importers that they had good reason to stand together on matters that jeopardized trade. In fact, according to William L. Saunders, a mining equipment executive active in the NAM foreign trade committees, it was this case that prompted exporting manufacturers to look again "toward a readjustment of our tariff laws."[11]

In the years immediately following the defeat of the Kasson treaties, NAM executives also began to sketch out a more sophisticated general approach to tariff revision. In his presidential report for 1903, David Parry reaffirmed that Blaine's "tropical reciprocity"—limited treaties facilitating exchange of U.S. manufactures for South American raw materials—was no longer sufficient. Even the few reciprocity treaties that had "passed muster in the Senate . . . seem[ed] only to come into existence to be abrogated after a few years." Calling the old strategy of reciprocity through commercial treaties a "failure," Parry was publicly acknowledging that the revisionist movement lacked the power to overcome protectionist logrolling in the Senate, which could block or cancel longer-term reciprocity with Europe through the two-thirds majority requirement for approving treaties. Thus, Parry offered a counterproposal. Drawing from the visible processes of European tariff making then under way, Parry endorsed a French-type maximum-minimum tariff system as a "general basis for reciprocity arrangements." Under such a system, both rates would be set in the legislature by simple majority vote, hence advancing the interests of export-oriented capitalists against the political power of entrenched protectionists.[12]

Another group became captivated and mobilized by the maximum-minimum tariff idea and played an instrumental role in the revival of reciprocity—the primary producers of livestock. American meat producers had been prominent in exporting circles since the 1870s. In value terms, meat products led American exports for most of the years between the late 1870s and the first decade of the twentieth century. Moreover, the livestock growers were no strangers to export problems. Many were veterans of the European pork boycotts of 1879–91, and most were conspicuous supporters of export expansion.[13]

In 1898, a group of western and midwestern cattlemen, stockbreeders, swine growers, sheep raisers, and other livestock interests had formed the National Live Stock Association (NLSA).[14]

Promoting export trade and pursuing government assistance in overcoming foreign obstacles to meat exports were on the agendas of the early livestock conventions, but reductionist activity among the stock growers was held in check into the twentieth century by divisions in the animal products industry as a whole. First, growers were suspicious of manufacturers' demands for tariff-free hides and wool, which many growers regarded as a threat to livestock prices. Perhaps even more significant was the mistrust engendered by the consolidation of the intermediate market for livestock by the so-called packing trusts—Armour, Swift, Morris, and others. Although the meatpackers were vigorous proponents of expanded foreign trade, the stock growers were reluctant to cooperate with them because they resented the packers' influence at the stockyards, where speculation, manipulation of prices for animals, and collusive pricing were thought to be everyday practices.[15]

Revisionist sentiment remained alive within the NLSA despite frictions with the packers. Part of the reason for the growers' continued interest in trade expansion lay in the fact that the growers stood to gain considerably from foreign trade. The concentration and centralization of meatpacking had led efficient processors to exploit markets abroad for animal byproducts that were not salable in the United States, from lard and cheap grades of canned meats profitably exported for European working-class consumption to a packaged bone-marrow "butter" sold in Africa. As Upton Sinclair wrote at the time, the packers sold "every part of a pig but the squeal." This foreign demand for packinghouse products was an indirect stimulus to production of livestock and reduced the risk to growers of falling domestic prices.[16]

Revisionism in the NLSA was boosted by the group's perennial president during its early years, John W. Springer. An articulate Colorado lawyer, banker, and mine operator who was later mayor of Denver, Springer, like David Parry, was a favorite-son vice-presidential candidate. Springer's uncle and mentor, Judge William McKendree Springer, served as the NLSA's legal counsel and representative in Washington, D.C., until his death in 1903. The elder Springer, an Illinois Gold Democrat, had been chairman of the House Ways and Means Committee during the early 1890s and was a well-known tariff liberal. Under the Springers, the NLSA supported trade expansion in tandem with politics intended to restrain the packers. For example, the NLSA favored the 1902 attorney general's suit against the "Beef Trust." To compete with the big packers on their own ground, the NLSA also tried to create an independent packing company financed by subscription among the livestock interests. Thus, on the whole, most growers aspired not to destroy the packers but to create conditions in the industry that would give growers some share of and control over the profits of an expanded trade in meats. Yet, up to 1905, their internal divisions had prevented them from pursuing reciprocity with vigor.[17]

In 1905–6, the industry erupted into open conflict that ultimately freed the organization to engage the tariff issue forcefully. The immediate occasion for the dispute was an attempt at the 1905 NLSA convention by the organization's leaders to formalize the NLSA's constitution and bylaws, which had been unofficial since the founding of the group. The leaders, though self-avowed trustbusters during the earlier years of the NLSA, had promulgated rules that would have admitted packer interests directly onto the NLSA's executive committee. Supporters of a modus vivendi with the packers included John Springer; Frank Hagenbarth, now the president of the organization; and executive committee members William A. Harris, a former Democratic senator from Kansas and now the spokesman for the Chicago-based Short-Horn Breeders Association, and Alvin H. Sanders, an NLSA executive committee member who was the editor of the *Breeder's Gazette*, published in Chicago, and the scion of an established midwestern family of stockbreeders.[18]

Why had Springer and company reversed field on their relations with the packers? It may be that they had come to view the packers as sufficiently restrained by law and regulation so that the common interests of large-scale growers, feeders, breeders, and packers outweighed their conflicts. Organizational unity thus might allow them to arrange cooperative domestic marketing practices for stock trade to some extent outside the conditions of competition in the marketplace. Moreover, it would facilitate cooperation on common goals such as expansion through reciprocity. Whatever the underlying motives, ex-senator Harris defended the proposed merger of interests vigorously at the 1905 NLSA convention by portraying the leaders' move to admit the packers into the NLSA as an opportunity for the noncorporate growers to get inside the packers' "breastworks" and to call them to account "before the Central Committee."[19]

The rhetoric of Harris failed to quell spirited resistance to the leaders' plan from the floor of the convention. Most of the opposition came from western stock growers who mistrusted the packers' motives and money. Opponents of the merger pointed out that because the NLSA was financed from contributions that were proportional to the size of the member firms, the huge and wealthy packers would soon dominate the organization. Colorado rancher Murdo Mackenzie, a dissident executive committee member, bluntly pronounced himself "opposed to the packer. I don't want him mixed up with the live stock raiser." Association attorney Samuel H.

Cowan, a Texan who was also a vigorous proponent of railroad rate legislation, assailed the mostly Chicago-based NLSA leaders: "The packing houses are in absolute control of the proposed organization," he argued. Springer, Sanders, and others were unable to appease the organization mavericks, and Mackenzie and Cowan led a walkout from the convention. Although the rump assembly approved the new constitution, the secessionists retaliated by forming the American Stock Growers Association (ASGA), a group explicitly open only to livestock producers.[20]

The walkout of western livestock growers at the January 1905 livestock convention pulled away a sizable fraction of the NLSA membership, but it did not impede the NLSA leadership's effort to establish a regime of cooperation with the meatpackers in pursuit of reciprocity. Even as dissidents stampeded from the convention floor, executive committee member Alvin Sanders was calling for "the packers and everyone else to put their shoulders to the wheel" of tariff revision. Sanders's 1905 proposal was similar to the one made by David Parry in 1903: The reciprocity sections of section 4 of the Dingley Tariff should be transformed into a law that would constitute a maximum-minimum tariff approved by the legislature and administered by the executive branch. The resolution passed, and Sanders and Harris began to organize a conference for the summer of 1905 to promote the idea among other manufacturing and trade groups.[21]

The immediate focus of the proposed national convention was the threat embodied in the new German tariff. The maximum or general rates of this tariff had been passed by the Reichstag in the last days of 1902. A complete, dual tariff was scheduled to go into effect in March 1906, after German trade representatives had finished negotiating a series of commercial treaties whose composite base rates would make up its minimum or conventional rate. American revisionists anticipated that because the United States had failed to modify the Dingley Tariff or to conclude any comprehensive trade accommodation with Germany, the Germans would apply the maximums to the United States as a retaliation. The German maximum rates would effectively close out American meats and other agricultural and manufactured products, sales of which were already declining in the face of intensified European competition and the protectionist hostility of the German Agrarian party. Conference organizers feared as well that German reciprocity agreements with other European states would be constructed— as, in fact, they were intended to be—to create a more self-sufficient European trading system, which would permanently exclude American goods. Thus, not only the German trade was at issue: What loomed was the perennial bogey of American foreign trade proponents, the European *Zollverein*, or tariff union.[22]

As Sanders later recounted, he was soon approached by "other export interests" who wanted to support the proposed conference. These included "millers, Board of Trade people, [and] some of the large manufacturers of agricultural implements, like the Deerings and McCormicks." These groups provided funding, and soon protectionists began accusing the convention of being under the sway of the "packers, or the so-called Beef Trust, and the so-called Harvester Trust." The Call to the convention showed, however, that the sponsoring groups included midwestern livestock raisers, commercial crop growers, and smaller agricultural implement associations as well as the "trusts." In addition, the conference organizers sent a second call to manufacturers and merchants, notably easterners, inviting them to "make common cause with agriculture . . . not for . . . radical Tariff legislation but simply to secure an equalization of the benefits which all industries are taxed to support."[23]

Finding an acceptable and workable format for reciprocal trade and for integrating diverse regional agricultural, manufacturing, and trading interests was the underlying purpose of the convention. The midwestern groups had been concerned with preserving European markets for meats, agricultural goods, and machinery. But the eastern interests, more closely tied to the banking and import-export houses, were preoccupied with obtaining cheaper or free raw materials, extending markets in South America, and facilitating shipping and import of German manufactures for retail sale in the United States. The conference conveners hoped to promote a maximum-minimum tariff system as a new organizing tool for "reciprocity." They also hoped to form a national movement for presidential appointment of an advisory tariff commission to assist Congress and the executive in setting the minimum rates under the proposed dual-tariff system.[24]

The attempt by conference organizers to shift the focus from reciprocity via commercial treaties to a dual, maximum-minimum tariff system with rates administered by the executive branch was similar to David Parry's suggestion of two years before and represented an important development in revisionist activity. As the organizers contended, the rudiment of a maximum-minimum system had been outlined already in section 4 of the Dingley Tariff, under which the major Kasson treaties had been negotiated. This provision, it will be recalled, authorized the president or his designee to reduce duties up to 20 percent, thus setting a minimum duty, as part of treaty conventions to be ratified by a two-thirds vote of the Senate. The revisionists now sought to implement this system outside the treaty format and the requirement of a two-thirds Senate majority by making it the president's firm prerogative to set the minimum rate, though still within a lower limit set independently by a majority in Congress.

Although apparently a relatively minor shift in procedure, the setting of a legislative minimum tariff would allow the revisionists to use executive branch support to take the initiative in commercial policymaking away from traditional home-market protectionists, because legislating an across-the-board 20 percent tariff cut as a minimum rate would block protectionist logrolling—the system of supporting protectionist duties for each others' home-state industries. In effect, it was a direct challenge to traditional congressional prerogatives in tariff making. Because varieties of the dual-tariff system were becoming the rule in Europe, the convention organizers hoped to portray this shift as no more than a modern and efficient adaptation to contemporary commercial exigencies and as an alternative to exhausting tariff bickering in Congress.[25]

The organizers' plans for reciprocity were both coherent and astute. Apparently, however, the organizers had not yet become politically adept enough to secure extensive prior support among the myriad prorevision groups. Thus, divisions sprang up immediately between eastern proponents of free raw materials, who were touting free hides and cheap coal, and proreciprocity midwestern agricultural interests, who were cool to agricultural imports. Protectionists commenting on the conference were quick to seize on the confusion and delighted in retailing how a provocateur from the ultraprotectionist Boston Home Market Club had sown confusion at the opening of the convention by handing out unsigned pamphlets contradicting the organizers' assertions about German tariff threats.[26]

That the conference in some respects highlighted disunities is clear, but the positions outlined there reveal much about how the revision movement evolved. The politicians who attended the conference did not markedly assist the organizers' objectives. Senator Shelby M. Cullom (R.-Ill.) gave the warm-up speech, beginning and ending with paeans to the expansion of foreign trade. In between, he predicted increased European resistance to the "American invasion" of goods, warned of the dampening effects of the new German tariff, and endorsed a reading of the Dingley Act that stressed its rates as a conservative maximum from which reductions of up to 20 percent easily could be made along the lines of a maximum-minimum tariff scheme. Cullom, the chairman of the Senate Foreign Relations Committee, thus endorsed the maximum-minimum idea as a practical revision measure.

Yet almost in the same breath, Cullom, up for reelection to the Senate, hedged by implying that the Dingley rates might well be taken as a minimum, thus making the tariff into a punitive or retaliatory measure.[27]

Like Cullom, Republican Governor Albert B. Cummins of Iowa sought a Senate seat and gave enthusiastic but ambiguous support to the convention's objectives. Unlike the senator from Illinois, however, Cummins's commitment to tariff reduction was not in question. Cummins was a longtime "radical" revisionist who had challenged an entrenched standpat group in his home state and had popularized the "Iowa idea" of using the tariff against the trusts. But Cummins was lukewarm toward the legislated dual-tariff idea and the notion of executive branch administration of the lower rate. In the convention's floor debate, Cummins worked to dilute the endorsement of a maximum-minimum tariff by adding the qualifier that it was the only practical method "at this time" of relieving foreign trade constriction. Cummins thus tried to preserve the older reciprocity ideas. It is probable that Cummins was uneasy about ceding too much power over the tariff to the executive branch, which might pass into control of those unsympathetic to a tariff reduction beneficial to midwesterners.[28]

Conference delegates also differed on the proposed redirection of reductionist efforts. The organizers tried to exalt the new "maximum-minimum reduction" idea, much as the promoters of the 1901 convention had tried to deify reciprocity as a suprapartisan concept. But some groups could not be deterred from focusing on specific industry and political interests. The boot and shoe manufacturers, for example, wanted to promote free hides and were miffed when their resolutions on these matters were shunted into committee in the interest of "harmony." They later grumbled that they would make no sacrifices on imports of foreign shoes unless the meatpackers supported commensurate concessions on hides. Nonetheless, although suspicious about specifics, the shoe producers were receptive to the general ideas of a dual tariff and an advisory commission.[29]

Other groups viewed the controversies over specific items more lightly. After the sessions were over, cotton mill operators speculated that the western interests would preponderate in the conference's executive committee, which was charged with creating a permanent organizing body. The cotton producers were confident, however, that "eastern interests have not been neglected." Urging cotton producers to rally around the new organization, they praised the aggressiveness of the western sentiment for reciprocity and urged that "there should be no criticism of the sectional composition of the committee." Likewise, H. C. Staver, of the Carriage

Builders National Association, described the conference as having passed "strong resolutions" that his constituents—mainly midwestern carriage and automobile shops—could support. He added that the conference was carrying on the work begun by the earlier manufacturer-inspired meetings, and he urged "hearty cooperation" in securing "reciprocal treaties or maximum and minimum tariffs."[30]

Another controversy surfaced on the second day of the meetings. Like Governor Cummins of Iowa, delegates from Illinois, Wisconsin, and Kansas opposed taking tariff-making power away from Congress and handing it to nonelected "outsiders." A man from Indiana averred that he was not afraid of his congressman and that he preferred to have his policymakers accountable to him at the polls. To an extent, these complaints may have represented fears of too-sweeping tariff revision. But they also reflected uneasiness of proprietary manufacturers about the movement of the tariff revision cause into the hands of an elite of organizers and appointed commissioners. The same sorts of arguments erupted over the constitution of the proposed tariff commission and of the executive committee charged with forming a new lobbying organization.[31]

The most tangible result of the conference did not accommodate rank-and-file fears of elitism. This was the formation of a permanent reductionist lobby group, a move initiated by the propacker board member of the NLSA, Alvin H. Sanders. The midwestern convention organizers retained tight control, quickly electing Sanders chairman and co-opting prominent easterners onto the board of directors—notably, Gustav H. Schwab, the New York representative of the North German Lloyd shipping lines and an officer of the Merchants Association of New York; A. B. Farquhar, the Pennsylvania Democrat and implement manufacturer; and Eugene N. Foss, of the B. F. Sturtevant Company of Massachusetts, then a Republican but later a Democratic congressman and governor of Massachusetts.[32]

In fact, Sanders had anticipated shaping the lobby group's approach all along. Even before the convention, he had met with President Roosevelt to solicit an endorsement for the new lobby. Sanders had mused to Roosevelt that "the word 'reciprocity' is so closely related in the public mind with the defunct treaties [that it might] be well for us to drop the use of that term entirely in christening the organization." As alternatives Sanders proposed "The American Exporters' Association, or The Foreign Market Club, or the Dual Tariff League." But Roosevelt refused to become the group's godfather, and in the end Sanders chose the title American Reciprocal Tariff League (ARTL).[33]

The board of the ARTL included not only NLSA members and associated eastern revisionists but all the major members of the stock-growing industry, including Mackenzie and Cowan of the secessionist ASGA. Their presence no doubt reflected an impending reconciliation with the NLSA. By January 1906, the feuding groups had formalized a new working arrangement. The meatpackers were enjoined from formally entering stock grower groups, but would cooperate "at the executive level" on matters of mutual interest such as tariff reduction. Satisfied that these terms preserved their prerogatives as growers, the rebel western stock growers agreed to disband the ASGA and to unite with the propacker NLSA faction as the American National Live Stock Association.[34]

It is interesting to note that at the first convention of the newly reunited growers—in contrast to the antipacker diatribes of the previous meeting—a mood was set for an emerging cooperation and coordination between primary product producers and the semimanufacture and transportation "trusts." For example, James M. John argued that meat growers, like cotton growers, could best adjust to conditions of combination among the processors by combining among themselves to restrict production and gain leverage in the market. Foreign markets, it may be added, would stabilize the restriction of production by providing a vent for "surpluses." Not all revisionist politicians, stock growers, or manufacturers were sanguine about combination, of course, but the rhetoric, like the reconciliation, epitomized the burgeoning of a "cooperationist" synthesis between proprietary and corporate organizations—to coordinate a national price policy and expand foreign trade as a profitable and stabilizing component of American capitalism.[35]

Early in 1906, the ARTL began its work for a tariff commission and a maximum-minimum tariff. The new lobby circularized the national legislature, arguing that the Dingley Tariff had already authorized the House to fix the limits of a maximum-minimum tariff within which the executive branch could "adjust duties as may be necessary for the common welfare." The ARTL now proposed going a step further and replacing the partisan, logrolling system of shaping tariffs within the House Ways and Means Committee by an advisory board that would formulate tariffs based on unified national principles. Effective tariff revision along such lines was one of the "active steps" the United States had to take to keep pace with "an enormous advance in productive power, commercial activity and increased consumption everywhere." American bars against foreign manufactures were accelerating a process that could isolate the United States commercially. For example, the rapid development of the Argentine economy was leading Britain to reorient its commerce to exchange its manufactures for Argentine wheat and beef. In Asia, Japan threatened to redirect its agricultural imports. And more generally, "the great consuming masses of Europe are seeking and finding elsewhere supplies which under a proper adjustment of affairs should continue to flow from this country."[36]

The shift of tactics toward a commission and a maximum-minimum tariff signaled a revival of tariff agitation along new lines. But the new direction was filled with ambiguity. As in the reciprocity period of 1897–1901, concerns about U.S. foreign trade and about retaliatory foreign tariffs were important themes. In the earlier period conflicts between proprietary manufacturers and the emergent corporate groups had been mostly latent, submerged in a common enthusiasm for expansion and opposition to "Bryanism." By 1905, however, two distinctive positions on the proprietary-corporate issue were emerging. The new spirit of cooperationism, as epitomized in the meat industry, sought to emphasize trade expansion and would mute opposition to the system of corporate combination.

But proprietary manufacturers sought to preserve what they believed was a popular voice against the interests of raw material and semimanufacture trusts. Although radical tariff reductionists were not much represented at the reciprocity convention, Republican future "progressives" such as Albert B. Cummins had begun to work to make their voices heard in the revision movement. They faced a serious dilemma. The movement was becoming more elitist by seeking to use a commission and the executive power to circumvent protectionist practices of the legislature. Resistant at first, the radical revisionists could not deny the "practicality" of bypassing entrenched legislative protectionism. Because they were politically disinclined to ally with the Bryan Democrats to promote tariff reduction, the radicals remained in close, though skeptical, alliance with the cooperationists.

What purposes tariff revision would serve in the domestic political economy, and what role a more powerful executive would exercise in promoting revision, therefore remained unclear, as the pressures of adapting to the new German tariff increased.

4 The German Imbroglio, 1905–1907

It is not at all impossible that the German Reichstag may decide to draw the sword and throw away the scabbard. . . . Our government must be prepared for the contest and whatever it may bring.—U.S. Ambassador to Germany Charlemagne Tower, Personal and Confidential Dispatch to Secretary of State Root, September 27, 1906

In the period from 1905 to 1907, commercial frictions between the United States and Germany epitomized the complexity of the tariff question at an international level and drew both the administration and revisionist groups into the process of policymaking.

Contention in U.S.-German trade relations was far from new by the early 1900s. German capitalists had been decrying the damage done by "made in America" goods at least since the late 1870s, when the Agrarian party had pressed Bismarck to declare the pork boycott. Some German manufacturers, capitulating to the growing popularity of U.S. manufactures, had begun to forge American trademarks on their own copies of popular imports such as American shoes. But many other manufacturers had begun to demand exclusion of foreign goods.[1]

The ambiguous status of most-favored-nation relations underlay much of the controversy between Germany and the United States. Public opinion in both countries was divided on whether the two nations actually had most-favored-nation relations. Belief that they did was bolstered in Germany, at least, when the two nations signed the Saratoga Convention of 1892. In 1894, however, the Democratic Wilson Tariff repudiated the Republican reciprocity agreements, thus abrogating the Saratoga Convention. Germany protested, claiming that the United States was still flouting an 1828 most-favored-nation treaty with Prussia. The protests were aimed specifically at the "countervailing" duties imposed by the Wilson Tariff on German sugar. These extra imposts were aimed at neutralizing German government subsidies to beet sugar producers. President Cleveland and his secretary of state, Walter Gresham, were inclined, at least for a time, to remove the duties, but they were unable to persuade Congress to cooperate.[2]

During the remainder of the 1890s, the Germans continued to grant the United States unconditional most-favored-nation status informally, thus giving the United States rates equal to those granted all favored trading partners. For its part, the United States, with its conditional most-favored-nation policy requiring it only to give Germany rates it considered equivalent to the value of German concessions, would not concede that the countervailing duties were unfair. In fact, the Dingley Tariff in 1897 reaffirmed those duties, and the U.S.-German Argol Agreement of 1900, negotiated by the Kasson Commission under section 3 of the Dingley Tariff, gave reductions to only a few German products—namely, argols, brandies, still wines, and works of art. Nonetheless, Germany did not press the tariff issue during the 1890s. The central reason probably was because revolution and war had so disrupted Cuban sugar exports that German sugar sales in the United States grew despite the duties. It was the U.S.-Cuban reciprocity treaty of 1902, which gave a recovering Cuban sugar industry an exclusive preferential rate 20 percent below the Dingley tariff rates, that rekindled the dispute. Now the Germans protested strenuously that under most-favored-nation relations Cuba's sovereign status required the United States to grant Germany reductions commensurate with those granted Cuba. The United States, invoking its conditional interpretation and what some officials later called relations of "proximity" or "propinquity" with Cuba, rejected the German claim. Essentially, the United States was equating its tariff relations with Cuba to European colonial preference systems, a view that the "open-door" Germans refused to recognize officially.[3]

According to Germany's tradition of making long-term tariff agreements, the Caprivi treaties of the early 1890s generally were not due for revision until 1903. But the increase of foreign exports to Germany and other tariff conflicts prompted Germany in 1897 to appoint a tariff commission, composed of thirty representatives of industry, commerce, and government, to begin a review of the imperial tariff schedules. In 1902, the commission recommended a general tariff of markedly higher rates, and between 1902 and 1905, German emissaries negotiated conventions of reduction with many European states. Germany's complete dual tariff was scheduled to take effect in 1906.[4]

The protracted and public tariff making of Germany was designed partly to urge the United States to join the series of new treaties and perhaps to move toward European unconditional most-favored-nation relations. In the Argol Agreement of 1900 the United States had accorded Germany a limited array of reduced rates. Yet although the Germans exported quantities of these items, German exports to the United States as a percentage of all German exports had declined. Moreover, whereas U.S. exports to Germany rose by 131 percent in the 1890s, German exports to the United States increased only by 12 percent. German manufacturers resented this and were increasingly irked by the more noticeable American commercial intelligence gathering that had come with the reorganization and upgrading of the U.S. consular service in the early twentieth century. Of course, Americans merely regarded activities such as researching the daily and monthly consular reports for the Department of Commerce and Labor as parallel to the commercial intelligence activities of the European states, and even then as not offsetting the abilities of foreign companies to combine to force out American trade. The Germans, however, viewed the enormous productive power of the United States as threat enough.[5]

It was implicit, then, that when the new German schedules took effect on March 1, 1906, the United States no longer would receive the minimum rates. Moreover, the new German maximum rates effectively excluded American exports except for some raw materials, such as copper, that Germany could not get in acceptable quantity elsewhere. Thus, the shaky status quo of U.S.-German trade relations appeared to be broken, and several new options—reflecting the shifting balances of commercial and political power between the two nations' commercial systems—presented themselves. The United States might continue to expand trade with Germany by promulgating a new tariff law of its own that Germany would accept as equivalent to the German conventional tariff rates. Or the United States might offer a new commercial treaty or other concessions to prompt Germany to grant its conventional rates. Or the United States might take a protectionist hard line, insisting that concessions already made under the Argol Agreements constituted the United States' most-favored-nation treatment and demanding the German minimum, imposing counterdiscriminations against German exports and threatening escalating tariff sanctions or complete embargo if Germany failed to relent.

The United States and
Germany Risk Tariff War

The drawn-out development of the new German tariff had occasioned only episodic concern in the United States until 1905. By then, however, the terms of the new German conventions with European nations were being published, illustrating the serious relative handicap the new German maximums would pose if applied to American export trade. In addition, German government and commercial interests fostered a spirited discussion in American public and private circles of an impending "tariff war" between the two countries.[6]

In a tariff war the United States had a powerful opening hand against Germany because German industry relied heavily on American raw material exports such as cotton, copper, and oil. American exporters of such products, and American producers of domestic goods with which German products competed, might be sanguine about prospects of a tariff war. But American importing manufacturers, shippers, and exporters of manufactures were threatened. For example, textile makers were dependent on proprietary German chemicals and dyestuffs; freight and passenger lines risked losing their customers; importers of specialty German manufactures such as optical instruments would be stripped of supplies; and American exporters of bicycles, typewriters, boots, and shoes would be set at a crippling disadvantage by the German maximum rates. Especially vulnerable were the meatpackers and the producers of machinery and tools, who clearly would be excluded from the German market by the rates of the German general tariff.[7]

Worsening the situation, some German official and commercial interests appeared eager to punish the United States for failing to adopt a compatible unconditional European conception of most-favored-nation relations, which would have integrated the United States more fully into the German and East European trading system. Resentful that German exports to the United States were only half those of the United States to Germany, an editorialist in the manufacturer-oriented *Kölnische Volkszeitung* warned that any attempt by "the Americans . . . to stretch out the Monroe Doctrine also over the territory of commerce and trade" would be met by "a united Europe; and statistics will show what that would mean to the export trade of the United States."[8]

American manufacturers were anxious about such threats. At the May 1905 meeting of the National Association of Manufacturers (NAM), Eugene N. Foss of Massachusetts warned that Germany's "tariff thunderbolt" could devastate not only selected U.S. interests but all U.S. trade with Europe. Foss explained that the German law's harsh punitive provisions would impose surtaxes, even extending to free-list items, if the United States retaliated against German commerce. Foss here appeared to be highlighting the features of the *Kampfzoll* ("tariff war") paragraph of the 1902 German law, section 10, which called for up to 50 percent ad valorem duties in case of discrimination against German exports. In explicating the new German law, Foss was trying to show how even exporters who did not feel threatened by the German maximums could be harmed in a contest of escalating sanctions. Similar concerns were evident in the broad support for the Chicago Reciprocity Conference of August 1905 and in the involvement of agricultural, manufacturing, and East Coast commercial capitalists in the organization that grew out of that conference, the American Reciprocal Tariff League (ARTL).[9]

U.S. government experts also reacted to news of the German commercial conventions with Eastern Europe. Consul General Frank H. Mason wrote Secretary of State John Hay from Berlin that the signing in February 1905 of the Russo-German commercial treaty, the last in the series of German tariff agreements, marked "an epoch in the history of German economic legislation." The new agreements, Mason said, united European nations as a "formidable" threat to U.S. export trade. Nahum I. Stone, tariff specialist in the Department of Commerce and Labor, concurred. During Germany's tariff war with Russia in the 1890s, Stone wrote, the United States had been an alternative source of raw materials. Now, Germany's new agreements implied a turnabout—an "intention to use Russia as a whip against the United States." Stone noted further that in applying its general tariff to the United States, Germany, then second only to Britain as a customer for U.S. exports, would be increasing not only the disparity between the prices of German domestic products and American-made goods but also that between American goods and those of Europe receiving the conventional tariff. Given the projected growth of German and European manufacturing in general, Stone concluded, Germany could successfully cut off all its trade with the United States "in lines in which we have not a world monopoly."[10]

In general, American officials were concerned but not panicked over the trade situation. Ambassador to Germany Charlemagne Tower regarded the German threats as "serious" in tone, but he viewed the Germans as predominantly "conciliatory," aiming not at a trade war but at forcing U.S.-German reciprocity onto a broader basis. Consul General Mason believed that tariff war talk stemmed mainly from the agrarians and other high protectionists, whereas the "commercial and industrial classes generally," though frustrated by U.S. trade barriers, valued U.S. markets and U.S. raw material and agricultural exports and feared the social effects in Germany of a rise in the "price of bread." These more moderate views were grounded in the diplomats' balanced reading of the German press and other commercial intelligence sources. The diplomats cited, for example, a German trade editorialist who cautioned that "in view of the enormous interests involved in the international trade between America and Germany, the word Tariff-War should upon no conditions be pronounced in the course of our negotiations."[11]

Sentiment in both nations thus was volatile when, in summer 1905, Secretary of the Treasury Leslie M. Shaw indicated that the Roosevelt administration, recognizing the protectionist complexion of the Senate, would not seek a treaty adjusting U.S.-German relations. The Germans reacted angrily but, seeing and perhaps exploiting the political exigencies of the situation, immediately advanced two new proposals that would not involve the Senate in approval. In private negotiations with the Department of State, German Ambassador Hermann Speck von Sternberg suggested that Roosevelt bend the U.S. interpretation of the most-favored-nation clause to make it more compatible with German practice. Second, Sternberg asked Roosevelt to extend on a provisional basis, again without congressional action, the existing Argol Agreement to include a wider array of trade items. Roosevelt naturally abjured such politically risky steps, however, and in the fall of 1905, the Germans, now able to claim they had made every effort to avoid conflict, announced that they would cancel their most-favored-nation treatment and apply their new maximum tariffs to the United States on March 1, 1906.[12]

The Merchants Association and Proposals for Customs Revision

The announcement that Germany soon would apply its general tariff to the United States propelled New York importers and shipping agents to Washington to beseech Roosevelt and Root to find a politically viable compromise. By winter, the German embassy had advanced this process by outlining new demands that were more accommodative of the political character of American tariff making. Instead of requiring the executive to make changes in the broad principles of the American tariff system, the Germans took an oblique approach, demanding administrative changes in the U.S. customs system. Here, the Germans, who for years had developed their own elaborate customs regulations designed to bolster protectionist policies, were quick to see in American practices discriminations that cried for alleviation. Their outline for U.S. reforms, although apparently technical, had considerable importance for the commercial relations of the two nations. Germany sought (1) public hearings for customs appraisal disputes; (2) modified procedures for assessing the dutiable value of German goods entering U.S. ports; (3) permission for importers and consignees to change the declared value of the goods after their arrival in the U.S. but before they were formally declared for customs appraisal; and (4) lighter penalties for undervaluation of goods presented for appraisal. The German focus on customs procedures would emphasize the role in the revision movement of a group that had not been prominent in previous reciprocity talk—importers and exporters represented by the Merchants Association of New York (MANY) and other East Coast commercial associations.[13]

Before mercantile revisionists could mobilize to support conciliatory U.S. customs changes, however, protectionists in Congress lashed out at the German tariff maneuvers. Ways and Means Committee member James Thompson McCleary (R.-Minn.), an outspoken critic of Republican revisionists, introduced two bills designed to set the general Dingley rates as a minimum and to levy 25 percent penalties in response to any nation's refusal to give the United States its conventional or favored-nation tariff rates. Lest anyone misunderstand the bills' purpose, McCleary announced that he intended them as "a means of making Germany sick of the maximum-and-minimum tariff scheme." In the Senate, Henry Cabot Lodge offered similar, although slightly less punitive, legislation.[14]

Supporting the congressional attack on the revisionists' demands for accommodation with Germany, Secretary of the Treasury Leslie M. Shaw, in whose department customs resided, urged Roosevelt to confine new commercial negotiations strictly to section 3 of the Dingley Tariff. Shaw pooh-poohed the concerns about German trade retaliation emanating from the Chicago Reciprocity Conference as "catching at straws" and implied that broadening reciprocity with Germany would only encourage tariff radicals within the party. Brushing aside Germany's concessions in its minimum-tariff conventions, the secretary opposed all special tariff treatment. This hard-line position may have derived partly from Shaw's ambition for the presidential nomination for 1908. By hinting that there were worse things than a tariff war, Shaw declared his fealty to the Republican Old Guard and implicitly reminded Roosevelt of its power to make not merely laws but politicians as well.[15]

Shaw pursued the protectionist case with the public, as well, opposing any tailoring of American commercial legislation to the demands of revisionists or foreign commercial interests. In attacking compromise, Shaw emphasized Germany's commercial advantages in world trade, citing low German wages, German export market targeting, dumping at below production cost through selling at high protected home prices, and discriminatory customs administration that admitted of no appeals such as the Germans were demanding of the United States. Shaw also contended that the wily Germans intended to exploit liberalized American customs rules to increase their writing of double invoices—one for the actual purchaser and one, undervaluing the goods, for American duty inspectors. Thus, where revisionists praised German commercial acumen as exemplary, Shaw cited it to inspire suspicion.[16]

The McCleary and Lodge bills failed to clear committee during the first session of the Fifty-ninth Congress, possibly because of pressure from New England textile interests and importers who feared losing their supplies of German dyestuffs. Then, in February 1906, as the March 1 deadline approached, Roosevelt called Shaw to a White House conference with Secretary of State Root and a group of importers. The participants drafted a compromise measure on customs administration that they hoped would mollify the Germans. The details, worked out between Root and German Ambassador Sternberg, provided that Shaw and the Treasury Department would allow open customs appeals unless the secretary considered "public interest" prejudiced. Further, importers would not have to appear personally before U.S. consuls to declare their goods; invoices could be validated either in their district of manufacture or of purchase abroad; and U.S. consuls were directed to confer with German chambers of commerce in determining valuations for goods. The Germans, sensing these proposals as embodying the current limits of compromise, grudgingly accepted them and, in the "Provisorium" of February 26, 1906, extended their deadline for the new tariff to June 30, 1907. Roosevelt issued a concurring proclamation the next day.[17]

By the time the two nations were formalizing their agreement, importing and exporting merchants in the United States had mobilized to press Congress for a longer-term modus vivendi with Germany. On February 23, the Ways and Means Committee opened hearings on two bills, one introduced by committee chairman Sereno E. Payne, the upstate New York protectionist, and the other by Representative Jacob Van Vechten Olcott, a low-tariff Republican from Manhattan's Upper West Side. The Payne bill did only a little more than codify the concessions that Secretary Shaw had already made to the Germans. The Olcott bill, however, had been drafted originally for possible use in reciprocity negotiations by a committee of the MANY in 1899–1900, in response to a request from President Mc-Kinley. In 1905, the MANY secured Olcott's sponsorship and updated the bill, which called for broad, statutory changes in the customs law that amounted, in the words of a contemporary observer, to "a decidedly radical change [in] the existing methods of valuing goods and making appraisements." The MANY also elicited fresh endorsements of its revisions from importing merchants in Boston, Chicago, and St. Louis—among them Sears, Roebuck and Montgomery Ward.[18]

As presented by Wickham Smith and Thomas H. Downing, counsel for the MANY and chairman of the MANY Committee on Customs and Revenue Laws, respectively, the Olcott bill contemplated significant changes in customs procedure. First, the bill would have permitted consignees of imported merchandise to make alterations in the declared value of their goods during the appeals process of customs appraisals. As Smith described it, this procedure would allow importers whom customs appraisers believed had undervalued merchandise to avoid paying a penalty on similar merchandise imported between the original customs appraisal proceeding and the final decision. In practice, this would enable large importers to avoid almost all penalties by offering a small shipment as a "straw in the wind" for initial appraisal. Also, the MANY wanted to enable importers to adjust their invoices if the market value of consigned goods had dropped in the United States after the goods entered the country. The law then in force, which dated from the McKinley Tariff of 1890, forbade importers to claim a market value below the invoice value. The overall effect of this change would allow importing merchants, who often bought on consignment, to stockpile goods and save duties by declaring their value during periods of low market values.[19]

A second change envisioned in the Olcott bill was extending the margin of error for undervaluation of declared goods, within which the penalty of 1 percent per percentage point of disagreement in valuations would not be assessed. The merchants first sought to negate penalties in cases in which the differences in appraisals would not have resulted in a jump to a higher ad valorem duty level. They also proposed extending the basic margin of error to 5 percent and giving the secretary of the treasury the option of extending it to 10 percent, if he considered the error an "honest difference of opinion" on the value of the goods. Moreover, the Merchants Association proposed that the secretary have the power to remit penalties altogether if he deemed it "wise or expedient" to do so. Clearly a sympathetic executive branch would have considerable latitude to countenance low customs valuations.[20]

The final section of the bill would have authorized open hearings in customs cases by statute, and not simply by executive decree, which Shaw had conceded in the negotiations that led to the Provisorium. In seeking to codify the practice, Smith argued that Treasury Department agents were responsible for collecting evidence on prevailing market values, but foreign chambers of commerce and merchants were under no obligation to the United States to report the truth. The result, Smith claimed, was a "star chamber" proceeding in which importers and consignees, excluded from knowing the sources and details of the information used to nullify their valuations, could not mount adequate defenses. Therefore, the MANY wanted a statutory right to appeal to the federal courts in cases in which differences with the Board of General Appraisers could not be resolved.[21]

Secretary Shaw also testified at the hearings, and his forceful reaction to the Olcott bill suggests some of the significance of its proposed changes. Shaw complained that statutory rights to open hearings would threaten business competition by revealing the sources and prices paid by competitors; that many importers in the MANY opposed open hearings; and that German customs administration was far worse than that of the United States. Yet, significantly, perhaps under pressure from Roosevelt, Shaw acceded to the remission of penalties for undervaluation of less than 5 percent and to extending the remissions on the authority of the secretary of the treasury to 10 percent. Discussion of the measure in the Ways and Means Committee indicates that its members saw the concession as tantamount to inviting "the German exporters [to] uniformly undervalue the goods" by 5 to 10 percent. In essence, of course, this constituted a limited and somewhat disguised form of reciprocity intended as a quid pro quo for the German conventional tariff.[22]

The Olcott bill never came to a vote, but the Payne bill, which incorporated the 5 and 10 percent plan, did. After it passed the House, however, the bill was pigeonholed in the Senate Committee on Finance by Senator Nelson W. Aldrich of Rhode Island. Discussion of the Payne bill, and of the McCleary bill, which remained on the congressional agenda into the fall of

1906, revealed that the Republican party remained deeply divided on tariff matters. It remained, then, for Theodore Roosevelt to attempt to break the impasse in Republican policy on the German trade and tariff issue.[23]

The Roosevelt Administration and the North Mission to Germany

Because Congress had failed to forestall the expiration of the provisional agreement with Germany, Roosevelt took the initiative. To begin, he solicited opinions from both sides of the controversy. On accommodation with Germany, Roosevelt consulted Ebenezer J. Hill (R.-Conn.), a member of the Committee on Ways and Means. Although nominally a protectionist, Hill had assisted Roosevelt in convincing Connecticut tobacco growers to accede to the special reductions of the Philippine tariff, recognizing Roosevelt's concern for integrating and developing the United States' outlying territories. A loyal party man, Hill declared himself ready to vote the anti-German McCleary bill, with its punitive provisions, out of the Ways and Means Committee, if the president desired it. But he told Roosevelt that "the passage of the bill would be ruinous to the Republican Party."[24]

Hill's arguments were not unlike those developed by the MANY and other revisionist groups. He maintained that by provoking Germany into escalating retaliations, the McCleary bill would alienate "the entire textile industry of this country because of the increased cost of dyestuffs and chemicals." In addition, the bill would provoke the "agricultural sectors" of the United States dependent on German markets for animal products, and it would open the door to a Democratic tariff revision of major proportions. Hill argued against his Minnesota colleague's scheme by suggesting that the original basis for protection, the high cost of American labor, had lost force with the relative rise in European wages during the previous ten years.[25]

To support his position, Hill shared with Roosevelt a Ways and Means Committee tabulation of comparative average ad valorem duty rates of the major industrial nations. The elaborate compilation showed that the United States tariff in any case far exceeded the differences in labor costs that McCleary and his supporters used to justify current levels of protection. The American duty according to the study was 26.9 percent, compared with Germany's 9 percent. Other nations in general were much closer to the German rate than to the American. With the exception of Russia's 35.6 percent and Canada's 19.46 percent (not including Canada's preferential tariff with Great Britain), the rates of Britain, France, Switzerland, Belgium, Holland, and Italy were all 10 percent or less. U.S. rates, Hill concluded, could be reduced materially without threat to American wages and with possible benefit to the competitiveness of American exports in international markets.[26]

Hill was sensitive to the implications of high tariffs as an aid to combinations, arguing that "the best Republicans" were concerned "that combinations . . . are shielding themselves behind a tariff wall and extorting from the American people higher prices than they are glad to sell at in foreign countries." Hill acknowledged that protection's "perfect work" was to develop domestic industry to a point of parity with Europe. "But," he continued, its "whole purpose" was "completely nullified when the combination steps in and throttles domestic consumption and makes of a protective tariff a perpetual bounty to the home producer, and this is what the American people are criticizing now." As Root had suggested in 1904, Hill now insisted in 1906 that convincing the public of the Republican party's independence of high-tariff special interests was politically vital: "My judgment is that as a Party we have got to face this question . . . for it is surely going to be forced upon us."[27]

On the other side of the issue, Secretary Shaw, having acquiesced to the minimal concessions of the Provisorium and the Payne bill, urged the president to support the McCleary bill. Shaw insisted that Germany's tariff was high compared with its wage rates—in essence that German prices were lower to begin with because of lower rates of labor. To equalize the tariffs on the basis of cost of production (presumably as determined by German domestic prices) would enable Germany to "dump" goods at 5 to 25 percent below German home cost and, Shaw said, to "close every factory in the United States."[28]

Shaw's advice was to defy the Germans and "meet discrimination with discrimination." Arguing that Germany required U.S. cotton, copper, and lard, whereas the United States could dispense with German exports, Shaw contended that the United States would win a tariff war and find other markets for goods excluded from the German market. Although he admitted that there would be some political cost to the Republicans, especially in the meat-raising states of Wyoming, Montana, and the Dakotas, Shaw suggested that he and Roosevelt should not "supinely surrender" to German demands but instead should "defend retaliation from the stump."

Revisionist opposition could be sapped by striking individual groups at their weakest point—by demanding reductions in the rates of their own constituents. Jabbing by implication at Hill, whose letters Roosevelt had sent him, Shaw challenged "Connecticut" to first "consent that the tariff on hats be materially reduced."[29]

By mid-September, Roosevelt had come down clearly, in a practical sense at least, on the side of Hill. Although he acknowledged, with Shaw, that general revision of the tariff was best postponed until after the 1908 elections and he complimented Shaw on his "mighty strong letter" in support of the "standpat position," Roosevelt absorbed Hill's concern about the growing sentiment for reform of the tariff, not only among the ardent revisionists such as the agricultural implement makers—whom Roosevelt recently had received at the White House—but among manufacturing interests in general. Noting Indiana Senator Albert J. Beveridge's complaint about the many who were resentful of the "Joe Cannon and Congressional Committee attitude" on the tariff, Roosevelt lectured Shaw that Republicans had to express "a willingness to revise the tariff whenever it is necessary, but at the same time cautioning people against jeopardizing our general prosperity by such a revision until they are absolutely convinced that it is necessary." In a letter to Root, however, Roosevelt suggested that his interest in accommodating revisionist sentiment was partly based on fear that intransigence would give free rein to radical tariff reform directed against large capital. Scorning Bryan's advocacy of "warfare on the trusts . . . by taking off the tariff on all trust-made articles" as "folly," Roosevelt implied that it was equally important to take the initiative away from insurgent Republicans who were espousing the identical idea. The division in the party, he suggested to Root, was serious:

> The tariff is of course what will cause us the most trouble. The demand for its immediate revision is entirely irrational; but this does not alter the fact that there is a strong demand; and as Cannon and the Congressional leaders will not—and I believe really cannot—say that there will be an immediate revision, I should not be surprised to see this issue used to defeat us.[30]

Such considerations clearly led the politician in Roosevelt to favor opening diplomatic negotiations on customs reforms with the Germans, because their technical nature and distant venue would allow him to secure changes that would pacify revisionists in the party without publicly involving or alienating the standpats. In addition, the political support of the meatpackers, influential in midwestern politics and won at considerable effort in the struggle over the Beveridge bill on food inspection just months before, may have been on Roosevelt's mind. At an international level, Roosevelt's recent relations with Germany may have predisposed him to seek an effective compromise on U.S.-German trade. Having frustrated at Algeciras Germany's desire for a commercial open door to French-controlled Morocco, Roosevelt may have wished to assure Germany, at what appeared a minimal cost, that even if their outlets to colonial markets were to be restricted, their access to the American market would not be cut off.[31]

Thus, to overcome the impending renewal of a tariff crisis, Roosevelt appointed a three-member commission to negotiate with the Germans in Berlin during late 1906 and early 1907. As chairman, Roosevelt chose Director of the Census Simon Newton Dexter North. S. N. D. North had been secretary of the National Association of Wool Manufacturers during the 1890s and therefore had good protectionist credentials, but he was also a thoroughgoing commercial expansionist, an advocate of capital and manufacturing exports who anticipated the eventual lowering of tariffs as an aspect of American integration into the world economy. Moreover, North had been a member of the MANY committee that had drafted the original customs law revisions for the McKinley administration. Commerce and Labor Department tariff expert N. I. Stone was the commission's second member and its principal statistician and translator. He had emigrated to the United States from Russia as a teenager in 1891, studied economics at Columbia University with E. R. A. Seligman, and accompanied Root to the Rio Conference of summer 1906 as a commercial attaché. The author of a number of influential articles on European tariff developments, Stone also corresponded with and informally advised the ARTL and the NAM Tariff Committee. The chief of the customs division of the Treasury Department, James L. Gerry, was included in the mission because of his detailed knowledge of customs statutes.[32]

Conditions for commercial agreement between the United States and Germany appeared inauspicious in fall 1906. "The German business world is dissatisfied, [and] German commercial writers are against us to a man," wrote Ambassador Charlemagne Tower to Root in September. The German legislative session, scheduled to begin on November 19, would concentrate on U.S.-German tariff matters, and, Tower added, the Reichstag might "decide to draw the sword and throw away the scabbard." On the other hand, the imperial government "would go to the limit of concession rather than break with us," Tower noted. The problem was that because of the tumult in the German commercial community, imperial officials who had been sympathetic to revision, such as Interior Minister Posadowsky, had to have convincing U.S. concessions to bring to the Reichstag.[33]

The North Commission assembled in Berlin in mid-November 1906 and met a well-prepared staff of ten German commercial and manufacturing officials who represented the German Foreign Office and the departments of Interior, Commerce, Agriculture, and Treasury. In addition to urging the Americans to revise customs procedures, the Germans revived their original demands for a broadened reciprocity treaty. On these subjects, the Americans and Germans held a series of twenty meetings, lasting until late January. Root, Ambassador Tower, and the large American commercial community in Berlin offered advice. In addition, Consul General Frank H. Mason, an expert on German affairs, was recalled from his post in Paris and appointed a full American commissioner.[34]

As the North Commission performed its work, American revision groups informally pressed the State Department for both customs modifications and a commercial treaty and poured advice into the department on specific concessions the U.S. export interests desired. Alvin H. Sanders and the ARTL had lobbied unsuccessfully to add to the commission an Agriculture Department expert to advise on "western meat product" export needs, but Sanders remained confident that the North Commission would "uphold the meat trade." Sanders was not above some saber rattling of his own, however, telling the State Department that "our packing house friends" remained skeptical of its efforts and that it was the ARTL's lobbying in James McCleary's Minnesota district that had caused the protectionist Republican's defeat in the 1906 congressional elections.[35]

At least in part, Sanders aimed at promoting the demand of western meat producers for the import into Germany of live cattle, which the Germans were blocking by nontariff sanitary inspections they refused to relax without a broader reciprocity treaty. This demand—as Ike T. Pryor, president of the Cattle Raisers of Texas, confirmed—stemmed from the cattle producers' attempt to widen the power of the export market as a control to the base prices domestic packing trusts paid for beef on the hoof. If the large German market for meat was opened to live cattle shipments, the meat-packers would have to match the German price, Pryor argued, and "export buyers can compete in our market centers with the Packers for such beef as is suitable for export." Thus, Sanders urged Root to invite German health experts to the United States to inspect all phases of American cattle production and pushed for the western cattleman's demands as part of the ARTL's program of packer-grower cooperation on reciprocity. He wrote Root that "if as a result of special endeavors the commissioners secure substantial concessions on our agricultural products, I believe the President could safely appeal to Congress or even the Senate for ratification."[36]

The MANY also actively sought to inform and influence the North Commission. Thomas H. Downing, chairman of the MANY committee on revenue laws and customs, provided the State Department with customs information, forwarded information and resolutions from the New York League of Customs Brokers, and summarized the views of American commercial interests on the political and tariff views of German foreign trade interests in response to State Department requests. The MANY, its officials repeatedly reminded the State Department, stood ready to help at any time "in matters relative to tariff relations with Germany," and considered a "proper Treaty with Germany . . . an absolute necessity."[37]

The MANY and the ARTL also cooperated in influencing the work of the North Commission. William R. Corwine, the MANY member who was head of the New York ARTL office, had a long conference with S. N. D. North on November 5 at the Murray Hill Hotel before North sailed for Germany. Corwine took up with North an ARTL and MANY proposal for investigating comparative costs of production as a guide to setting boundaries for negotiation on specific items of U.S.-German commercial trade. Corwine's motive here was to set an official check on the broad claims of damage that protectionists—especially textile makers— would voice as the result of a "scaling down" of rates via a Kasson-style reciprocity treaty. Although the State Department believed that this was not something the North Commission could accomplish on its own, it facilitated the contact between Corwine and North and continued to pass information from the MANY and from the ARTL's New York and Chicago offices to the commission in Germany.[38]

In Berlin, the discussions covered a variety of customs and commercial topics, with the Americans claiming that a major concession was in permitting the Germans to use export pricing, as determined by German chambers of commerce, as the basis for customs valuations. Because the Germans produced quantities of specialized goods for export, these goods could not be given an official domestic market valuation. Acceptance of German export pricing therefore could lead, N. I. Stone argued, to as much as a 25 percent reduction on those items. The Germans were unwilling to divulge the extent of German export-pricing procedures and also claimed that the Americans already accepted export pricing for some products, which would reduce the gains to be made from this concession. Nonetheless, they agreed on this cardinal point: Germany now would be allowed to use export prices as the basis for valuation of goods when an established domestic price was not available. Thus, only the international market value of a commodity, if such could be established by comparing the selling prices of identical items in other foreign markets, would act as a check on German valuations.

In addition, the North Commission offered to broaden the German-U.S. Argol Agreement made under section 3 of the Dingley Tariff to German champagnes and sparkling wines. Also, U.S. commercial officials sent to Germany to investigate valuations now would use "official facilities" for securing pricing and marketing information. This change was made to quell German concerns about the "economic espionage" of American commercial agents.

Another American concession would permit consignees to alter the valuation of their shipments after arrival in the United States. In addition, open hearings in U.S. customs cases would be the rule (rather than an exception granted by the Board of General Appraisers with the permission of the secretary of the treasury), except when the secretary ruled that publicity was prejudicial to the public interest. Because it had been announced in October 1906 that Leslie Shaw would relinquish his post to George Cortelyou, who was sympathetic to the agreement, this concession was meaningful.

Last, American customs courts would now accept German Chamber of Commerce appraisals of goods as competent evidence of valuation. This could mean little or much, depending on the weight American customs administration gave to German declarations compared with other competent evidence, but it at least provided a basis for argument on valuations, and a sympathetic administration certainly could facilitate the import process.[39]

All the American changes were real concessions to Germany because State and Treasury Department officials made them in the belief that they would lead to increased German imports at effectively lower rates of duty. They are perhaps more notable because they followed the spirit and sometimes the letter of the recommendations originally offered by the MANY through the Olcott bill, which had died in the Ways and Means Committee. Recognizing this, the Germans offered to grant conventional rates on most of their tariff items.[40]

The North Commission also sent back a draft of a new reciprocity treaty, whose negotiation Root had authorized in December. The treaty broadened U.S. rate concessions along lines of the 20 percent reductions called for by the Dingley Tariff's section 4 provisions, as had the major Kasson treaties of 1898–1901. In return, the Germans had offered a long-term guarantee of German conventional rates, relaxation of sanitary inspection of packaged American meat products, and—a key ARTL demand—import of live cattle.[41]

By late April, the State Department and the German Foreign Office had agreed on the nature of a customs agreement involving the exchange of the German conventional rate on nearly all items for concessions made by the North Commission. The pact would run for a year and would be renewed automatically unless six months' notice of cancellation was given. The agreement contained six articles, which recapitulated nearly all of the customs recommendations that stemmed originally from the MANY and were reiterated in the German Reciprocity Commission Report. Also included were the extensions of the Dingley section 3 items. But missing from the final report was the Dingley section 4 draft reciprocity treaty, which the Roosevelt administration shelved because it was "too late" for Congress to consider it in the current session.[42]

Predictably, the agreement, which did not require ratification by Congress and hence went into effect almost immediately, was met with indignation by protectionist groups. Samuel S. Dale, editor of the *Textile World Record*, denounced North and the State Department for keeping the terms of the agreement secret until after it was signed. Dale reiterated the "cheap German labor" argument and insisted that the United States was better off risking a tariff war with Germany. Whatever the overall balance of U.S.-German trade, Dale maintained, Germany was selling ten times the value in textiles (more than $30 million) to the United States as the United States exported to Germany. The new customs changes would exacerbate the damage to the U.S. textiles and woolens, encouraging German dumping and confirming the Germans in their "watchword, 'Deutschland ueber Alles.'" Textile manufacturers, Dale complained, were the sacrificial victims of the treaty and did not want German dyestuffs at such a price. The National Association of Wool Manufacturers was also quick to assail North by quoting their former secretary's 1904 denial of the likelihood or danger of a trade war with Germany.[43]

The NAM gave S. N. D. North scope to defend the agreement in its biweekly, *American Industries*. North minimized complaints that the open hearings would expose to retaliation those who testified contrary to German export interests, claiming that the agreement merely formalized what Secretary Shaw had agreed to a year earlier in the Provisorium. On export pricing, North noted that it was limited to German articles produced for export only, and that even in those cases, "international valuation" would check discrimination against the United States.[44]

Others defended the commission's work in the popular press. John Ball Osborne, chief of the Bureau of Trade Relations of the Department of State and a former member of the Kasson Commission, minimized the degree to which it represented a descent from the protectionist heights of the Dingley Tariff. Osborne glossed over the American concessions as administrative and of minor significance. He also pointed out that the Germans had conceded to the United States its conventional or minimum rates on 96 percent of tariff items, whereas the United States had conceded preferences to only 1.4 percent of the German exports to the United States (referring to the extension of the Argol Agreement).[45]

Roosevelt, too, was pleased by the agreement and confided as much to Root shortly after it was put into effect:

I am receiving various howls over the German agreement, coming from people who are vitally interested in the protective tariff and in business stability, and who therefore clamor for us to follow a course which would cause ruin to the protective tariff, and which would probably bring about a revision next winter, with attendant widespread disaster to the business community.[46]

Although some defenders of the arrangement with Germany supported it by minimizing its effect, many others involved in the controversy—both defenders and detractors—described the agreement as a radical change. Such characterizations voiced truths as well as exaggerations. Although not the broad-scale commercial disaster protectionists accused it of being, the agreement did invite further inroads of German exports such as textiles into the American market and therefore established a principle that had failed during the Kasson debates several years earlier: The immediate interests in protection of certain domestic groups could be modified to meet exigent commercial considerations of the economy and of international harmony in general. In addition, contrary to Secretary Shaw's wishes, the agreement was closely tailored to the requirements of German exporters and chambers of commerce, and it appeared to grant substantially greater power to German groups organized for commercial export activity to influence the valuation of German-made goods for American customs purposes. Certainly in the hands of sympathetic appraisers and a sympathetic treasury secretary, the agreement promised—without congressional approval—at least a 5 percent cut in duties as well as other benefits to large German-American traders. Here then was Roosevelt's tariff revision "by ukase."[47]

Open hearings in customs cases would now also make it more difficult for the government to establish willful undervaluations. Although Root was quick to announce that similar concessions were available to other nations that could comply with customs procedures, their initial grant to Germany, a nation well organized for export trade, probably represented, under the U.S. conditional most-favored-nation practice, a guarantee of discrimination in Germany's favor for a specified period. Moreover, the executive offer to generalize customs revisions to other exporting nations was testimony to the administration's desire to overcome the political restraints the constitutional system imposed on its commercial policymaking activity. In sum, the agreement did mark a distinct departure from the United States' position of protectionism as established by the rejection of the Kasson treaties at the turn of the century.

Certain limitations of the treaty are apparent as well. The Roosevelt administration declined to put the broader section 4 reciprocity agreement negotiated by the North Commission before Congress. This was probably not merely because of the difficulty of completing the agreement on time, as Roosevelt claimed. Very likely, Roosevelt was afraid to risk the symbolic test of a wider reciprocity agreement, because raising the issue directly would highlight polarizations in the Republican party, and failure would damage and further divide the administration. In addition, judged from a reductionist viewpoint, the German agreement was cumbersome and vague in principle, appeared unequal in favoring Germany, and seemed either to constrain future revisions or to risk being canceled by an administration seeking to placate other constituencies.[48]

Probably the 1907 agreement was the most in the way of revision that the Roosevelt administration could have accomplished, given the continued strength of congressional protectionists such as Cannon, Aldrich, and Payne, for they had stymied the legislative passage of a similar agreement in the Olcott bill. The Germans also seemed to appreciate this, despite their continued claims that they had made "one-sided" concessions. The ease with which the United States obtained nearly the entire German conventional tariff was a measure of that nation's dependence on U.S. raw materials and interest in U.S. markets. Thus, Germany's accommodation of American protectionism likely represented Realpolitik as much as fundamental contentment with the terms of the 1907 commercial agreement. That meant that the Europeans expected the United States to seek further means to coordinate its most-favored-nation clause and overall tariff policy to support the internal social stability of European states and to avoid overtaxing the conciliatory capacities of the general system of multiple bargaining tariffs then in force on the Continent.[49]

In a domestic context, the German agreement appears most significant as a mark of the practical—as opposed to the solely ideological—inclination of the Republican party to effect downward revision. Roosevelt had determined to postpone overall revision until after the 1908 election and the end of his presidential tenure. But he had clearly rejected the protectionist Shaw's approach to the German problem, and the two leading candidates for his succession—Root and Taft—had publicly declared support for downward revision and for a dual tariff that could provide for executive-level bargaining on U.S. rates. Both men were aware that continued intransigence by the United States in the context of increasing exports risked stimulating anti-American combinations in foreign trade. Therefore, the Roosevelt administration and executive leadership of the party were more willing to respond to the demands of reductionist groups such as the ARTL, MANY, and NAM. Thus, as a contemporary observer noted, the "German imbroglio" was

> only the temporary and unessential form in which an issue of world-wide importance and of great national moment is presented. For this reason no answer can be finally given to the demands of Germany which does not in some measure commit us to the acceptance of a definite policy with regard to the other phases in which the question may offer itself. The decision . . . will be the first step on a road that may lead to an entire change in our present commercial policy.[50]

The agreement also marked the unification under the banner of the ARTL of agricultural, manufacturing, and import-export groups, who exerted public and informal policy pressure in favor of the German agreement so far as their still-limited organization permitted. But even among Republican revisionists, conflicts were apparent between those who favored more radical—that is, antitrust-inspired—tariff reform and cooperationists who sought revisions favorable to large capital. Agricultural revisionists had cooperated in pressing for live meat exports, a tactic that had united forces supporting and opposing the meatpackers for a reciprocity treaty. But the treaty was not consummated, and proprietary-corporate conflicts threatened to further divide Republican movement for a full-scale revision. This was especially so among manufacturers. Because Roosevelt had shied away from a large-scale German reciprocity treaty and had created an agreement sustained by executive decree alone, Republican revisionism had not had a full legislative and public test of its coherence. The nature of these internal conflicts and the drives to resolve them would become manifest as Republican revisionists organized for a new tariff and for a tariff commission.

5 A Big Stevedore

Origins of the Tariff Commission Movement, 1906

America is still a big stevedore bearing down to the ships of the sea crude and semi-crude materials. Reciprocity and Revision with their present large trading margins will further increase the worth of those highly finished products which alone will disclose to the world the degree of our efficiency as a manufacturing people.—Special Tariff Committee of the National Association of Agricultural Implement and Vehicle Manufacturers, 1906

Tariff revision had acquired new momentum by 1906, as agricultural and mercantile revisionists mobilized for commercial accommodations with Germany and for expansion of executive branch authority in customs administration. Yet even the revisionists' small victories in commercial diplomacy and customs rulings highlighted their deficiencies in the central arena of tariff policy, Congress. Recognizing the power of the national legislature and the pitfalls to reduction in its tariff-making process, revisionists thus sought to integrate legislative and executive tariff authority through a new instrumentality: a dual-rate tariff approved by Congress and administered by a presidentially appointed tariff commission. It was this new strategy, emphasizing a maximum-minimum tariff and a tariff commission—rather than reciprocity, as such—that revisionists chose to promote as a more stable, durable, politically acceptable, and "progressive" path to lower rates, expanded trade, and institutionalization of their political-economic outlook.

The movement for a tariff commission was initiated by manufacturers and was supported by agricultural and mercantile interests. Like the reciprocity push at the time of the Kasson Commission, the tariff commission movement was hampered by conflicts between raw materials producers and finishing manufacturers and between reductionists of differing interests and ardor. As revisionists pressed for actual legislative changes to the tariff-making infrastructure, tensions between corporate and proprietary capitalists emerged as a basic dynamic of the struggle to define and control U.S. tariff policy. Here, conflicts between steel manufacturers and manufacturers of finished metal products such as agricultural implements were central.

Origins of Radical Revisionism

Among manufacturers, the putative relation between trusts and tariffs was given popular expression in the dictum "The mother of all trusts is the customs tariff bill." The phrase, uttered before the U.S. Industrial Commission in 1899, was that of Henry O. Havemeyer of the American Sugar Refining Company—that is, the "Sugar Trust." Although, or possibly because, Havemeyer immediately followed his startling statement by issuing a blizzard of self-exculpatory verbiage, his words on the genesis of trusts were singled out and widely repeated as an insider's confession of a broad truth.[1]

In politics, the linkage between high tariffs and trust abuses was popularized further by Republican Governor (later Senator) Albert Baird Cummins of Iowa, as the "Iowa idea," a plank in that state's 1901 Republican platform that called for reciprocity and urged depriving monopoly-made goods of all tariff protection. Distinct from the Democratic-inspired national platform, which had condemned the protectionist tariff in 1896 and 1900 and had spoken of it as a "prolific breeder" of trusts, this Republican antimonopoly statement spoke not for agrarian radicals but for midwestern manufacturers who now were pressured by the spread of consolidations. Sentiment—in Iowa, at least—was strong enough so that Cummins would state flatly in his 1902 gubernatorial address that "corporations, as such, should be vigorously excluded in every form from participation in political affairs." Thus, the anticorporate position in the Midwest gained a durable Republican embodiment.[2]

One of the salient factors in the reemergence of tariff revisionism after the breakdown of the McKinley-Kasson reciprocity initiative was the emergence of the National Association of Manufacturers (NAM) as a combative representative of the owners of smaller and medium-sized businesses in the Midwest and elsewhere. These manufacturers, many of them in the forefront of industrial finishing manufacture, were seeking to compete and to preserve traditional entrepreneurial liberties in the face of an expanding system of large, integrated corporations.

The NAM, of course, had led the reciprocity drive of 1897–1901 under Theodore C. Search. In 1902, however, Search and his supporters were overthrown by a group that would dominate the organization for the next decade and more. Led by vehicle builder David M. Parry, stove maker James W. Van Cleave, and railroad equipment manufacturer John Kirby, Jr., the new NAM was marked most visibly by its hostility toward organized labor. Whereas Search had played down the union question within the NAM, the alliance of Parry, Van Cleave, and Kirby made opposition to unions a paramount purpose of the organization. Rhetorically associating trade unions with "mob power," the "hired thug and assassin," and "treason pure and simple," the new leaders fought the eight-hour-day movement and sought judicial rulings that applied the Sherman Act more broadly to labor combinations.[3]

Beneath the NAM's hostility toward unions was its concern for defending proprietary enterprise from organized threats of all kinds, including those from corporations that sought to dominate markets and absorb businesses. The NAM chiefs were convinced that in the twentieth-century context of labor and corporate combinations, proprietary entrepreneurs also required unity and, perhaps paradoxically, the intervention of the state to preserve what Parry called "the individual liberty" of the marketplace. For the majority of NAM members, this liberty meant nineteenth-century capital-labor relations of paternalism, expanding production and employment, and low wages. Thus, they sought to discredit workers' claims for organized influence on wages and conditions. Symptomatic of the NAM leaders' approach was the sometimes obsessive crusade James Van Cleave waged against the AFL-associated Metal Polishers' Union in a protracted antiboycott suit on behalf of his Buck's Stove and Range Company.[4]

The new NAM stance seemed to put it at odds with Theodore Search's effort to take regulatory matters "out of politics." In fact, as NAM president after 1906, Van Cleave exhorted members to "go into politics." This meant contesting with labor in the factory and judicial arenas and representing proprietary enterprise vigorously through lobbying and electioneering— for which the NAM was exhaustively investigated by Congress in 1913, after sensational newspaper revelations by its chief lobbyist and purported bagman, "Colonel" Martin M. Mulhall. But despite the apparently furious and reactionary tenor of its activity, the NAM, in its own view, was using the legislative process as it and all interests had done, by pursuing its own conceptions of "efficient" and "nonpartisan" solutions to public questions.[5]

The NAM's continued advocacy of tariff reduction aptly illustrated its self-conceived progressive ideology. Although eclipsed temporarily by the general waning of reciprocity after 1901, tariff revisionism quickly recovered prominence in the NAM's overall outlook. In one sense, tariff reduction complemented the "new" NAM's labor concerns: Lower duties on working-class consumer goods would relieve wage pressures and thus would undergird the NAM's claim to concern for workers, as opposed to unions. More immediately, like the Search regime, the new NAM leaders saw reduction as a tool for expanding foreign markets and for securing cheaper raw materials. Overall, this approach—it might now be called a high-value-added export policy—sought to expand employment and profits and to restore a harmony that comported with the proprietary manufacturers' image of their paternalistic role in society.

David M. Parry articulated this viewpoint in the *Annals of the American Academy of Political and Social Science*, writing of American destiny as a manufacturing nation and the need for "a foreign vent for the surplus" of its products. As Parry argued, the nation should not "exhaust its mineral wealth and denude its forests" by exporting raw materials. Instead, it should lower tariffs on "coal and lumber . . . pig iron, bar iron and kindred products" to encourage their importation and to nurture U.S. capacities for finishing manufacture.[6]

In calling for expanded low-tariff raw material imports, the Republican Parry sought freedom from the control of raw materials by domestic producers. His view paralleled that of Democrats David A. Wells and Edward Atkinson, who had called for "free raw materials" in the 1890s. But whereas Wells and Atkinson in a practical sense spoke mainly for New Englanders facing rising competition from the Midwest, Parry now spoke for manufacturers in the Midwest whose views and interests had converged not only ideologically but to some extent practically with those of the easterners. This expressed the potential for the interregional political alliance for reduction that nineteenth-century expansionists had failed to forge.[7]

As early as 1902, the NAM newspaper, *American Industries*, began to emphasize tariff and raw materials questions. Especially noteworthy—and possibly symptomatic of the convergence of Democratic and Republican views—were the writings of A. B. Farquhar, the popular economist and implement entrepreneur (and a Democrat), who challenged President Roosevelt's assertion that the trusts could not be "disarmed by cutting down a protective duty." In 1903, Farquhar complained that the steel corporations had finishing manufacturers "bound hand and foot." Only by winning "the national power to our side," Farquhar said, could finishing manufacturers counterbalance extortionate pricing by the steelmakers.[8]

Like Parry, Farquhar sought "less regulation" to protect and more to guarantee equal rights in the marketplace. In pursuit of these goals, Parry had advocated a maximum-minimum tariff system, a theme echoed by the Merchants Association of New York and the livestock interests in the 1905 reciprocity conference. Yet in 1906, those two organizations were focusing principally on customs reform in pressing for diplomatic agreements with Germany. In fact, although a NAM executive privately described securing tariff revision as potentially the "second greatest triumph of the Association"—presumably behind extirpating the labor unions—the NAM under Parry had failed to inspire the administration or the legislature to make broad changes and thus to advance the tariff revision cause.[9]

One of the roots of the problem was that the opinions of Farquhar or even of Parry, however eloquently expressed, had not been translated into a program of action for the NAM itself. Clearly, NAM leaders feared to revive within their own ranks the traded accusations of self-interested partisanship against the reductionists and narrow and unpatriotic insularity against the protectionists. This was the same dilemma that Henry R. Towne of the Merchants Association had aptly outlined after the 1901 Kasson treaties debacle. Parry understood the problem, as well. Reciprocity that does not "injuriously affect any home industry," he wrote ruefully, was "practically no reciprocity at all." Thus, a NAM executive informed Parry's successor privately in 1906 that on tariff matters, the organization was "to-day just where we were a year ago and two years ago." The memory in the NAM of the divisive controversy over the Kasson treaties was such that in 1905, the fervent trade expansionist George Seabury seemed to speak for many when he publicly decried any return of the organization's "reciprocity fever."[10]

Yet the tariff controversy would not just disappear. The calls of Parry and Farquhar for a renewed reciprocity, dual tariffs, and free raw materials struck increasingly resonant chords within the NAM membership because the availability of low-cost crude products was becoming a serious problem for many proprietary manufacturers in the first years of the twentieth century. The growth of raw material and semimanufacture corporations—and the market policies they pursued—played a substantial part in the evolution of the controversy and the revision movement.

The Steel Industry and Tariffs

In many cases of raw material or semimanufacture production, the American market was dominated by large corporations protected by high tariffs—a concern that had been prominent in industrial circles at least since the hearings of the U.S. Industrial Commission of 1899–1900. At that time, conservative Democrats such as Edward Atkinson deemed "extravagant" the description of the tariff as the "mother of trusts." Still, testimony before the commission revealed that control of prices was well within the capacity of the major corporate combinations, including important raw material producers of coal, rubber, lead, tobacco, paper, chemicals, and steel.[11]

At least one witness before the Industrial Commission, singling out steel, petroleum, copper, tin plate, borax, and plate glass, directly linked higher domestic raw material prices to the tariff and to combinations' policy of export pricing. This process, also known as dumping, essentially meant the selling of "surplus" production abroad at below-domestic prices, a process sheltered by protectionist tariffs that prevented foreign competitive challenges to corporate-set domestic prices. Here, Atkinson allowed that high tariffs had prevented a "natural equilibrium" of investment across national boundaries. Data on this process came heavily from the Democratic-oriented New York Reform Club, which had been issuing pamphlets detailing price differences in U.S. and foreign markets since the 1890s. But this was not a Democratic party issue alone. As the German tariff controversy illustrated, export pricing was an important feature of foreign commercial practice. And, according to an economist who studied the subject during the 1920s, dumping was practiced in the prewar period by the basic industries of Britain, France, Japan, Germany, and, "on a substantial scale," by the United States.[12]

Among the large protectionist interests, the steel industry was central to the proprietary-corporate conflict over raw materials in the early twentieth century. By 1900, the American iron and steel industry was the world's most powerful, accounting for 34 percent of the global output of pig iron and 37 percent of steel. It was also a key factor in American export trade. In 1900, exports of structural steel, rails, and semifinished products such as bars, plates, ingots, and billets represented more than 25 percent of all U.S. exports; in 1905, such exports were more than 22 percent, compared with only about 13 percent in 1890.[13]

Steelmakers' interest in foreign markets expanded when the United

States Steel Corporation was formed. Part of the basic reason for the consolidation, as a historian of the industry put it, was to build a "steel empire . . . that would have worldwide influence." The tool for creating this empire was to be the Steel Products Export Company (SPEC), formed in 1903 under the guidance of Elbert H. Gary and Charles M. Schwab, the chairman and president of U.S. Steel, respectively. The SPEC itself was headed by James A. Farrell, who had worked his way up in the wire business of the steel company and had experience in international operations.[14]

In the pre–World War I period, the steel industry was a notable practitioner of export pricing, as Schwab readily acknowledged before the Industrial Commission. Some steel was sold abroad, Schwab said, at $23 per ton when the domestic price for that steel was $26 to $28. In 1904 hearings, witnesses made similar charges of dumping—that American shipbuilding materials that were selling at $24 per ton c.i.f. Belfast were priced at $32 per ton f.o.b. Pittsburgh.[15]

U.S. Steel's leaders did not envision export pricing as an optimal or permanent strategy. In March 1903, at a private corporate meeting, James A. Farrell said that "it is impossible to condemn too strongly the . . . supplying [of] our European competitors with cheap material with which to compete with the various companies' finished products." But deplore it as they might, steel executives appear to have restricted their efforts to minimize export pricing in the prewar period largely to the exports of U.S. Steel's constituent companies—attempting to promote exports of their finished wire, for example, over their semifinished rods or other crude forms. Thus, as E. H. Gary testified in 1905, U.S. Steel continued to find it advisable at times "to use foreign countries as a dumping ground." Moreover, steel executives blithely defended high steel tariffs on the ground of not disturbing "present prosperity," although they candidly admitted that most low-labor-value steel items produced in the United States needed no tariff.[16]

When pressed, steel executives defended high tariffs and export pricing by arguing that they sustained employment and helped to capture distant markets, even though it later came out that in some steel operations, the companies had imposed wage reductions to sustain low-cost foreign sales. On balance, in this period, the executives may have favored higher tariffs to help them consolidate the industry in coastal and port areas that remained vulnerable to imports and as a holding action for protection, guaranteeing good domestic prices and ample export opportunities.[17]

The steel industry's fundamental orientation toward the tariff in this period may be epitomized by the fact that it seemed to support tariff revision in only one important respect—with regard to foreign countervailing duties. These alone SPEC President Farrell regarded as "undue discrimination," whose imposition on U.S. exports would interfere with corporation attempts to supply branch plants and building operations in Canada and elsewhere. Because countervailing duties by definition could meet any price inequality, they threatened even the lowest-cost, lowest-price exporters.[18]

In contrast to large raw material or semimanufacture corporations, many manufacturers who were consumers of crude and semicrude steel products believed that reducing U.S. iron and steel tariffs would facilitate the entry of cheaper foreign raw materials or would at least force the steel corporation to meet a lower "international price." Domestic users of steel, especially exporters, resented steel dumping not only because foreign purchasers were getting better prices but because they were convinced that foreign manufacturers were using cheap U.S. raw materials against them in foreign markets. As one exporter complained, "We have to pay a high price for our material and ship [our finished products] to Argentina . . . and the Englishman may use this same American steel and beat us all to pieces in the neutral market."[19]

Domestic users of steel and their representatives in Congress became increasingly skeptical of U.S. Steel's position on the price issue as corporate enterprise made further inroads into independent businesses. In hearings, Gary and Schwab were interrogated repeatedly on export pricing. Schwab was assailed with his less-guarded testimony before the U.S. Industrial Commission, for example. And James H. Bridge's "inside" *History of the Carnegie Steel Company*, published in 1903, reproduced a letter Schwab had written in 1899 boasting that U.S. rail production costs of only $12 per ton, compared with British costs of $19, would enable it to sell surpluses abroad and, Schwab had said, "control the steel business of the world." As with Henry Havemeyer's statement about tariffs and trusts, and despite Schwab's efforts to "clarify" his remarks, popular attention was focused on what appeared as a confession of the trusts' designs for dominating domestic and export markets. This helped push the tariff issue from an arcane dispute over imposts toward a potential public challenge to corporate control of industry.[20]

One of the chief problems of dealing with export pricing by U.S. corporations was that within the U.S. system, charges of dumping could not be

well substantiated. Roosevelt was disinclined to pursue the steel corporation in the antitrust arena, and Congress lacked a specific mandate and
technique for monitoring the accounting and pricing procedures of large
corporations. Gary and Schwab used this in their appearances before Congress, minimizing the degree to which the company engaged in dumping
and airily attributing most domestic and foreign price differentials to differences in the sizes of orders and to price compensation for transportation
expenses. Irritated Democrats sought to shape a general indictment of large
exporters as discriminating against American consumers of raw materials.
But Republican protectionists shifted under the Democratic attack from
denying the existence of substantial dumping to defending it as a legitimate
tool for acquiring foreign markets. Thus, export pricing was an economic
practice for which effective political mediation or regulation did not yet
exist in the United States.[21]

In Germany, the foremost European practitioner of export pricing, the infrastructural arrangements formed an interesting counterpoint to the United States, one that American proprietary manufacturers viewed with interest and, possibly, envy. In Germany, protests against the dumping of pig iron
in Europe by the *Stahlwerksverband* had spurred an official inquest and led
German raw-material-using industries in 1902 to organize an intermediate
consumer cartel. To defuse controversy and accommodate the new cartel,
the larger steel organization initiated a system of export bounties in its sales
to domestic intermediate consumers. That is, the large semimanufacture
cartel granted rebates to domestic consumers of pig iron that exported
finished manufactures of steel, regulating this system by establishing its own
clearinghouse for export bounties. Germany's predominantly horizontal
integration structure thus was conducive to a concerted pricing and export
policy that gave a state- and industry-sanctioned place in the political economy to banded smaller producers, at least to the extent that these smaller
industries were able to sustain their own syndicates.[22]

In the United States in the prewar period, in contrast to Germany, the
diverse intermediate consumers lacked the unanimity, political organization, and legal mandate to create an intermediate consumer cartel or to
engage in formal export cartelization. Many U.S. businesses believed that
such combinations, though legally in a "gray area," were under the jurisdiction of the Sherman Act, and they feared to take action.[23]

Two means of subsidizing exports did exist, however. First, federal
drawback provisions, long a feature of American tariff law, technically
permitted manufacturers to recoup some 99 percent of their tariff expendi-

tures on foreign raw materials destined for reexport. But the drawback law was difficult for smaller manufacturers to use, because it required manufacturers to track imported raw materials pound-for-pound through the production process to show that the actual imports had been reexported in manufactured form. The process could result in disaster to a manufacturer who had purchased foreign raw materials if an export consumer reneged on a purchase or an export market failed to materialize. Moreover, smaller manufacturers who produced for both domestic and foreign consumption often simply could not afford to segregate foreign materials in production and storage or to conduct or concoct the accounting necessary to comply with filing requirements. Brokers who specialized in drawback filings did exist, but their commissions represented a burden.[24]

Seeking to make the drawback process more advantageous for smaller manufacturers, the NAM supported a bill introduced in the House in 1904 by William C. Lovering of Massachusetts. The bill would have dropped the requirement that the actual imports be reexported and instead called only for proof of pound-equivalent exports as sufficient to qualify for rebates. Protectionist Congresses rejected the bill, however, although Lovering and NAM members continued to try to insert the liberalized drawback provisions in new tariffs.[25]

Another accommodation to intermediate consumers was made by the U.S. Steel Corporation itself, which privately offered rebates to some 158 companies on steel for goods manufactured for export, a procedure that accounted for some $30 million of U.S. Steel's sales in 1911. For example, U.S. Steel would price sheet steel to a domestic manufacturer of boilers or oil tanks so that the exported finished product, shipped and marketed with U.S. Steel products, would be competitive in the foreign market. U.S. Steel's rebates constituted a single-corporation system parallel to that of the German steel cartel, but it also resembled advantageous rates given by U.S. railroads for freights destined for export. Or, it might be considered as a selective domestic analog of the drawback provisions of the tariff. The steel corporation, like the *Stahlwerksverband*, actually maintained an office and kept track of manufacturers' exports to verify compliance with the export provisions of its special sales agreements. Of course, the steel corporation controlled arrangements to target markets, grant price reductions, and ship products. Thus, manufacturers who were allowed to participate were consenting to becoming part of U.S. Steel's marketing apparatus and to sharing profits with the steel company.[26]

In general, groups such as the NAM resisted being drawn into the steel company's orbit in export matters. They did not exert the kinds of organized and recognized pressures within the political economy that the German finished manufacturing syndicates did, one that would have had the state validate, supervise, or regulate price relations between the two sectors. As for the existing American regulations, many NAM members lacked the resources to comply with drawback accounting procedures or did not purchase for export in the kind of bulk that would make them attractive clients for reexport rebates from the steel corporation. The exclusion of the medium-sized and smaller American manufacturers from effective participation in governmental and private rebate systems thus channeled their protest logically toward tariff reductions on foreign raw materials and a tariff commission, which they believed would relieve price pressures in the domestic market and remedy the structural inadequacies of the current system to respond to their requirements. That is, whereas German and other manufacturers formed cartels, the American manufacturers were moved to revive the Wellsian emphasis on lower raw materials tariffs and a commission as a means of state support for finished manufactures and as a "progressive" attack on the trusts.

The early twentieth-century tariff situation illustrated the uneven development of corporate integration in the United States, especially with regard to the timing and character of tariff changes. This lack of coordination or consensus was clearly the case in the agricultural implement industry's relations with the steel corporation and helps to explain the prominence of the implement makers in the "progressive" political movement for tariff revision, multiple tariffs, and a tariff commission.

The Implement Makers and the Broadening Struggle for Revision

Independent agricultural implement manufacturers, like other finishing manufacturers, faced increasingly difficult conditions in the early twentieth century. Whereas International Harvester was rapidly expanding its foreign and domestic operations in the quantity and diversity of sales, the independents were nurturing an array of complaints: against catalog houses that sold their own brands of implements by mail, against high rail freight rates, against union activities in their factories, and—most important—against rising materials costs and shrinking market shares many attributed to corporate consolidations.

Expansion of combinations and restriction of access to raw materials were for many manufacturers critical problems. In the central trade organization of the industry, the National Association of Agricultural Implement and Vehicle Manufacturers (NAAIVM), sentiment on trusts had gone from a nervous ambivalence in 1901 to an "Iowa idea" suggestion in 1902 by executive committee chairman Martin Kingman that for iron and steel trusts "we are in favor of free trade." Kentucky implement manufacturer W. G. Munn summarized the problem: The consolidated iron and steel rolling mills had created a pricing and supply system that required "enormous advances" of capital and cumbersome delays in securing orders of modest size. Munn mused that the implement makers, following the "drift of modern business enterprises," might have to own their own "blast-furnaces, rolling mills, bolt factories, sawmills, etc." to assure their supplies of raw materials. But he knew that such activity was beyond the immediate capacity of the myriad, dispersed implement makers, just as capitalizing an independent packinghouse proved beyond the capacity of individual ranchers in this same period. Moreover, for the implement makers, the overweening power of two giant enterprises, International Harvester and U.S. Steel, was a goad. By 1904, the NAAIVM president was declaring the combination question "the order of the day," and by 1905, NAAIVM members were petitioning President Roosevelt for relief from Harvester's efforts, "closely allied with the steel trust . . . to command and control . . . other lines of farming machinery and kindred manufacturing." As the implement men put it, the injustice was that their competitor was manufacturing "its own iron and steel, while the independent manufacturers . . . are buying at high prices in a tariff-protected market."[27]

It was under such pressures that in March 1906 the NAAIVM delegated members of its executive committee to confront the officers of the "steel pool"—that is, the general sales managers of the U.S. Steel Corporation. The implements group sought relief on steel bar prices, which had doubled since 1899. The delegation was led by H. E. Miles, chairman of the NAAIVM executive committee and soon to become a major figure in the movement for a tariff commission. Miles was president of the Racine-Sattley Company of Racine, Wisconsin, formed in 1904 from the merger of his own Racine Wagon Company and the Sattley Implement Company of Springfield, Illinois. A medium-to-large operation fairly typical of the independent implement concerns of its time, Racine-Sattley produced farm wagons, buggies, and smaller implements such as sulky and gang plows. The company had branch offices, essentially wholesale outlets, in a dozen midwestern states and in California and employed over 1,500 workers in its Racine and Springfield plants.[28]

As a manufacturer, manager, employer, and self-made millionaire, Miles was a "big businessman" in his own sphere, but conspicuously a nonintegrated one, a consumer of raw materials for manufacture—steel, lumber, and leather. Miles's committee blamed the trusts for the inflation of primary materials costs, which had outpaced agricultural income, undermined the independents' relationship with farm consumers, and put them at a further disadvantage relative to highly capitalized companies such as Harvester, which offered extended terms of credit to farmers. In addition, the price inflation affecting raw materials was fatal to the once highly competitive export trade of the independent manufacturers. As proprietary entrepreneurs, the manufacturers considered it manifestly unfair that the power of the Harvester Corporation in credit and raw materials in the long run threatened the independents' viability, no matter how efficient and "progressive" they were as manufacturers.[29]

In approaching the steel company, the NAAIVM committee had arranged to represent the entire agricultural implement industry as a buyers' combination. In this capacity, it asked for a reduction on the rates of domestic bar steel to $26 per ton. The implement manufacturers argued that independents could not afford to meet the competition of International Harvester in the domestic market at the current prices of $30 per ton. The manufacturers also scored Harvester's expansion from the big harvesting machines into the smaller implement and vehicle lines. In essence, the implement makers had combined informally to demand recognition of their collective needs and power as steel consumers.[30]

After some discussion, the steel executives decided to take the "rather unusual expedient" of quoting to a single industry, the implement makers, a special price of $28 per ton for the remainder of the 1906 buying season, which was for 1907 production. This offer was to last for fifteen days, after which prices were to return to the market level of $30 per ton.[31]

The manufacturers accepted the steel company offer, and at a farm equipment dealers' convention soon after, H. E. Miles touted the session as an example of the efficacy of joint action on the part of the implement makers and between the implement makers and the steel manufacturers. But the implement manufacturers actually believed that the meeting had yielded far less than the steelmakers could have offered on the basis of their current bar steel production costs, which the implement men estimated at no more than $18 per ton. As the implements negotiators reported privately to their superiors, after they had raised the question of the low—and, they believed, declining—costs of steel production with the corporation executives, "a prominent officer" of the steel corporation, although conceding the slight reduction, had scoffed at their rationale as a basis for future arrangements, saying that the steelmakers' policy was to "get for their goods all that they can without reference to cost." In the words of one of the steel executives, the implement manufacturers received this news indignantly and "said they were going to call a meeting of the association in Chicago and start a tariff agitation among the farmers against the Steel Trust."[32]

The implement manufacturers did not intend an "agitation among the farmers." As a group mostly comprising Republicans who continued to benefit from protection of between 20 percent and 45 percent ad valorem on agricultural implements, the NAAIVM shunned precipitant action on the tariff and too-close association with "radical" Democratic revenue-tariff or free-trade ideas, especially because low-tariff agrarian groups sometimes accused the independents themselves of price gouging and export dumping. Nonetheless, the meeting confirmed implement makers in their view of the trust's intransigence and in the tariff as a source of high domestic raw material prices.[33]

As a first step against the trusts, the implement negotiators secured a mandate from the NAAIVM for an investigation of competitive conditions and tariffs in the raw material end of their business. This Special Tariff Committee comprised principally large independent manufacturers who were then struggling to remain clear of entanglement with the Harvester Corporation and to regain the foreign trade into which they had expanded in the "American invasion" of the 1890s. The energetic H. E. Miles was selected as chairman and as president of the NAAIVM for 1906–7.[34]

By July 1906, the Special Tariff Committee had formulated a report—really, an indictment—analyzing and protesting raw materials prices and concomitant dumping of raw materials at cut prices abroad by the major steel producers and by primary producers of lumber and leather. The committee had drawn its material from published documents, surveys of the NAAIVM membership, and from contacts it had developed with other tariff revision groups, including the Free Hides League, which represented independent leather tanners in the Northeast and Midwest. The report called for a tariff commission—one of the earliest distinct revivals of the commission idea. The report also evoked a national viewpoint of independent manufacturers by noting that "much is said of the large amount of our manufactured goods exported. Not enough is made of the fact that these exports consist principally of materials like copper, petroleum and steel bars—products which are advanced little beyond the crude state." The report went on to invoke an image H. E. Miles would repeat in subsequent years: The United States was "still a big stevedore bearing down to the ships of the sea crude and semi-crude materials."[35]

In the report, Miles and associates condemned the tariffs on steel and hides, arguing that the "nation's ore beds have now in great measure come under monopolistic control," and charging that the monopolies such as the "lumber association, or pool" were manipulating prices. The report denied that the independents engaged in export dumping and called for reciprocity, especially with Canada. The report also epitomized some of the main tenets of the proprietary manufacturers' tariff argument in the coming years, extolling American finishing manufacture and the necessity of tariff reduction to the retention of foreign markets. The report was adopted without dissent by the NAAIVM executive committee.[36]

The fact that the report was accepted unanimously meant that even the representative of International Harvester who served on the committee, Edwin D. Metcalf of the D. M. Osborne Harvester Company of Auburn, New York, had approved the independents' attempt to secure cheaper raw materials. This is not too surprising, because along with other Morgan-organized corporations in this period, Harvester was attempting to deflect or absorb attacks on its market expansion and status as a "trust." Metcalf and C. S. Funk, Harvester's general manager, served on the NAAIVM committee on national legislation, supporting reciprocity and tariff reduction initiatives designed to maintain open markets for farm equipment in Europe, Canada, and South America. In part, Harvester's support for lower tariffs in this period may have been expedient. Harvester was building and equipping plants abroad, particularly in Canada and Russia. In the Russian case, it was specifically Harvester's ability to finance and build factories on Russian soil, a $40 million investment, that gained the company favor over other American and European implement makers. Once built, the factories would put Harvester's foreign production inside the walls of high foreign tariffs. But until the foreign plants were completed, Harvester needed lower foreign tariffs to export finished goods and materials to construct the plants. On a broader international level, however, Harvester continued to support the NAAIVM's general tariff initiatives because Harvester sold in many foreign markets and had begun to take over foreign marketing functions for a number of independent companies that manufactured in lines in which Harvester was not yet strong. Harvester thus profited from general tariff flexibility.[37]

For its part, the independents' group welcomed the support of the Harvester representatives, noting that "even members who have factories already established in Canada" favored Canadian reciprocity and the German Provisorium of 1906. The independents were aware that it was possible to "sell out" profitably to the rising corporations—Metcalf himself was an example, because as one of the principal stockholders of D. M. Osborne, a concern employing about 3,500 workers, Metcalf, along with company president Thomas Osborne, had done just that in 1903. Implement makers occasionally joked that their members opposed the trusts so vehemently only because they were not themselves part of a trust. The effect of the ambiguities of the situation, as with the relationship between the livestock producers and the meatpackers, was to tend to shift the focus of industry members toward cooperation in common goals of trade expansion and away from intraindustry conflicts.[38]

Even reductionists such as H. E. Miles, who vociferously opposed the inroads of corporate enterprise on proprietary capitalist activity, recognized that the secular rise in prices led by the raw material corporations was reflected in rising prices and profits for finishing manufacturers. Miles knew that this tendency could not be reversed entirely, and he knew that it would not be profitable for manufacturers to reverse it completely. "The steel Trust," Miles said in a tariff campaign letter, "takes possibly fifty thousand dollars more annually from my company but I . . . profit on that fifty, . . . charging my customers well above sixty. . . . I cannot say I lose a penny."[39]

It may be suggested that what even the most militant of implement manufacturers looked for was not a reversal of corporate power but an adjustment of influence that would stabilize the place in domestic and foreign markets of the independents—essentially through government intervention in the tariff rates and in the processes of tariff making. These reforms would prevent the foreclosure of foreign markets and would moderate the raw materials and capitalization advantages of the harvester combine by challenging the steel corporation and promoting expanded foreign trade in implements.

The fall of 1906 was a problematic period for the NAAIVM to raise the tariff question, however. As a predominantly Republican group, the organization understood that the year's congressional elections gave them political leverage with their representatives. But the revisionists also risked alienating the Republican leadership if they pushed too hard. Thus, before they began to "agitate" the tariff question with anyone, the NAAIVM executives decided to sound out President Roosevelt and other prominent Republicans in the hope of influencing the party to preempt Democratic calls for tariff revision. As H. E. Miles described it, the implement makers wanted to persuade Roosevelt, "for the infinite good of the party," to support revision and a tariff commission with the same vigor he had applied to his other reform efforts.[40]

Toward the end of influencing the Republican party, a NAAIVM committee, led by then-president C. F. Huhlein, met in Chicago with Illinois Republican Senator Shelby M. Cullom, who had supported revision at the Chicago Reciprocity Conference of 1905, and with Speaker Joseph G. Cannon, chief of the House standpat faction. Cullom encouraged the implement makers to forward their protest to Roosevelt, but Cannon flatly told the NAAIVM to make its own steel if it did not like to buy it, and he denounced any tariff "tinkering" by the Republican party, likening revisionist talk to "the Democratic tariff for revenue and antitrust rhetoric." Cannon relented, in a sense, only by urging the manufacturers "not to go into the camp of the enemy if they desired to accomplish results, at least during this election."[41]

Roosevelt, in more temperate terms, advised the implement makers similarly. Although professing his personal sympathy for free hides and other tariff reductions, Roosevelt argued that Congress would not pass such reductions and that to raise the question would divide the party. Roosevelt also urged the manufacturers to get off the tariff-trust hobbyhorse, saying that it was neither the trust question nor any bias toward "wealth, corporations or monopolies" that kept Congress from acting but rather the multifarious interests of the members and their constituents. Yet Roosevelt was concerned enough about the party's electoral base in the Midwest to invite Miles privately to discuss postelection approaches to the tariff question. This "audience" had its intended effect. Miles and the implement makers were persuaded to quash their tariff report and all tariff commission organizing until after the 1906 elections.[42]

Writing to his standpat secretary of the treasury, Leslie M. Shaw, Roosevelt summarized the situation:

I got the agricultural implement makers—that is, those western reciprocity people, to agree not to try to do anything this year; but they
say they are perfectly willing to have a cut on their own implements
and warned me fairly that after this Congressional campaign was over
they should begin a serious fight for revision—a fight which of course
will need to be taken into account in connection with our attitude in
1908.[43]

6 The Tariff Commission Movement, 1906–1908

> Give us a commission and we guarantee that it will find out
> what is wrong at the bottom of the Tariff schedule[s] and
> how far they are Congressional permits to create Trusts.
> —H. E. Miles, Chairman of the National Association of
> Manufacturers Tariff Committee, open letter to Senator
> Joseph Benson Foraker, August 28, 1907

In the latter part of 1906, the National Association of Manufacturers (NAM) joined the implement manufacturers in pursuit of revision and a tariff commission. The accession of James W. Van Cleave to the NAM presidency in 1906 may have cleared the way for more purposive action on tariff matters. A former Democrat from Kentucky who had shifted to the Republicans during the "free silver heresy" of 1896, Van Cleave was an intense, politically ambitious leader whose health was tried by his crusade against the American Federation of Labor. Resolving to extend the NAM's lobbying activities in tariff reduction, Van Cleave sought to delegate much of the actual work to a man of his own vision and forcefulness. That man would be H. E. Miles.[1]

Organizational and Conceptual Initiatives

Van Cleave moved toward reconciling the NAM's feuding tariff factions by dropping the emphasis on reciprocity and dual tariffs as such and taking up a tariff commission as a "scientific" and "businesslike" way to adjust tariff rates. In theory, a tariff commission would be able to investigate dispassionately and to determine "correct" maximum and minimum tariff rates independently of traditional free trade versus protection biases and more independently of the pressures of Congress and international diplomacy.

Van Cleave's advocacy of the commission idea, which had been proposed on and off since the time of the Arthur Tariff Commission of the 1880s, was politically astute. As Van Cleave framed it, a tariff commission was a minimalist tactic, vague enough to tie trade expansion groups together and to gain the approval of politicians who wished to endorse "scientific" and "fair" methods without actually committing anyone to defining actual tariff rates or levels in advance of the legislation. In addition, manufacturers could be reassured by the fact that a commission's powers would be limited by Congress and by the commission's own investigatory mandate.[2]

The tariff commission idea was also in a swing of increasing popularity within the NAM. At the 1905 convention, George Seabury, the critic of "reciprocity fever," had proposed a commission that would consist of expert economists "representing our interests in agriculture, mining, manufacturing, labor and transportation on land and sea." In essence, Seabury's commission was a powerful committee of committees, comprising cabinet, customs, and technical officials. Seabury outlined his rationale:

> A tariff commission of experts is needed now more than ever to analyze the power of our great American commercial trusts and industrial combinations, . . . to contrast their productive facilities with their European competitors and to investigate the regulation of prices and ascertain as to whether their increase has been due to the laws of supply and demand or to their greed . . . on speculation or to the so-called cornering of manufacturers that is not due to any legitimate cause.[3]

Van Cleave was confident enough to seek an audience for his tariff plans before the Boston Home Market Club, the bastion of high protection. There, the NAM leader called on "all protectionists" to unite to modify the tariff sensibly to forestall conceding the initiative to the Democratic free traders. He supported the value of tariff reduction as a thrust against the trusts, citing federal legislation inspired by the "Iowa idea" and introduced in 1902. Van Cleave also said that even the staunchest administration protectionist, Secretary of the Treasury Leslie M. Shaw, expected "a Roosevelt tariff commission to be formed for revision in 1909." The NAM president thus urged the Home Market Club to support a commission to "go over the entire Dingley law, schedule by schedule, and make a report to Congress which can be used as a basis for revision." Although the secretary of the Boston group, Colonel Albert Clarke, predictably opposed a commission and sought to cast doubt on the solidity of NAM support for it, Van Cleave had established his revisionist credentials under fire, moved toward generalizing the view among proprietary manufacturers, and set an important activist direction for the NAM.[4]

In September 1906, Van Cleave appointed H. E. Miles, already a member of the NAM tariff committee, as its chairman. Miles was well known within the NAM as a revisionist and by virtue of his work for the National Association of Agricultural Implement and Vehicle Manufacturers (NAAIVM). No doubt, too, the NAAIVM document proposing a tariff commission was a source, if not the only source, of Van Cleave's tariff commission ideas. In any case, Miles's appointment signaled the beginning of a five-year public crusade for revision and a tariff commission along lines that would foster the continued role of proprietary capitalism within the American political economy.[5]

In his new role as NAM tariff committee chairman, Miles immediately began to make frequent trips to Washington and New York, where he pushed Van Cleave's "scientific revision" scheme for a tariff commission. Miles was the energetic partisan Van Cleave had sought—and more. He presented a strongly worded report to the May 1907 NAM convention committing the organization to the commission movement. Against accusations, already afloat, that Miles was promoting revision purely as a self-interested implement maker, the committee chairman produced a survey indicating that 1,221 of 1,384 (more than 88 percent) NAM members polled favored the committee's campaign for a tariff commission.[6]

Perhaps more significant, and possibly going beyond what Van Cleave had envisioned, Miles called for a commission with considerable power. Like the Interstate Commerce Commission, Miles said, a tariff commission should have the power to summon witnesses and examine business records on a "semi-judicial" basis—that is, by subpoena—to compel accurate testimony on costs and pricing. Miles reassured his Republican fellow manufacturers that "we are all protectionists" and declared that a commission's role was to ensure that industries were amply but not excessively protected. Acceptance of this principle and of the fruits of its execution, Miles implied, was the price manufacturers would have to pay to control the trusts. The convention approved the full report and passed a resolution favoring revision at the earliest practicable moment. The resolution specifically approved "semi-judiciary" powers, a clear indication that a majority had accepted Miles's conception of a regulatory tariff commission.[7]

Van Cleave and Miles immediately embarked on a more extensive campaign of speaking and writing, reinforcing the view that manufacturers had to expand beyond "tropical reciprocity" by giving up some protection from competitive European products. They also insisted that a commission would bypass the heretofore insuperable legislative barriers to reduction by treaty and would assure manufacturers that the burdens of reduction were being distributed more fairly. Marking the increasing interest the issue was generating, the *Annals of the American Academy of Political and Social Sciences* dignified the cause by publishing special tariff issues coinciding with the 1907 and 1908 NAM conventions and containing tariff speeches by Elihu Root, as well as articles by Miles, Van Cleave, and East Coast revisionists.[8]

Miles and Van Cleave also sought to capitalize on Roosevelt's vague preelection promises to respond to the revision initiative by identifying the president with a commission. In the summer of 1907, Miles again met with Roosevelt. Although Roosevelt apparently promised little, Miles was bold enough to tell the *New York Herald* that the president might well make the tariff commission another reform coup, to match his activities in food and drug and railroad regulation. More plausibly, Miles and Van Cleave gave wide publicity to the public prorevision statements of Taft, Oscar S. Straus, and Root and pressured Congress by publicizing the 1904 Republican platform's statement that the minimum measure of tariff protection ought to be the "difference in the cost of production in this country and abroad."[9]

As part of its organizing, the midwestern Republican commission partisans invited cooperation with eastern manufacturers, merchants, and Democrats. The commission format, the midwesterners argued, would protect manufacturers from a destruction of the tariff altogether, which they believed would open the U.S. market too widely to foreign competition and allow only the trusts to survive; but it would also provide a broader, more practical base for Democratic "free raw materials" ideas. Coming from former Democrats such as Van Cleave, the call for cooperation could have some degree of sincerity. Miles, too, encouraged the easterners. Writing to Franklin Pierce, the New York mercantile attorney and author of the *The Tariff and the Trusts*, Miles granted that Pierce's advocacy of free raw materials was "entirely right," and that anything he said about the tariff would be helpful, but he cautioned that if Pierce pressed issue in that way, "various interests would put us off with theorizing" whereas with "a commission . . . we are on very strong ground." Whether the ideal or "scientific" level of protection could accomplish the balancing act of curbing the trusts while preserving proprietary manufacture had yet to be tested in practice, however.[10]

The revisionists also began to invoke the ideals of resource conservation after Miles and other NAM members attended Roosevelt's historic Governors' Conference on Conservation. Although discussion of the tariff as such was barred in that context, the issue was implicit in the idea that freer trade might be a solution to the problem of scarce domestic materials. In letters, Miles enthusiastically paraphrased a conversation he had had with railroad baron James J. Hill, who had endorsed the association between conservation and revision, telling Miles that within fifty years, domestic ore, forest, and other resources would be threatened if the tariff continued to put "a premium upon the wasteful and speedy exhaustion of raw materials." The consequent crisis of scarcity, Hill added, would challenge democracy itself and leave the nation vulnerable to the rule of the "man on horseback."[11]

Despite the significant support for revision within the NAM, protectionists rejected the commission initiative as a Trojan horse for free trade. Particularly vehement was the *American Economist*, house organ of the American Protective Tariff League (APTL), representing members of the glass, dye, railway, machine tool, cutlery, and cotton mill machine industries. The APTL, reviewing Miles and Van Cleave's alliance-building efforts, sarcastically proposed a "merger of tariff wreckers" to include the NAM, the American Reciprocal Tariff League (ARTL), Merchants Association of New York (MANY), and the generally Democratic organizations such as the American Free Trade League of Boston and the Reform Club of New York.[12]

The continuing resistance of some sectors of proprietary manufacture that were not heavily invested in foreign trade and that feared the competition of powerful European industries may have had an important effect in shaping the tariff reduction initiative. Their opposition may have pressed "radical," antitrust revisionists toward a wider coalition with procorporate elements, such as the meatpackers in the ARTL, International Harvester in the NAAIVM and NAM, and large retailers and import-export merchants in the MANY. Hence, as the movement went forward in favor of a commission and reciprocity, it encompassed forces that sustained its views on trade expansion and a tariff commission but that may have undermined its radical proprietary commitment. This development appears to have laid the groundwork for a dynamic of opposition and conciliation between "radical" proprietary versus "cooperationist," corporate-oriented versions of revision and a commission.

The effort to widen the coalition of tariff commission proponents gained impetus early in 1907, when more than nine hundred delegates assembled for the National Convention for the Extension of the Foreign Commerce of the United States, held at the New Willard Hotel in Washington, D.C. Organized by the New York Board of Trade and Transportation, the convention featured Secretary of State Elihu Root and Secretary of Commerce and Labor Oscar S. Straus, speaking on trade expansion topics, including ship subsidies, an issue then before Congress. Maximum and minimum tariffs were endorsed by Root and even by House Speaker Joseph G. Cannon. Moreover, Roosevelt himself, in what the press described as a "ringing speech," endorsed Root's address, again hinting that he might be amenable to tariff revision. Alvin H. Sanders of the ARTL called for reciprocity in U.S. commercial relations with Germany, then under negotiation by the North Commission in Berlin, and Thomas Osborne of International Harvester called for immediate tariff reform, which the conference "greeted with great enthusiasm." Van Cleave was elected conference chairman, and, most significantly, the conference endorsed "a permanent nonpartisan advisory board or commission charged with the duty of studying at all times our trade relations with foreign countries, with a view toward recommending . . . modifications in customs duties."[13]

It seems clear that the conference, coupled with Van Cleave's and Miles's leadership, spurred coalition building. Now, Miles began to meet with Alvin Sanders, and they attempted to hammer out a common position that would overcome some of the historic divisions between agricultural and manufacturing revisionists—that is, the conflict over import of agricultural crude products, such as hides. Both men were readers of Commerce and Labor Department tariff expert N. I. Stone's articles on European tariff conditions, and in fact it was Stone who brought them together and may have provided the intellectual foundation for their admiration of German commission-style tariff making and for integrating their agrarian and manufacturing positions. On the latter subject, Stone had suggested that in effect U.S. raw material exports were vital to American manufacturing exports because they gave the United States leverage in foreign markets.[14]

An early result of the NAM-ARTL collaboration was the publication in the NAM's *American Industries* of an article by William R. Corwine, the ARTL's New York secretary, entitled "Tariff Should Be Adjusted in a Businesslike Way." The article, following the "Stone" line, argued that the NAM and the ARTL's policies were in harmony. Lower tariffs, obtained scientifically through a commission, would be fair and would "benefit our export trade, not only of raw material but of partly and highly finished manufactured products."[15]

The cooperation of "trusts" such as the Harvester Corporation and the meatpackers in the tariff commission movement, though it stimulated the jibes of the protectionists, did not blunt Miles's attack against the large semimanufacturing corporations that were the object of the NAM's tariff campaign. "Give us a commission," Miles challenged protectionist Senator Joseph Benson Foraker (R.-Ohio) in an open letter, "and we guarantee that it will find out what is wrong at the bottom of the Tariff schedule[s] and how far they are Congressional permits to create Trusts."[16]

The Beveridge Bill and the "Progressive" Tariff in Congress

As the chairman of the NAM tariff committee, H. E. Miles began a legislative initiative by writing to a number of senators and congressmen, including those favorable and unfavorable to downward revision. Movement on actual legislation to establish a commission was vital, Miles wrote in October 1907, so that the commission would be prepared to participate in the revision Republicans were promising after the 1908 election.[17]

With Alvin Sanders of the ARTL, Miles focused particular attention on Senator Albert J. Beveridge. The charismatic Indiana Republican was a credible and creditable ally of the tariff movement because he had influence with President Roosevelt and because he had proved his credentials both as an expansionist and as a reformer in the meatpacking industry. Moreover, Beveridge was a close friend of former NAM president David M. Parry, also of Indiana. The relationship between Parry and Beveridge gave the movement an important entrée into the national political arena. No less important, the link provided Beveridge and other "progressive" politicians with an organized and vocal constituency whose activism could carry forward their own careers.[18]

Beveridge was already known to favor tariff revision and the commission idea. But Miles's initial attempts to accelerate Beveridge's motion in this direction were only equivocally successful. Miles tried to convince Beveridge that the cabinet and the country were on the verge of a tariff revolt, but the Indiana senator was politically too sophisticated to accept Miles's partisan view or to back openly a commission with the extensive tariff-making powers Miles wanted. However he may have felt personally, Beveridge remained sensitive to the views of congressional Republicans—telling one House colleague that "on the general question of protection, I am with you horse, foot and dragoons"—and to President Roosevelt's reluctance to move on the tariff issue.[19]

Yet Beveridge—like Roosevelt, Taft, and other prominent Republicans—also feared conceding the mandate for change to the Democrats. And perhaps because his position in the legislature and his home-state support enabled him to speak more freely than the executive branch revisionists, and because the Panic of 1907 brought the need for economic reforms to a higher pitch, Beveridge soon promulgated a revision plan encompassing a maximum-minimum tariff and a tariff commission. He privately urged the protectionist congressman and Ways and Means Committee member John Dalzell (R.-Pa.) to support a commission "to get at the *facts*" and publicized his plan in a dual-column magazine debate that featured William Jennings Bryan taking the revenue-only tariff stance on one side and Beveridge espousing a commission along "German" lines on the other. Beveridge cited N. I. Stone as an authority on the German commission's scientific work.[20]

Beveridge's views and basic strategy for a commission clearly owed much to his contacts with the revision movement. Parry and Van Cleave had interceded with Beveridge on behalf of H. E. Miles, and Beveridge had privately asked Parry for "a brief of a bill such as your permanent tariff commission of experts." Van Cleave soon gave Miles a full go-ahead to "draft a bill for a national permanent tariff commission to be established just as quickly as practicable." Whatever spurred him, Beveridge soon was inviting the NAM tariff committee to meet with him in Indianapolis, and by November, Beveridge and Miles were exchanging views on the possible makeup of a tariff commission. Miles imagined that Democratic as well as Republican support could be enlisted for a commission bill; he tried to convince Beveridge that farmers were "rising" in support, possibly basing this assumption on the endorsement of a tariff commission by the National Grange, whose annual convention had just taken place in Hartford, Connecticut. Beveridge privately waved away Miles's contention that the Grange was a bellwether for the Democratic party and insisted, probably for political as well as practical reasons, that passage of any commission bill must depend on the Republicans in Congress. Yet, despite serious misgivings about the chances of a tariff commission bill in an election-year Congress, Beveridge began work on his own draft of a bill during November and December of 1907. He may have feared that other progressive Republicans might preempt the issue. In addition, Beveridge had "talked with a very large number of manufacturers and other producers and I [had] yet to find one who [was] not insisting" on revision, a commission, and a maximum-minimum tariff. Further prompted by a raft of mail on the subject, Beveridge concluded that "some of our smaller manufacturers are in a pretty bad case and are getting pretty well heated up upon this whole question," and he hurriedly completed his bill and planned its introduction for early 1908.[21]

If Beveridge was dubious about the prospects of his legislation, not so the indefatigable H. E. Miles, who immediately set out to rally support among the revisionists. Van Cleave for the NAM, Sanders for the ARTL, and William McCarroll, the New York leather manufacturer who had been chairman of the National Foreign Trade Convention earlier in 1907, issued a joint communiqué in support of revision in 1909 by a tariff commission. Miles also enlisted a blue-ribbon delegation to meet in Washington to bolster Beveridge's efforts. For the delegation, Miles drafted Van Cleave and other midwestern delegates from the Millers National Federation and the American National Live Stock Association. Miles also co-opted his successor as NAAIVM president, G. A. Stephens of Moline Plow, a company with a long record of support for reciprocity. Also to be present were Nahum Batchelder, master of the National Grange, and a contingent of eastern revisionists including Henry R. Towne of the MANY and E. S. A. DeLima of the New York Board of Trade and Transportation. Joining the group were Alvin Sanders of the ARTL; Arthur B. Farquhar, the political economist and manufacturer; and representatives of the South's export-conscious cottonseed oil association. In Miles's view, the trip was an opportunity not only to lobby for the Beveridge bill but to create a "central or executive committee" of procommission organizations endowed with a fund of $10,000 to $20,000 for further work.[22]

Miles also hoped, along with Beveridge, to use the delegation's Washington trip to press prorevision members of the executive—notably Taft, Root, and Straus—to come out fully for a commission, as a way of putting pressure on Roosevelt and on Congress to take decisive action on the tariff matter in the 1908 election year. Both Beveridge and Van Cleave, however, attempted to muzzle Miles's avowed intention to "talk truth, naked and unadorned" in Washington on specific tariff schedules, on the inequities of German-American trade relations, and on the injustices of the trusts. Although Van Cleave, not the most temperate of men, himself had been flaying opponents of the commission scheme as "dumb, deaf and blind reactionaries," he was enough of a politician to warn Miles that his singling out of specific interests as overprotected was causing resignations from the NAM. Pursuing his minimalist tactic, Van Cleave wanted to make the commission do the dirty work of cutting the schedules. Beveridge, too, warned the Wisconsin manufacturer against arousing "opposition [that would] prevent passage of the bill." For his part, Miles complained to Beveridge that Van Cleave had told him on the one hand to "shoot to kill" and on the other "not to raise hell," but he acceded, at least temporarily.[23]

As the progress of Beveridge's proposed legislation would show, a key area of contention was over the makeup of the proposed commission, its powers of investigation, and its mandate to advise Congress on the "difference in the cost of production at home and abroad." At one end of the spectrum were Miles and midwestern Republicans who favored an independent and powerful commission explicitly serving proprietary ends. At the other were protectionist Republicans, such as Cannon and Nelson Aldrich, who favored the traditional congressional committee system and who were willing, as Aldrich remarked, to vote for 300 percent of protection if it was needed to bar foreign competition. In between were Republicans who favored a powerful commission, such as Van Cleave and Beveridge, but for political reasons were unwilling to push quite as hard as Miles, and others who were willing to allow a commission of "experts" a limited, strictly supervised role in assisting the Ways and Means Committee to formulate schedules.[24]

Miles's radicalism on the tariff and commission, it is worth stressing, was not merely the expression of a naive or overenthusiastic personality, although he may have behaved that way at times. In political-economic terms, Miles and the proprietary groups' chief interest in revision was to undercut "tariff-fed trusts"—the corporations that controlled manufacturers' access to raw materials such as steel, coal, and lumber. Adjusting the tariff "adequately, but not excessively" was the radical revisionists' Republican version of Democratic tariff-trust arguments that took into account manufacturers' continuing need for protection against European industrial exports.

To define what they considered an "adequate" level of protection, Miles and other "progressives" took an ideological initiative by seizing upon the heretofore vague utterances of the Republican party about equalizing the "cost of production" at home and abroad. This, they believed, would serve as a lever with which to master trust power and to implement their conceptions of the proper definition of productive enterprise.

The notion of equalizing domestic and foreign costs of production was, in the words of a contemporary political-economic writer, "as old as protection itself." But the greater development of cost accounting in the early twentieth century by businesses gave a scientific cachet to the idea. Many proprietary businessmen, victors in the marketplace struggle of competitive capitalism, were confident of their superior productivity; knew their labor, materials, and selling costs to within a few percentage points; and were prepared to compete with corporations in many aspects of manufacture itself. This was especially true of noncorporate finishing manufacturers such as Miles and lockmaker Henry R. Towne, an innovator in production engineering whose writings inspired Frederick W. Taylor's later work. Conspicuously missing from the political-economic arsenal of proprietary business was control of raw materials, however. High materials costs would force proprietary manufacturers to raise prices and to economize on labor expenses. Here, they would lose ground to integrated corporations whose greater control of materials, capital, and the market system would allow them to raise wages—or armies of strikebreakers—to purchase "labor peace" or to lower prices to extend control over an increasing share of the market.[25]

The problem for proprietary manufacturers was to find not only an instrumentality but a principle by which to modify protection so that the tariff would enable efficient manufacturing plants to compete without having to integrate vertically—essentially to be absorbed by or form a "trust" with control of raw materials. The cost-of-production theory was amenable to this purpose because it implicitly tied protection to a formula of average cost across the nonintegrated, proprietary majority of businesses in an industry. This would mean that the existing configuration of manufacturing operations, taken horizontally by industry, would set a standard of protection, discriminating against only the weakest producers in an industry. Serious commitment to reduction meant that proprietary manufacturers had to reach a consensus on a minimum level of productive efficiency that in effect defined the market via a state mandate, the tariff. Under such a system some inefficient producers would have to be sacrificed, but those such as Miles and Towne would have a barrier against imports. At the same time, the generally low production costs of the large corporate raw materials and semimanufacture corporations would bring their tariffs down, and foreign production economies at the raw material level would become available in the American market. In theory, thus, American trusts would be brought into horizontal competition with foreign combinations in the domestic market, giving intermediate consumers greater leverage in domestic and foreign markets. In the hands of Miles and associates, then, the cost-of-production formula was a new incarnation of the old "god" of reciprocity, but one specifically intended to predicate commercial expansionism on state support for proprietary capitalism.

Thus, speaking to the exigencies of international commercial relations, the position of the proprietary manufacturer in reference to those relations, and the domestic conflicts between proprietary manufacturers and corporations, Miles sought to convince Beveridge that a commission following cost-of-production methods was responding not to the self-interests of particular manufacturers but to a particular conception of "national and international needs and ethics."[26]

Early in February 1908, the delegation organized by Miles met with Ways and Means Committee Chairman Sereno E. Payne (R.-N.Y.) and Speaker Joseph G. Cannon (R.-Ill.). Perhaps influenced by the cautions of Van Cleave and Beveridge and possibly by an assurance by Cannon that he would go along with a tariff commission plan if party harmony was not disrupted by strong attacks on protection, the delegates gave rather tame résumés of their demands. Miles, for the manufacturers, asked that the Ways and Means Committee delegate individuals to investigate tariff abuses. Samuel Cowan of the American National Live Stock Association complained of a falloff in meat exports to France and Germany. Batchelder of the National Grange and G. A. Stephens of Moline Plow supported the commission idea, although Stephens bristled at the suggestion that implement manufacturers themselves engaged in dumping.[27]

Payne and Cannon rebuffed the commission idea, however. Both had agreed with Roosevelt and Root that the United States should adopt a maximum-minimum tariff structure to adjust to European multiple-tariff systems. In fact, Payne had defended such notions since the 1890s, when he attacked the Wilson Tariff with the club of reciprocity—that is, he accepted effectiveness of tariff bargaining. Yet although both Payne and Cannon allowed that revision legislation would come up after the election and that the tariff adopted would employ some new bargaining system that would have to be administered, they balked at a substantive commission, defending Congress's abilities and prerogatives in managing tariff tasks. They questioned the adequacy of the Arthur Tariff Commission of the 1880s and portrayed the Republican party, the House Ways and Means Committee, and the tariff's old schedules as protecting not "interests" but business stability itself.[28]

After the meeting had ended and the delegates had returned to their home states, Miles began to fume. Feeling gulled by the promises of House leaders to entertain the delegation's ideas, only to have them fobbed off in practice, Miles scathingly attacked "Old Schedules" Payne in the NAM newspaper. Apparently Miles and Van Cleave felt sufficiently frustrated with the lack of congressional response and the ambiguity of presidential support for the core elements of their program that they were willing to risk another slew of protectionist resignations from the NAM to press their case in public in a continuing series of articles in *American Industries*. Although Miles continued to try to associate Roosevelt with support for a commission, privately he was still asking Roosevelt for an unequivocal statement that might move the congressional leadership.[29]

A development in the revision movement's strategy came about, however, after Nelson Aldrich, through George W. Perkins of the Morgan banking interests, approached Beveridge in search of support for the Aldrich currency bill, then coming before the Senate. Beveridge believed that some political horse trading might enable passage of his own bill in the Senate. In addition, he wrote Miles, "House leaders are evidently so scared that they have practically agreed upon a joint resolution directing the Treasury Department to gather the data provided for in our Tariff Commission bill." To this half step toward a commission Beveridge had not agreed, though he felt he might have to at some point.[30]

The legislative complexities involving the commission bill highlighted differences between Beveridge and Van Cleave, who had larger political agendas, and Miles, the manufacturer and tariff agitator. Whereas Beveridge was inclined to accept compromise to pass the measure, Miles was exasperated at the idea of having Treasury Department or customs officials do the work of a tariff commission. As he protested to Beveridge, this "lot of appraisers"—that is, the customs officials—"know nothing about costs, nothing about the real inside. . . . [But] what has the sales or market price of steel, petroleum or sugar to do with the protection needed by those industries[?] A trust makes its prices with no regard to its own needs or its costs, and protection is nothing but a question of cost and need."[31]

Miles also believed that a "lot of appraisers" would lack status and power vis-à-vis Congress. Miles wanted not an advisory committee of customs clerks but a presidentially appointed regulatory commission of notables commanding the services of technical experts on industrial costs, a structure on the lines of the German model. Miles's commission would effect a cost-of-production system of determining economically appropriate tariff rates that Congress would be impelled or intimidated into following. Miles specifically wanted on this commission influential representatives of industries or economic sectors, "practical outsiders," in essence manufacturers sympathetic to proprietary conceptions of revision. Even the "experts" Miles had in mind for the commission were of greater stature and different orientation from the customs clerks. For example, Miles named the Commerce Department's N. I. Stone, who had participated in the German tariff negotiations of 1906–7, and S. N. D. North, who had led the German commission and who was director of the Census, both sympathetic to a tariff commission. In short, Miles insisted on a commission with teeth, one that could supersede congressional logrolling on the tariff, and that had the "power to summon witnesses and compel the submission of testimony to investigate the books."[32]

In attempting to shepherd Beveridge's negotiations on the bill, Miles was adamant on the integrity of his program, insisting several times that "the difference in the cost of production here and abroad . . . is the gist of our entire contention." As Beveridge tried to finesse the bill with Aldrich, Miles dunned Roosevelt with letters that mixed cajolery and threat, beseeching the president to support the commission in his upcoming message to Congress and inveighing against the notion that tariff changes would destabilize the economy. Miles lauded the countercyclical economic effect of foreign trade and reminded Roosevelt of the "two million voters" his organization represented, presumably referring to employers and employees of NAM industries. Pressing Roosevelt to break with Payne, Cannon, and Aldrich, Miles also organized a letter-writing campaign aimed at the Senate Finance Committee and discussed raising an extensive fund from the constituent organizations of his Washington committee.[33]

Miles's hopes of moving the Republican party were raised when Senator Robert M. La Follette of Wisconsin introduced a tariff commission bill in the Senate whose merits even Beveridge acknowledged. Supported by Halvor Steenerson of Minnesota in the House and by Missourian William Warner in the Senate, the La Follette bill called for a bipartisan commission with power vested in the president to act on its findings to restrain monopolistic pricing abuses through the suspension of the tariff duties. Thus, the early "insurgent" Progressives were extending the vague threats of the "Iowa idea" by grafting Miles's formulations onto their tariff plank.[34]

Still, Miles recognized that the chances of a substantial commission were slipping, because he began to telegram Beveridge not to compromise or to "hurt nation ten years by half measure." Miles begged Beveridge not to give Congress an opportunity to create a powerless commission but to stick to "the substance of our contention[,] treasury experts and option with Roosevelt to add [a] few practical outsiders and power to compel evidence."[35]

Miles's efforts were unavailing, however, against the combined influence of Payne, Cannon, and Dalzell in the House and Aldrich in the Senate. In conference with Aldrich and Roosevelt on March 16, Beveridge was told that a commission with "outside" experts would not pass in the current Congress. The most that could be done would be to get a joint resolution urging revision by a special session of Congress after the next presidential election, the revision to be prepared by a House subcommittee with "departmental experts" advising. "It is either this or nothing," Beveridge wrote Miles.[36]

The defeat of the Beveridge and La Follette initiatives and the approval of only a few Treasury and Commerce Department clerks to assist the Ways and Means Committee meant that the 1909 revision would have to proceed without a tariff commission. Hence, it would still reflect the "old" methods and schedules that Miles and his group excoriated. Still, the Senate resolved that the Ways and Means Committee and its assistants should seek information on "the relative cost of production in this and in principal competing foreign countries on dutiable items for which some change was anticipated." This, at least, preserved the cost-of-production formula and encouraged the Miles group to continue to push their tariff views within the Republican party. As Alvin H. Sanders wrote to Beveridge in May, the gains might be the "thin edge of the wedge."[37]

For his part, Miles redoubled his tariff activities, establishing a Joint Committee for a Tariff Commission that included members of tariff reduction groups from across the nation. He also continued his work within the NAM, with an eye toward exerting some influence on the Republican party platform for the 1908 election. Miles's May 1908 report to the NAM again evoked the image of the United States as a "huge stevedore" and urged manufacturers to press the government to emphasize labor-intensive manufactured exports as against raw materials exports that could help foreign manufacturers beat Americans in third markets. Miles was even more specific in a private response to a request from Van Cleave to draw up a position paper on the tariff for Van Cleave's use in an anticipated meeting with the Republican platform committee. Miles held that the NAM should insist that the Republican party take a strong stand against monopoly through the tariff: "This monopoly clause must be enlarged upon enough to take the thunder away from the Democratic guns," he wrote. In addition, Miles stressed that the concept of cost of production must be included. Miles referred to this as "international cost," by which he meant using the tariff to equalize U.S. raw materials prices with prevailing international commodity rates.[38]

After firing off this agenda, Miles departed for Europe, ostensibly for a rest after his grueling tariff campaign. In fact, he used the trip to meet with English manufacturers and to accumulate further data on "international costs" of making steel. The Republican convention, meanwhile, though it failed to approve a suggested tariff commission plank, showed the influence of revisionist sentiment: It called for revision, and Taft, the new candidate, who had spoken generally in favor of revision and a commission for several years, announced that his conception of revision was with only a few exceptions a downward revision and would very likely enable the creation of a tariff commission.[39]

Between 1906 and 1908, the tariff revision movement among manufacturers developed rapidly, moving from an effective standstill to a central place in the Republican party electoral and legislative agendas.

In place of "reciprocity," the guiding ideological conception of the tariff movement from the time of McKinley, the movement for reduction and trade expansion had adopted a tariff commission that would shape a "scientific" dual tariff based on a formula that compared domestic and foreign costs of production. In its minimalist form, this change sought to transcend the limitations of reciprocity by bypassing the treaty system; by adopting a progressive, reform tenor; and by avoiding the divisiveness of specifying rates on particular commodities. The movement's program mimicked German commission ideas that sought to institutionalize the relations among producers.

The movement also had developed a better-defined proprietary capitalist faction, of which H. E. Miles of the NAAIVM and the NAM was the primary and maximalist spokesman. This faction now more effectively embraced disparate regional groups, particularly in the Midwest and New England: The Democratic emphasis on free raw materials of the 1890s was now incorporated into the standard of a bipartisan, national group of finishing manufacturers who sought to use their advantages of numbers to influence tariff legislation to preserve their place in a political economy increasingly dominated by large, integrated corporations. The transregional character of the movement was recognized in the cooperation of groups such as the midwestern ARTL and NAM with the MANY and other eastern mercantile groups. The implement makers and the NAM, loyal Republicans for the most part, lent considerable lobbying power and established a durable presence and impact on the national policy agenda.

The tariff revision movement also recognized that it shared common ground with some export-oriented corporations, especially those that supported tariff reduction and that provided foreign marketing assistance to proprietary businesses as an effective way of competing in Europe and the neutral markets. This cooperation blunted the anticorporate character of the movement and tended to narrow its focus to criticism of the large semimanufacture corporations such as United States Steel. In addition, the participation of procorporate revisionists may have tended to check more radical midwesterners who sought to keep the movement focused on anticorporate strategies epitomized by the "Iowa idea." The movement hence tended to stress cooperative adjustment of interests between proprietary and corporate groups.

The tariff revision movement developed important support in this period from major executive branch leaders, such as Taft and Root. Whereas Roosevelt tended to avoid a public airing of the revision question and sought to defer the matter, both Taft and Root openly declared the need for revision from both international and domestic standpoints. Along with the revision movement, they advocated coordinating the U.S. tariff system with that of Europe and the undeveloped world as an important condition for U.S. commercial expansion. Concerned with Republican party credibility and their own political futures, they acknowledged the tariff issue as central to domestic electoral politics and economic equity, as well.

The legislature, especially Joseph G. Cannon's House, where logrolling tariff legislation methods were strongly entrenched, proved less responsive to revision initiatives. Although bills for a tariff commission were drafted as the result of the cooperation of the tariff revision movement and "progressive" Republican congressmen, the legislation failed in 1908. Nonetheless, it gained legitimacy and support among reductionist Republican legislators and among those who opposed Cannon's domination of the House. In addition, many state party organizations came to support the commission, and it received at least lip service in the seconding of executive department experts to assist the Ways and Means Committee in the upcoming revision.

In sum, the revisionists, though divided, had ensured that their priorities would dominate the Republican legislative agenda after the elections of 1908—and the session that would produce the Payne-Aldrich Tariff of 1909.

Part Two

The Payne-Aldrich
Tariff and Revisionist
Policy

7 Tactics and Testimony, 1908

> It is a great question whether you can save the manufacturers—the independent manufacturers—of the higher product or not from absolute trust domination. But you ought to try it.—H. E. Miles, testimony in tariff hearings before the House Ways and Means Committee, December 1908

The revisionists had assured that a new tariff would be at the head of the congressional agenda of 1908–9, much as earlier revision impulses had placed the tariff on the agendas of the postelection Congresses of 1896–97 and 1900–1901. But unlike the reciprocity coalitions of the McKinley era, the movement of the Taft period had a more specific ideology, greater organization, and a more elaborate policy agenda. Working with the president-elect, revisionists sought to confront congressional logrolling and to create, in what would become the Payne-Aldrich Tariff of 1909, a more effective infrastructure for expansionism. In addition, as all tariff makers recognized, the new tariff law would codify the evolving political-economic relations of domestic producers. Thus, as revisionists pressed for lower tariff rates, a maximum-minimum duty structure, and a tariff commission, they redefined their stance toward the rising corporate system.

Taft and the Tariff Factions

President-elect William H. Taft knew that the tariff would be the first crucial issue of his presidency. Although upholding protection in his campaign against William Jennings Bryan, Taft had described tariff revision as not only expedient but necessary. In part, Taft was answering Democratic calls for revision. But Taft also pursued revision because of his global experiences—in Asia and as overseer of the Panama Canal effort—and from a belief that periodic tariff adjustments were necessary to govern powerful sectors of the economy.

Taft's conception of "balance" in the economy encouraged those who conceived of the tariff as an instrument for regulating trusts. Taft never identified with radical reductionism in this sense, but his orotund self-description as "a tariff revisionist since the question has been mooted" was more than campaign flummery; it was a forthright statement of his orientation. In fact, Taft insisted during the campaign that "in accordance with the pledge of the Republican platform," he intended "on the whole a substantial revision downward." In private, Taft vowed to overcome standpat protectionism even if it risked splitting the party.[1]

As a reductionist, Taft the candidate had accumulated the backing of many state organizations of the Republican party. In the Midwest, the Illinois and Indiana state Republican conventions had given strong support to revision. In the Northeast, party organizations had declared for revision in New York, New Hampshire, and Massachusetts. The national platform, of course, already had called for a special session of Congress to frame a new tariff after the election. That platform specified, and both Roosevelt and Taft had endorsed, a tariff that would reflect "the difference between the cost of production at home and abroad, together with a reasonable profit to American industries."[2]

Yet if Republicans had joined Taft in opposing Bryan, they soon divided again over the president-elect's attempt to guide revisionism from pronouncement to policy. Within weeks of his election, Taft would become enmeshed in a three-way struggle between traditional Republican "home market" protectionism, moderate reductionism, and a revived and often radical revisionism of the developing Insurgent movement.

Protectionists sharply challenged Taft's desire to lower the tariff. Especially hostile were iron and steel producers, glassmakers, certain wool growing and manufacturing industries, and the makers of hats and gloves. In these and myriad smaller domestic industries, protectionism remained akin to gospel. Moreover, protectionists swayed many state Republican legislators—a threat to Taft's power at the national level before the popular election of senators. In all, protectionists remained in command of the logrolling system that for the past forty years had enabled legislators from diverse sections to secure high protective rates for disparate local interests.

The revisionists had developed a distinctive power base as well, however. Manufacturers who favored tariff reduction were organized in groups such as the National Association of Manufacturers (NAM), in the Merchants

Association of New York (MANY), and in industry organizations, state manufacturers' groups, boards of trade, and chambers of commerce. These groups had a fairly sophisticated understanding of international market politics. Many reductionists admired the German syndical arrangements in which the combined interests of chambers of commerce, industrial organizations, and legislative and executive agencies promulgated and implemented tariff and commercial treaty legislation and so retained independent influence in a larger system. The NAM consistently publicized German commercial and tariff-making methods in its newspaper, *American Industries*, and the German model remained something of a paradigm for many of the tariff commission proponents in the United States. New York commercial and banking figures in this period of immigration and emulation knew and popularized German business methods. Gustav Schwab of the MANY, a representative of German steamship lines, is a good example.[3]

Expansionist proprietary manufacturers represented a powerful group within the Republican party. McKinley had addressed the founding convention of the NAM in 1895; the manufacturers had supported the party's war with Spain and the expansion of American commercial activity through construction of the Panama Canal. Although economically eclipsed by the rising corporations, the proprietary manufacturers represented a constituency to which Republican leaders, including Taft, continued to turn for support and as models of American entrepreneurial possibilities.[4]

At their most radical, the low-tariff manufacturers saw the tariff in the terms of the "Iowa idea," popularized by Albert Cummins in the early part of the decade and repeated and developed by proprietary manufacturers in subsequent years. The "Iowa idea" argued for eliminating the tariff on trust-made goods to allow cheaper foreign raw materials to enter the United States, thus restoring the competitive pricing—and lower prices—of laissez-faire capitalism. The doctrine, though certainly not publicized as such by its proponents, was close in content to the Democratic positions of the 1890s, which also stressed antitrust themes, cheaper raw materials, and the superior value of manufactured exports.

But not all reductionists were radicals. East Coast manufacturers and traders, livestock growers and processors, cottonseed oil pressers, flour millers, and other exporters may have sought stable and secure markets for their products in Europe more than they desired any restructuring of the emerging order. Import and export merchants, primarily on the east and gulf coasts, though also including developing midwestern retailers such as Sears, Roebuck, sought lower tariffs. Newspapers, which thrived on retail advertising and sought cheaper imported pulp for papermaking, also tended toward lower tariffs. Bankers, who had tended toward low tariffs in the nineteenth century, may have become more protectionist with the development of markets for industrial investments, yet commercial bankers close to the New York merchant community were putting aside fears that tariff changes would destabilize the economy or the social order and were calling for judicious revision.[5]

Tensions over the tariff were expressed politically in the dispute between the Republican Old Guard, led by longtime protectionist legislators such as Joseph G. Cannon, Nelson W. Aldrich, and Henry Cabot Lodge, and politicians who explicitly favored downward tariff revision. These latter included members of the future Insurgent movement such as Robert M. La Follette, Albert B. Cummins, Jonathan Dolliver, and George Norris, all midwesterners. They were the natural allies of the radical revisionists in the manufacturing community. But others in Congress also leaned toward revision, including E. J. Hill of Connecticut, Edgar G. Crumpacker of Indiana, William C. Lovering and Samuel W. McCall of Massachusetts, and Jacob Van Vechten Olcott of New York. These nonradicals were responsive primarily to local reductionist interests and to the party executive's leadership.

At first, Taft was committed definitively to no party group. His choices for cabinet positions were mostly corporate lawyers, whom he explicitly hoped to use to elaborate new and judicially more adequate conceptions by which to regulate the new corporate order. In this context, Taft regarded Cannon's backroom influence peddling in committee appointments and logrolling on tariff rates as unprincipled and obstructive. Yet although Taft approached some midwestern Republicans on the feasibility of ousting Cannon as Speaker, he soon backtracked, concluding that the Speaker would be too dangerous a political opponent if aroused and not defeated.[6]

At Roosevelt's urging that the Old Guard could be worked with on the tariff, antitrust, and interstate commerce law, Taft met with the Speaker, the Ways and Means Committee, and Nelson Aldrich in December 1908 and extracted a promise of a "genuine effort" to cooperate with his program. The relationship was to be somewhat adversarial, Taft understood, and he wrote Root that he was determined to "fight" if he found the Republican legislative leaders "in a spirit of recalcitrancy" on the tariff question. Taft's basic orientation, therefore, was to attempt to get the best tariff bill he could by working with the regular Republicans, beginning with Sereno E. Payne and the Ways and Means Committee and including such Republicans as Hill, Crumpacker, McCall, and others. Yet, clearly, Taft was determined not to be held captive by the Old Guard.[7]

Given the ambiguities of his political situation, Taft continued to regard revisionists outside Congress as important to his tariff strategy. In fact, after the election, Taft met with tariff reductionists in the Midwest, Northeast, and West. The support of reductionists was important not only because their legislators counterbalanced the protectionist Republican congressional leadership but also because the manufacturers, traders, and raw material exporters who had formed the tariff movement represented the basic Republican constituency for tariff change. Thus, if Taft was to influence the Republicans who wavered on the tariff question, he would need to draw on the public organizations of businessmen for strength in effecting the executive's conception of the public will in the legislature. The opening of tariff hearings by the Ways and Means Committee slated for November 10, only a week after Taft's election, marked the beginning of this process.

The House Ways and Means Committee, under Chairman Sereno E. Payne, had begun to prepare for a new tariff as early as May 1908. In part this was a response to the push by Albert Beveridge and the NAM in 1907–8 to create an independent tariff commission for the pending revision. That attempt had failed, but Payne sought to forestall its renewal by authorizing his own commission of "departmental experts"—that is, the committee clerks and some special agents borrowed from the Department of Commerce and Labor—to research the comparative costs of production of schedule articles. These materials were hastily compiled into two volumes that, although praised by Payne, fell far short of what the proponents of a tariff commission wanted in the way of a "scientific" analysis of comparative production costs.[8]

Disappointed with the Ways and Means Committee's tariff study, revisionists also were apprehensive about other aspects of the tariff process of 1908. It appeared that the scheduled testimony at the committee's formal tariff hearings would be biased heavily toward protectionists. Clearly, if revisionists failed to make an effective public impression before the committee, Taft's case for reductions would be undermined. Taft plainly had this in mind when he publicly and privately encouraged revisionist leaders to enlist manufacturers and merchants to testify before the committee. The development of Taft's relationship with the revisionist groups reveals important dimensions of the evolution of the Republican revision movement.[9]

Among the revisionist figures the president-elect consulted from his winter quarters in Virginia and Georgia was John Candler Cobb, head of the Boston Merchants Association, a member of the NAM, and a Taft activist in the recent campaign. Cobb had sent Taft his notes on the tariff situation after observing the early hearings and meeting privately with some of the deponents and committee members. In Cobb's view, many congressmen leaned toward revision, but they might well be intimidated by Speaker Cannon from voting for substantial reductions. In addition, now that actual revision impended, "many of our leading manufacturers are being forced into line for the stand-pat principle, against their convictions, by the argument that if the bars are once let down, there is no knowing what may happen." At Taft's encouragement, Cobb pressed the New England cotton and woolens manufacturers, who were critically divided on the tariff, to support reductions on "all the lines" possible. Cobb apparently was unable to enlist members of the Boston Merchants Association to testify at the hearings, but he did get the group to pass a unanimous resolution in favor of tariff reduction.[10]

Cobb's perspectives on the tariff commission movement in this period are also revealing of the outlook of some Republican revisionists. In the course of a national campaign to discuss revision and tariff commission issues, Cobb became wary of raising the commission movement during the current tariff-making process. He feared that when Congress began full discussion of a tariff bill, after Taft's inauguration, the "demand for lower duties and immediate action may wear itself out and give the opportunity . . . to put the whole matter over by the appointment of a commission." Thus, Cobb decided to work with Taft to subordinate all efforts for a commission to the tariff reduction task itself.[11]

Taft and Cobb may have had more than tactics in mind. They may have feared that control of a commission could fall to the Old Guard or to reductionist radicals; formalizing a commission's powers in the current volatile situation thus could be dangerous. Cobb had supported this cautious approach by amending to the Boston Merchants Association tariff resolution the stipulation that appointment of a commission should be delayed until after the present tariff deliberations. Taft agreed that an immediate demand for a commission would be seen as a threat to congressional prerogatives, and he endorsed Cobb's "quiet" diplomacy in deferring the matter. Thus, a pattern of cooperation and communication between Taft and one of the leaders of the eastern revisionist movement was established.[12]

Taft also met and consulted with Alvin H. Sanders, publisher of the

Breeder's Gazette and chief executive of the American Reciprocal Tariff League (ARTL), which represented midwestern and western livestock, packinghouse, and stockbreeding groups. The ARTL also had co-opted members of the MANY and the New York Chamber of Commerce onto its board of directors. Here, too, a pattern of cooperation emerged similar to that between Cobb and Taft. Sanders, like Cobb, had been an active Republican campaigner. He had been mentioned in the agricultural press as a possible successor to James Wilson as secretary of agriculture, as well. His particular concern of the moment was that the new tariff include maximum-minimum provisions favorable to the livestock industry. In addition, as the hearings progressed, Sanders editorialized against the Ways and Means Committee's protectionist orientation and encouraged letter writing by agricultural revisionists to support Taft's revisionism.[13]

Sanders and Taft's agendas intersected in late November 1908, when James M. Swank, the perennial protectionist secretary of the American Iron and Steel Association and a frequent correspondent of Senator Aldrich, appeared before the Ways and Means Committee to condemn the revisionist movement. Swank derided the proposed maximum-minimum provisions as a ploy by free traders to destroy American industries by lowering both rates below those of the existing Dingley Tariff; he assailed the North Commission's 1907 agreements with Germany as encouraging tariff cheating in customs valuations; and he drubbed the cost-of-production theory of tariffs as unwieldy, impractical, and incapable of compensating for dumping by foreign combinations.[14]

Sanders saw Swank's testimony as a machination by Cannon. The Speaker, Sanders was convinced, "had nurtured a carefully planned scheme to hold a few hurried hearings, take the Dingley rates substantially as they stand as a minimum, fix a maximum duty at a much higher range and railroad the whole business through." The ARTL chief tried to bolster revisionism by sending Payne and Aldrich a memorandum written by N. I. Stone, the Commerce and Labor Department's tariff expert, on the concept of the maximum-minimum tariff that Payne subsequently forwarded to Taft. Stone's note, "Dual Tariff System," plainly reflected the personal priorities of both men—that is, Sanders's desire to lever open German tariff doors for U.S. meat products and Stone's hope to serve on an American commission modeled on the extensive German tariff body. But the memorandum—later published nearly verbatim in the American Economic Association proceedings—succinctly articulated in comparative international perspective the principles and current applications of dual-tariff systems, and Sanders may well have hoped to contrast its scholarly revisionism to the polemical protectionism of the nineteenth-century holdover, Swank.[15]

Because it was read by the major policymakers, Stone's memorandum is worth exposition and analysis. It began by addressing the form that an effective tariff reduction had to take. The author noted that the predominant European system of general and conventional tariffs, because it was based on treaties, was politically unworkable in the United States on the "constitutional" grounds that treaties were too easily defeated by minorities in the Senate. In addition, Stone maintained, the United States' seemingly fixed conditional interpretation of the most-favored-nation clause complicated any U.S. attempts to promulgate reduction through a commercial treaty system because it would require separate reciprocity treaties for every nation. This, in turn, would create a confusing tariff schedule that would engender enmity among the European nations, who would hesitate to sign a treaty if they believed that the United States might negotiate agreements that would render its previous concessions "nugatory."[16]

Stone was suggesting that, although American reciprocity treaties resembled the conventions of the European treaty-tariff systems, the American conditional interpretation of the most-favored-nation clause defeated the entire purpose of such conventions by thwarting uniform treatment of particular articles in international commerce. Put another way, whereas the European system was a truly multilateral approach that created a composite minimum rate from many treaties, the American was a multiple, bilateral approach that created "equitable" but different rates for identical items from different countries. Thus, the U.S. system could not achieve parity in commercial treaties on European terms and represented a basic conflict with European nations that practiced unconditional most-favored-nation relations.

Despite the prevalence of general and conventional treaty tariff systems in Europe, then, Stone's preference, supported by Sanders and the ARTL, was for a U.S. maximum-minimum system with the minimum schedule withheld as a bargaining concession and the maximum fixed on a cost-of-production basis. A legislative revision of this type, of course, fixed U.S. minimum rates uniformly, superseding the conditional clause, and represented a substantial lowering of American tariffs, because nearly any measure derived from a "cost-of-production" scheme would result in a lowering of tariffs that were sometimes 100 percent ad valorem.[17]

Stone argued against a U.S. tariff with a "punitive maximum," an idea then being promoted by protectionists. Such a tariff, Stone contended, was unduly confrontational. European states might refuse to recognize the U.S. minimum as a sufficient concession for their minimum schedules, because the European tariff rates were generally low, and the U.S. rates, even under considerable reduction, still would be relatively high. Then, the United States would have little alternative but to take the European maximum without protest or to invoke its own punitive maximum. This, Stone observed, could lead European nations to impose countervailing duties. In short, it meant tariff war.[18]

In this last argument Stone may have overstated the likelihood of European retaliations. The crucial element in whether Europe would accept an American tariff was not necessarily the form of the maximum-minimum provisions but rather the uniformity of rates they would create and the actual level of the American minimum. If the new tariff's rates were an improvement over the Dingley Tariff, and if they were uniformly applied, European nations might well accept them, though unhappily. Such was the conclusion that politicians might have drawn from the experiences of the Roosevelt years, in which, despite considerable grumbling, European nations had accepted high American rates and exchanged them for their own minimums.[19]

Taft, however, had concluded that the new tariff needed to offer foreign nations substantial improvements over the Dingley Tariff. Stone and Sanders were not the only ones informing the policy process on this issue. Charles M. Pepper, a special agent of the Department of Commerce and Labor assigned to investigate foreign trade conditions, advised the president-elect directly on trade matters. Writing from Europe, Pepper told Taft that European "industrial and commercial classes" would retaliate if Congress failed to pass a tariff reduction. Warning that the United States had "pretty near reached the limit," Pepper argued that "the efforts of these countries to approximate to our level cannot justly be regarded as a tariff war against us." The Europeans required some "basis of trading on lower rates, for which they will reciprocate." Pepper thus advised the president-elect as had Stone. If Taft wanted good commercial relations with Europe, Congress had to pass a dual tariff "with the minimum as the persuasive factor."[20]

Root had reached similar conclusions in calling for a maximum-minimum tariff in his speech before the National Conference for the Expansion of Foreign Trade in 1907, and even Cannon and Payne had agreed that the United States had to offer a "minimum" tariff to exchange for European minimum tariffs. The Republican platform itself had called for a maximum-minimum tariff with a "punitive" maximum, but because it had not defined clearly how the minimum would be determined, except for vague reference to cost of production, it gave little guidance. In principle, then, the executive branch, legislators, bureaucrats, and business groups had agreed on the need for a dual tariff, but they had not agreed on how much of a reduction such a tariff would embody or on its exact form. This matter would be decided in the politics of tariff making.

The Tariff Hearings of 1908

Perhaps the most active revisionist group was the NAM, which had made the tariff commission its cause. Surprisingly, the manufacturers greeted the Ways and Means tariff hearings by declaring a boycott. In an exchange of letters with Chairman Sereno E. Payne, NAM president James W. Van Cleave denounced the "old manner" of tariff revision—that is, revision by the House Committee and without the advice of a full-scale tariff commission. Taft, having deferred the commission plan, wanted the NAM to testify on schedules and was quoted in a newspaper as asking, "Where are the members of the National Association of Manufacturers?" Van Cleave huffily responded, however, that to appear at the hearings would "mean to acquiesce in the superficial and unbusinesslike methods of investigation against which we protest."[21]

Van Cleave's avoidance of the hearings had motivations apart from pique and principled abstention from logrolling politics, however. First, Van Cleave was becoming concerned about the diversity of sentiment within the NAM on the tariff, and he feared to associate the NAM with discussions of specific schedules when NAM members, even within the same industries, disagreed on specific rates. Although Van Cleave had always defended the tariff commission activities of the NAM, he had shunned comment on specific schedules because this would preempt his insistence that revision was the "scientific" work of experts. When a NAM tariff radical such as tariff committee chairman H. E. Miles made one of his outspoken attacks on trust privileges, the tariff commission proposal appeared more clearly as a general reductionist effort, and it raised all the conflicting demands of industrial and regional groups that Van Cleave was trying to subdue. During 1908, these differences had led to demands from NAM protectionists for Miles's resignation. Van Cleave had upheld Miles, but to protect the commission plan the NAM president had admonished the Wisconsin manufacturer to restrain his rhetoric and to confine NAM tariff work to "the commission only."[22]

Furthermore, Van Cleave and his associates' views on the labor question dictated a less confrontational stance toward Old Guard congressmen who were supporting the NAM. As Van Cleave's Buck's Stove and Range Company suit against the AFL-associated Metal Polishers' Union and Samuel Gompers proceeded, he grew even more convinced, in the words of his secretary, Ferdinand C. Schwedtman, of "the necessity of handling Mr. Payne, Mr. Dalzell, Mr. Cannon and others known to be absolutely sound on the labor question with the utmost policy on other matters." As Schwedtman continued, Van Cleave had "no doubt . . . that Mr. Payne and his stand-pat associates are all wrong on tariff," but attacks on their views on schedules could not appear to come from the NAM so that the organization could "show proper strength and concentration when the labor question again takes the Congressional limelight." Thus, in response to the House hearings, Van Cleave apparently envisioned only a magazine campaign stressing the tariff commission idea. In addition, the NAM supported Cannon's bid for the House speakership.[23]

H. E. Miles, on the other hand, was convinced that revisionist testimony at the hearings was essential, if not to the NAM then to the independent implement makers and the cause of opposition to the trusts. Miles wrote to Taft urging him to take up the progressive reform stands of Roosevelt and apply them to the tariff issue, as his campaign seemed to indicate he would. Complaining to Taft that Payne had left practically no room for testimony on the metals schedule, Miles asked the president-elect to secure an extended hearing for revisionists before the committee. Miles's action may have marked the beginning of an outright split in proprietary ranks that would foreshadow the emergence of the Insurgent Progressive movement. At the time, however, Miles considered both Van Cleave and Taft as potentially sympathetic to the antitrust tariff revision stance, and he was responding to Taft's call. Promising the NAM that he would not associate his statements with its official policy, Miles decided to respond personally to Taft's call for testimony on schedules. In doing so, Miles noted, he also would follow Taft's admonition not to "make faces at the Committee without offering your evidence."[24]

Miles's mission, worked out with Taft at Hot Springs, Virginia, on November 29, 1908, was to concentrate on specific tariff items such as steel, lumber, and hides. The president-elect also apparently reinforced his warnings to Miles to cooperate as far as he could with the Ways and Means

Committee, and Taft may also have encouraged the committee to extend the hearings, because on November 30, newspapers noted that the hearings had been extended specifically to afford scope for the testimony of Miles and others. This extension also would give Payne and Dalzell, the longtime protectionist powers on the committee, a chance to cross-examine the man whose critical statements about the committee had been widely publicized.[25]

Miles intended to support the NAM's campaign for a tariff commission, but the brunt of his planned testimony, as he told Taft and Van Cleave, would center on the trusts. Miles also was initially encouraged to testify after conversing with Edwin Metcalf, of International Harvester, who told him that the Morgan steel interests would not oppose reduction directly. They were, as Miles paraphrased Metcalf, "too big to object to our presenting our cause." Miles believed, however, that the steel industry would try to intimidate the reductionists by threatening to reduce wages if the tariff was cut. Hence, Miles felt that his testimony on the real costs of steel production—information he had derived from his research in England during the previous summer and in his U.S. tariff organizing—would constitute a vital riposte to such threats.[26]

H. E. Miles appeared before the Ways and Means Committee on December 5, 1908, and again on December 8 and 11. His testimony ranged far more widely than his original indications to the NAM tariff committee, covering issues devolving from the Dingley Tariff, including the nature of trust development in the steel industry, the decline of the independent manufacturer, the methods of determining "fair" levels of protection, and the need for a tariff commission. Heeding the strictures of Taft and of the NAM, Miles sedulously dissociated his testimony from the official policy of specific national organizations. But he made it quite clear that he spoke for myriad smaller businesses and associations that had explicitly delegated him to pull together their critique of the U.S. industrial system. Miles thus was conscious that his appearance on the public stage represented a critical opportunity to advance the proprietary viewpoint. Speaking as "one of about 150,000 manufacturers who are greatly injured by the present tariff," Miles asked the committee to recognize the claims of "the independent, 'nontrustified' manufacturer" who was threatened with "destruction or absorption by trusts."[27]

In his testimony, Miles publicized charges that the trusts engaged in cut-rate export pricing to show that the tariff stood as a defense behind which trusts were able to maintain high domestic prices. He drew examples of "excessive protection" from a wide variety of industries, the information having come to him from correspondents and in the course of his tariff commission organizing under the aegis of the NAM and the National Association of Agricultural Implement and Vehicle Manufacturers (NAAIVM). Miles picked out Standard Oil's labor costs at about 6 percent versus its protection of about 99 percent—far more than the advantages of foreign "cheap labor" could account for. Miles also cited comparative statistics on a variety of other "trust tariffs."[28]

Miles's main attack was on the steel industry, however. Brandishing Moody's *The Truth about the Trusts* and James H. Bridge's *History of the Carnegie Steel Company*, Miles asserted that the costs of steel production were "as little in this country as anywhere on earth." Predictably, he cited Bridge's reproduction of the letter of Charles M. Schwab to Henry Clay Frick, written when Schwab was president of the Carnegie Steel Company, in which Schwab had claimed that Carnegie's rail production costs were $7 cheaper per ton than the British costs and that the company could "control the steel business of the world." Miles did more than rehash old information, however. He recounted information gleaned from an investigation of the Homestead Works and from correspondence with independent steel manufacturers in the United States and England. Tariffs on steel and other basic industries, Miles attempted to show, were far higher than warranted by "legitimate" protective principles because they outweighed differences in domestic and foreign production costs by any form of calculation. In addition, Miles argued, recent innovations, such as automatic conveyor belts, were decreasing labor costs.[29]

Miles argued that profits extracted by the steel industry were largely at the expense of the "intermediate consumer." Miles related that before the Dingley Tariff and the incorporation of United States Steel, his steel costs were about 80 cents per hundred pounds; in 1908, they were about $1.60. In his own lines, though threatened by the expansion of International Harvester into implements and wagons, Miles could pass along higher raw materials costs to the jobbers who handled his goods. But even here Miles noted a problematic effect: Increased basic costs created an inflationary multiplier. His additional cost of $2.00 on the four hundred pounds of steel that made up one of his farm wagons would become $2.40 to the jobber, who would make it $2.60 or $2.70 to the dealer, who would charge the farmer $3.00. "We do business on a percentage basis," Miles told the committee, arguing that the parties involved had "to get the same profit on one part of [a] purchase as on another." Miles added that such inflation was ultimately destructive of trade in the implement business because prices were advancing faster for manufactures than for farm products. Independent farmers were thus less able to buy products made from expensive raw materials. Some relatively well-off farmers could buy automobiles, he conceded, but the average farmer could barely afford to buy necessary wagons.[30]

The inflationary effect of the tariff was highly relevant to the foreign trade of the implement manufacturers as well, Miles argued. Perhaps expressing the frustration of exporters whose trade had expanded greatly during the "American invasion" of Europe in the late 1890s and early 1900s, Miles suggested that foreign tariffs and the rising costs of American production were hurting sales abroad. Implement manufacturers, Miles continued, including "one of the three largest in America," were losing foreign business not only in South America but in Europe and in South Africa because of high materials costs. Although gross trade in implements was increasing, this was largely the exports of International Harvester, which made its own steel at 30 percent or more below the cost to the independent manufacturer. Nor were the independent manufacturers, Miles stressed, able to organize production to take advantage of the existing tariff drawback system. Hence, tariff reduction on raw materials represented an essential "equalizer" that would allow independent manufacturers to recoup their foreign trade.[31]

High domestic—and low international—raw materials prices were thus at the center of Miles's complaint against the trusts. The solution, he argued, in terms similar to those he used among his fellow manufacturers of the NAAIVM and the NAM, was to shift American export emphasis toward finished manufactures. This shift could be accomplished, Miles said, echoing the "Iowa idea," by cutting the tariff on raw materials whose prices were held up by domestic combinations. He was not naive, however, about the possibilities of multinational price cooperation, which, he understood, would negate the effects of tariff revision.[32]

The alternative to revision, Miles argued, was further trustification of the economy through inflation and combination. The current tariff not only protected trusts but also subverted entrepreneurship and marketplace equity. The tariff, said Miles, "has been an invitation to independent men to get together and form a trust as to their prices." He protested that "an excessive rate is nothing less than a congressional invitation to people to consolidate and use the excess against the consumers of their own country." Miles thus spoke not merely for the survival of individual proprietary manufacturers but for the perpetuation of the proprietary system itself.[33]

Miles's colloquy with protectionist committee members Dalzell and Payne and with Tammany Democrat William Bourke Cockran pushed him into an interesting expansion of his viewpoint on the question of the adequate degree and determination of protection. Noting that costs among producers of raw materials differed, committee members asked Miles if the less efficient producers did not deserve protection as well. Miles replied that within the steel industry, production costs were basically the same, and that differences resulted from unequal access to raw materials. He thus asked the producers that lacked access to raw material to come out for free ores.[34]

But Miles also had to refine his previous statements on the adequate level of protection due to industries when Dalzell pointed out that Miles had dropped his support of the Republican plank calling for protection to guarantee a "reasonable profit" in addition to compensating for differentials in costs. Although Miles had supported the reasonable-profit idea in May 1908, he had rejected it in July, fearing that the clause would be used to keep tariff rates up. Miles thus had to stand by his later statement, which excluded the profit guarantee. The implication was that efficient producers had to be taken as the benchmark for the appropriate rate of profit in an industry. Miles was thus ruling out protection for inefficient finishing manufacturers as well as for overprotected trusts, and he was implicitly defining equity as the policy that favored efficient but not necessarily integrated producers. The criterion of competitiveness in foreign expansion thus militated that even proprietary radicals had to countenance abandoning some of the "crossroads" manufacturers whom James Deering had derided in 1901. Miles himself suggested that with interest rates of 6 to 8 percent on bank capital, an appropriate rate for business returns would be about 15 to 20 percent. The state thus would play a role in the regulation of profitability at the highest and lowest levels of the private sector.[35]

In Miles's view, regulation of business along such lines was precisely the work of a tariff commission. The state had to scrutinize manufacturers' production costs to determine rates. This meant that the commission had to have the right to "go to the factories, investigate . . . cost, compel the submission of testimony, administer oaths and act upon the principle of a just and fair protection as defined by the President-elect and by the Republican party."[36] In short, Miles sought a tariff and a tariff commission influenced by the broad sector of successful proprietary businessmen that would act as an instrument for the wider distribution of the profits of domestic and foreign expansion among corporate and proprietary producers.

The criticisms made by H. E. Miles and by other revisionists of the "overprotection" of special interests may have had some impact on the public postures of a number of industries, including some important export-oriented groups. They quickly rallied to define their own versions of tariff revision and foreign trade expansion.

Among the more publicized reactions were the Ways and Means interviews of Charles Schwab, now of Bethlehem Steel, and E. H. Gary, the current chairman of U.S. Steel. Schwab had to explain his boast that Carnegie could make steel at $12 per ton versus the $19 English cost. Schwab complained that animadversions on his integrity in defending protection were unfair because he was citing "actual mill cost" and leaving out interest charges and depreciation. He had omitted these in his letter to Frick because, "as an enthusiastic and optimistic young man seeking preferment in a great company," he had sought to put the best light on the operation of the plants under his management. Schwab claimed that since the time of the letter and his similar testimony before the U.S. Industrial Commission, European costs of production had decreased and that German and English costs were now about equivalent to those in the United States. Thus, Schwab announced, wage cuts were inevitable if the tariff was reduced.[37]

What Schwab could not explain, however, was that after the formation of U.S. Steel, rail prices rose from about $17 per ton to $28 per ton, with no commensurate increase in cost of production. The steel companies, he could not deny, were making about 100 percent profit on rails at the stabilized $28 price, a rate he justified only by claiming that the profits were needed for reinvestment and retooling for more efficient technologies. His industry required, he said, a minimum of 25 percent overall profit to underwrite consolidation and rebuilding of plants. This stance, of course, conceded his critics' point, that the steel companies were using high profits, in part preserved by the steel tariff, to finance expansion and integration of the corporate system rather than to protect their ability to compete as such. When Schwab affirmed that American producers dumped rails at as much as $10 per ton cheaper abroad, he reinforced his critics' conviction that protectionist tariffs were being upheld to rationalize the corporate system.[38]

E. H. Gary conceded that high tariffs were no longer necessary to protect the steel industry, although, as H. E. Miles had predicted, Gary, like Schwab, threatened wage cuts in response to drastic tariff changes. Gary agreed with Schwab that steel production costs in Germany and England were not greatly different from U.S. costs, though he did acknowledge that U.S. ores were about a third more concentrated than the German. But in

Gary's view, what kept the Germans out of the American market was their current inability to produce sufficient surplus quantities of steel to make an appreciable offering to American steel consumers. The Germans, understanding that they could not market pig iron or rails profitably in the United States, were selling most of their steel in Europe and in their domestic market, where it could be converted into steel manufactures that had higher rates of profit in export trade. Implicitly, Gary was dismissing the tariff as irrelevant to steel production except on the coasts. His mild resistance to reduction suggests that he was defending coastal producers, who participated in U.S. Steel's controlled pricing system. Gary's concern, then, like Schwab's, was stabilization, not survival, and his acquiescence in a moderate reduction conceded little to the independent steel buyer.[39]

The positions taken by the American National Live Stock Association (ANLSA) also illustrate the effects of concentration on tariff matters. Since the time when it was instrumental, as the National Live Stock Association, in organizing the Chicago Reciprocity Conference of August 1905, the group had agitated for a tariff commission and for reciprocity agreements, particularly with Germany, that would ensure the freer export of American meats to Europe. The 1905 conference had spawned the American Reciprocal Tariff League (ARTL), headed by ANLSA board member Alvin H. Sanders, the publisher of the Chicago-based *Breeder's Gazette* and one of the board members who had favored the packers in the organization's 1905–6 constitutional crisis. Ultimately, the crisis had resulted in the formal exclusion of the meatpackers from the ANLSA, but it had set up the means for grower-packer cooperation for foreign trade expansion through the ARTL. Under Sanders, the ARTL had expanded its offices to engage in lobbying in Washington and had established a bureau in New York headed by William R. Corwine, a member of the MANY who also held an executive position in the corporate-oriented National Civic Federation. The ARTL was particularly active during the negotiations with Germany to encourage arrangements that would assure the continued entry of American meat products and livestock into foreign markets. In this, the ANLSA cooperated fully. Significantly, it was Murdo Mackenzie, the ANLSA president, and Samuel H. Cowan, its attorney, the leading opponents of the meatpackers during the constitutional crisis of 1905–6, who now in 1908–9 pressed the cooperative approach.

The underlying reasons for grower-packer cooperation may be found in the development of their respective industries during this important transitional period in the industry. In 1905, Argentine beef production for export, which had been booming under the influence of heavy British investment, surpassed U.S. production, which, though it declined from 1905 to 1909, still remained substantial. During this period, meatpackers and cattlemen were especially vociferous and cooperative in supporting export and tariff legislation intended in part to recapture markets lost to more efficient Argentine and Uruguayan producers and to stabilize prices and supply in the United States. Resistance to—and then acceptance of—the meat inspection legislation sponsored by Senator Beveridge in 1906 was a cooperative effort of meatpackers and cattlemen, who at first feared the costs of inspection but later saw it as a way to argue that foreign sanitary import regulations were unnecessary.[40]

In addition, although the formal integration of the meatpacking industry through umbrella companies such as the National Packing Corporation was primarily horizontal and not backward into cattle production itself, the meatpackers were becoming heavily involved in the financing of cattle raising and the rediscounting of cattle paper with eastern banks. The ownership and control of cattle loan companies through at least eighteen packer-controlled livestock banks gave the meatpackers a direct interest in stabilizing the price and production of cattle in the United States.[41]

In 1907, the independent cattlemen had cooperated with the packers in supporting the German reciprocity agreement in the hope that the agreement would permit live cattle sales to Europe, which the independents saw as a counterweight to the packers' U.S. buyers' market for export-grade live cattle. The agreement was not consummated, however. But even at less advantageous terms, cattlemen continued to look to the packers' export connections to exert a "flywheel" effect in the market, because meatpackers could buy stock even in times of slack domestic demand, and then can or store the meat, hides, and other products for later export sale. As ANLSA president Murdo Mackenzie noted at the 1908 association meeting, the packinghouses, through their efforts in maintaining foreign agencies and in tailoring the marketing and export of meats to fit foreign consumption patterns, had been "large factors" in the export expansion so profitable to the meat growers. Mackenzie suggested that an export policy was vital to the profitable production of meat by American livestock interests because "the price of the surplus part is the most forceful factor in establishing the value of the whole." Collective cooperation of growers and packers in regulating the domestic market prices thus had come to assume great importance in the public activities of the agricultural revisionists.[42]

Packer-grower interests were not identical, however. Responding to a secular decline in beef production in the United States and to the loss of export markets after 1907, the packers themselves began to invest heavily in Argentine, Uruguayan, and later Brazilian packing operations. Growers, on the other hand, continued to insist on adequate protection from Canadian and Latin American beef production. Packers and growers would alternate between periods of conflict and concord into the 1920s; but expectations of cooperation to stabilize domestic prices were high at the time of the Payne-Aldrich Tariff.[43]

In the tariff hearings, the ANLSA continued to press for a maximum-minimum tariff schedule that could be used to negotiate entry of American meat products into Germany and France under their minimum tariff rates. Extension of the German agreement, new reciprocity treaties, and a tariff commission all would be vital to the future interests of livestock producers. A tariff commission, Mackenzie believed, might assist the western stock-growing interests to press their claims for a proper balance of protectionist and trade expansionist ideas by defending exports of agricultural surpluses. But it would not be a tool of antitrust activism.[44]

In their desire to balance protection and expansion, the stock growers were in harmony with the NAM and the eastern manufacturing groups. On the issue of hides, however—a traditional conflict between the raw material producers and raw material users—the stock growers and packers vehemently opposed the demand of Miles and numerous shoe and independent tanning interests for negating the 15 percent duty. Miles had argued that the duty was unfairly imposed in 1897 and that most of the profits went to the packers and not to the growers, because the packinghouses were expanding into the tanning business and were cutting the prices on hides to their own operations. The independents charged that their only means of survival was to move their businesses out of the country to take advantage of cheaper South American hides available in the free port of Antwerp.[45]

The ANLSA was quick to counter the contention that stock growers could do without the duty on hides and with reductions in the duties on wool. In the tariff hearings of December 1908, ANLSA attorney Samuel H. Cowan argued that whereas Miles and the leather manufacturers had portrayed the packers as a "trust," the tanners were seeking to get the whole profit from the removal of the duties on hides. Thus, the livestock interests would accept free hides only if the "leather people" agreed to deep cuts in duties on finished leather products. The ANLSA would agree to no more than keeping the 15 percent duty as a maximum and offering 25 to 30 percent reductions, to about 10 percent duty, as a reciprocal concession.[46]

By early 1909, the stock growers had diverged even further from the manufacturers on the tariff question, when H. H. Jastro, a California rancher who was Mackenzie's successor as ANLSA president, announced the organization's withdrawal from the "Committee of One Hundred" organized by Miles and the NAM for revision and a tariff commission.[47]

Miles's position itself was assailed publicly by Harvester executive Edwin D. Metcalf. Metcalf had become chairman of the executive committee of the NAAIVM and apparently had encouraged Miles to testify for the agricultural implements industry. But Metcalf had been disturbed all along by what he called the radical tone of Miles's remarks and wrote to Taft repudiating Miles's testimony. In his own testimony before the Ways and Means Committee, Metcalf maintained, contrary to Miles, that smaller companies could succeed in the export market by using existing drawback legislation and by producing specialized items that addressed markets left open by consolidated manufacturers. Companies that did not specialize in this way, he implied, had failed to recognize the exigencies of the foreign trade situation of the day.[48]

Concomitantly, Metcalf avoided endorsing removal of duties on raw materials, claiming that "the foreign market is open at the present price of the raw material." The tariff was irrelevant to the price of materials, Metcalf argued, and Harvester met increases in its own costs by "improved methods of manufacture." Metcalf denied that Harvester's raw materials and steel-making capacity influenced its view on the matter. He claimed—contrary to the findings of the 1913 investigation of the Harvester Corporation— that Harvester's steel plants sold to its implement plants at market rates. Metcalf confined himself to supporting a maximum-minimum tariff with implements on the free list, with a duty held in reserve for cases of discrimination.[49]

Here, Metcalf showed clearly the divergence of corporate and anticorporate sentiment within the implement industry that had occurred since James Deering's activity in the agricultural implement association earlier in the decade. In the face of high foreign tariffs, Harvester had begun to build factories in Canada, Russia, Sweden, France, and Germany. Harvester even expected to use the 1907 Canadian-French preference treaty to get the French minimum rates by exporting through its Canadian subsidiary. In Metcalf's view expansion now had to take place not within the priorities of a broad revisionist movement but under the aegis of a corporate-led system.

That is, independents ought to fill the niches left open by the corporations in the foreign market and refrain from contesting for them by appealing to the regulatory power of the state. Harvester's position was thus now much closer to that of U.S. Steel.[50]

Through the early stages of the Payne-Aldrich Tariff process, revisionism retained its impetus as part of a broad strategy of the executive and foreign trade interests to coordinate American tariff policies with those of Europe. Yet, hobbled by commitments to Old Guard Republicanism or interlinked with powerful consolidated interests within their own industries, manufacturers and stock growers were unable and unwilling to join in a consistent proprietary "progressive" antitrust version of expansionism of the kind H. E. Miles was proposing. Even as they entered the tariff-making process they had sought for three years, agricultural and manufacturing revisionists struggled to contain not only the traditional antagonisms of competing immediate interests but the newer conflicts over their respective relations with an emergent corporate system. As the tariff issue came before Congress, these conflicts would be politicized, and Insurgent Republican legislators would become a focus of the proprietary antitrust tariff initiative.

Framing a Tariff, 1909

There is one great fact that makes a new tariff epoch. That
fact is that the Republican party has changed its front.
Whereas it has been marching toward higher and higher
tariffs, it has now faced about and is marching, no matter
how slow any one may think its present pace is, toward
lower tariffs. It has recognized changed conditions. This is
a wonderful, radical, and fundamental change, the importance of which has not been sufficiently recognized.
—Secretary of the Treasury Franklin MacVeagh, Address to
the Massachusetts Bankers Association, December 8, 1909

After December 1908, tariff revisionism divided more markedly into camps
allying themselves with a strategy for a moderate tariff reduction led by
President Taft and Congress and for a more forceful opposition to protection emphasizing an independent tariff commission and based on opposition to the trusts, a position typified by individuals such as H. E. Miles
among the industrial interests and by the developing Insurgent movement
in the legislature.

Revisionism and Its Discontents

H. E. Miles's relations with the National Association of Manufacturers
(NAM) during the early months of 1909 reveal some of the political and
ideological dimensions of the tariff revision movement. After his tariff
testimony before the Ways and Means Committee in December 1908,
Miles sought to sustain revisionist pressure on Congress. Encouraged by
his success in presenting the revisionist view before the committee and by
the strong support he had received from many smaller Republican businessmen, Miles began to see the revisionists as central to Taft's attempt to
influence the tariff. In turn, Miles was convinced, or acted as if he were
convinced, that Taft was depending on outspoken Republicans to revise the
tariff downward.

Acting on this mixture of confidence and audacity, Miles arranged for N. I. Stone, the tariff expert of the Department of Commerce and Labor, to intercede with NAM president Van Cleave to put Miles forward as a candidate for secretary of the Department of Commerce and Labor in the new administration. Restless in Racine, Miles told Van Cleave that he thought Taft already had "something in mind for me." Miles's surmise was not preposterous. Unlike Van Cleave and Parry, also men of ambition, Miles had no public history of antilabor activism. Miles thus saw himself as an ideal "manufacturer's" candidate. In addition, Miles was close to the revisionist industrial and commercial groups, including the Grange, the meatpackers, stock raisers, boards of trade, and some textile manufacturers. Of course, Miles had alienated many protectionists and even some revisionists through his forthright testimony at the tariff hearings. Nonetheless, Miles had gained political experience, credibility, and connections by participating in the National Council of Commerce, a quasi-governmental business organization initiated by Roosevelt's Department of Commerce and Labor secretary, Oscar S. Straus. There, Miles noted, he had just been appointed to the advisory committee by the council's chairman, Gustav H. Schwab, an important figure in the Merchants Association of New York (MANY).[1]

Van Cleave furthered Miles's political prospects to the extent of sending a letter of extravagant praise on his behalf to Taft. No doubt Van Cleave genuinely appreciated the Wisconsin manufacturer's unremitting efforts for a tariff commission. But it seems probable that Van Cleave had already begun to divorce Miles's perspectives and positions from those of the NAM. In promoting Miles for a politically sensitive office, Van Cleave may have hoped to impress him with the need for a less radical approach to the tariff. Moreover, Miles may have been only a stalking-horse for the NAM's prime candidate for the Commerce and Labor post, James E. Watson, the former Indiana congressman and majority whip who was a close ally of former NAM president David Parry and of Speaker Joseph G. Cannon. For at the same time as it deplored influence peddling and recommended Miles for the position, the NAM was working covertly through its Washington lobbyist, Martin M. Mulhall, to secure the job for Watson.[2]

One reason for the NAM's cooling relationship with Miles may have been the labor question. Miles, disappointed with the meager showing of other reductionist manufacturers at the Ways and Means Committee hearings, had been developing support for revision among midwestern manufacturers. Recently, he had addressed the Midwestern Manufacturers' Association, composed of many small Republican manufacturers. That association had issued a resolution along the lines of the "Iowa idea," castigating "monopolistic interests" that "control . . . the production of many articles" and "exert a powerful interest toward directing congressional action with regard to the import duties upon these articles." Along with its antitrust tariff language, the resolution specifically condemned House Speaker Cannon. Moreover, Miles had been asked to assume the chairmanship of the organization.[3]

Such developments alarmed Van Cleave. He lectured Miles that no group should "attack a member of Congress" and said that many NAM members now felt that the word "trust" was being used "irresponsibly" as an attack on business in general, citing NAM member Charles M. Jarvis, a hardware manufacturer from Connecticut who had been an important supporter of the tariff movement. Van Cleave also had acceded to advice from Edwin D. Metcalf, the International Harvester official and friend of Ways and Means Chairman Sereno Payne, to dissociate himself from Miles's radical viewpoint, and when Miles criticized Metcalf's testimony before the Ways and Means Committee, Van Cleave pronounced Miles's actions not in line with "constructive statesmanship."[4]

In an attempt to dissuade Miles from undertaking an alliance with radical midwestern businessmen and insurgent politicians, Van Cleave had his associate Ferdinand C. Schwedtman write to the Wisconsin manufacturer explaining and softening the NAM leader's criticisms. Schwedtman wrote that if Miles persisted in inflaming antitrust sentiment, he soon would find himself described to a jury as "a man of the style of Rockefeller or Gary." Of course, Schwedtman acknowledged, the proprietary manufacturers of the NAM were "crushed between the Labor trust and the Material trust." But, he continued, the "forces that are considered trusts on tariff matters have given a most helpful hand" on labor questions, whereas only U.S. Steel "is found wrong both on labor and on tariff matters."[5]

The NAM thus appeared unwilling to press the antitrust implications of tariff revision because of its desire to conserve an alliance with anti-union forces in Congress and among the corporations. Miles could only respond by reminding Van Cleave and Schwedtman of their previous opposition to both "combinations of labor and capital." Although Miles agreed that "the large unit is a business and national necessity," he opposed "the real trusts like Standard Oil" as a public duty. He would not dispute the NAM's policy, but he would not abandon his viewpoint. Someone, he contended, had to stand up for "our old-fashioned way of thinking."[6]

At the same time, Miles was disillusioned of the possibilities of an extensive trust-limiting tariff reduction by Taft. Frustrated by revisionists' lack of militancy, Miles asked Taft—as he had asked Roosevelt—to declare himself more specifically on the tariff and commission. Miles wrote that many manufacturers were withholding tariff information that would justify reductions because they were waiting for political reassurance from Taft. If this was not forthcoming, Miles warned, the militant revisionists might have to force the issue by revealing their confidential sources of information on the "dishonest and wretched" schedules. But Taft called Miles's hand and snapped that he, Taft, had made all the statements he believed appropriate. "You are continuously threatening to make disclosures," Taft wrote, "and I have earnestly been urging you to make them as fully as you can."[7]

If H. E. Miles was reluctant to trim his social views to comport with association, executive, and legislative priorities, other tariff reductionists were falling into line with the Taft strategy of mild reduction and maximum and minimum schedules. Alvin H. Sanders of the American Reciprocal Tariff League (ARTL) soon was urging Nelson Aldrich and Sereno Payne to formulate a bill that would contain little more than a maximum-minimum rate structure and retaliatory provisions that could be used to counter nontariff trade restrictions, such as the health regulations being used against American meat exports by Germany. Sanders confided that instead of a tariff commission as such, empowered to investigate and recommend rates, he now favored a board of tariff commissioners appointed by the president and confirmed by the Senate that would have power only to administer the maximum-minimum provisions of the new law. Sanders implored Aldrich to see him as an ally within the commission movement. Noting that a businessmen's convention on the tariff commission impended—it was scheduled for mid-February 1909 in Indianapolis—the ARTL chairman told Aldrich that "it is my present purpose to attend this convention and take the ground that it is inadvisable to press for a commission at this time." If the convention did demand a tariff commission, Sanders said, Republicans in Congress could offer a more limited tariff board with power to monitor the maximum-minimum provisions of a new tariff as a compromise that could secure revisionists' cooperation in passing the tariff measure.[8]

Van Cleave and the NAM also recognized that a commission was not immediately or easily obtainable. According to the NAM's Washington lobbyists, of 195 congressmen surveyed, only 91 favored some kind of commission, and 33 of these were Democrats, whose ultimate vote for a Republican measure was questionable. Even generally revisionist Republicans such as Ebenezer Hill of Connecticut were spurning a commission in the current Congress on the ground that support was disorganized. The strongest supporters were the Insurgent Republicans, midwesterners such as George Norris, who were taking the side of H. E. Miles and the smaller midwestern manufacturers.[9]

The focus of the persistent reductionists' tariff commission ambitions was a bill recently proposed by Congressman Charles N. Fowler (R.-N.J.). It called for an independent commission with powers to investigate rates and recommend changes. Senator Beveridge's bill of 1908 was also of interest, although it was more limited in scope. Other commission proponents, such as Sanders of the ARTL and Henry R. Towne of the MANY, favored "more practical" proposals for a less powerful institution whose primary role would be to investigate foreign costs and negotiate reciprocal trade agreements. The differences within the movement thus centered around the ultimate focus and responsibility of a commission: Was it to investigate and regulate American business, as the radicals wanted? Or was it to be a consultative body of economists and customs experts that would look into foreign tariff structures and advise Congress on them, as the more conservative revisionists urged?[10]

The idea for the Indianapolis Tariff Commission Convention to which Sanders had alluded in writing to Aldrich had emanated from Henry Riesenberg, an Indianapolis cigar manufacturer who was close to Senator Beveridge. But its main organizer was the NAM. Perhaps the NAM had gone ahead with the convention, despite its misgivings about the solidity of support in Congress, to maintain its long-term presence in the tariff issue. Almost immediately Riesenberg was co-opted to work with the NAM tariff committee in Washington to drum up support. To broaden the political appeal and impact of the meeting, the NAM arranged for a wide group of organizations to issue the call. These included the MANY, the Boston Merchants Association, the Farmers National Congress, and the National Association for the Extension of Foreign Commerce.[11]

At the convention, procommission politicians and most of the organizational constituencies were able to go on record on the tariff system. Beveridge and Fowler discussed their respective bills, with Beveridge emphasizing the extensive commercial intelligence gathering and cooperative industrial, legislative, and executive tariff-making processes of Germany. Louisiana Congressman Joseph E. Ransdell spoke for Democrats who favored a commission removed from partisan politics, and John Barrett, director of the Pan-American Union, endorsed a tariff commission as essential for U.S.–Latin American trade.[12]

The industrial and agricultural groups praised the intrinsically greater fairness and utility of a tariff commission to determine rates and expand American commerce. But conference organizers failed in efforts to bar all talk on specific rates. Unable to press the stock raisers and the shoemakers into quiet agreement on hide tariffs, the organizers reiterated that a "fair, scientific" commission would determine rates in a way that all industries could—but obviously did not—accept as nonpartisan. This was the reciprocity dilemma in reprise.

Despite continued conflicts, however, the philosophy and support of a scientific tariff commission had far more substance than the "benignant deity" of reciprocity. A very specific structure—the German syndical model of joint industrial, executive, and legislative activity popularized by N. I. Stone—undergirded the tariff commission idea. Moreover, the commission idea had a distinctive American expression in "The Neutral Line," a key paper read to the delegates by longtime tariff activist Henry R. Towne of the MANY. Although Towne originally had supported a less independent tariff board within the Department of Commerce and Labor, his paper revised this view and proposed a commission with rate-setting influence. Towne's commission would assist Congress in finding the "correct" degree of protection for each industry by determining the comparative costs of production of U.S. and foreign goods. Thus, tariff rates would become a product not of congressional logrolling but of "science."[13]

Noted as a venerable and innovative industrial efficiency and cost-accounting expert, Towne gave prestige to the commission idea. He envisioned an American commission quite similar to the European tariff bodies. It would assemble and analyze foreign and domestic statistics and report on prices, wages, costs of materials, and probable revenue impact of different tariff rates. The commission also was intended to harmonize the interests of labor and capital by promoting the wealth of society as a whole through the export of finished manufactures. Such manufactures incorporated a greater amount of domestic labor, and, concomitantly, at each stage of manufacture, profits accrued to domestic interests. Thus, finished manufactures were the most socially valuable class of exports, Towne argued. Although he acknowledged the rights of domestic raw material producers to export their surpluses, Towne stressed the importance of holding down the inflation of basic materials and foodstuff prices as a protection against labor militancy. Towne did not attack the trusts directly, as H. E. Miles had done, but he implicitly articulated the dilemma of manufacturers of finished goods and criticized the large corporations for destroying the putative bond between small capitalist and worker that had led the economy out of the depression of the 1890s. Towne thus posited that expanding production and marketing, at home and abroad, of finished goods would benefit all classes. If tariffs were forced to toe the "neutral line," Towne hypothesized, traditional social harmonies might be restored. It was a view that was widely popular at the convention.[14]

Before adjourning, the Tariff Commission Convention issued a series of forceful resolutions calling for the immediate creation of a tariff commission to collect data and arrange for reciprocal trade agreements, under provisions modeled on the Dingley Tariff's sections 3 and 4, within maximum and minimum limits set by Congress. The effective impact of the rank-and-file movement for "immediate" revision by commission was blunted, however, when the delegates stipulated that current tariff making should proceed "with the best information presently available." This clause confirmed that delegates actually had abandoned the commission as a basis for the upcoming revision. Tariff activists sustained their momentum, however, by creating a Committee of One Hundred, headed by John Candler Cobb, as the core of a lobby to be called the National Tariff Commission Association (NTCA).[15]

The Politics of Tariff Making

The framing of the Payne-Aldrich Tariff illustrated the movement of the Republican party toward a lower-tariff position, reflecting the spread of a consensus for revision and new tariff structures among legislators and capitalist interest groups. Although accomplished at some political cost to the party—notably the alienation of the Insurgents—the political-ideological achievements of Taft's tariff revision often have been under-recognized. They included an attempt to quell popular discontent with the Republican party as the refuge of privileged trusts and entrenched legislative influences, development of a more stable setting for economic growth, movement toward revenue reform, and greater stabilization of the United States' relations with European tariff systems.

Taft set the tone for the tariff discussion in his inaugural address on March 4, 1909. The new president sent a message both to Republican radicals and standpats about the revision he sought. Taft said questions involving the trusts were properly addressed through interstate commerce and antitrust law. There, he would sustain "the right of people to avail themselves of those methods of combining capital and effort deemed necessary to efficiency, at the same time differentiating between combinations based upon legitimate economic reasons and those framed with the intent of creating monopolies and artificially controlling prices." Taft thus implicitly excluded the trust argument from the tariff issue.[16]

Taft was equally clear about the priority of tariff revision based on "the difference between the cost of production abroad and the cost of production here." Taft knew that revision was necessary to fulfill Republican campaign promises, and he was cognizant that the tariff question itself was affected by the expanding role of the state in national and international economic affairs. This expansion meant greatly enlarged revenue needs that essentially outmoded the revenue-versus-protection debate over tariffs. Hence, Taft recommended an inheritance tax to reverse current federal deficits of $100 million.[17]

The revision process began formally when Sereno Payne, chairman of the House Ways and Means Committee, introduced his bill on March 16, 1909. The bill was the product of the committee's efforts over nearly a year of investigations and hearings. But it was also influenced by the president-elect, who had sent Payne memorandums and emissaries to explain and argue aspects of the tariff question. The bill also showed the impact of the public debate not only at the hearings but over the previous three years of tariff agitation. Reciprocity as a theme had disappeared as the Republican standard.[18]

Payne's speech introducing the bill affirmed the Republican party's changed orientation toward the tariff. Payne began by reviewing Republican tariff legislation since the 1890s. The chairman praised the reciprocal tariff provisions of the McKinley and Dingley tariffs as appropriate to their time. But he suggested that those provisions had proved politically flawed and were now out of date. This was an important—perhaps even historic—statement, coming from Payne, a longtime protectionist and staunch advocate of congressional privilege in tariff legislation. Now the chairman took the role of critic. He reminded his auditors that the trade gains secured by the McKinley Act had been negated by the Democratic Wilson Tariff, thereby seriously undermining U.S. international commercial credibility. More important, he contended that the limited adjustments provided by the existing U.S. reciprocity provisions could not secure a growing trade: "We saw our rivals for the trade of the world getting conventional rates that we could not get, partially because . . . under the Constitution no change can be made in the tariff except Congress takes the initiative." Significantly, Payne was telling his fellow congressmen to change the system by delegating some of their authority: "We must pass legislation to enable the Executive to offer favorable trade agreements. It is with us here to originate it."[19]

In this context, Payne urged adopting, as formulated by the committee, a maximum-minimum tariff to replace the old system of reciprocity treaties. The new system would create minimums that were sometimes moderate reductions from the Dingley Tariff. It would set a maximum rate at 20 percent above the minimum (that is, the maximum rate would add 20 percent of the original duty imposed), to take effect after a sixty-day period. During this interim, the president or an official of the executive branch would consider whether other nations had proffered rates and trading conditions (implicitly to include nontariff discriminations) that would justify retaining the U.S. minimum and canceling the imposition of the maximum rate.[20]

This system, it is clear, was in form the "punitive maximum" tariff that experts N. I. Stone and C. M. Pepper had warned against. But it was a very mild version, with the maximum duties not much above the minimum and the minimum duties constituting the "persuasive factor," the reduction, that the experts had deemed essential. Payne may have cast his bill in this way because of domestic politics and practical international considerations. On the first point, it may be observed, a punitive maximum form allowed Republicans in Congress to assure protectionist constituents that they had been tough on the tariff. On the second point, Payne noted that the contemporary policy in Europe invited equality of access through international tariff bargaining. Payne quoted McKinley's Buffalo Address to buttress his point and emphasized that a modern American tariff system must have similar objectives—to eliminate needless duties, not to attain free trade.[21]

That Payne's bill was intended to accommodate European practices was underlined in subsequent discussion, when Payne noted that his bill specifically excluded colonial preferences as discriminations warranting imposition of the U.S. maximum tariff. The principle of bilateral metropolitan-colonial preferences, practiced not only by Europe but by the United States—in Cuba and the Philippines, for example—was thus to be preserved for colonizing powers. The doctrine of equality of access (that is, the open door) was to apply principally to neutral markets and the metropolises.[22]

As a stalwart Republican, Payne would not denounce the doctrine of protection outright, but he did establish a philosophical justification for tempering it when he declared that the United States had to begin to define effective methods to limit the home-market ideology. In remarks apparently directed at Aldrich and Lodge in the Senate, who were known to be resistant to downward revision, Payne announced that rates in excess of cost-of-production differences were illegitimate: "He is the better friend to protection who tries to keep the rates reasonably protective to the people engaged in the industry," Payne warned. "Old Schedules" Payne had begun to sound a little like H. E. Miles.[23]

Like Taft, Payne also hinted that the old issues of protective versus revenue tariffs were outmoded. The new bill contained a provision for the issue of $250 million in 3 percent certificates to relieve the debate on schedules of revenue considerations. Payne suggested with some wit that tariff making had become not so far different for Democrats and Republicans: The Georgia peanut growers were ostensibly revenue-tariff proponents, but, Payne mused, they would not protest if the duty were raised from a half cent per pound to a half cent per peanut. He thus implied that all legislators, although cognizant of their constituents' interests, had to operate on the basis of a bipartisan awareness of the impact of tariff rates on American foreign trade expansion. Such sentiments had been expressed in the nineteenth century by David A. Wells and James G. Blaine. But this statement came not from party theoreticians and executive branch officers but from a Republican leader in the House, a bastion of interest politics.[24]

The Payne bill's provisions reflected its framers' intent to revise the tariff along the moderate principles enunciated by Taft. Duties on coal, hides, and iron ore were eliminated completely. The impact of public criticisms of the steel rates, and probably of E. H. Gary's admissions that rates could be cut substantially without great harm, was apparent in the marked reductions on pig iron, cut from $7.00 per ton to $2.50 per ton, and on other steel products, where cuts averaged about 50 percent. In addition, lumber duties were slashed by 50 percent, and newsprint, the subject of considerable controversy and a congressional investigation spurred by press interests, was cut from $6.00 per ton to $2.00 per ton.[25]

But the Payne bill still bore the residual features of traditional political tariff making. Hosiery duties were raised; duties on gloves, Payne's home-state industry, were more than doubled; certain cotton schedules were hiked; wool was clipped only slightly; and sugar duties were left virtually untouched.[26]

The House discussed the Payne bill for fifteen days, a debate that was largely pro forma because the rules of the House restricted amendments to members of the sponsoring committee. Nonetheless, the debate served as a platform for the parties to declare their positions on the bill. Republicans broadly supported the bill, although some standpats criticized reductions. Ways and Means member Edgar G. Crumpacker (R.-Ind.) gave a major address defending the bill in which he praised the measure's retaliatory powers, emphasizing that Payne had not pulled the party's protectionist teeth. This obligatory bellicosity aside, however, Crumpacker stressed the advantages of a flat minimum rate over the "system of international dickers" that had prevailed before—that is, the reciprocity of commercial treaties. Crumpacker thus rejected the multiple bilateral system of previous U.S. tariffs for a more frankly multilateral one. "Conditions have materially changed" since the Dingley Tariff, Crumpacker reasoned. Foreign trade expansion, not protection of the home market, was at the root of the new Republican tariff approach, as Crumpacker concluded in an oratorical flourish, pointing to "the paramount importance of creating conditions that will enable the great lines of industries in the United States . . . to arm and equip themselves for further conquests of the neutral markets of the world."[27]

In response to the Republican bill, House Democrats accepted the principle of reciprocal reductions but stressed the dangers of trade wars that would follow use of maximum or retaliatory provisions. But Republicans countered that the maximum-minimum system represented a practical advance over sections 3 and 4 of the Dingley Tariff because the new system corresponded in form to European tariff making and because it could be put into rapid practical use. Illinois Republican Frank O. Lowden cited Commerce and Labor Department tariff expert N. I. Stone as the authority for this view.[28]

Some Democrats applauded this broadening of Republican tariff doctrines. The Democratic minority, it appeared, was flummoxed in that the Republicans had adopted the cheap raw material position while they, the Democrats, had done little more than advocate reciprocity. One effect of their response was the removal of petroleum duties, and another was the insertion of a proposal for a graduated inheritance tax, which Taft had recommended in his inaugural. But it was clear that although the Democrats could snipe at the Taft proposals for failing to go far enough, they had yet to propound a systematic alternative to the Republican position. Moreover, their programmatic adherence to revenue tariffs subverted their attempt to attract Insurgent Republicans to oppose the Payne bill. In light of the rising revenue requirements of an expanding state, the Democrats' tariff stance was increasingly anomalous as a low-tariff concept, even though they endorsed income tax measures as a solution to government requirements.[29]

Taft, although to this point publicly silent on the tariff, was generally satisfied with the House effort, with the exceptions of the hosiery and glove schedules, which he considered embarrassing to the party at the national level. The Payne bill, Taft wrote a Chicago merchant when the bill was reported to the Senate in April, "was as near [to] complying with our promises as we can hope." In a retrospective letter to his brother, Taft reiterated that he felt that Payne had sought "to work conscientiously to carry out the plank of the platform" and that the bill was "a genuine effort in the right direction."[30]

The tariff bill ran into serious difficulties in the Senate, however. Nelson W. Aldrich, chairman of the Committee on Finance, was committed to protectionism and to the textile industries of Rhode Island. He was also intent on preserving congressional tariff-making prerogatives. Along with Henry Cabot Lodge of Massachusetts, Aldrich immediately denied that the Republican platform had committed the party to tariff reduction. Soon Aldrich declared that he would as cheerfully vote for 300 percent rates as for 25 percent rates if he believed them necessary for protection. Aldrich was not completely hostile to Taft or to Taft's objectives, but he was determined to establish a strong negotiating position for a more conservative revision of the tariff. In response to the Payne bill, Aldrich's committee prepared a separate schedule that restored duties on hides, iron ores, coal, and petroleum, reclassified cotton goods to increase the rates, raised lumber duties to $1.50 per thousand feet, and increased newsprint from the House's $2.00 to $4.00 per ton. In addition, the committee struck out the nontariff revenue measures, including the graduated inheritance tax.[31]

Aldrich's provocative move, though aimed primarily at Taft, mobilized the Senate Insurgents, led by Robert M. La Follette of Wisconsin. They reacted to the tariff "graft" represented by the Aldrich bill in increasingly agitated terms. Senators Bristow, Cummins, Dolliver, Clapp, Nelson, Crawford, Brown, and Burkett, all midwesterners, along with Beveridge, formed the salient of this opposition, which La Follette later identified as the formative experience of the Progressive movement. Although themselves inconsistent on tariff reduction when important midwestern interests were threatened, the Insurgents joined with Senate Democrats in denouncing the Aldrich alterations in the administrative and nontariff revenue features of the bill. The midwesterners were also responding to the conspicuous neglect of the smaller proprietary manufacturers' demands for antitrust tariff legislation and a tariff commission. But La Follette failed in an attempt to amend the tariff to assure a reduction of up to, but not more than, 20 percent below the Dingley Tariff rates—that is, to take the Dingley section 4 reductions as the standard for a new U.S. minimum tariff.[32]

Taft was also intent on trimming the Aldrich version of the tariff bill. Politically he was in a difficult position, however. He recognized that the Senate leaders were testing his power and resolve by propounding high rates. Yet Taft believed that the vociferous reductionism of the newspapers, the Insurgents, and the Democrats was disruptive to his overall political program. This conflict was exemplified by the revenue question. Many Insurgents and Democrats favored making an income tax provision part of the tariff bill, rather than an inheritance tax or a corporation tax, whose burdens could be sidestepped or passed along to consumers. Taft came to favor the last measure, in good part because he felt that a corporation tax would more effectively enable "federal supervision of corporations, which is quite a step in the direction of similar reforms . . . with which Senator Aldrich has pledged himself to help me." Although Taft did not oppose the income tax in principle, he believed that the Pollock case, in which the Supreme Court struck down the Populist-inspired income tax attached to the Wilson Tariff of 1894, illustrated the futility of imposing such a measure without a constitutional amendment. But it seems likely that Taft was also resisting leveling initiatives tied to the tariff. Increasingly alienated from the "so-called 'progressives'" and their "yelping and snarling at Cannon and Aldrich," Taft committed himself to negotiating the tariff with the Old Guard leadership in the course of House-Senate conferences on the bill.[33]

Taft's contacts with Aldrich, Cannon, and Payne were extensive over the summer of 1909, during which the final shape of the tariff bill was hammered out. At White House dinners and in "roaming over the countryside in the [presidential] automobile," Taft, with considerable help from Payne, obtained a fair amount of compromise on the tariff rates. Taft was particularly intent on restoring to the free list items such as coal, iron ore, oil, wood pulp, and hides, which he believed created the predominant public impression of the House bill as a sincere reductionist effort. Given his broad support in the House, Taft hoped to persuade Aldrich to prevail on about thirty protectionist diehards in the Senate to compromise on the rates and on the maximum-minimum features to avoid a veto confrontation. Cognizant that Aldrich's position was "complicated with some objections that association in the Senate imposes on him," Taft concluded that Aldrich's bill was really not so far different from the House bill, when the salient examples of the raw materials rates were overlooked.[34]

As it emerged from the conference committee, the Payne-Aldrich bill did appear, on most rates, as the compromise Taft had sought. The duties on hides were dropped. On coal, duties were reduced from the Dingley rate of 67 cents per ton to 45 cents per ton; iron ore was reduced from 40 cents to 15 cents per ton (as opposed to the Senate's original 25 cent rate); lumber was cut from the Senate's $1.50 to $1.25, replacing the Dingley rate of $2.00. Steel tariffs were cut substantially: Pig iron was lowered from $4.00 to $2.50 per ton; scrap steel, at $4.00 per ton in the Dingley Tariff and at 50 cents in the Payne bill, was compromised at $1.00; rails were dropped from $7.84 to $3.92 per ton; and bar iron went from 0.006 cents per pound to 0.003 cents. In all, more than 80 percent of the metals rates were affected, and cuts averaged about 50 percent.[35]

Changes in the administrative features of the bill were significant, though less extensive than those originally conceived by the tariff revision movement. The Payne-Aldrich Tariff embodied maximum-minimum provisions, as the revisionists of the ARTL and the NAM had been demanding and as the House had stipulated. The Senate and final versions of the bill, however, increased the maximum, or penalty, duty from the modest 20 to 25 percent surcharge on the rates to a heavy 25 percent surcharge on the entire value of the imported item, to be invoked if foreign "tariff rates or provisions, trade or other regulations, charges, exactions," export bounties, or duties of foreign nations were altered to the detriment of the United States. The maximum duty was to go into effect after March 31, 1910, unless the president declared that a lack of discrimination warranted continuing the minimum rates. The final version, the result of political compromise, thus contained a much more punitive maximum than what Taft had approved in the House bill. Yet this dramatic increase, striking in the public mind and in the reactions it evoked from reductionists, was paradoxically neutral in effect, because it was a commercial doomsday weapon that could be invoked only against most extreme discriminations. That is, its use seemed guaranteed to produce a tariff war.[36]

The maximum-minimum provisions, conservative as they appeared, had another innovative effect. They provided an opening for a sort of tariff commission as had been advocated by the revisionists. Reluctant to empower any authority that would seriously undermine Congress, House and Senate conferees resisted the attempts of the tariff commission movement and its legislative allies to shape an effective rate-making or regulatory-type commission. But revisionist legislative leaders were partially successful. Beveridge, pressed by Senate Insurgents, insisted—as he had not in early

1908—on following the Miles formula for the president to appoint "outside experts" to an independent tariff bureau rather than accept the delegation of clerks by the Treasury or Commerce and Labor departments to work under the Ways and Means Committee.[37]

Beveridge was also supported by H. E. Miles and the Committee of One Hundred, formed as the result of the Indianapolis Tariff Commission Convention of February. In addition, the NAM had enlisted former House majority whip James E. Watson, who after his defeat for the governorship of Indiana and his failure to be named to the Taft cabinet had gone to work for the NAM in Washington. Ultimately, however, the revisionists accepted, at Taft's urging and Aldrich's insistence, a diluted formula that allowed the president to "employ such persons as may be required" to aid in the administration of the maximum-minimum provisions of the tariff. This was the objective that Sanders had expressed to Aldrich in January and with which Van Cleave urged compliance in May. The language, Beveridge and the more radical tariff revisionists understood, limited the role that the Tariff Board, as it came to be called, could play in formulating tariff rates by reducing its scope to investigating domestic and foreign costs of production. Nonetheless, Taft mollified the revisionists by promising to create an effective board by the nature of his appointments and by securing a $100,000 appropriation from Congress. It is interesting that both Van Cleave and Miles, who were probably anxious to see results from their years of activism, acceded to Taft's limitations, whereas Beveridge and the Insurgents voted against the diluted conference committee provisions. Thus the center of tariff radicalism appeared to be shifting from the revisionist business community to the legislature.[38]

President William H. Taft signed the Payne-Aldrich bill into law on August 5, 1909. The act was not all he had hoped for in reductions, especially on schedules such as wool, which was largely untouched. But Taft had been far from the veto he had originally feared; the new tariff eliminated or substantially reduced duties on hides, leather, coal, iron ore, and lumber—most of the original targets of the executive's reduction effort. In the deliberations and consultations over the bill, Taft had induced a majority of moderate Republican protectionists to vote for a reductionist bill, and even Frank Taussig, the Harvard political economist and free-trade advocate, acknowledged the effort as—if not a Democratic-style reduction—at least an apparent turning point in Republican tariff policy.[39]

Like Roosevelt before him, Taft had also headed off the attempt, first by H. E. Miles and then by the Insurgents, to make of the revisionist movement and of the proposed tariff commission an independent antitrust force with powers to subpoena evidence and to recommend tariff rates designed to limit corporate power in the domestic marketplace. Instead, Taft had channeled reductionist demands more narrowly by creating a tariff board whose powers were limited to the investigation of costs of production in the domestic and foreign markets.

Moreover, Taft dignified the revisionists by appointing a three-member Tariff Board composed of moderate protectionists: Henry Crosby Emery, a Yale political economist and former Gold Democrat with strong interests in Asian trade expansion; James Burton Reynolds, former assistant secretary of the treasury; and Alvin H. Sanders, the ARTL chief who seemed anxious to work with the administration and Congress. Emery would serve as chairman, and the knowledgeable N. I. Stone was appointed as chief economist of the Tariff Board. H. E. Miles was specifically denied a position on the board, and soon it would become apparent that the lead in analysis of foreign and domestic commercial legislation would be taken primarily by the Department of State's Bureau of Trade Relations, to which Taft appointed his adviser Charles M. Pepper. Taft thus appeared to have rallied Republicans for tariff changes and to have contained proprietary antitrust tariff movements.[40]

In a political sense, however, the tariff was a disaster for Taft. In part, this was because a tariff bill always alienated someone—a notion epitomized in the popular wisdom that a ruling party often lost an election after a tariff bill. In addition, the tentative nature of the bill, although obviously necessary in a transitional ideological period, ran against the grain of many businesses' desires for tariff stability. But a chief problem Taft faced was caused by his underestimation of the public and legislative influence of the Insurgents. Rankled by the executive's acquiescence in Aldrich's changes in the tariff, they scored the Payne-Aldrich Act as a token reduction reeking of collusion between the executive and the Old Guard. Their criticisms, though at times inaccurate—as when they claimed that the tariff was not in fact a reduction—were a renewed and forceful expression of the original standpoint of H. E. Miles and the antitrust tariff radicals who sought to use the state to limit corporate power.

In an ideological and political-economic sense the Insurgents were on target. Miles had believed from the start of the tariff agitation that proprietary manufacturers required a 66 to 75 percent reduction in the steel schedules to combat the trusts, whereas the 50 percent reductions passed "would keep the market in the control of the domestic users [that is, producers]" but would not lower prices sufficiently to steel consumers. The Payne-Aldrich reductions thus promoted foreign trade expansion to a degree, but they seemed insufficient to challenge the continued power in the economy of the integrated semimanufacture corporations. That is, the new $4.00 rate on steel rails was very little less protective than was a $7.00 rate, given the inland position of most U.S. markets and the limited export capacity of Europe. As the steel industry well knew, the new tariff would require minor adjustments only.[41]

Taft, it has been remarked many times, exacerbated the political problem, with the help of a hostile press disgruntled over compromises on reductions of paper pulp, by remarks such as those made at Winona, Minnesota, where he praised the Payne-Aldrich Act as "the best tariff bill that the Republican party ever passed."[42] Yet, although he clearly erred in injudicious self-congratulation at Winona, Taft, from his own point of view, had succeeded under trying circumstances in moving the Republican party from protection to reduction within a procorporate framework. Taft acknowledged the problems with the lumber and wool schedules, and he did not pretend privately that the tariff was an unqualified triumph. Still, the Payne-Aldrich Tariff was an achievement in the view of Taft and his administration, and his words at Winona thus might be taken at face value:

> On the whole . . . I am bound to say that I think the Payne tariff bill is the best tariff bill that the Republican party ever passed and that in it the party has conceded the necessity for following the changed conditions and reducing tariff rates accordingly. This is a substantial achievement in the direction of lower tariffs and downward revision, and it ought to be accepted as such. Critics of the bill utterly ignore the tremendous cuts that have been made in the iron schedule. . . . The severe critics of the bill pass this reduction in the metal schedule with a sneer, and say that the cut did not hurt the iron interests of the country. . . . It was not expected to hurt them. It was expected only to reduce excessive rates.[43]

Taft had struggled to achieve a new direction for Republican tariff policy, which now had accepted the need for accommodating itself more fully to the international dimension of tariff making and had reoriented its initiatives toward the executive branch. Moreover, Taft had provided the direction that had helped to meld the perspectives of revisionists such as Alvin

Sanders with those of congressional leaders such as Payne and Aldrich and had created an outlet for the energies of revisionists in a new tariff board. Some radicals, such as H. E. Miles, were intent on working within the National Tariff Commission Association to enlarge the tariff board's abilities to empower proprietary business regulation of corporate activities. But it appeared that the Republican party mainstream was successfully incorporating the main thrust of proprietary business revisionist movement while limiting its aims to promoting its interests within the context of an overall corporate system.

Still, the ideological gains Taft had won in the tariff were not guarantees of his political popularity, especially with the Insurgents. Moreover, the Payne-Aldrich Act and its infrastructural innovations had to be tested in at least three distinct arenas: as an instrument of international tariff adjustment; as a feature of domestic policy in which the cost-of-production doctrine would be assessed as a means for adjusting corporate-proprietary relations; and as a means of forging greater political consensus on the tariff.

Part Three

Revisionism
in Practice

9 Commercial Policy, 1909–1912

The new law provides for the termination of . . . special agreements. . . . [It will] constitute a uniform plan to be extended to all foreign powers alike. This is a great advantage. Many foreign nations have the same scheme in what is known as the regular (or maximum) and conventional (or minimum) tariff. That plan is in line with the strong modern practice of thus comprehensively and automatically extending tariff concessions to all foreign nations uniformly and without preference upon considerations of mutual advantages. It is a sort of tariff union.—John Ball Osborne, Chief of the Department of State Bureau of Trade Relations, "Memorandum on the New Tariff Law" for Secretary of State Philander C. Knox, September 16, 1909

After the passage of the Payne-Aldrich Tariff, the Taft administration attempted to carry out the ideas that had motivated its push for a change in traditional Republican high-tariff policy. At the level of international relations, the administration tested the capacity of the new U.S. dual-rate tariff to elicit enduring minimum or treaty tariff concessions from well over a hundred nations and colonies. Along with the State Department's Bureau of Trade Relations (BTR), the newly created U.S. Tariff Board participated in important minimum-tariff negotiations, especially with Canada, Germany, and France.

Formation of Taft Administration Commercial Policy

Section 2 of the Payne-Aldrich Act permitted President Taft to "employ such persons as may be required" to advise on the application of the new maximum-minimum provisions of the tariff. It was under this vague authority that Taft created the Tariff Board and that Treasury Secretary Franklin MacVeagh made its principal appointments. As chairman, MacVeagh selected Henry Crosby Emery, a Yale political economist who was, like MacVeagh himself, a Gold Democrat who had switched to the Republican party. Emery had strong interests in Asian trade and had recently urged cooperation between his generally Democratic and free-trade-oriented academic colleagues and the predominantly Republican revisionist business organizations in effecting gradual tariff reduction.[1]

Also selected for the Tariff Board was Alvin H. Sanders, editor of the Chicago-based *Breeder's Gazette*, head of the American Reciprocal Tariff League (ARTL), and executive committee member of the American National Live Stock Association (ANLSA). Sanders, a leader of the business revisionist movement, was a "cooperationist" who urged intra- and interindustry accommodation with corporate tariff goals. His policies were sometimes at odds with those of the proprietary "radicals" who sought to turn the tariff against the trusts, and his appointment was the more notable in that one of the prime movers of the tariff commission movement, H. E. Miles of the National Association of Manufacturers (NAM), was specifically rebuffed for a board position.[2]

The third appointee, James Burton Reynolds, was reputedly the most protectionist of the group. A former Massachusetts Republican party chairman, Reynolds was close to Henry Cabot Lodge. He was also the assistant secretary of the treasury and had been responsible for many years for customs administration. MacVeagh chose, and Taft approved, N. I. Stone, the tariff expert of the Department of Commerce and Labor and former member of the North Commission to Germany, as the board's chief economist and statistician.

Taft's authority for creating the Tariff Board and the board's first challenges of advising on the maximum-minimum provisions seemed to draw it into the foreign arena. The tariff law of August 5, 1909 stated that the maximum rates were to be applied on March 31, 1910, unless discrimination was found not to exist or not to be "undue." Thus, a determination of the facts of commercial practice and the position the United States would take with regard to foreign tariffs in negotiations had to be arrived at quickly. Yet Taft's underlying purpose in creating the Tariff Board was to constitute a group outside the Ways and Means Committee for investigating domestic industries and evaluating their tariff requirements. Hence, the board's provenance and mandate regarding international aspects of the tariff were uncertain.[3]

The board's scope of authority regarding the maximum-minimum tariff was all the more uncertain because Taft entrusted the BTR of the Department of State with the primary responsibility for formulating U.S. policy in tariff negotiations. In the BTR Taft and Secretary of State Philander C. Knox had established a group of experienced diplomats, foreign trade experts, and administration loyalists. Chief of Bureau John Ball Osborne was a former member of the Kasson Commission who had been a vigorous defender of Roosevelt's tariff initiatives toward Germany. Assistants were Charles M. Pepper, a former international business journalist and Taft foreign trade adviser during the preinauguration period, and M. H. "Mack" Davis, a career State Department analyst. Department Counselor Henry Martyn Hoyt had served as U.S. Solicitor General under Roosevelt. A Philadelphia investment banker and Yale law graduate, Hoyt had close personal ties with both Knox and Taft.[4]

Even before the passage of the Payne-Aldrich Tariff, the BTR was assessing the United States' new tariff posture in terms of the expansion of American influence in the international competition for markets and economic influence. Naturally, the bureau supported Taft's strategy of moderate reduction and changes in rate structures and customs valuation as effectual in domestic and international contexts. But it also delved into technical tariff details and considered the political-economic implications of the general trends in tariff duties. BTR policy analyses were read by Knox and probably by Taft and may have had important effects on their thinking in commercial policy matters in the period after passage of the Payne-Aldrich Tariff.

One of the most striking commercial essays was a memorandum by BTR assistant chief Charles M. Pepper, "The Open Door to Canada." Written during the House-Senate conferences on the Payne bill, Pepper's paper strenuously argued for retaining the reductions embodied in Payne's House version of the tariff and criticized Aldrich's Senate alterations. Although Pepper focused on Canada, he addressed much broader issues involving U.S. treatment of preference tariffs and the general principles of U.S. conduct vis-à-vis European tariff systems.[5]

Pepper's immediate point was that the United States should retain the reductions embodied in the Payne version of the tariff because they represented not merely an advantage for certain interests but a crucial weapon for U.S. foreign trade as a whole. The memo pointed out that as of 1907, more than half of Canada's external trade was with the United States. But, Pepper noted, Canada's preference tariff of 1907 threatened this arrangement. The new three-level Canadian tariff would give Britain the lowest, imperial preference, rate. Then it would give reciprocal treaty signatories such as France, which was in the midst of such negotiations with Canada, an intermediate rate. Last, it would leave the United States with a maximum duty on its exports to the Dominion. Undisturbed, such an arrangement would foster a West-East flow of Canadian goods that would channel Canadian trade away from the United States and toward Europe. But, if the United States retained the Payne reductions and thereby qualified for the intermediate or treaty rate of the Canadian tariff, the United States would assure the continued development of North-South, Canadian-U.S. trade. The United States needed only the intermediate rate to outcompete both English and French exporters, Pepper believed, because the United States' large output and geographical proximity to Canada gave it an inherent advantage. In effect, he argued, U.S. receipt of the intermediate rate would "nullify the British preferential rate."[6]

The immediacy of the problem was Pepper's consistent theme in the memorandum. Trade relations involved not only economic flows but acute political sensibilities. Canadians, he noted, were no longer actively seeking reciprocity as they had done in the late nineteenth century, because Canada's progressing industrial and national development now made that nation's industrial bourgeoisie economically vulnerable to the incursions of American products. In addition, Anglophiles in relatively developed Ontario and Francophiles in Quebec had developed a more sophisticated nationalist strategy: They sought to avert shifting Canada's neocolonial status from Britain to the United States by playing European export markets off against the American.[7]

U.S. concessions at this point, however, would have the advantage of appealing to Canadian agricultural exporters and to western Canadians, many of them immigrants from the United States, who wanted readily available U.S.-made goods. In addition, many Canadian raw material producers in the East, such as the Nova Scotia coal and iron mining interests, were funded by U.S. capital and saw the United States as a natural market. But the United States had to act now, Pepper warned, before the national-industrial interests of Canada solidified against the Canadian liberal party, headed by Sir Wilfred Laurier, which was sympathetic to increased trade with the United States.[8]

Pepper also noted that the current U.S. climate, as embodied by the numerous business revisionist groups such as the "New York Chamber of Commerce, Chicago Commercial associations, and similar bodies," indicated a positive U.S. public sentiment for trade accommodations with

Canada. Unification of American political opinion to support the Payne reductions at this critical juncture in empire politics would help ensure that "the British imperial system will prove non-workable." The Canadian tariff issue and the Payne reductions thus appeared to some U.S. analysts as interlinked with U.S.-European commercial struggles of the period.[9]

Although the administration failed to implement the Payne version of the tariff bill, the BTR determined nonetheless to pursue the broad open-door aims Pepper had outlined in his memorandum. Immediately after the passage of the tariff act, BTR experts—principally Pepper and Osborne—began to assess the new U.S. tariff policy in a series of memorandums written to define and articulate the U.S. position vis-à-vis various sections of the world and the interests of U.S. industries in trade expansion.

Pepper began with a careful analysis of the iron and steel schedules. His view forms an interesting counterpoint to the attitude of radical revisionists such as H. E. Miles, whose emphasis in public debate on the tariff was also on the metals schedule. Miles had argued that proper reduction in iron and steel required 66 to 75 percent cuts rather than the approximately 50 percent reductions made. In "Effect of the Iron and Steel Schedules," Pepper argued that the Taft policy, as embodied in the final tariff bill, could still accomplish much of what the revisionists sought. It would bring in cheap ores, at 15 cents duty per ton (12 cents for Cuban ores under the still-operative 1902 reciprocity treaty), scrap iron, and high-speed and specialty steels. A signal benefit of these reductions would be in making more economic the inland shipment of items not produced in the United States such as British tin and Swedish (that is, high-speed) steels. The cuts probably would not affect the market shares of U.S. producers of bar iron, rails, and other semifinished and finished basic steel products, because of the tight corporate control of production—the point H. E. Miles had made consistently during the tariff debates. But, Pepper maintained, the new rates might encourage foreign tenders for U.S. contracts at Antwerp and might thereby tend to drive down the U.S. prices to the benefit of steel-using finished manufacturers such as the machine tool, agricultural implement, and hardware industries, the industries that had conducted "the most vigorous agitation for a reduction of the metal schedule." Thus, Pepper reasoned, actual imports might not measure the salubrious effects of the new tariff accurately; the revision might cheapen raw material prices and thus play a role in "enabling the European market to be maintained."[10]

Pepper's generally sanguine attitude about the adequacy of the Payne-Aldrich Tariff metals schedules conformed well with the approach of the steel industry. President James A. Farrell of the United States Steel Products Export Company summarized company policy in a letter to his export sales manager, who was concerned about U.S. Steel's exports to the Hamilton (Ontario) Bridge Works. Farrell argued that the new tariff's maximum-minimum provisions should be used only to guarantee equality of access by serving as a counterweight to Canadian and European antidumping provisions or countervailing tariff clauses. Farrell appeared concerned that the maximum might be invoked against the British preferential rate in Canada and elsewhere. This would be a mistake, he suggested, because such preferences were similar to the ones the United States implemented vis-à-vis Cuba, the Philippines, Puerto Rico, and even Alaska. Farrell hoped that the maximum-minimum clauses would be used to secure "equitable and just treatment as compared with the exporters of any other country." But what U.S. Steel needed—and was confident of getting from the Taft administration, Farrell suggested—was a lenient definition of foreign discrimination that emphasized as "undue" only retaliations in the form of antidumping provisions or import quotas. In short, the steel industry had acquiesced in moderate rate reductions and was now seeking to avoid tariff conflict by encouraging an "open door," or unconditional most-favored-nation tariff.[11]

The Pepper memorandum and the steel industry communications thus suggested that despite the changes made to the Payne version of the new tariff, the rates and benefits of the present revision appeared adequate to the domestic and foreign requirements of U.S. industry—a position that would have failed to satisfy fully H. E. Miles but that appeared to conform to Taft's own view of the tariff as he was then expressing it at Winona and elsewhere.[12]

A series of summary memorandums, apparently written by John Ball Osborne, chief of the BTR, concurred in the utility of the administration's tariff policy. The writer noted that the tariff constituted a significant reduction, decreasing the duty on 650 items, increasing it on 220, and leaving the remainder (about 1,130) the same. Although acknowledging that the Payne-Aldrich Act was a compromise "between strong and antagonistic forces," the writer considered the law a "distinct advance in the direction of tariff reform and reduction" that would correct domestic tariff injustices and allow the rectification and reciprocation of U.S.-foreign rate imbalances.[13]

In addition, the administrative revisions of the tariff should make the negotiation of tariff adjustments with foreign powers easier than heretofore. This was a point that Osborne, a longtime State Department official and member of the Kasson Commission, was well qualified to make. On the maximum-minimum features of the law, one of the memorandums noted that terminating special specific agreements would enable the United States to exchange its minimum rate for the conventional or minimum rates of European nations, a plan consonant with the "modern practice of . . . comprehensively and automatically extending tariff concessions to all foreign nations uniformly." Osborne noted that the United States' previous agreements had given the nation "a very limited list of articles to trade with . . . and what we received . . . in exchange was often less important to us than other items as to which an agreement could not be made." He added that the United States often got the benefits of other nations' conventional tariffs but could not reciprocate without negotiating a special treaty, thus automatically putting the United States outside the "most-favored-nation" community. "The maximum and minimum section accomplishes a great and much needed reform in our methods," he concluded. Thus, Osborne was arguing that the maximum-minimum provisions could substitute for a formal revision of the U.S. conditional most-favored-nation clause toward the European unconditional interpretation. That is, by creating a uniform minimum rate and by abrogating previous special arrangements, the United States would be generalizing its minimum tariff in the way that the European nations automatically extended their greatest concessions to any one nation to all most-favored-nation treaty signatories.[14]

On the customs administrative features of the new tariff act, Osborne appeared equally enthusiastic. The new act reversed the procedures of the 1907 agreement with Germany, which construed "market value" for customs appraisals as an "export price" that could be verified by German Chambers of Commerce. That is, the old practice allowed German testimony on the foreign selling price of German goods as valid, though not necessarily definitive, evidence in U.S. customs valuation cases. Elihu Root had later generalized this concession to all foreign nations, removing foreign resentments of favoritism toward Germany. But U.S. protectionists accused the system of placing far too much power in foreign hands and of inviting undervaluations. The new act avoided these conflicts by allowing appraisers who dealt with merchandise subject to ad valorem duties to use data on cost of production gathered by American agents abroad. In no case would appraisers assign a price less than the U.S. wholesale price. The Payne-Aldrich Tariff also provided, it may be added, for a Customs Court of Appeals, which would centralize and make uniform heretofore heterogeneous decisions made by the local circuit courts, which formerly had jurisdiction over cases referred from boards of general appraisers. The customs system was thus more effectively institutionalized and rationalized and made distinctly less susceptible to regional differences in interpretation of valuation procedures.[15]

Administration policy, as expressed by the State Department and the BTR, then, tended strongly toward justifying the Payne-Aldrich Tariff as a step toward potentiating the productive advantages of U.S. industry through an open-door tariff system that emulated the European unconditional most-favored-nation systems and that comported well with the strategy of major exporters such as the steel industry.[16]

The BTR, as the effective center of commercial policy formulation, and the Tariff Board, appointed to assist with maximum-minimum negotiations and with developing new methods of forming U.S. tariff policy, had partially overlapping jurisdictions. Their conflicts over their respective responsibilities, and over some important political and philosophical matters, would become clear as the United States worked to apply the new tariff legislation to foreign nations—in particular, to Canada, Germany, and France.

Implementing the Maximum-Minimum Provisions

December 1909 found the State Department's Bureau of Trade Relations and the Tariff Board ready to begin negotiations with foreign governments over the application of the U.S. minimum tariff. Taft authorized the Tariff Board to render judgments on what constituted "undue discrimination" in foreign tariffs and to make recommendations on the concessions the U.S. might demand in addition to or aside from minimum tariff rates to ensure equality of treatment. The State Department, however, would handle all direct communications and inquiries from foreign sources.[17]

The power the tariff act conferred on the executive to apply the heavy 25 percent ad valorem duty in the case of discrimination raised some initial anxieties on the part of foreign nations, principally Germany, France, and Canada. Because the final version of the tariff bill had dropped the House's exclusion of imperial preference tariffs for colonies from the definition of "discrimination," even the British were concerned about the new tariff, although Britain's home policy of virtual free trade essentially guaranteed it the extension of the U.S. minimum. The United States thus was pressed to resolve the question of how it would apply the maximum-minimum clause of the new tariff.[18]

U.S. negotiations with Canada over the application of the Payne-Aldrich Tariff minimum rates were an important step in defining U.S. flexible tariff policy. They were also a prologue to the Canadian reciprocity controversy. Because that controversy has been treated so extensively elsewhere, it may be summarized here. In negotiations held in Ottawa, Albany, and Washington, the United States sent Charles M. Pepper of the BTR and Chairman Henry C. Emery of the Tariff Board to meet, along with U.S. Consul General J. G. Foster, with representatives of the Ottawa government of Sir Wilfred Laurier, including Finance Minister W. S. Fielding. In line with his strategy of making the British Empire system "non-workable," Charles Pepper sought to press Canada to extend its intermediate, or French treaty, rate to the United States in return for the Payne-Aldrich minimum. Pepper recognized that in many products, especially metals and electrical apparatus, the United States already had the preponderance of trade and would not lose it by virtue of the 2.5 percent reductions in the French rate. But, as a matter of practicality and principle, the BTR did not want to waive its right to the Canadian intermediate or French treaty rate. Doing so would give European beneficiaries of Canada's intermediate rates an advantage in lines in which the United States was not yet dominant, especially in manufactures. In addition, if the United States and Canada exchanged other concessions different from or more favorable than the French rate in a separate agreement, it would call into question whether the United States had given European states most-favored-nation treatment in granting the United States' regular minimum tariff and might appear as a U.S. challenge to the British preferences in Canada. Thus, Pepper believed, the United States should seek the best agreement possible with Canada within the maximum-minimum format, focusing on the French rate as Canada's "minimum." Pepper also felt that if the United States secured France's own minimum tariff in its concurrent negotiations with that country, Canada would lose its advantages over the United States in the French market and therefore would have less motive to "maintain the Franco-Canadian treaty rates unimpaired as to French products entering Canada." Hence, the BTR sought to use the U.S. dual-tariff system both as an instrument of expansion in Canada and as a tool to ensure U.S. access to European most-favored-nation rates.[19]

The Canadians, however, were not easily swayed by the United States' offer of the Payne-Aldrich minimums and held out on conceding the intermediate rate. Here, the Tariff Board and the BTR came into conflict. Emery and Sanders recommended that the "policy adopted toward European countries should be given up in the case of Canada." The board wanted to offer Canada the U.S. minimum even without Canadian concession of the intermediate rate to strengthen the Canadian government and public's confidence that the United States was not seeking to dominate Canada. Certain that the application of the U.S. maximum to Canada would lead to a mutually destructive tariff war, Emery and Sanders hoped to preserve a basis for future concessions by making a unilateral concession to Canada. This the State Department vigorously opposed. Taft, agreeing, quashed an early concession of the U.S. minimum, telling Emery that he was "unwilling to 'eat dirt.'" Still, as he wrote his wife a month later, he was "very anxious" to avoid a tariff war with Canada and basically wanted a concession "upon which I can hang a decision . . . and make the announcement." Following Taft's lead, Pepper, Hoyt, and Emery convinced the Canadian negotiators that the United States would not grant its minimum tariff without some Canadian concessions. These the Laurier government provided in the form of reductions on thirteen items in their tariff, and the United States responded by issuing a proclamation of its minimum tariff in return.[20]

Taft attempted to portray the Canadian negotiations in the best light. He claimed that the reductions Canada had offered were on the most significant articles of competition between the United States and the intermediate-rate beneficiaries. Yet he also had to admit that the geographical proximity of the United States and Canada—that is, the implicit ability of the United States to dominate Canada's trade completely under reasonably favorable trade conditions—"justifies a different policy as to imports and exports between the two countries from that which obtains in regard to European and oriental countries." To secure the full intermediate rates of Canada, Taft believed, the United States would have to offer unusual and commensurately greater concessions on Canadian raw material exports that could be secured only through a reciprocity treaty.[21]

In promoting a Canadian reciprocity treaty Taft was conceding the principle of exceptional treatment of Canada, for which his advisers on the Tariff Board had argued, and he was seeking the same open-door ends outlined in the BTR memorandums, as well. Special concessions beyond the U.S. minimum tariff were both necessary and advisable, however, to gain the intermediate rate of Canada, Taft believed. As he later wrote

Roosevelt, reciprocity and a cost-of-production tariff that recognized the approximate parity of U.S. and Canadian raw materials production costs would allow Canadian natural products to flow freely into the United States. This would antagonize U.S. agricultural interests, but it was consistent, he said, with "the principle of protection as we laid it down in Chicago." Canadian reciprocity, Taft believed, would make that nation a raw materials hinterland of the United States—or as he put it to Roosevelt, it "would make Canada only an adjunct of the United States." In Taft's view, reciprocity "would transfer all their important business to Chicago and New York, with their bank credits and everything else, and it would increase greatly the demand of Canada for our manufactures." Taft added that he had seen "this as an argument against reciprocity made in Canada, and I think it is a good one."[22]

In effect Taft was including Canada in a neocolonial class with nations such as Cuba, which enjoyed similar special "relations of propinquity" that the United States treated as exceptions to the most-favored-nation structure. Here, Taft echoed his State Department advisers, who characterized Canada and Mexico as geographical "prolongations" of the United States and as "within the sphere of a North American commercial policy." Yet, of course, Canada, unlike Cuba, had substantial political autonomy that did not derive from—and in fact was partly defined in opposition to—U.S. intervention. Here, Charles Pepper's original prognostication in his "Open Door to Canada" memorandum might be considered prophetic. The failure of the Taft administration to pass the lower Payne rates may have pressed the Laurier government into forcing complete exchange of minimum rates into the reciprocity format. Although Taft would succeed at some political expense in passing reciprocity in the U.S. Congress, Canadian nationalists were able to highlight the neocolonial implications of a reciprocity agreement with the United States, as Taft had acknowledged. The Canadians rejected the agreement and the Laurier government. Thus, Taft's earlier inability in the Payne-Aldrich conferences to make the U.S. minimum a sufficiently "persuasive factor" to gain concession of the Canadian intermediate minimum may have impeded U.S. expansion into Canada through tariff measures and compromised the effectiveness of the U.S. dual tariff as an approximation of the European most-favored-nation system.[23]

During the Canadian negotiations, the State Department and Tariff Board were also testing the maximum-minimum system as a basis for adjustment of commercial relations with Germany. These negotiations were important because Germany's trade relations with the United States had been tentative and contentious for some years. During the tariff debates in Congress, the German ambassador in Washington, Count Johann von Bernstorff, had expressed to the State Department a substantial concern over the future of German-American commercial relations. Bernstorff's focus was the abrogation of the provisional agreement negotiated by the North Mission of 1906–7, which had granted Germany relaxations of customs valuation and had reduced rates on exports to the United States of certain German products. The particular value of the concessions was somewhat diminished when Secretary of State Root generalized them to all nations. But they were still of sufficient importance to Germany that when the concessions were rendered void by the new American tariff, the German ambassador declared that Germany had regarded them as a necessary part of the quid pro quo for the extension to the United States of Germany's conventional, or minimum, tariff. Thus, the entire question of U.S.-German commercial relations was reopened.[24]

The United States, for its part, was aware of German sentiments that would make the negotiation of a new tariff agreement difficult. German exporters feared that the Americans would use the tariff to seek repeal of all German restrictions on American meat products, a demand the protectionist German Agrarian party would be sure to use its power in the Reichstag to frustrate. In addition, German manufacturers were heavily dependent on low-price U.S. raw materials such as copper and petroleum, and they feared that intransigence by American exporters and German Agrarians would lead to a tariff war and consequent disruption of German industrial production. Knox had tried to placate the Germans after the passage of the Payne-Aldrich Tariff by reassuring their ambassador that the new tariff was not punitive in intent and demanded removal of only "undue" foreign discriminations, a concept that Knox implied would be interpreted elastically. Although the United States had powerful commercial weapons—the value of its domestic market to German exporters and the value of its raw material exports to German industries—State Department officials were aware that Germany was beginning to wean itself of its dependence on U.S. basic products. The Germans were investing heavily, Knox learned, in Austro-Hungarian oil fields in Galicia and in the Russian oil fields in the Caucasus. Because Germany had now established most-favored-nation and conventional treaty tariffs with these nearby countries, their resources could be expected to supply increasing proportions of German industrial needs, particularly under tariff conditions more favorable than those obtaining with the United States. Cognizant of these considerations and under pressure from German exporters, industrial nationalists, and domestic protectionists, the German foreign office was bent on pressing claims to an equitable exchange of commercial concessions with the United States. The State Department thus recognized that negotiations of pivotal importance were imminent, and it instructed its consular and diplomatic officers to collect information on German discriminations that State could use in the bargaining process.[25]

As it established itself in its Treasury Department offices, the Tariff Board also sought to gather information and to assure its participation in the negotiations scheduled for December 1909 between the Bureau of Trade Relations and the German embassy's commercial envoy, G. D. Waetzoldt. Treasury Secretary Franklin MacVeagh, who had informal jurisdiction over the Tariff Board, had expressed to Taft and Knox his resentment over the de facto exclusion of the Tariff Board from arrangements for the maximum-minimum negotiations, which had begun in November. In a letter to Taft, MacVeagh deplored the tendency of Knox's department to "take into its own hands the entire business of determining for the President the terms of agreement with . . . foreign countries, to the exclusion of the Tariff Board." Taft responded by instructing the State Department to develop positions, to communicate regularly with the Tariff Board, and to include the Tariff Board in the commercial negotiations. The BTR, under John Ball Osborne and represented by Department Counselor Henry M. Hoyt, was to take the lead in the conferences, however. The controversy between MacVeagh and Knox thus resulted in greater coordination between State and the Tariff Board, but it also set the stage for some differences of opinion and emphasis in the commercial objectives of negotiation.[26]

The Germans opened their tariff initiative along the lines intimated by Bernstorff—that is, by complaining that the Payne-Aldrich Tariff was punitive and had dropped concessions of particular value to German exporters. Furthermore, Bernstorff, taking a page from the dissatisfied U.S. reductionists, complained that with the failure to pass the Payne bill or House version, the U.S. minimum tariff failed to offer significant new concessions. The Germans also revived their argument that in retaining a treaty of reciprocity with Cuba that allowed a 20 percent reduction from the United States' minimum rate the Americans had favored a sovereign state with rates to which Germany, as a most favored nation, was also entitled. Soon, Baron Wilhelm Von Schoen, then in the German Ministry of Foreign Affairs, was pressuring the U.S. ambassador in Berlin, David Jayne Hill, with threats of the imminent application of German maximum rates. As the Americans discovered, the Germans were very reluctant to grant their own minimum tariff and to make particular concessions on nontariff discriminations such as the waiver of German sanitary inspection of American meat products in return for the Payne-Aldrich minimum rate. In part, their threatening rhetoric may have reflected the fact that the structure of the new American law prevented them from making definite demands with regard to particular U.S. rates, as they might in a commercial treaty system. The legislatively fixed, or "autonomous," U.S. tariff prevented this in principle, so the central issue of the negotiations, and of U.S. participation in European commercial systems, had become the concessions Europeans would make to get the U.S. minimum as set by Congress. That is, as Knox had indicated earlier to Bernstorff, the sole subject of negotiation was whether the Americans were satisfied with German concessions.[27]

The Americans had compiled a long list of German discriminations. These included the German refusal to accept American certificates of inspection of U.S. pork for trichinae and German demands to inspect U.S. canned meat products—a virtual prohibition, because German discretion in opening cans could spoil the product and cripple the trade. In addition, the United States claimed discrimination in the German government's railroad freight rates and in flour drawback regulations. The State Department and the Tariff Board agreed on the basis of the U.S. negotiating position—the equivalence of the U.S. minimum tariff rate with the German conventional rate. Knox immediately dismissed the German argument on Cuba by maintaining that Cuban relations with the U.S. were a special case of quasi-colonial relations and were thus not applicable in the present instance.[28]

There were differences in BTR and Tariff Board approaches to Germany, however, and in a sense they reversed the positions the two groups had taken regarding Canada. In general, the BTR now took the conciliatory approach. Recognizing the tariff rates of the Payne-Aldrich Act as comparatively high, the State Department compensated by softening its demands. Like Nelson Aldrich, who in September and October 1909 was discussing the tariff that bore his name at state dinners in several European capitals, the BTR seemed to hope to bolster American public opinion of the tariff act by rapidly concluding the maximum-minimum negotiations. With respect to Germany, the BTR was prepared to leave aside the rail discriminations, flour drawbacks, and live cattle imports and to accept the extension of German minimum rates on only the salient U.S. exports, if the pork inspection statutes were waived. As State Department counselor Henry M. Hoyt put it, the United States in the negotiations should "be disposed to concede everything possible, and then if at the end negotiations fail . . . we shall feel . . . that we have done everything possible to avoid that result."[29]

From the outset, however, the Tariff Board insisted on a tougher negotiating position. The general position of the board, along with the Republican revision movement, had been to seek to use a dual tariff to elicit concessions from Europe as a way of differentiating its policy from the unilateral reductionism of the Democrats. Doubtless the Tariff Board members and the revisionist movement felt that the Payne-Aldrich rates were not as low as they might be to give the United States a persuasive minimum rate for exchange with foreign minimums; such substantial reductions in the tariff were to be the incentive for foreign concessions and were to rationalize the enforcement of maximums. Yet the revisionists had made the bargaining aspect of reduction a cardinal point of their strategy to sell tariff revision to expansionist capitalists, and they seemed pressed to respond to the constituency of exporting manufacturers and agricultural interests that had lobbied for its formation and expected it to win tangible concessions. The board's apparently harder line, then, was not necessarily a shift toward greater protectionism. Rather, it seemed to reflect the board's view that its constituency would scrutinize an official proclamation of an exchange of minimum rates more critically than would Congress or the general public.

N. I. Stone fired the board's first salvo by criticizing the BTR's willingness to accept the extension of German minimum rates on only important U.S. export items. If Germany, as a sovereign and most favored nation, was allowed to offer less than its complete schedule of conventional rates in return for the U.S. minimum, other European nations might be tempted to trim their own concessions. Stone also criticized the BTR's position from the vantage point of the German reciprocity treaty negotiated but not signed under the Dingley Act's section 4 provisions in 1907. That treaty, which Stone had helped to negotiate as part of the North mission to Germany, had gained the extension of the full German conventional tariff, relaxation of the meat inspection fees, elimination of pork inspections when U.S. goods were accompanied by U.S. certificates of inspection, readjustment of German rail rates for U.S. lumber products, and promise of consideration of live cattle imports. The treaty had not been submitted to Congress then because Root and Roosevelt feared its protectionist mood. The Payne-Aldrich minimum tariff, Stone contended, represented at least an equivalent concession to the 20 percent reductions of the 1907 Dingley reciprocity treaty. The United States thus would be conceding ground it had virtually gained if it failed to secure equivalent German concessions in the current negotiations.[30]

Tariff Board chairman Emery and board member Alvin Sanders were even more emphatic, writing to Hoyt that although the Tariff Board, like the BTR, desired to "avoid tariff wars with other countries," the maximum provisions in the Payne-Aldrich Tariff were "designed to force concessions . . . impossible to secure by ordinary diplomatic negotiation." They continued in the same vein by asserting that "the business interests of the country expect the Act to be used vigorously to secure better treatment for their products . . . [and] that the responsibility of the administration to such business interests should be given due weight." Much of the impetus for this posture may have come from Sanders and the meatpacking interests. In fact, Sanders produced a detailed memorandum arguing for special attention to the export priorities of the diverse American meat products and live cattle exports. These views were based in good part on an extensive conference with livestock and packing interests the Tariff Board had held in Chicago in early December 1909. In fine, then, the board was ready to use the maximum as a threat, especially in the light of the implications of the impending extension of the U.S. minimum to German export competitors such as low-tariff Belgium and Britain, which could be expected to expand into markets from which the Germans were excluded.[31]

Tariff Board and BTR disagreements on U.S.-German commercial strategy were resolved in conferences with Taft and Knox. The two agencies decided to make as a preliminary demand of the Germans the essence of the Tariff Board proposal: the complete German conventional tariff, waiver of the microscopic inspection of pork, and German agreement to import live cattle from the United States. The Germans refused to consider the cattle proposition and the full minimum, however. After several interchanges, the United States agreed to defer the cattle question, and the State Department delegates argued to Knox that the United States ought to accept the German stance as adequate for the extension of the U.S. minimum rate. But Knox accepted the Tariff Board view that although the German Agrarians would block cattle imports, the full minimum tariff could be obtained. A further meeting with the Germans was held in late January 1910. At this colloquy, the Americans held that the U.S. minimum rate constituted "most-favored-nation treatment practically as that expression is accepted in Europe." In other words, the Americans argued that the effect of granting the U.S. minimum was equivalent to the extension of unconditional most-favored-nation treatment. Although it must have appeared implicit that the United States had not formally renounced its conditional interpretation of the clause and thus technically was free to alter its policy, the Germans were intended to understand that the United States would not alter or impair the quality of its agreement with Germany because the U.S. minimum tariff would represent a constant and uniform rate in international commercial agreements. These assurances appeared to satisfy the Germans, who accepted the American demands for waiver of pork inspections and granted the full German conventional tariff on February 5, 1910.[32]

The new German agreement appeared to be a victory for the United States and for the Tariff Board in particular, because it was the insistence of the board that led to pressing of the full minimum agreement with Germany. Although the live cattle issue was again deferred, Sanders argued to both livestock producers and shippers who had a direct interest in promoting increased sale of U.S. meats to Germany that the question was just too touchy to press with the Germans at present, and that at least they had secured German promises to consider cattle imports in the future. For his part, James B. Reynolds considered that the negotiations had "ended very successfully."[33]

The agreement of 1910, it may be noted, was defined by Congress when that body set the terms of the American maximum-minimum system. But its details were worked out substantially by the executive branch, principally through the State Department and the Tariff Board. These agreements, unlike previous reciprocity treaties, required no subsequent congressional approval. Moreover, the framework of the negotiations, particularly as carried on by the Tariff Board, allowed for the input of interested industries, such as the meatpackers, independent of the legislative processes of committee hearings and tariff making and largely independent of public scrutiny. To this extent, and as the originators of the revisionist movement had hoped, the new arrangements had taken the tariff "out of politics," unifying U.S. commercial priorities and making them more effective and compatible with European commercial systems. In essence, the new policy instituted an implicit unconditional most-favored-nation principle without specific congressional approval.

The new tariff was also more consistent in its application; the concessions it offered did not represent accommodations to specific groups favored by the executive branch, such as the Merchants Association of New York, which had pressed for the export pricing clauses of the 1907 agreement. Rather it offered broader and less ambiguous advantages in the customs system, such as recourse to a Customs Court of Appeals (which the Merchants Association had opposed) and a fixed minimum tariff rate.[34]

Subsequent developments would show, however, that the German agreement of 1910, like that of 1907, was provisional. By late 1910, the United States was embroiled in a controversy over the export price policies of the German potash syndicate in which invocation of the U.S. maximum tariff was one of the few retaliatory options. By November 1911, the Germans were again excluding the United States from the concessions of their new conventions with Sweden and were selecting certain U.S. products—notably, boots and rubber shoes—for application of the German maximum rate. By 1912, Knox was wondering whether the maximum-minimum system could be altered toward selective enforcement of maximums—a question that was not answered until after World War I. In 1910, however, the view was toward resolving the crises of the previous decade. In this connection it is useful to consider briefly U.S.-French trade relations.[35]

The conclusion of successful maximum-minimum negotiations with France was vital for several reasons. France's exports to the U.S. had grown by 100 percent from 1899 to 1909 and exceeded U.S. exports to France. Yet during the decade ending in 1909, France had extended only parts of its minimum tariff schedule to the United States, by virtue of the agreements of 1898 (the Kasson Treaty, signed in 1899, even though not ratified by the U.S., was honored in part by France) and 1908 (an agreement pursuant to the U.S.-German agreement of 1907). During this period U.S. exports to France ranged between about 7 and 10 percent of all U.S. exports to Europe, and U.S. analysts believed that American trade to France could be expanded with more extensive reciprocity or a minimum tariff agreement—a point that the revision movement, conscious of France's less developed and hence less competitive industry, had made consistently during this time.[36]

By the latter part of the first decade of the twentieth century, the need for a U.S.-French commercial agreement became more urgent. The Canadian-French treaty of reciprocity, which exchanged the Canadian intermediate rate for the full minimum of France, was approved. By virtue of European unconditional most-favored-nation relations, France would generalize its concessions to Canada broadly to Europe; U.S. exclusion from a most-favored-nation agreement with France thus represented exclusion from an entire system of commercial advantages. Moreover, the tension between the United States and France was heightened by the termination of the U.S.-German understanding of 1907, which had been generalized to

France in 1908. Because France had not negotiated directly with the United States for these concessions and had thus not set a specific date for their expiration, the concessions were immediately voided by passage of the Payne-Aldrich Tariff, whereas the identical advantages had been guaranteed to Germany into 1910. The French retaliated against this by stipulating that their entire maximum tariff was to apply to all U.S. products as of October 31, 1909.[37]

Technically, U.S.-French commercial relations were at a low point in late 1909, an incentive in itself for U.S. negotiators to begin bargaining seriously. But obtaining an agreement with France also had a bearing on U.S.-Canadian trade negotiations. As Charles M. Pepper had argued in his Canadian tariff memorandum, if the United States could secure equal benefits in France to those available to Canadian exporters (for example, on agricultural implements, a major export item of both the United States and Canada), the Canadians would lose part of the French market and would thereby have less incentive to preserve Canadian markets for French products. Thus, a commercial agreement with France that broke into the European-Canadian most-favored-nation system could be highly beneficial to the United States in Canada as well as in Europe.[38]

The United States, through the efforts of the U.S. ambassador in Paris, Henry White, and Senator Nelson Aldrich, on tour in Europe following passage of his tariff bill, attempted to pacify French indignation over the expiration of American concessions by claiming that they were handcuffed by the nature of the 1907 agreement with Germany and the wording of the Payne-Aldrich Tariff. The U.S. statesmen tried to persuade the French that U.S. consumption of French products affected by the increased duties (including wines and other luxury products) would not be substantially curtailed before the two countries could come to a satisfactory new commercial agreement. U.S. diplomats also went on the offensive, waxing indignant over French discrimination against U.S. paraffin exports. Aldrich and White assured the French that the United States would not demand the entire French minimum tariff but that the United States only sought to ensure the absence of "undue" discrimination against articles in which the United States was "interested." The French were to anticipate that the United States wanted to apply its minimum tariff to France, Aldrich confided at a dinner meeting with members of the Bank of France. Although State Department officials believed that Aldrich had given away a bit too much of the U.S. position, they approved Aldrich's and White's general representations to the French.[39]

The final American-French negotiations saw the Americans demand equalization of U.S. and Canadian rates on agricultural implements, French acceptance of U.S. pork inspection certificates, and, the Americans hoped, French permission to import live American cattle. In early 1910, the French agreed to the essence of the American proposal, granting minimum French rates on about eighty tariff items in which the United States was "interested." Included were cottonseed oil, U.S.-inspected pork, and U.S. sulfur. In all, the United States did not gain a literal extension of the complete French minimum, but the general character of the agreement paralleled that made with Germany. The United States thus finally had a French treaty of the sort John Kasson had negotiated ten years before. At least temporarily, the United States had advantages equivalent to those of the European most favored nations and had extended its own minimum tariff unconditionally in return.[40]

By April, the maximum-minimum negotiations were complete, and Taft was announcing that proclamations had been issued to 134 countries; the State Department published a résumé of the agreements in June. Although actual negotiations had shown that the new U.S. minimum tariff was not quite equivalent to an unconditional most-favored-nation clause, and that special agreements would continue as aspects of U.S. policy, the implementation of the maximum-minimum clauses did represent a singular step toward a modified commercial open door and a real departure from the predominant treaty format of American commercial agreements of the nineteenth century. Meanwhile, the Tariff Board, which, overshadowed by the BTR, had been disengaging itself from the maximum-minimum process since late March, now moved on to concentrate on its cost-of-production investigations.[41]

10 The Tariff Board and the Tariff Movement, 1909–1912

Do not expect too much of your Tariff Commission. Do not think that it is going to operate as an artificial deity that will separate you from all your tariff troubles. Not all the sins in making tariff laws are sins of ignorance.
—Congressman Samuel W. McCall, Address to the Convention of the National Tariff Commission Association, January 1911

In concluding maximum-minimum tariff agreements with foreign nations, the Taft administration had defined, at least for the moment, the United States' international commercial posture. The new Tariff Board had played a role in this process by participating in and advising on the negotiations with other countries, particularly Canada and Germany. In fact, the Tariff Board had been created under the authority of the maximum-minimum provisions, "to secure information to assist the President in the discharge of the duties imposed upon him by this section, and the officers of the government in the administration of the customs laws."[1]

Yet the maximum-minimum negotiations were only a preliminary function of the board. Using the vagueness of the Payne-Aldrich statute, which authorized him to appoint such people "as are necessary," Taft hoped to use the Tariff Board as a seed for a permanent domestic tariff commission that would help shape future domestic legislation and as a counterweight to the "political" tariff making of the House Ways and Means Committee. To this end, the board was charged with implementing the heretofore vague professions of the Republican party that tariff rates should represent "the difference between the costs of production at home and abroad."[2]

Developing a working cost-of-production tariff system required the board to consider the intricacies of industrial cost accounting. Here, the technical aspects of a board-administered cost-of-production tariff were laden with political-economic implications. Defining costs of production required making empirical investigations of actual industrial operations that would render tariff rates measurable for compliance with a specific policy and formula.

Thus, cost-of-production tariff making would involve the continuous cooperation of industrial and mercantile interests with the tariff investigatory body. In addition, policies that attempted to measure and enforce an equilibration underwrote general acceptance of a flexible protectionist strategy in international tariff negotiations. Such a strategy would put the resource of information and the power of regulation—not only of trade but of business as a whole—more firmly in the hands of state agencies. Hence, the validity and workability of the cost-of-production tariff theory itself became an important underlying source of tension and conflict not only between those who favored differing tariff levels but also between those who favored differing degrees of state intervention in political-economic affairs.

The Tariff Board and
the Revision Movement

Because it was formed as a consequence of a new tariff, and because a cost-of-production tariff was still largely theoretical, the Tariff Board could not contemplate immediately formulating revisions of tariff rates. Necessarily its role had to begin as investigative, as it had been in the maximum-minimum negotiations. In addition, where the board had been secondary to the Bureau of Trade Relations in international affairs, it also was secondary to the House Ways and Means Committee and the Senate Finance Committee in domestic matters, and it depended on yearly appropriations from a Congress only barely willing to tolerate an agency whose day-to-day operations it did not control and whose functions impinged on those of its own committees.

Nonetheless, the board clearly was intended to assume and expand functions that the congressional committees had exercised by compiling statistics, updating commercial information, and holding hearings in the development of a new tariff bill. And unlike the House Ways and Means Committee, whose concentration on the tariff was episodic and marked by partisan agendas, the board was to work on a more systematic and extended basis, open to sustained input from industrial and trading groups interested in tariff matters. Thus, in Chairman Henry C. Emery's view, despite the ambiguities of its mandate, the board was a useful experiment, because it was freed of "statutory provisions" and the political pressures of framing a new tariff bill. It could evolve and work out its relations with Congress and capitalist groups so that a permanent commission under more direct legislative scrutiny would have greater credibility and chance of success.[3]

Much of the board's effectiveness and claim to unique value would depend on its ability to offer greater accessibility to and mediation among interests whose official outlet for tariff views historically had been limited to appearances at Ways and Means Committee tariff hearings or irate letters to members of Congress. Board members thus were anxious to develop the support of the business and exporting manufacturers. In fact, one of their first official acts was to travel to meet with exporting industry associations, including the livestock and agricultural machinery interests in the Midwest and chemical manufacturers in New York. They also corresponded with steel exporters.[4]

The board tried to systematize its links to export-oriented businesses by developing its relations with the National Tariff Commission Association (NTCA), a group that had been informally constituted as a "Committee of One Hundred" in the wake of the February 1909 Indianapolis Tariff Commission Convention. Actually, the organization really came to life only in late 1909, through the efforts of H. E. Miles, the Wisconsin implement maker and National Association of Manufacturers (NAM) official. To meet as an NTCA executive board, Miles recruited Henry R. Towne, of Yale and Towne Lock Company and the Merchants Association of New York (MANY); John Candler Cobb, the Boston railroad and shipping entrepreneur; and Daniel A. Tompkins, the Charlotte, North Carolina, textile manufacturer and NAM activist. The revived NTCA now had the immediate goal of supporting the investigations of the Tariff Board and the long-term objective of expanding and legitimizing the board as a full-fledged tariff commission. The NTCA's official statement actually called for a tariff commission that would not have the power to make laws or rates, as such. But, the statement continued, the commission should administer a staff of technical cost-finding experts and could act in a judicial sense "in making findings on the evidence so obtained, and in compiling reports of conclusions so reached."[5]

The matter of structuring the state's relations with its foreign trade constituencies was a concern of both the Tariff Board and NTCA executive committee when they conducted a joint session at the Tariff Board offices in February 1910. The groups listened with interest to N. I. Stone's lecture on the only existing permanent tariff commission, the German "Imperial Commission for the Elaboration of Economic Measures." The thirty-two-member German group, the board's chief economist told the meeting, was a permanent commission drawn from the major segments of the German capitalist class, as represented by the major German agricultural, manufacturing, and commercial organizations. The German chancellor appointed half the membership, but the industrial organizations appointed the other half from within their own ranks. Thus, the commission was organized not along political party lines but "along lines of industrial cleavage."[6]

Members of the board and the NTCA were interested in the Germans' commission because of their own ambitions to enhance the influence of the board in a way that avoided giving it an overt partisan complexion. It was in that spirit that Secretary MacVeagh had appointed the board, noted Emery; that all three current members turned out to be Republicans was not strictly intentional, but perhaps constituted in present political circumstances a liability. In fact, board and NTCA executives generally agreed at their meeting in early 1910 that the board should add at least two more full members to diversify its personnel and facilitate its work.[7]

Despite their agreement on the advisability of expansion, board and NTCA leaders differed on how the board was to grow. H. E. Miles, the "radical" NTCA executive committee member, wanted the board to evolve rapidly toward the German "industrial cleavage" model. Miles proposed that the National Council of Commerce (NCC), a quasi-governmental business advisory organization that had originated in 1907 under Roosevelt and Oscar S. Straus in the Department of Commerce and Labor, might be the model for, or even serve as, an official industry affiliate of the Tariff Board. In its present status, under the Department of Commerce and Labor, the NCC was enjoined from political discussions, and hence from making any direct pronouncements on tariff rates and methods. But linking it specifically as a special advisory body to the Tariff Board would create a connection between industrial and commercial groups and state tariff policy along the lines spoken of by Stone. The affiliation, Miles asserted, would not usurp the board's powers but simply would enable the industrial and commercial groups to exert a "corrective effect" on the government-appointed board through "friendly criticism."[8]

Miles's suggestion was more than idle speculation. It revealed a serious ambition to use state power to effect the goals of foreign-trade-oriented proprietary manufacturers. Largely because of the leadership of Secretary Straus and NCC Chairman Gustav H. Schwab, both connected with New York commercial and shipping interests, the NCC's dominant constituents were the same foreign trade groups that were involved in the tariff reduction and tariff commission movements: the NAM, the Meat Packers Association, the New York Board of Trade and Transportation, the National Association of Implement and Vehicle Manufacturers (NAAIVM), the New England Shoe Manufacturers Association, and the MANY. As a member of the NAM, Miles had become a part of the NCC advisory committee in 1908. By June 1909, with his influence as a tariff reductionist within the NAM under challenge, Miles had become the chairman of the NCC's Committee on Foreign Commerce. He used the position as a platform to repeat his theme: The United States was a "huge stevedore," depleting its natural resources by shipping them abroad at low cost for foreign manufacture. Assisted by N. I. Stone, then the Commerce Department's tariff expert, Miles studied German commercial practices and sought to encourage the development of a parallel structure for commercial information gathering within the Department of Commerce and Labor. Here, his efforts were parallel to those of the Commerce Department Bureau of Statistics. Under O. P. Austin, the bureau had been working as a commercial information-gathering body for several years, in cooperation with secretaries Straus and Root.[9]

The desire to use the NCC as a lever to influence tariff questions was not unique to Miles. George L. McCarthy, New York representative of the American Meat Packers Association and Miles's fellow NCC Foreign Commerce Committee member, suggested to Miles that he promote the NCC to the Tariff Board as a source of information and that the NCC should attempt to influence the maximum-minimum negotiations of the Bureau of Trade Relations and the Tariff Board with Germany. The configuration of interests in the NCC necessarily gave representation to corporate-oriented export groups as well as to proprietary manufacturers. Miles's radicalism, then, was somewhat defensive, or perhaps just realistic, and his letters to Emery on trust-related subjects had some of the same plaintive militancy of his earlier correspondence with NAM president and tariff revisionist James W. Van Cleave. Yet, as Gustav Schwab had reported to Emery, Henry R. Towne and the executive committee of the NTCA generally sought to head off demands for immediate tariff action by "impetuous tariff reformers" within their Committee of One Hundred in favor of a longer-range, more institutionalized strategy supporting a tariff commission. Understanding the situation, Miles thus sought to develop and preserve a voice for proprietary interests rather than to capture the tariff-making institutions for proprietary manufacturers.[10]

The board could do little in the way of developing its structure or pursuing its cost investigations during the maximum-minimum negotiations and before a new appropriation was made to supplement its original $75,000 funding. But after the negotiations, the board obtained Taft's permission to travel to Europe to investigate tariff commissions there. Emery visited Germany, Austria-Hungary, and England between May and July 1910; Reynolds traveled from July until October. On his return, Emery presented a lengthy disquisition to Secretary MacVeagh and President Taft on the operation of European tariff investigatory bodies and on how the projected operation of the Tariff Board would work within the distinctive parameters of the American political system and Taft administration commercial policy.[11]

Emery's report was clear evidence of the development of his thinking about the uses of a tariff board and of a cost-of-production tariff system. The German and Austro-Hungarian boards, falling under the Imperial Department of the Interior and Ministry of Commerce, respectively, used interdepartmental cooperation to accumulate statistical material, Emery reported. Where the European boards differed from extant American practices was in scope of study and administrative structure. Their investigations, highly touted in the United States, were similar to ones carried out by the Census Bureau's census of manufactures and were actually not so extensive as those contemplated by the Tariff Board. It was not so much in tariff "science" but in the practical elaboration of measures that the Europeans had the advantage of the Americans, Emery believed. They supplemented their statistical and commercial information not by boards of accountants but by frequent conferences with interested industrial parties. Here, European commission experts served as effective mediators among industrial and commercial interests because, unlike the Ways and Means Committee and its open tariff hearings, they were making tariff inquiries as technicians and not as political theater for public consumption. In Germany, therefore, there was "not the same feeling of attack and defense," of "tension on the tariff question." This was not to say, of course, that the European tariff-making systems were apolitical. Government officials who mediated among competing groups—as in Germany between exporting manufacturers and the Agrarian party—had to take into account the political influence of those interests. The difference was that these demands were worked out in private before a tariff measure was given to the full legislature: "That is, the tariff commissioners can go down on the floor and work out the details of compromises beforehand." Thus, unlike Stone and Miles, who emphasized the proportional and collegial representation of manufacturing interests in the board, Emery focused on the capacity of the board to formulate and represent executive branch conceptions to Congress. The continuous working relationship between executive experts and legislators, as Emery noted, insulated the executive from criticisms of the kind leveled at Taft after the Winona speech.[12]

As Emery pursued his European studies, H. E. Miles sought to promote his conceptions of the proper role for an American tariff commission in countering the trusts. Miles tried to get Emery to meet with English cotton entrepreneur Sir William Holland and with Sir Hugh Bell, president of the British Iron and Steel Institute, as a way of getting information on U.S. dumping and the costs of production of British goods. Although welcoming Miles's involvement and offers of help and minimizing the differences between their views, Emery preferred to keep the Wisconsin manufacturer at ideological arm's length. Emery resisted Miles's repeated entreaties to press investigations in the context of the trust issue. Emery wrote to Miles that the board's tariff work should go forward, but that the cause of a permanent commission would be hurt if the board were to "go off at half-cock because of political pressure." And in reporting to Taft and MacVeagh, Emery strongly advised against any need for the board to exercise any legal power to call for the books of businesses. Rather, the board should seek cooperation, Emery believed. Foreign tariff officers lacked compulsory powers, Emery said, and he feared, though he did not specify, the uses to which an independent "inquisitorial authority" might be put. A better check on business veracity, he suggested, might be through comparative statistical work by experts and application of information, gained from "knowledgeable men in the industry," that would highlight anomalous testimony.[13]

Miles's conceptions of a regulatory tariff commission with subpoena and "semi-judiciary" authority were thereby rejected, though within the general membership of the NTCA, Miles's calls for a "commission with power" remained popular. His suggestions for creating a link with the NCC were rejected as well. Rather than set up the NCC as a quasi-governmental organization with a strong voice for proprietary foreign-trade-oriented manufacturers, Taft and Commerce and Labor Secretary Charles Nagle deemphasized the NCC's connections with the government. They appointed John Candler Cobb, the NTCA president, as part of an NCC reorganization committee, with the purpose of broadening the base of NCC support and of transforming it from a quasi-governmental group into an independent business lobby. Cobb quashed discussion of a quasi-governmental role for the NCC or a similar body in tariff matters, and in 1912, the NCC became the United States Chamber of Commerce. Thus, the Taft administration ruled against giving the Tariff Board direct political-economic power but would recognize expansionist capitalists generally by seeking to moderate protectionism by developing the board's investigative capacities.[14]

Cost of Production: Theory, Practice, and Denouement

In its less than three years of operation as a tariff and industrial investigatory body, the Tariff Board was dogged by controversy—attacked by Democrats as avoiding wholesale reduction, by protectionists as too reductionist, and by Insurgent Progressives as discriminating against the Midwest. Moreover, the ideologies of tariff revisionism were divided by internal debate among Republican revisionists and against increasingly powerful conservative Democratic tariff theorists on the implementation of cost-of-production investigations.

From the outset, the Tariff Board's effort to determine the costs of production of various manufacturing operations was an ambiguous task. Although appreciative of a speech Taft gave in New York supporting the board's efforts, Chairman Emery was skeptical of Taft's idea of creating a definitive tariff "Glossary." In a February 1910 meeting with the executive committee of the NTCA, Emery had already alluded to "the care one must take in talking about the cost of production." Emery opined that Taft talked "more glibly about it than the business man. . . . He does not recognize that there is a difference in cost in January from that in March; a difference in cost on the north side of the street from the south side."[15]

The board's European trip convinced Emery that a cost system had to be more complex than Taft envisioned. Noting that there were no effective European precedents for cost-centered investigation, Emery wrote Mac-Veagh and Taft that among American businesses as well "there is no uniform method of cost accounting," and on specific practices of cost apportionment "the most expert opinion is divided." He cautioned Mac-Veagh and Taft that "in many lines of industry, products are not standardized," and even "a progressive manufacturer . . . sometimes finds it impossible to determine [his] exact cost of producing any particular article." Thus, "cost of production" could be gotten only approximately, through averages and by applying "business acumen." This meant, Emery told Taft, that the board could not produce the kind of "Glossary" that would allow the "layman unfamiliar with the conditions of the industry casually [to] look up a certain article under an alphabetical list and get a clear understanding of the situation regarding that article in relation to the tariff, including its cost of production." Emery stated that there could be no useful "translation of the tariff into English" as Taft had hoped, and that the tariff could not be so "taken out of politics." In any case, Emery said, the tariff was at base a question of economic policy: "Should certain industries be protected or not?" Power to make such decisions should not be vested in a Tariff Board, Emery believed. The board should remain subordinate to "properly constituted authorities."[16]

Nonetheless, Emery said that economic studies would be highly useful from a policy standpoint. The board could prepare a technical glossary of production figures, calculating the relation of production to imports and exports, and figuring the current protection ad valorem for individual articles of the tariff. This expert's glossary, Emery believed, could serve in commercial policymaking, especially if it was distanced—as it was in Europe—from "political advantage in the play of party interests."[17]

The board was determined, then, to proceed with designing and implementing an investigatory system, if not for using it as a definitive authority for tariff rate setting. In this effort, the board depended explicitly on the "business acumen" of Henry R. Towne of the NTCA and the MANY. President of the Yale and Towne Lock Company, Towne had been an engineer and manager for more than forty years. He was also the originator of the Towne-Halsey plan of shop management, a precursor of the Taylor System. Emery had Towne meet with the board and its economists in September 1910 for a long session on cost accounting. Towne's system was to sum labor and material as prime cost, to add factory expenses to that sum to arrive at shop cost, commercial expenses to that to get actual cost. It was agreed by Towne and the board that interest on invested capital and dividends, however, would be excluded "to place all the returns from all the manufacturers on a comparable basis in this respect." Depreciation would be included in factory expenses.[18]

Detailed as his methods of accounting were, Towne shared the original views of Emery that finding precise costs in many cases would be difficult; he had not gotten his own exact costs in lock manufacture yet, he said. For it was one thing, Towne noted, to deal with an industry that was "devoted to [producing] one thing; where everything is going into a hopper . . . and coming out of the spout," and quite another to deal with "the great majority of products in large manufacturing plants" that are "greatly diversified." Moreover, Towne believed that getting costs for any but a few domestic products "would approximate to a physical impossibility" because factories making "hundreds or even thousands" of diversified products would require cost estimates on all of them to apportion effectively factory and commercial expenses. He advised that the board go ahead with its effort for the "educational experience it affords . . . and still more because its abandonment now without longer effort would be misinterpreted by the public." But cost finding should be limited to "a comparatively small number of simple and staple products."[19]

Towne and the board agreed that ascertaining the size of the producing unit would help the board to get a sense of whether an anomalous low production cost of a trust, for example, represented an artifact of accounting. But Towne's recommendation for the legitimate and reasonable activity of a tariff commission was to concentrate not on costs and the productive process but on a "second line of approach" focusing on "minimum selling price" to be obtained from large distributors and importers. "I believe that here can be found a basis for comparing domestic and foreign values, which will be more accurate and reliable than any attainable information concerning 'costs of production.'" Towne averred that manufacturers would respond more readily to price inquiries, without a need for compulsory investigation and regulation, and that anomalies between domestic and foreign prices would be readily apparent.[20]

In marked contrast to the Towne-Emery view, H. E. Miles continued to maintain that actual production costs were central to a tariff commission and that if the board departed from the "principle of the difference in cost" it would "at once fall into a mire of uncertainty, and be substantially where the Ways & Means Committee were in their hearings, . . . without chart or compass." Although not present at the September NTCA meeting with the board, Miles argued in a lengthy letter that his own thirty years of experience as an implement manufacturer and his long work in the revision movement had convinced him that there was a useful comparability in costs in most industries, and he cited figures on vehicles, flax, chemicals, steel, and others. Miles acknowledged that "in an absolute sense you cannot arrive at the difference in cost here and abroad." But he believed that it could be gotten to within 3 percent or so, and he argued that the variations were "minute and immaterial, [differences in] quality considered." However much they protested, manufacturers knew their costs fairly well, Miles maintained, and for the Tariff Board to cede authority in this area would be a "complete undoing" of its work. Miles was as acerbic on the idea of using selling prices as an index to protection as he had been on using customs price appraisers as members of a tariff commission during the push for the Beveridge commission bill in 1908. Prices, he believed, were far too subject to manipulation by businesses—especially trusts, domestic and international. "The basic principle is of cost, not of distribution," he insisted.[21]

Together with the NTCA, Towne made recommendations on the proper personnel and methods to carry out studies. The NTCA suggested multiple investigations, travel by the board abroad to review European tariff commission efforts, and advertising to recruit experts from within industries, "but quite broadly so as to avoid placing men who are controlled" by special interests. Possibly as a first step in a push for a permanent commission, Emery went public on the investigation strategy of the Tariff Board. It would comprise the experts' glossary on supply, production, and use of tariff schedule articles; inquiries into actual costs of production for selected products, mostly raw materials; and studies of prices at home and abroad. Thus, although the board and Taft had vetoed giving proprietary manufacturers a quasi-governmental voice in controlling tariff rates and the board appeared to be shifting its focus somewhat away from costs of production, they continued to develop an independent governmental system to monitor claims for tariff protection.[22]

Emery had written Taft that a staff of about twenty temporary experts would be necessary to carry out the investigations. To fulfill these ends, the board hired a staff to work in assembling the glossaries and assessing the "cost of production" of various articles of domestic manufacture, including cotton and wool textiles, chemicals, oils and paints, and newsprint and pulp. In addition, studies on metals, including iron and steel, leather products, grains, and other agricultural products were begun. At times, over seventy experts were working for the board.[23]

"Field investigations" began in earnest in October 1910, with board experts circularizing and visiting plants and requesting books and records. The pulp and paper and wool investigations were the first priorities. In November, the board met with its agents in New York and advised them on questioning of manufacturers. There was to be no coercive power, but the cost inquiry was to be presented as equivalent to a direct request from the president. In addition, the board worked to secure returns from the Bureau of Corporations under the corporation tax regulations.[24]

Almost immediately, however, the Tariff Board's future was called into question by the Democrats' capture of Congress in the 1910 elections. The Democrats were expected to oppose the board and a permanent commission as attempts to "legitimize" protection. Probably as an effort to pass a tariff commission before the new Sixty-second Congress convened, Republicans introduced bills to create an expanded permanent commission. James W. Good of Iowa and Irvine Lenroot of Wisconsin offered bills that were the subject of Ways and Means hearings in December 1910. Good's bill, reflecting the views of House Insurgents, and a bill that succeeded it by Nicholas Longworth of Ohio, both offered the Miles-Beveridge formula of a "semi-judiciary" commission with power to subpoena witnesses and business records. These powers had failed in tariff commission bills Miles and Beveridge had submitted in 1908 and during the 1909 House-Senate conferences on the Payne-Aldrich Tariff. Now they were opposed again by Republicans aligned with the administration. John Cobb favored only the Lenroot bill's version of compulsory testimony, which would give a commission no power to apply penalties for noncompliance. And at the NTCA's convention the following month, Ways and Means member Samuel W. McCall of Massachusetts rejected the subpoena power and the cost emphasis adamantly. Although favoring a permanent commission, McCall opposed arming a commission with "inquisitorial powers to summon every businessman in the United States, perhaps . . . to testify under oath as to his business secrets, if not to the public . . . to some political organization or . . . dishonest administration which may . . . happen to be in power." Taft, however, seemed to temporize publicly on subpoena power. Seeking popular support and addressing the same convention at which Miles, to applause, had called for a "commission with power," Taft opposed power for a commission to compel testimony but allowed the acceptability of the Lenroot formula giving contempt powers to Congress.[25]

The cause of a full-scale commission was aided by the Tariff Board's work on pulp and paper and raw material production costs. During the Canadian reciprocity debates in February 1911, the board was called on by the Senate to prepare a report on commodities named in the Canadian reciprocity treaty. By drawing in its field agents, the board was able to prepare the report, principally on wood products and wheat and other grains, between

February 23 and 28, 1911, and thus demonstrated its ability to provide quantities of relevant statistical material at congressional request.[26]

But the Longworth bill failed to pass the Sixty-first Congress in the face of Democratic filibustering and protectionist opposition. In effect, this was one of the last gasps of the "insurgent" or "radical" construction of a tariff commission within the Republican party. Despite the defeat of a permanent commission, Taft gained a large appropriation for the board to carry its work through the year ending in June 1912. On March 4, 1911, Taft also appointed two Democrats to the board to buttress its nonpartisan image. These were University of Virginia economics professor Thomas Walker Page and former Georgia congressman and attorney William M. Howard, whom Taft had intended as members of an expanded permanent commission.[27]

But the appointment of the Democrats to the Tariff Board did little to allay the political conflicts over the tariff. By pressing for Canadian reciprocity, Taft had alienated the Insurgents. Although Taft believed that Insurgents' opposition to Canadian reciprocity showed their calls for tariff reductions to be hypocritical and self-centered, Insurgents such as La Follette saw Taft's willingness to promote reductions on Canadian wheat and his failure to press effectively for broader reductions and a regulatory tariff commission as discriminating against the Midwest. Taft had suggested the usefulness of a tariff commission in conducting piecemeal investigations and tariff revisions, as a way of forestalling logrolling on rates. Now the Democrats sought the same high ground by offering the so-called pop-gun bills, seeking to revise Schedule K, the wool schedule, which Taft had admitted was too high. By passing the bills before the Tariff Board's wool study was complete, the Democrats sought to show that revisions could be accomplished without a commission and to place Taft in the position of having to veto reduction measures. In addition, once the study was complete, La Follette and Albert Cummins of Iowa introduced bills to compete with Republican Ways and Means bills in the House and the Senate Finance Committee's wool bill. H. E. Miles encouraged Taft to support La Follette's bill. Miles was here supporting an Insurgent position, which held up higher wool rates than the Ways and Means version and demanded that Taft use the revised Schedule K as a lever to gain reciprocal concessions in the German tariff. But Taft identified the Ways and Means bill as the only one representing Tariff Board findings, and no wool bill was signed into law.[28]

In addition to the political confusion surrounding the board, prominent academic experts on the tariff, notably Frank W. Taussig, James Laurence Laughlin, and H. Parker Willis, all Democratic reductionists, had been sniping at the board since its inception and now began to attack the Republican cost-of-production theory on political-economic grounds. A University of Chicago economist had suggested in 1909 that the history of comparative cost investigations dating back to the Arthur Commission was really ephemeral. Then, in 1910, Taussig described cost finding as a "vogue" and caricatured the logical problems of a cost-based policy by demanding to know whether cost inquiries were intended to advise on the appropriate protection for "grapes grown in Maine" and other marginal enterprises. Equalizing costs led to inefficiency, Taussig said, because such a system could be used to protect weak producers. This, of course, was really a more extreme statement of the Republicans' own reservations, and Taussig did suggest some economic investigations to clarify whether "undue" or monopolistic gains were at issue or to demonstrate efficiency that would undermine tariff needs altogether. Laughlin attacked costs as an unnecessarily complicated method of reduction and suggested that the international movement of goods now involved requirements for balances of payments that made horizontal comparisons of production costs of like goods less useful. Others, including Willis in 1911, cited Ricardo's doctrine of comparative advantage as the basis of international trade to denigrate the relevance of cost-based theories. Finally, in 1912, Willis, quoting Taussig, attacked the implicit labor theory of value in the cost studies and brought marginal utility theory to bear on cost-based tariffs by maintaining that costs of production did not measure the effective basis of exchange in laws of price and demand. Willis in particular seemed to stress the dangers of a commission's "scientific" cost inquiries because they would force public adjudication among producers of differing efficiencies. Taussig, too, returned to the fray by attacking the Tariff Board's wool report.[29]

This political and ideological onslaught put the board on the defensive. Emery disputed Willis in front of the American Economic Association, saying that "we have been forced against our will into the limelight when it was our desire to keep quietly at work . . . until the results of such work could be presented and stand on their own merits." Emery and other board members and staff supported the board's work in the maximum-minimum negotiations and cost investigations. The exhaustive wool report, issued at the end of 1911, contained statistics on production in the United States and foreign producing nations and a glossary for Schedule K. It also revealed discriminations in classifications, and hence duties, on certain foreign wools. The pulp and paper report, issued earlier, represented surveys of 116 mills, about 80 percent of the productive capacity, and arrived at what were called reasonable figures for costs with cooperation from mill owners. And the cotton report of March 1912 revealed conclusively that, no matter how calculated, the rates of the Payne-Aldrich Tariff on yarns and threads exceeded the differences in the production costs of the principal competitor, England. L. D. H. Weld, an economist who had worked on the wool report and who later taught at New York University and the University of Minnesota, also disputed Willis's interpretations of Ricardo and Cairns's doctrine of comparative costs and marginal utility. But in the theoretical dispute, he, Emery, and other board members ended closer to their Democratic critics when they suggested that costs might be considered as one aspect of tariff studies of "relative prices, costs, and all other market conditions."[30]

By 1912, the Republican revisionists were in stalemate, with neither Taft nor the Insurgents having sufficient power to effect legislation. The Democrats, in control of Congress, now were preparing to formulate a new tariff bill under the leadership of Ways and Means Chairman Oscar Underwood of Alabama. Taft invited Underwood and the Tariff Board to meet at the White House in an effort to preserve a role for the board, the dual-tariff system, and the cost investigations in a new tariff. But Underwood, supported by a legislative majority and by the broad-scale academic attack on the cost theory, anticipated a single, lower tariff made without the board. When Congress refused to renew the board's funding, it had to disband in June 1912.

Ironically, Roosevelt, as the 1912 candidate of the Progressive party, now took up the cause of the tariff commission along "German" lines as he had not done during his administration as Republican president. He called for a schedule-by-schedule downward revision as a means of forestalling tariff logrolling and for expert investigation with "ample powers" to secure information. But this revisionism was now outside the Republican party, and with the defeat of Roosevelt—and Taft, as well—by Woodrow Wilson, it was stymied. Thus, the board's work was never consummated directly, although in the board members' view, politics were more responsible than was dissent from the utility of economic tariff investigations. The sine qua non of any commission, commented L. D. H. Weld, would be recognition by the Democrats of protection and not revenue as the basis from which tariff policies would be effected. The Underwood Tariff recognized this basis by substantially lowering, but not eliminating or placing on a "revenue" basis, the rates of the Payne-Aldrich Tariff. Moreover, as the conclusion of the present study seeks to show, the Wilson administration confirmed the revisionist view of executive branch tariff investigations in finally creating the U.S. Tariff Commission, on which Frank Taussig, William S. Culbertson, and Thomas Walker Page served. But so far as dual tariffs and cost studies were concerned, the Tariff Board had become, in James B. Reynolds's words, "a mere prologue without a play."[31]

11 Conclusion
Revisionism's Ambiguous Legacy, 1912–1916

We are sending altogether too great an amount of our natural resources out of the country in the raw state. More of them should be manufactured here, and would be if, by our own laws, we did not forbid American producers and manufacturers to meet foreign competition on even terms.

—John D. Ryan, president, Anaconda Copper Company, to the National Foreign Trade Council, 1915

Between 1897 and 1912, tariff revisionists took crucial steps toward transforming the U.S. tariff system. As Treasury Secretary Franklin MacVeagh claimed in 1909, the Republican party had "changed its front." That is, despite an apparently slow pace of reductions, the party had committed itself to downward revision and had abandoned the staunch home-market protectionism that had dominated party ideology and legislative activity in the late nineteenth century. As MacVeagh said, the party had inaugurated a "new tariff epoch."[1]

In place of the high-protectionist home-market system, the Republicans had implemented a dual tariff via the maximum-minimum provisions of the Payne-Aldrich Act. This system, intended to allow the United States to secure concessions from foreign nations in exchange for a uniform lower U.S. rate, was portrayed by U.S. policymakers as equivalent to the European or unconditional form of most-favored-nation treatment. The new U.S. minimum was not a marked reduction in terms of the expectations of the Democrats and many revisionists, but it served as the basis of more than a hundred conventions with other nations.

The salient weakness of the maximum-minimum system was that it proved rigid in operation. This flaw may have been built into the system by the Taft administration's failure in 1909 to influence the Senate to lower the U.S. minimum rate sufficiently to approximate European minimums and by the fact that U.S. maximums could not be invoked "flexibly"—that is, selectively by commodity—but only as a full-scale retaliation. These shortcomings of the Payne-Aldrich Tariff as a basis for enduring commercial relations forced the debate back into Congress. There, disputes over reciprocity arrangements and individual schedules reopened the political conflicts that an executive-based maximum-minimum tariff system operating through a Tariff Board was intended to moderate. In an atmosphere of contention, a Democratic majority quickly abandoned the dual tariff in favor of a wholesale reduction and a single rate. Thus, although the Republican revisionists had provided a sophisticated infrastructure, they could not establish it firmly. Nonetheless, the Democratic single rate resembled a Republican minimum rate more than it did a revenue-tariff rate. Moreover, by 1912, Republican tariff policy had effected what both section 4 reciprocity of the Dingley Tariff of 1897 and the Democratic Wilson-Gorman Tariff of 1894 had not: a consistently applied moderation of U.S. rates. In carrying out the moderation, the Republican revisionists had undermined Grover Cleveland's taunt that protectionism could not be revised by its "friends." Thus, they underscored their leadership credentials and the credibility of the overall U.S. effort to establish a U.S. open-door ideology among the world economic powers.

In revising the U.S. tariff stance, President Taft had challenged the legislative dominance of tariff making by creating a prototype tariff commission, the Tariff Board. Appointed under provisions Taft had worked with a protectionist legislature to insert into the Payne-Aldrich Act, the board played a dual role—advising the president on the maximum-minimum provisions and developing an investigatory system for assessing tariff rates based on "differences in costs of production" in the United States and abroad. Like the dual tariff, the Tariff Board was an unstable first attempt at systematizing U.S. tariff policy, one that quickly became enmeshed in partisan contention. Yet, here, too, the Taft regime established an initial direction in U.S. policy by shifting the emphasis of tariff investigation from the legislature to experts in the executive branch, a function modeled on European precedents. In addition, creating a commission enhanced executive branch facilities for bringing academic economics into the process of tariff investigations and for establishing systematic contacts with foreign-trade-oriented businesses.

Thus, by 1912, despite the political furor over Taft's tariff policies, the question had become not whether to revise the tariff downward, but how. Typical of the consensus that underlay the partisan conflict were the revised wool bills introduced in Congress in 1912: Different versions of Schedule K were offered by Taft Republicans (through the Ways and Means Committee), Progressives, and Democrats: All purported to be "scientific" and equitable reductions.[2]

The Transition to Wilsonian Policy

The policies of the Roosevelt and Taft periods provided an important impetus for later commercial policies—one that was accelerated in some respects by World War I but that had emerged clearly before the United States entered that conflict.

Although the Democratic House majority abolished the Taft Tariff Board in June 1912, Congress preserved the principle and practice of economic tariff investigations under the aegis of the Bureau of Foreign and Domestic Commerce (BFDC), created as part of the Commerce Department from the merger of its bureaus of statistics and manufactures in August 1912. In part, the Democrats may have acquiesced in this act as an alternative to an executive-based tariff commission. It was Congress, not the executive, that delegated the BFDC to conduct studies under cost investigation provisions originally given the Bureau of Labor in 1888 but long inactive because of protectionist opposition. Thus, although the BFDC was an independent executive-branch institution, its mandate was similar to the seconding of clerks to the Ways and Means Committee that had supported the promulgation of the Payne-Aldrich Tariff of 1909.[3]

The BFDC investigations were in subject generally continuous with those of the Tariff Board, in the view of BFDC chief Edward Ewing Pratt. They concentrated on textiles, especially hosiery and knit goods, men's clothing, and cotton-spinning machinery, but also covered sugar, pottery, and glassmaking. The BFDC "broadened the scope of the inquiries and made them complete economic surveys of each industry studied—not mere analyses of costs of production," Pratt claimed. But the appropriation from Congress for BFDC's cost-of-production section was meager—about $50,000 for fiscal 1916, compared with the $250,000 given the Tariff Board for fiscal 1912. Thus, the BFDC could not undertake the extensive "glossary" work of the board, employ "outside" experts, conduct hearings and conferences, or (partly because of the outbreak of the world war) investigate foreign costs. Pratt defended the BFDC work in relation to that of the Tariff Board as "no less comprehensive, in comparison with the magnitude of the industries studied." But he readily admitted that the BFDC's subordinate status, low funding and salary levels, and restricted investigative tools made it far less effective than a full-scale tariff commission would be.[4]

A full-scale commission, however, was not on Woodrow Wilson's immediate agenda. Like most Democrats, Wilson had opposed creating a formal tariff commission on the grounds that revision could be accomplished more swiftly and equitably by wholesale congressional reductions. This strategy the Democrats had followed during the Taft era, in the electoral campaign of 1912, and in the making of the Underwood Tariff, which Wilson signed into law in October 1913. Wilson's attacks on Republican tariff doctrine and his stress on the tariff issue in part may have reflected deference to powerful southern Democrats such as Oscar Underwood of Alabama and John Sharp Williams of Mississippi, who continued to oppose a commission and a systematized rate structure as "protectionism reduced to a science." Yet although Wilson, like Theodore Roosevelt, had political debts to senior party members, his own views, again like Roosevelt's, were not derived fundamentally from partisan considerations. In fact, Wilson's image of the gradual reduction of the tariff as a means to economic expansion echoed theorist David Ames Wells and owed much to the ideas of Harvard economist Frank Taussig and American Manufacturers Export Association (AMEA) official William C. Redfield.[5]

Although the Democrats rejected a commission, the newly organized, nonpartisan U.S. Chamber of Commerce supported one and distributed a complete poll on the issue to its membership almost as soon as the Underwood Tariff was signed. The bill the chamber supported was one that Sereno E. Payne, former House Ways and Means Committee chairman (now ranking minority member), had offered in 1911. That bill had passed both houses but was tabled when the session expired before the House could consider Senate amendments. Reintroduced twice as an amendment to the wool and general excise tax bills in the following session, the Payne measure succumbed to partisan conflict. As written, it would have endowed a tariff commission with subpoena power and the authority to carry out the cost-of-production investigations begun by the Tariff Board. The chamber members polled approved it by a vote of 724 to 9, but the Democrats in Congress remained suspicious: Though sedulously nonpartisan, the chamber seemed to echo the views of the now-defunct National

Tariff Commission Association (NTCA), which had worked openly in support of the Republican Taft's tariff policies.[6]

Over the first three years of the Wilson presidency, demands for a tariff commission continued among business groups, especially as the nation lapsed into recession. No longer, however, was the commission idea led by tariff radicals such as H. E. Miles. After supporting Roosevelt's Progressive party candidacy, Miles was working within the National Association of Manufacturers (NAM) and the U.S. Chamber of Commerce on the subject of industrial education, the cause with which he would be associated for the remainder of his public life. N. I. Stone, now out of government, also worked with the chamber, but on U.S. agricultural statistics. James Van Cleave had died in 1910. The NAM itself, under the leadership of John Kirby, Jr., and George Pope, had become generally more protectionist. In addition, extensive congressional investigations of NAM lobbying, the result of revelations in 1913 by former NAM agent Martin M. Mulhall, kept the NAM relatively quiet on the tariff commission issue.[7]

Now, however, the Merchants Association of New York (MANY), which had proposed a tariff commission as early as 1907, became a major force promoting a commission and in other matters of national economic policy. Here, the original MANY supporters of the commission such as the small manufacturers, dry goods wholesalers, textile dealers, commission merchants, and shippers were joined by a marked influx of new members representing nearly all the major New York commercial banking and investment brokerage firms and large exporting corporations, including the National City Bank; Kuhn, Loeb; U.S. Steel and the Steel Products Export Company; International Harvester; Westinghouse, Western Electric, and General Electric; and the Guggenheims. The MANY assisted the commission campaign with a large meeting of its Members Council that included speeches from former MANY president and NTCA treasurer Henry R. Towne, Senator Thomas P. Gore of Oklahoma, and John H. Fahey of the U.S. Chamber of Commerce.[8]

By July 1915, the U.S. Chamber of Commerce had enlisted broad support for a commission, and a Tariff Commission League (TCL) had been founded in Chicago. The new league shared some members with the tariff commission movement of the Roosevelt-Taft period: Eugene N. Foss, former governor of Massachusetts; J. M. Studebaker, automobile manufacturer and member of the National Association of Agricultural Implement and Vehicle Manufacturers; Nicholas Murray Butler, president of Columbia University, who had spoken out in the NAM newspaper in favor of tariff revision and a commission; and members of the MANY. Like the earlier tariff commission movement, the TCL deplored "unscientific" legislative techniques and upheld the "German system of tariff making" as the epitome of nonpartisan tariff organization. But whereas the commission drive of the first decade of the twentieth century had been organized around the NAM and insurgent Republican proprietary businessmen, the TCL of 1915, also seeking popular support, had a quite different executive core. Rail and financial figures were prominent: George W. Perkins, the former Morgan bank man and Roosevelt supporter; James J. Hill of the Northern Pacific Railroad; William Hamlin Childs of the American Coal Products Company and the MANY; E. P. Ripley of the Atchison, Topeka, and Santa Fe Railroad; H. U. Mudge of the Chicago, Rock Island, and Pacific Railroad; E. J. Buffington, president of Illinois Steel (part of U.S. Steel); Cyrus McCormick of International Harvester; C. S. Funk, former export manager of Harvester; John V. Farwell, Yale-educated Taft associate, backer of Marshall Field, and central banking advocate; and Waldo H. Marshall, president of the American Locomotive Company and first vice-president of the MANY. The TCL was headed by H. H. Gross, head of the National Soil Fertility League. Still, the push for a commission was stymied, as Wilson continued to oppose a commission, and the Democratic Ways and Means majority resisted new legislation.[9]

Another factor diverting the flow of energy for a tariff commission was that some of the tensions between proprietary and corporate capitalists that had marked the tariff issue of the Roosevelt-Taft period had shifted under Wilson into the issue of combination in American export trade and the activities of the Federal Trade Commission (FTC). In part, this diversion devolved from the passage in 1913 of the reductionist Underwood-Simmons Tariff. At first, the Underwood Act blunted immediate demand for tariff changes. But the recession that followed made the Democratic tariff less satisfactory as an adjunct to economic expansion, especially because, as passed, it had no retaliatory provisions and therefore seemed to make the United States vulnerable in the atmosphere of economic nationalism engendered by the European war. Calls for U.S. measures against anticipated European postwar dumping proliferated. In the absence of a formal tariff commission and a multiple or flexible tariff system, some suggested that the FTC control such measures, whereas others wanted to develop special exclusionary antidumping legislation, and still others saw the need to study the problem as an argument for a tariff commission. The outcry against possible postwar dumping was especially marked in industries such as chemicals and dyestuffs; newly stimulated by the interruption of Central European exports, they wanted immediate guarantees of protection against postwar German price cutting. But fears of European economic nationalism were not restricted to a few interested industries. They reflected a broader preoccupation with questions of postwar world commerce in the context of European state-capitalist and cartel combinations. Germany was already poised for a "new conquest of the world's trade," observed Charles A. Conant in 1915, in part because its state ownership of railways provided an inbuilt "opportunity for discriminating tariffs on exports" and threatened the overall stability of the British free-trade system.[10]

Concerns such as these helped spawn the movement for U.S. export cooperation, which drew in many of the prominent advocates of a tariff commission. Here, the FTC took an important role in investigating foreign trusts and cartels and in promoting the modification of the Sherman and Clayton antitrust acts, which seemed to prohibit explicit U.S. combinations in export trade. The FTC, although nominally domestic in focus, thus became an important early forum and instrument through which capitalists sought to redefine the contours of American export trade. Ultimately, this led to the Webb-Pomerene Act of 1918, which legalized export combinations. Although often treated in the context of the war, the export combination issue, seen in retrospect, recast issues that had been central to the tariff disputes of the previous decade. Now, however, in the second decade of the twentieth century, procorporate and "cooperationist" proprietary businesses led the legislative initiatives, whereas proponents of the proprietary business sector played a more secondary and defensive role in seeking to shape the legislation and institutions to sustain an independent power vis-à-vis corporations.[11]

In examining the origins and early work of the FTC, it is useful to note that procorporate efforts to define, and thereby regularize, administration of antitrust statutes had an early prominence in the proposed Hepburn bill of 1908, formulated by the National Civic Federation (NCF) in close cooperation with President Roosevelt and Commissioner of Corporations Herbert Knox Smith. This measure was vehemently opposed by the proprietary businesses of the NAM and by New York commercial interests, including the MANY. In addition to deploring the Hepburn bill's exemption of labor unions from the Sherman Act, opponents feared the establishment of executive-branch regulatory powers within the Bureau of Corporations and the Commerce Department and the extraordinary latitude this gave to corporations by default of definitive legal regulatory principles. Although the Hepburn bill failed, the NCF proposals were realized in slightly altered form when President Wilson, allied with former Progressive party leaders and NCF figures such as Seth Low, came out for a "quasi-judicial" Interstate Trade Commission as a more acceptable means to stabilize and limit the boundaries of trust—and antitrust—activity. In January 1914 Wilson portrayed this approach as a means of applying the rule of reason derived from the Taft-era antitrust cases while avoiding the "menace of legal process." The final FTC measure signed by Wilson in September 1914 established a bipartisan commission assigned to review annual corporate filings on activities and competitive practices and empowered to investigate, hold hearings, and regulate corporate practices under the rule of reason doctrine. The passage of the Clayton Act in October further defined FTC authority with regard to price discriminations, tying contracts, holding companies, and interlocking directorates.[12]

Capitalists in general were much more supportive of the more explicit FTC and Clayton legislation than they had been of the Hepburn bill. The MANY was now solidly behind the legislation, for example. President Henry R. Towne testified that the proposed commission would be an important adjunct to small business, but he carefully stipulated that his group opposed more radical proposals empowering a commission to scrutinize corporations only above a certain capitalization. The ultimate purpose of a commission, Towne declared, should be to regularize and define the application of the Sherman Act in terms of "unreasonable" restraint of trade. The MANY also delegated a special committee, headed by Towne, Waldo H. Marshall, William Hamlin Childs, and attorney Gilbert H. Montague, to support and advise the FTC. Where capitalists of imperial imagination remained particularly critical was in the failure of the legislation to rule specifically on the issue of combination in export trade, which many businesses were beginning to approve as means of competing with European combinations.[13]

The maturation of central banking legislation, as well as the passage of lower tariffs and the evolution of trust regulation, brought the foreign-trade combination question and proprietary-corporate relations to the fore. Between 1908 and 1912, the National Monetary Commission (NMC), drawing on ideas posed earlier by Charles Conant, outlined the need for foreign branch banking as an important aspect of the attempt to establish American commercial and financial power. In 1910, the New York Chamber of Commerce, the American Academy of Political and Social Science, and the MANY cosponsored a conference to discuss and pursue NMC goals in promoting American foreign branch banking. The framers of the Federal Reserve Act, following this impulse under Wilson, provided the authorization for major U.S. banks to establish foreign commercial operations and to rediscount foreign bank acceptances. These capabilities would assist American exporters in financing their businesses domestically and in withholding information on American credit and financing practices and commodity movements from the foreign institutions that had dominated commercial finance in neutral markets. In September 1916, bank branching was given further latitude by an amendment to the Federal Reserve Act that allowed interbank cooperation in foreign branch activities.[14]

The leading commercial banks involved in foreign expansion, such as the National City Bank (NCB) under Frank Vanderlip, and the major foreign trade organizations, such as the AMEA and the National Foreign Trade Council (NFTC), welcomed bank cooperation but believed that industrial export cooperation was also necessary to developing U.S. international commercial and investment potentials. They had begun to work in 1914 to see that the Sherman Act was amended to complement the enhanced banking cooperation provided by Federal Reserve legislation. Secretary of Commerce William C. Redfield, a former officer of the AMEA, proposed and secured authorization for the FTC to study the effects of foreign export cooperation and to make recommendations on U.S. responses. It is worth noting, however, that this study was not an innovation of the Wilson administration but an expansion of the Bureau of Corporations' Foreign Trusts Investigation, which also contemplated American industrial combination measures.[15]

Taking a lead in offering a discussion agenda for the extensive FTC investigation of export cooperation was the MANY committee on the FTC headed by Henry R. Towne. According to MANY attorney Gilbert H. Montague, the organization had drafted preliminary legislation on industrial export combination as early as 1914. Montague, presenting the MANY committee report to open the FTC's June 1915 New York hearings, expressed the hope that the FTC study would "reveal means to enable competing manufacturers to cooperate in export trade, as done in Germany." Also appearing at the FTC hearings as supporters of export combination legislation were Henry Davison of the Morgan Bank; W. S. Kies of the NCB; Joseph P. Grace, of the W. R. Grace shipping lines; Edward M. Herr and Maurice Coster of Westinghouse; Waldo H. Marshall and Charles Muchnic of the American Locomotive Company; and John D. Ryan, of the

NFTC and Amalgamated Copper, a holding company for Anaconda Copper and other properties that were closely allied to Frank Vanderlip of the NCB, the Rockefeller and Standard Oil interests, and Guaranty Trust.[16]

Ryan and Vanderlip led the propaganda for legislation to modify the Sherman Act as part of their effort to assure corporate and bank leadership in systematically developing foreign trade and investment. The new NCB-organized American International Corporation (AIC), an investment trust intended to control transportation, financial, and construction facilities for foreign trade, was their instrumentality in this expansion, one that they wished to protect from antitrust prosecution via definitive legislation. The $50-million corporation solicited board members from Anaconda; NCB; Kuhn, Loeb; Chase National Bank; Guaranty Trust; Standard Oil; Armour; General Electric; W. R. Grace; the Union Pacific and Northern Pacific Railroads; and International Harvester. It purchased or formed shipbuilding and construction businesses and absorbed some of the older export commission houses such as G. Amsinck and Company as a means of developing its expertise in South American finance. NCB also began publishing a magazine, the *Americas*, to attract U.S. exporters to the bank. The NCB solicited and secured the informal blessing of Wilson and Redfield, and Vanderlip hired O. P. Austin of the Commerce Department as the NCB's chief statistical adviser.[17]

In the export business sphere, constructions of the ultimate purposes of combination and the scope of enabling legislation differed. Export commission houses doubted the motives of some of its proponents, as William Harris Douglas and Welding Ring testified before the FTC. Industry-bank cooperation would tend to eclipse their role in foreign trade finance and marketing. The NFTC, too, was divided. The group had supported a resolution in May 1914 calling for modification of antitrust laws to permit cooperation, but members were at odds over whether export cooperation required definite legal guarantees. In a January 1915 debate with John D. Ryan, Ingersoll-Rand chairman William L. Saunders, a member of the NAM who had been part of the U.S. Chamber committee that had drafted a proposal for cooperation, publicly supported combinations as most advantageous to small businesses. Saunders argued that current laws, regulations, and precedents already permitted legitimate foreign trade cooperation— that is, cooperation that did not affect domestic trade. Under the supervision of the FTC, argued Saunders and other business executives such as Harrison C. Lewis of the National Paper and Type Company, smaller businesses should be able to cooperate to economize on selling and market-seeking expenses, qualify for U.S. tax advantages, and engage in selling contracts in defined territories that would protect their profitability. The FTC, Saunders proposed, could administer current regulations to see that "the little fellow has a show equal to [the big combination]." In short, he maintained that the best way to intercapitalist consensus on the export combination issue was to support U.S. cartel-like arrangements to guarantee smaller businesses' place in the foreign market structure. Lewis, too, favored cooperation arrangements to support small manufacturers and wanted the FTC to assign exclusive rights to foreign contracts to small businesses' export associations. But Lewis, like many of the "cooperationist" businessmen, was caught between two millstones: He specifically opposed a more radical proposal by Massachusetts business statistician Roger Babson to limit the capital of combinations to a million dollars or less, because he believed this would inhibit the activities of businesses established in foreign trade and would prevent them from expanding by soliciting outside investment.[18]

Modifying the Sherman Act as a means to export combination was a cause Ryan and Vanderlip had taken up specifically more than a year before the FTC hearings. Ryan and the NCB, like the U.S. Chamber and Saunders, assiduously promoted export combination as an option for small capitalists, "for every business man in the country," who wished to join with each other and with the large commercial banking institutions to conquer foreign—particularly South American—markets. But unlike those who wanted structural legal or regulative guarantees for small businesses, such as Saunders and Lewis, Ryan worked to secure a consensus for industry-bank and interindustry combinations without limitations on the size of the company or the product exported. In fact, Ryan fulminated privately at proposals that would empower the FTC to give the combination legislation an explicit antitrust or pro-small-business spin. Writing to NCB Vice-president James H. Perkins in September 1914, Ryan fumed that the Manufacturing Chemists Association's support for a "political" commission to pass on export combinations, would end up prohibiting only the "conspicuous combinations. . . . People big enough to count for anything will not be allowed to work with other big people, and small manufacturers, on the plea that they have not the facilities or the means to fight for export trade by themselves, will probably get permission to combine, which is not at all what we are working for or what the country needs."[19]

Yet despite the clear intention of Ryan and Vanderlip to further the interests of the corporate AIC and NCB, they continued to cultivate smaller businesses to affirm and participate in a corporate-led expansion. Ryan exhorted smaller businesses to form "syndicates for the purpose of organizing selling campaigns abroad." Speakers at foreign trade conventions extolled the opportunities for smaller manufacturers and export houses in foreign trade and spoke of them in terms of specializing and retaining niches that the larger corporate enterprises did not or could not fill. Export combination in raw materials, in particular, Ryan argued, would enable U.S. producers of natural products to challenge the market strategies of foreign buying combinations. In addition to representing an interest-centered market strategy with its own historical rationale, this line of reasoning appeared to be aimed at assuaging the finishing manufacturers' complaints of U.S. corporations' dumping as an impediment to independent manufacturers' foreign sales. Now Ryan sounded a familiar note, saying that the United States was "sending altogether too great an amount of our natural resources out of the country in the raw state." Ryan argued that "the way to a constructive national policy" was to "draw a sharp distinction between domestic business . . . and business with the export markets in view . . . and make plain in our laws that all activities leading to the sale of our goods abroad are free from the restrictions that hedge the others about."[20]

Thus, Ryan, speaking for Anaconda, the NFTC, and the NCB, had come to express nearly the exact phraseology of David Parry and H. E. Miles of the NAM in the tariff commission agitation of the early 1900s. Yet now the language was appropriated for the reorganization of proprietary concerns within a corporate-led framework and not as an attempt to support the independent power of proprietary business. This was a realization of the expansive vision of U.S. capitalism so clearly expressed in James Deering's dismissal of the "crossroads" manufacturer in 1901. Lest anyone misunderstand, Ryan continued by noting that the "big people" required definitive, permissive export-cooperation legislation to remove the threat of antitrust prosecution or regulation: "American business men and heads of corporations will not attempt to increase their business and extend the benefits to their employees if there is any feeling of doubt upon their part as to their right to do so without violation of law or . . . of incurring penalties." In short, Ryan implied that small companies could expect to receive the advantages of alliances with large corporate, shipping, and financial institutions only if the export trade legislation assured that the FTC would not be used to constrain or counterbalance corporate export consolidation. "The law should be defined," said Ryan, "and the time is now propitious to make the definition."[21]

The FTC maintained close touch with the NCB's foreign trade experts, and the FTC report and survey, issued in 1916, strongly supported the broad Ryan-NCB construction of export cooperation, noting that "the Commission has been strongly impressed with the effect that the doubt as to the application of the antitrust law has had in the formation of cooperative export organizations among American manufacturers and producers." Although the FTC admitted that many smaller manufacturers eschewed foreign cooperation because they did most of their foreign marketing through export commission houses, the FTC interpreted its survey to mean that direct cooperative representation "with other small manufacturers is the best solution of the difficulty before them."[22]

In Congress, the export combination bill sponsored by E. Y. Webb of North Carolina and Atlee Pomerene of Ohio met concerted opposition mainly from midwesterners such as Albert Cummins of Iowa, George Norris of Nebraska, Dick T. Morgan of Oklahoma, and Knute Nelson and Andrew Volstead of Minnesota. As they had in associating the tariff and trust issues, they voiced skepticism over the latitude this legislation afforded "monopolies," whose power abroad might enable them to turn and devour their domestic competitors. Now, in wartime, they warned of the dangers of adopting "German" methods in trade. Like the export commission merchants and radical proprietary businessmen, the congressional critics were skeptical of the ultimate motives and fruits of corporate consolidation, and they managed to prevent passage of the Webb-Pomerene measure in 1916 and 1917. But smaller cooperationist manufacturers such as H. C. Lewis joined with the NFTC in supporting the Webb bill, and the U.S. Chamber and the MANY also endorsed positive legislation to remove doubts on export combination. Their support of the definitive and broadly permissive legislation demanded by the larger corporate capitalists in the Webb bill helped the measure to override objections in Congress in 1918. The final legislation did provide for FTC supervision of export associations and empowered the FTC to prosecute exporters who engaged in practices that clearly infringed on domestic competition. Still, the major thrust of the act was to relax antitrust and Clayton Act strictures regardless of the size of the combining entities. This empowered large corporations and commercial banking and industrial combinations far more than it guaranteed an independent role in the foreign market structure to small businesses or commission houses. Like the FTC itself, then, the Webb-Pomerene Act had adopted the form of the "semi-judicial" regulation advocated by the more radical progressives but had carefully circumscribed the judicial or political power of the commission in the defining legislation. President Wilson aptly described this process as substituting "the milder processes of helpful counsel for the harsh process of the law."[23]

In September 1915, Wilson wrote Ohio Governor James M. Cox that the BFDC and FTC comprised the full tariff "machinery" necessary. But as the 1916 election loomed, it appeared that the tariff and European dumping issues might be used to defeat the incumbent because the party might be portrayed as having pulled the retaliatory teeth of the Republican legislation. Pressures for a commission from Wilson's political allies and business organizations increased. Within the cabinet, secretaries Franklin K. Lane and William G. McAdoo leaned toward a commission. So did Agriculture Secretary David F. Houston, a self-described "Cleveland" Democrat and former student of Frank W. Taussig. Houston got the influential Harvard economist to support a commission, as did the academic leaders of Columbia, Yale, Johns Hopkins, Stanford, and the University of California. During the Taft era, Taussig had used marginal utility theory and the doctrine of comparative advantage to scoff at a commission with regulatory authority based on cost-of-production studies. But now he mused that a commission "could render important services" in assisting Congress to carry out policy by centralizing statistical information and organizing testimony on tariffs, classifications, and European commercial practices that could affect U.S. trade. Although Taussig continued to oppose a tariff commission with powers like those of the FTC or Interstate Commerce Commission, he now appeared amenable to a commission staffed by "independent persons . . . of larger caliber than can now be expected as sub-officials in the departments." This suggested that Taussig saw advantages to removing the tariff functions from the BFDC and FTC and centralizing them in a commission, as long as this did not support a commission with "political" policymaking or regulatory powers.[24]

The influence of his cabinet and the academics appeared to shift Wilson's view, and it was Houston's draft of a bill, worked out with Taussig, that Wilson forwarded to the House and Claude Kitchin of North Carolina. Wilson followed the Houston-Taussig formula of a nonjudicial commission and defended the idea against Commerce Secretary William Redfield's initial reluctance to cede functions of the BFDC to an independent agency and fear that the tariff would be "politicized" by a commission. Although Taussig had publicly dismissed the "preparedness" issue, Wilson centered his defense of a new "Tariff Board" on the grounds of the "extraordinary and far-reaching changes which the European war has brought about." This approach may well have reflected Wilson's view, but it was also the most politically appropriate stand, given his previous statements and the continuing opposition of southern and revenue-only Democrats, including Kitchin, to a permanent tariff commission. In fact, southern Democratic hostility forced Wilson to sidestep Kitchin and Underwood and have second-ranking Ways and Means Committee member Henry T. Rainey (D.-Ill.) introduce the bill. In addition, Wilson may have sought to placate "progressive" procommission forces who had been supporting his emphasis on a regulatory politics removed from proprietary capitalist control. These included Cyrus McCormick and a large number of the Progressive party's 1912 platform committee, which had endorsed a tariff commission, but excluded "Insurgents" such as Albert B. Cummins of Iowa and Miles Poindexter of Washington. Although favoring a new board, the Insurgents continued to seek a commission with power to adjust rates, to base investigations on a cost-of-production formula, and with commissioners who would receive salaries and exercise authority equivalent to those of the FTC officials.[25]

It is relevant that however much political considerations led Wilson to stress the war's "changed conditions" to justify a new tariff commission, the factors that Wilson enumerated in two public letters to Kitchin justifying his shift were thoroughly consonant with those that had motivated the prewar Republican revisionists. In addition to bureaucratic functions of coordinating information and advancing a nonpartisan tariff "science," a new Tariff Board, Wilson wrote, would "throw light from every possible angle on the tariff relations between the United States and foreign countries, the existence and effects of discriminating duties, commercial treaties and preferential provisions, the effects of any special or discriminating duties that might be levied by the United States." By 1916, Wilson was seeking to capture the initiative; he endorsed antidumping legislation and a tariff commission under Democratic auspices. In February, he declared to a foreign trade audience, "I am not interested in the doctrine of protection [or] the doctrine of free trade. . . . The facts of commerce and industry [have] nothing properly to do with party politics at all." Wilson told the U.S. Chamber of Commerce that he intended to put the resources of the government behind market expansion. In July, Wilson affirmed the flexible tariff philosophy and wrote to the president of the Illinois Manufacturers Association that a commission was a nonpartisan means "to make the question of duties merely a question of progress and development, a question of . . . facilitating and helping business and employing to the utmost the resources of the country." Wilson's commitment to foreign market expansion thus moved him toward support of a commission and tariff systematization from his earlier low-tariff viewpoint, just as the Republicans' commitment to expansion had moved them toward revision and systematization from the home-market stance. The tariff commission measure sponsored by Rainey passed as part of a larger revenue measure, and on September 8, 1916, Wilson authorized formation of a tariff commission.[26]

Wilson's appointments to the new U.S. Tariff Commission (USTC) paralleled Taft's efforts to shelter the Tariff Board from excessive partisan criticism. Wilson, assisted by Treasury Secretary McAdoo, originally sought Henry C. Emery, the chairman of the Tariff Board under Taft and a respected Yale economist, as chairman of the USTC. After Emery refused, Frank Taussig was chosen and was joined by Daniel C. Roper as vice-chairman (he soon resigned to head the Internal Revenue Service), and by William S. Culbertson and Thomas Walker Page, both of whom had served on the Tariff Board. Also appointed were Edward P. Costigan, a former Colorado Progressive who supported Wilson in 1916; William Kent, a former California Progressive who also supported Wilson; and David Lewis, a former Pennsylvania coal miner and Maryland congressman. Of these, Costigan still supported cost-of-production investigations as the primary basis of tariff legislation.[27]

The new USTC was largely insulated from taking an active role in shaping congressional tariff politics by its nonjudicial construction and by the general consensus of its mission as informational. The commission thus confirmed Wilson's intention to lead the Democrats away from the revenue-only position, the ideological shibboleth of their nineteenth-century politics, and to endorse officially the "revisionist" and executive-centered conception of a tariff system that the prewar Republicans had shaped as part of the United States' twentieth-century international strategy. Combined ultimately with a "cooperationist" framework established for export combination, Wilsonian trade policy had both absorbed and expressed the main forces of Republican revisionism.

Expansion and Equity

The ideological history of the revisionist movement as it arose in the early years of the twentieth century may be seen in one sense as a struggle to achieve hegemony against an entrenched home-market protectionism, as a movement to systematize an internationalist component of U.S. economic policy. Yet it may be productive as well to reflect on the history of revisionism in the context of its implicit tension between expansion and equity.

In the early period of tariff activism, 1897–1901, the term reciprocity took on an almost mythological cast. For the NAM and other groups, reciprocity promised to be a new and more "benignant" god that would unify and transcend the lesser deities of protection and free trade. Expansion, supported by reciprocity and fueled by American resources and productive power, would sustain the American "commercial invasion" of Europe and so enrich all—large capitalist and small. Such were the expectations of NAM president Theodore C. Search and harvester manufacturer James Deering, leaders in the early reciprocity movement. In their views, reciprocity served the "greatest good for the greatest number"; equity thus was a consequence of expansion. Industries "injured" by the reductions with Europe in the Dingley Tariff's section 4 would be few, and expansion would cushion the conflict between capitalists.

The NAM's somewhat delirious expansionism, referred to ironically as "reciprocity fever," was accompanied by calls to apply the "open door" to U.S. commercial policy and by warnings of European reactions to an inflexible U.S. protectionism. The movement may have drawn on the new sense of unity and purpose among Republicans and Gold Democrats that followed the defeat of Bryan and Populism in 1896 and that accumulated during the conquest of Spain in 1898 and the passage of the Gold Standard Act in 1900. Moreover, the Republican party had long used reciprocity as a counterweight to Democratic popular appeals against overprotected "interests." Republicans, though passing high rates in the Dingley Tariff, now appeared to be required to deliver on the promises of their critiques of the Wilson Tariff during the 1890s—that it was better to start with high rates and then "bargain them down." Thus, McKinley, Kasson, and the NAM worked toward reciprocity with a sense of urgency.

The failure of the Senate to pass any of the Dingley section 4 reciprocity treaties marked the end of a phase of the revision movement. As formulated in this period, reciprocity in competitive products lacked a sufficiently broad base of support to ensure passage of commercial treaties in the Senate, where a two-thirds majority was required. Moreover, it was programmatically too weak to unite disparate capitalist interests. In part this was because of the momentum and tenacity of protectionist opposition and the internal divisions of the movement—agricultural exporters against raw material importers, and so on. In addition, agreeing to reciprocal treaties meant accepting diplomatic terms of an agreement; the French treaty ended by excluding U.S. machine tools and industrial leather belting, industries that had been supporting reciprocity with one eye on their "new god" and the other on their main chance in the French market. Largely cut off from the treaty-making process and deprived of the support of McKinley at a critical juncture, the push for reciprocity faltered, illustrating that demands for class unity, the open door, and other forms of ideological special pleading were inadequate preparation for instituting what amounted to substantial social changes.

Between 1902 and 1907, revisionism gradually revived, acquiring increasing effectiveness by shifting its emphasis from lobbying the legislature for commercial treaties to pressing for changes that would increase executive influence in tariff affairs. European maximum-minimum tariffs now appeared to the NAM and others as models for U.S. revision because executive control over the second tariff rate would assist in removing the tariff from the logrolling or congressional tariff system and would free agreements from the requirement for congressional approval. In addition, revisionists pursued another executive-centered strategy by seeking customs accommodations with Germany. Here, American expansionists, including the MANY, the American Reciprocal Tariff League (ARTL), President Roosevelt, Secretary of State Root, and Census Director S. N. D. North, were seeking agreement to extend German-U.S. trade. In close concert they negotiated a revision of U.S. import regulations to favor European exporters, in effect creating a modest tariff reduction without congressional approval. The movement toward reduction thus was accompanied by a distinctive shift toward a more elitist and statist strategy.

The revisionists began to consolidate a national movement by about 1907. Agricultural revisionists, largely the stock growers and meatpackers, enlarged the ARTL by co-opting members of the MANY onto their board of directors, and they promoted greater communication between the eastern and midwestern revision movements. When the NAM reentered the national revision push in 1906–7, it, too, joined in this colloquy, exchanging information and helping to plan for joint conferences and lobbying efforts. Tariff revisionists met protectionist opposition from the Home Market Club, the American Protective Tariff League, the Old Guard congressional leadership, and Treasury Secretary Leslie M. Shaw. Yet as early as January 1907, the NAM, ARTL, and New York commercial revisionists were able to stage a large convention in Washington endorsing a tariff commission and maximum-minimum tariffs and featuring addresses by major business, executive, and legislative leaders. Thus they developed a policy agenda of considerably greater organization, with broader support within the executive branch.

Still Roosevelt refused to pursue an early, full-scale revision through Congress. Certainly this was partly because of the entrenched power of Republican protectionism. But the equivocal tariff policies of Roosevelt, and Taft after him, also reflected, this study suggests, their opposition to a programmatic alliance with the burgeoning Republican radical or anti-trust component of the tariff revision movement. Specific to the political-economic development of the early twentieth century were rising conflicts between proprietary finishing manufacturers and raw material and semi-manufacture corporations that began to surface in the Midwest as early as the 1901 "Iowa idea" tariff platform calling for regulation of "monopoly." Here, the notions that had animated the reciprocity drive—that equity among capitalist interests would be served automatically by lower tariffs, reciprocity, or expansion of trade—began to come into question. Instead, proprietary capitalists began to conceive of tariff revision as necessary to ensure equity by regulation of the pricing and market activities of corporations. It was this notion that was the primary stimulus to the early drive for a businessman's tariff commission, as supported by H. E. Miles and James W. Van Cleave of the NAM.

In a sense, this antitrust theme in Republican proprietary tariff revisionism paralleled the more extensive Populist protests of the 1890s. There, agrarian radicals sought to control the economic nationalization process through a focus on cooperatives and currency; that is, through economic legislation they sought to channel development to preserve widespread agrarian property holding against its consolidation in metropolitan and corporate hands. Likewise, Republican tariff radicals sought to shape reductions to promote their own export competitiveness, undermine corporate control of raw materials, and preserve independent proprietary capitalist power in American political and economic institutions. As president, neither Roosevelt nor Taft ever approved of this "independent" aspect of revisionism, and although both professed at times to be wholeheartedly in favor of revision and small business, and both courted the revisionists politically, both worked deliberately to minimize this radical influence for tariff revision in the Republican party.

Republican revisionism was not the victim of its "friends" in the executive branch, however, as some "Progressive" accounts have implied. Both radical proprietary and corporate-oriented revisionists largely agreed on an executive-centered strategy based on a dual tariff and tariff commission, and with sporadic exceptions such as Canadian reciprocity, both largely rejected alliance with radical agrarian Democrats and sought to strip Congress of some of its "political" tariff-making influence. The radical version of revisionism was not a broadly democratic or popular movement as such; its conception of equity centered around the ambitions of successful, nonintegrated proprietary businesses of the nineteenth-century mold, mostly in the Midwest. Although appealing to the "consumer," radical revisionists had mostly in mind the intermediate consumer of industrial raw materials and maintained generally paternalistic attitudes toward labor. H. E. Miles, for example, largely agreed with the more conservative Henry R. Towne's formulation of a "neutral line" on the tariff that would serve both corporations and proprietary manufacturers, and he recognized and sought to accommodate to the predominant "cooperationist" tendency within revisionism that accepted the leadership of corporate capitalism and sought to ally with it. It was the terms of the alliance that Miles sought to shape.

Despite its sometimes quaint insistence on the "old style" independent manufacturer, radical revisionism was neither a token resistance to corporate capitalism nor a retrogressive or antimodern movement. Rather, it drew upon current European (largely German) models to project an alternative form of industrial organization of structured, cartel-like, and state-regulated relations between components of the capitalist economy to assure a broader control of productive property than that evolving from a corporate-dominated economy. This was why H. E. Miles insisted, as "the gist of our entire contention," on a businessman's tariff commission armed with subpoena power over business records and employing a cost-of-production formula to guide rates, and it was why he insisted that the Taft Tariff Board cleave to "costs." Such a commission would have the power to make the majority of producers, the independent nonintegrated manufacturers, the measure of efficiency and would prevent corporate control of raw materials, capital, and markets from setting the standards for economic efficiency. For the same reasons, under Wilson, proponents of proprietary business sought to set capitalization limits for export cooperation to counterbalance corporate power, and they hoped to endow the U.S. Tariff Commission with substantial "political" regulatory powers. This conception of equity—stressing a labor theory of value and the independent influence of proprietary producers and consumers on a corporate market system—was fundamental to the "radical" or "insurgent" component of the revision movement but was shared to a degree by most revisionists. As implemented by the revisionists, this conception of equity played an important and creative role in the development of new tariff instrumentalities by motivating the revisionists to draw on European methods and American efficiency and cost accounting theories and by inspiring them to employ energetic and effective organizational, lobbying, and propaganda techniques.

For some tariff radicals, mainly those allied with the Insurgent Progressives, fidelity to the independent and creative conceptions of equity may have led to support for natural resource conservation, social reform, anti-war or anti-intervention sentiment, and more tolerant attitudes toward labor. Tariff reform remained an aspect of Progressive politics into the 1930s. Yet as an aspect of Republican policy, "radical" revisionism receded rapidly. Instead, the movement for tariff reductions and trade expansion moved ahead under a primarily "cooperationist" ideology, as reformers increasingly appropriated the ideas of a "semi-judicial" commission and of economic investigations to the ends of corporate-led expansion. There is an irony, then, in N. I. Stone's characterization some forty years later of H. E. Miles as the "father of the tariff commission," for Miles was the father of the established commission much more in form than in spirit.

The unification of a revision movement at a national level was a critical feature of the politics of the early twentieth century, representing a merging of the "free raw materials" and "reciprocity" revision frameworks that had been impeded by political and regional oppositions in the late nineteenth century. In part propelled by the conflicts between proprietary and corporate capitalism, the revisionist movement superseded the ideology of a self-sufficient home market and facilitated the broad acceptance of tariff reduction and systematization as beneficial, legitimate, and vital to U.S. open-door commercial policy. This, then, to recall Brooks Adams's phrase, was the alternative to reciprocity.

Notes

Abbreviations

ANLSA *Proceedings* American National Live Stock Association, *Proceedings*, 1906–11.

Annals *Annals of the American Academy of Political and Social Sciences.*

CTP U.S. Tariff Commission, *Colonial Tariff Policies* (Washington, D.C.: GPO, 1921).

FRUS U.S. Department of State, *Foreign Relations of the United States* (Washington, D.C.: GPO).

LHA U.S. Congress, Senate, Subcommittee of the Committee on the Judiciary, *Maintenance of a Lobby to Influence Legislation: Appendix. Exhibits Introduced during the Hearings*, 4 vols., 63d Cong., 1st sess. (Washington, D.C.: GPO, 1913).

MPP James D. Richardson, ed. *A Compilation of the Messages and Papers of the Presidents*, vols. 13–15 (New York: Bureau of National Literature, 1917).

NAAIVM *Convention* National Association of Agricultural Implement and Vehicle Manufacturers, *Annual Convention Proceedings*, printed in *Farm Machinery*, 1898–1910.

NAM *Proceedings* National Association of Manufacturers, *Proceedings* of Annual Conventions, 1895–1912.

NLSA *Proceedings* National Live Stock Association, *Proceedings*, 1899–1906.

NRC *Proceedings* *Proceedings of the National Reciprocity Conference Held under the Auspices of the National Association of Manufacturers of the United States of America*, NAM Circular of Information no. 43 (Philadelphia: National Association of Manufacturers, 1901).

RCT
U.S. Tariff Commission, *Reciprocity and Commercial Treaties* (Washington, D.C.: GPO, 1919).

RG 40
Record Group 40, Papers of the United States Department of Commerce and Labor, National Archives, Washington, D.C.

RG 59
Record Group 59, General Records of the Department of State, Numerical and Minor Files of the Department of State, 1906–10, National Archives, Washington, D.C.

RG 81
Record Group 81, Records of the United States Tariff Commission, Tariff Board, National Archives, Washington, D.C.

RG 122
Record Group 122, General Records of the Federal Trade Commission, National Archives, Washington, D.C.

Introduction

1. In the terms of Karl Mannheim, *Ideology and Utopia* (New York: Harvest Books, 1936), pp. 55–59, revisionism is seen in the context of a "total" rather than a "particular" conception of ideology; that is, revisionism purveyed a distinctive conception of social order, not merely an interest-centered rationalization of policy.

2. Republicans and Gold Democrats were already forging a suprapartisan alliance in the sound money and central banking movements of this same period. See, on banking, James Livingston, *Origins of the Federal Reserve System: Money, Class, and Corporate Capitalism* (Ithaca, N.Y.: Cornell University Press, 1986). For McKinley's views, see particularly his last speech, the "Buffalo Address" of 1901, favoring the Kasson reciprocity treaties. McKinley's speech was widely reproduced in contemporary newspapers and also can be found as "Last Public Address," *National Reciprocity* 1 (September 1902): 4–10.

3. Even the arch-protectionist Nelson W. Aldrich of Rhode Island—a vehement defender of traditional congressional tariff-making prerogatives and local protectionist interests—vigorously supported trade expansion, cosponsored the Payne-Aldrich Tariff of 1909, and defended his tariff's rate reductions in European capitals. Aldrich, then, could be considered a revisionist, or to have shared a revisionist outlook to some degree.

4. Democratic cabinet members David Houston, Franklin K. Lane, and William G. McAdoo and President Woodrow Wilson ultimately were most influential in forming the U.S. Tariff Commission in 1916; it was headed by Frank W. Taussig of Harvard.

5. Root to Roosevelt, November 16, 1904, Elihu Root Papers, Library of Congress, Washington, D.C.; Roosevelt to Root, August 18, 1906, Root Papers.

6. On the open door, see William Appleman Williams, *The Tragedy of American*

Diplomacy (New York: Delta, 1962), esp. pp. 37–50. See also Carl P. Parrini and Martin J. Sklar, "New Thinking about the Market, 1896–1904: Some American Economists on Investment and the Theory of Surplus Capital," *Journal of Economic History* 48 (June 1983): 559–78. See also David A. Lake, "International Economic Structures and American Foreign Economic Policy, 1887–1934," *World Politics* 35 (July 1983): 514–43, and *Power, Protection, and Free Trade: International Sources of U.S. Commercial Strategy, 1887–1939* (Ithaca, N.Y.: Cornell University Press, 1988), esp. chap. 4. Lake has emphasized the interest of American politicians in promoting an international system of trade and investment through the principle and practice of the open door. Following both Williams and models of "hegemonic stability" elaborated by economist Charles P. Kindleberger and other scholars, Lake has attempted to define U.S. and European roles as leaders, followers, and opportunists in an international economic regime. In treating early twentieth-century policy, Lake suggests—and I agree and try to detail later in this volume—that the maximum-minimum provisions of the Payne-Aldrich Tariff of 1909 in particular were attempts to embody the nondiscriminatory principles of the open door in American tariff policy, replacing the system of "international dickers" (as a Republican representative from Indiana put it) of earlier U.S. commercial treaty tariffs. On the theory of hegemonic leadership and the ideas of Kindleberger and Robert Keohane, see particularly Robert Gilpin, *The Political Economy of International Relations* (Princeton, N.J.: Princeton University Press, 1989), pp. 72–80.

7. Since 1948 the GATT has codified and attempted to regulate a multilateral system of trade to moderate the effects of differing state policies and the differing levels of development of economic systems. The "three pillars" of the GATT are the most-favored-nation practice, which automatically extends bilateral concessions to all participants; the prohibition of nontariff restrictions on trade; and the principle of reciprocal concessions that "balance" import tax revenues. See M. Abreu, "Developing Countries and the Uruguay Round of Trade Negotiations," *Proceedings of the World Bank Annual Conference on Development Economics, 1989* (Washington, D.C.: World Bank, 1990), p. 21. As the present study suggests, at least the first two of these were crucial factors in the international and domestic maneuvering around the tariff question in the early twentieth century. See also Angus Maddison, *The World Economy in the 20th Century* (Paris: Development Centre of the Organisation for Economic Co-operation and Development, 1989); Gilpin, *Political Economy*, pp. 73–74; Rolf J. Langhammer and André Sapir, *Economic Impact of Generalized Tariff Preferences* (London: Trade Policy Research Centre, 1987), pp. 2–3.

8. See chapter 2.

9. See Alfred D. Chandler, "The Beginnings of 'Big Business' in American Industry," *Business History Review* 33 (Spring 1959): 1–31; "The Large Industrial Corporation and the Making of Modern American Society," in *Institutions in Modern America*, ed. Stephen E. Ambrose (Baltimore: Johns Hopkins University Press, 1967), pp. 71–101; Glenn Porter, *The Rise of Big Business, 1860–1910* (New

York: Crowell, 1973); Ralph L. Nelson, *Merger Movements in American Industry, 1895–1956* (Princeton, N.J.: Princeton University Press, 1959); Louis Galambos, *The Public Image of Big Business in America, 1880–1940: A Quantitative Study in Social Change* (Baltimore: Johns Hopkins University Press, 1975); Naomi R. Lamoreaux, *The Great Merger Movement in American Business* (New York: Cambridge University Press, 1985). Figures on 1905 from U.S. Department of Commerce, Bureau of the Census, quoted by Livingston, *Origins of Federal Reserve*, p. 56. On the legal aspects, see especially Martin J. Sklar, *The Corporate Reconstruction of American Capitalism, 1890–1916: The Market, the Law, and Politics* (New York: Cambridge University Press, 1988).

10. Sklar, *Corporate Reconstruction*, esp. pp. 4–14; quotation from Sklar, "The Sherman Antitrust Act and the Corporate Reconstruction of American Capitalism, 1890–1914," paper presented at the meeting of the American Society for Legal History, Baltimore, October 1983. See also Livingston, *Origins of Federal Reserve*.

11. Sklar, *Corporate Reconstruction*, esp. pp. 4–14; see also Livingston, *Origins of Federal Reserve*. On the question of ownership and control under corporate capitalism, see, for example, Maurice Zeitlin, "Corporate Ownership and Control: The Large Corporation and the Capitalist Class," *American Journal of Sociology* 79 (March 1974): 1073–1119. The characterization is from Sidney Sherwood, "Influence of the Trust in the Development of Undertaking Genius," *Yale Review* 8 (February 1900): 362–72.

12. See Arthur Twining Hadley, "The Good and the Evil of Industrial Combination," *Atlantic Monthly* 79 (May 1897): 377–85; Edward S. Meade, "Financial Aspects of the Trust Problem," *Annals* 16 (November 1901): 345–403. Another prominent procorporate intellectual and government policy adviser was economist Jeremiah W. Jenks of Cornell University.

13. Frank W. Taussig, *Principles of Economics* (New York: Macmillan, 1911), 1:86–110.

14. On the economic crisis, see, for example, David Ames Wells, *Recent Economic Changes and Their Effect on the Production and Distribution of Wealth and the Wellbeing of Society* (New York: D. Appleton, 1889); J. W. Jenks, *The Trust Problem* (New York: McClure, Phillips, 1901). Cf. Sklar, *Corporate Reconstruction,* esp. pp. 14–20; Alfred D. Chandler, *The Visible Hand: The Managerial Revolution in American Business* (Cambridge, Mass.: Harvard University Press, 1979), chap. 5; Livingston, *Origins of Federal Reserve*, esp. chaps. 1 and 2.

15. Examples of the extended public forum given the trust question by procorporate groups are the proceedings of the *Chicago Conference on Trusts* (Chicago: Civic Federation of Chicago, 1900); the proceedings of the *U.S. Industrial Commission* (Washington, D.C.: GPO, 1899, 1900, and following), to which J. W. Jenks was secretary. Charles A. Conant's "The Future of Political Parties," *Atlantic Monthly* 88 (September 1901): 365–73, is a reflective conceptualization of the reorganization of the issue spheres under a corporate capitalist system. James Livingston has given

particular attention to the social character of the movement for banking reform that underlay the origins of the Federal Reserve System; see *Origins of Federal Reserve*, chap. 2, pp. 49–67. James Weinstein's treatment of The National Civic Federation, *The Corporate Ideal in the Liberal State, 1900–1918* (Boston: Beacon, 1968), shows how the NCF, in seeking to create a consensus between corporate, "public," and labor groups, became a lightning rod for the anticorporate animus of primarily proprietary capitalist groups such as the National Association of Manufacturers. Robert H. Wiebe's *Businessmen and Reform: A Study of the Progressive Movement* (Cambridge, Mass.: Harvard University Press, 1962), also touches on this theme. Political historians' treatments of the period include those of Walter Dean Burnham, "The System of 1896: An Analysis," in *The Evolution of American Electoral Systems,* by Paul Kleppner et al. (Westport, Conn.: Greenwood Press, 1981). Burnham argues that the "first wave" of the system of 1896, roughly to 1910, was the struggle over the issues of nationalization of politics and restriction of franchise— part of an "antiparochial" corporate ideal that sought to "dismantle older forms of partisan linkage and to reinforce the protections which the organization of the electoral mass market provided to industrial-capitalist elites" (p. 148). Thomas Ferguson, "Party Realignment and American Industrial Structure: The Investment Theory of Political Parties in Historical Perspective," *Research in Political Economy* 6 (1983): 1–82, also suggests that the agenda of this period was contention within the now-dominant antipopulist class, though his conception of it is somewhat different from Burnham's.

16. Sidney Sherwood, "Influence of the Trust in the Development of Undertaking Genius," *Yale Review* 8 (February 1900): 362–72; James B. Dill, "Industrials as Investments for Small Capital," in *Corporations and the Public Welfare*, Supplement to *Annals* 15 (1900): 109–19.

17. See Rudolf Hilferding, *Finance Capital* (1910; reprint and translation from the German, London: Routledge and Kegan Paul, 1981), p. 310. Hilferding wrote that protectionism had been transmuted "from a defense against the conquest of the domestic market by foreign industries [to] a means of conquest of foreign markets by domestic industries." H. E. Miles to Senator Joseph Benson Foraker, August 28, 1907, quoted in *American Economist*, September 13, 1907, p. 130; cf. copy in Albert J. Beveridge Papers, Library of Congress, Washington, D.C. Testimony of H. E. Miles, U.S. Congress, House, Committee on Ways and Means, *Tariff Hearings, 1908–1909; Free List and Miscellaneous*, vol. 7 (Washington, D.C.: GPO, 1909), pp. 7610, 7645.

18. See Lawrence Goodwyn, *Democratic Promise: The Populist Moment in America* (New York, 1976); cf. Livingston, *Origins of Federal Reserve*, pp. 42–43.

19. Representative "progressive" historical interpretations include those of Arthur Link (e.g., *Woodrow Wilson and the Progressive Era* [New York: Harper Bros., 1954]) and Arthur M. Schlesinger, Jr.; specific treatments include Kenneth Hechler, *Insurgency: Personalities and Politics of the Taft Era* (1940; reprint, New York: AMS

Press, 1970); for the organizational theories, see, for example, Wiebe, *Businessmen and Reform*, and William H. Becker, *The Dynamics of Business-Government Relations: Industry and Exports, 1893–1921* (Chicago: University of Chicago Press, 1982).

20. The study thus seeks to confront "the empirical record of the social relations within and among classes, the modes of consciousness, and the social movements, comprising, and relating to, the capitalist mode of production at the time." See Sklar, *Corporate Reconstruction*, p. 12. See also Sklar, ibid., "Class Metamorphosis and Corporate Reconstruction," pp. 20–33.

Chapter 1

1. I profited greatly in my understanding of the tariff policies of this period from reading Tom E. Terrill's *The Tariff, Politics and American Foreign Policy, 1874–1901* (Westport, Conn.: Greenwood Press, 1973), as well as the works of William Appleman Williams and Walter LaFeber.

2. Quoted in Terrill, ibid., p. 43.

3. See Stanley Coben, "Northeastern Business and Radical Reconstruction: A Re-examination," *Mississippi Valley Historical Review* 46 (June 1959): 68–71; see also Irwin Unger, *The Greenback Era: A Social and Political History of American Finance, 1865–1879* (Princeton, N.J.: Princeton University Press, 1964), p. 146.

4. Frederick S. Hall, "The Localization of Industries," in *Twelfth Census of the United States, 1900*, vol. 7, *Manufactures* (Washington, D.C.: GPO, 1902), part 1, pp. cxc–ccxiv. Cf. Harold U. Faulkner, *American Economic History*, 8th ed. (New York: Harper Bros., 1960), pp. 405–12; Harold G. Vatter, *The Drive to Industrial Maturity: The U.S. Economy, 1860–1914* (Westport, Conn.: Greenwood Press, 1975), pp. 102–5; Harvey S. Perloff, *Regions, Resources, and Economic Growth* (Baltimore: Johns Hopkins University Press, for Resources for the Future, 1960), p. 151.

5. Unger, *Greenback Era*, pp. 146–48, uses the term "old elite" to describe the eastern group. See also Robert Greenhalgh Albion, *The Rise of New York Port, 1815–1860* (1939: reprint, Devon, England: David and Charles, 1970), esp. pp. 260–85.

6. The policies of the eastern Republicans, leading to contraction of the wartime paper money issues, tended to reduce or eliminate the premium on gold that had been created by the inflated legal tender system of the war period. Contraction thus made it easier for Americans to pay for foreign goods, which were sold in gold terms. See Robert P. Sharkey, *Money, Class, and Party: An Economic Study of Civil War and Reconstruction* (Baltimore: Johns Hopkins Paperback Editions, 1967), pp. 149–52; see also Coben, "Northeastern Business," pp. 68–69.

7. See Frank W. Taussig, *Tariff History of the United States*, 6th ed. (New York: G. P. Putnam's Sons, 1913), pp. 451–52. The high-tariff regime heavily and

consistently protected basic industries such as iron and steel and decreased the differential between the price of capital goods and finished manufactures, thus making basic investment and development more profitable. This effort was undertaken at the cost of a more equitable distribution of goods and property that might have obtained if foreign goods at lower prices had entered more freely. And to a degree it was at the cost of northeastern influence. Although contemporary protectionists often defended their views on the Hamiltonian basis of nurturing "infant industries," the fact that they held the view long after the industries were established suggests that the "home-market" outlook more closely reflected the preoccupation with western settlement and resource development that had been a central economic and social issue of the Civil War and the nineteenth century in general. See Jeffrey G. Williamson, "Watersheds and Turning Points: Conjectures on the Long-Term Impact of Civil War Financing," *Journal of Economic History* 34 (September 1974): 657–58, 661. See also Jeffrey G. Williamson, "Late Nineteenth Century American Retardation: A Neoclassical Analysis," *Journal of Economic History* 33 (September 1973): 581–607. The early twentieth-century protectionist economist Alvin Saunders Johnson argued flatly that the primary function of the post–Civil War protectionist system had been to channel capital "from all other classes in society to the capitalist-manufacturer." Alvin S. Johnson, "Protection and the Formation of Capital," in *Essays in Social Economics* (New York: New School, 1952), pp. 120–41, esp. 129; this is a reprint of an essay originally published in *Political Science Quarterly* 23 (1908). On the actual levels of American tariffs, see Taussig, *Tariff History*, pp. 451–52.

8. Apart from Britain, Belgium, and a few other nations that maintained low single-tariff systems, most European countries maintained "multiple" tariffs, containing two or more sets of rates. The "general and conventional" system of tariffs was the most typical multiple system. In it, a national legislature adopted a general rate, which could be either high or moderate, depending on the commercial orientation of the government. Duties applied to the products of other nations then could be modified downward by "conventions," or treaties. The system formed policy by balancing legislative and international diplomatic initiatives. The higher, legislative rates could be changed at will, however, further jeopardizing the trade of nonsignatories.

The "maximum and minimum" system of tariffs was a second method of structuring rates. Here, both schedules were "statutory," adopted by the national legislature. Maximum-minimum systems necessitated that commercial negotiations could concern only the propriety of extending the minimum schedule already fixed by law, a point that would be embodied in the U.S. Payne-Aldrich Tariff of 1909. Extending a minimum tariff in this way established uniform minimum rates, but now both rates were subject to being raised or lowered as a whole at the will of the legislature. I try to show in subsequent chapters how the United States adopted the maximum-minimum system fixing a uniform minimum rate and maintain that it was a significant, although incomplete, step toward an open-door tariff system. Cf. David A. Lake, "International Economic Structures and American Foreign Economic Policy, 1887–1934," *World Politics* 35 (1983): 517–43.

"Preferential" tariffs were also multiple tariffs but embodied further schedules, lower than dual schedules adopted by the legislature or passed through treaties; preferences were often designed to foster exports or to create secure channels of trade by favoring specific countries' products, particularly those of colonies. Special schedules could also be constructed above the main schedules as "countervailing" duties—as retaliations to be imposed on nations that were considered to be discriminating.

Note that the most-favored-nation clause operated differently in Europe and the United States. European "unconditional" most-favored-nation status meant that a tariff concession made to any single nation with a most-favored-nation treaty was automatically generalized to all nations connected to it by such treaties. The United States, however (up to the 1920s), practiced "conditional" most-favored-nation treaty making, in which only the opportunity to negotiate for commensurate tariff concessions was promised to most-favored-nation treaty signatories. In the late 1890s, some European nations also began limiting their interpretations of the most-favored-nation concept. See *RCT*, pp. 389–456, 462–63; see also O[scar] P[helps] Austin, "Modern Tariff Systems: The Maximum and Minimum, Conventional, and General Tariff Systems of the Principal Countries of the World," in U.S. Department of Commerce and Labor, Bureau of Statistics, *Summary of Commerce and Statistics, 1902* (Washington, D.C.: GPO, 1902), pp. 3095–99.

9. After the Franco-Prussian war, Germany blocked French entrée into the developing German industrial market. France also was forced to extend to Germany the reciprocity provisions of the liberal-tariff-inclined Third Empire. This arrangement benefited Germany because France's still-operative most-favored-nation treaties with other European countries gave Germany access to the low-tariff European market system. *RCT*, pp. 468–70; Austin, "Modern Tariff Systems," p. 3098. Hans-Ulrich Wehler, "Bismarck's Imperialism, 1862–1890," *Past and Present* 48 (August 1970): 128–33, argues that important elements of "liberal commercial policy" remained in Bismarck's approach and that Germany's primary objectives remained European trade rather than territorial or colonial expansion, at least into the 1880s. See also Wehler, "Industrial Growth and Early German Imperialism," in *Studies in the Theory of Imperialism*, ed. Roger Owen and Bob Sutcliffe (London: Longman, 1972), pp. 71–92.

10. A French tariff of 1881 retained the general and conventional system but raised duties on manufactured goods by 24 percent. In some measure, the reflex toward protection was a response to the depressed state of French production. But it was also a reaction against the growing imbalances between French and German industrial strength in part made possible by the inroads Germany had made into the French market after the Franco-Prussian war. See *RCT*, p. 489. See also Michael

Stephen Smith, *Tariff Reform in France, 1860–1900* (Ithaca, N.Y.: Cornell University Press, 1980), pp. 197–235.

11. The main German treaties were with Austria-Hungary, Italy, Switzerland, Belgium, and later the Balkan states and Russia. *RCT*, p. 471. See also Alan Milward, "Tariffs as Constitutions," in *The International Politics of Surplus Capacity*, ed. Susan Strange and Roger Tooze (London: George Allen and Unwin, 1981), pp. 57–66.

12. *RCT*, pp. 473, 475–76; N. I. Stone "The New German Customs Tariff," *North American Review* 181 (September 1905): 396–97; Stone, "Dual Tariff System," Memorandum in the William H. Taft Papers, Library of Congress, Washington, D.C. See also H[einrich] Dietzel, "The German Tariff Controversy," *Quarterly Journal of Economics* 17 (May 1903): 365–416. None of these tariff systems had to exist in pure form. Both Germany and France in the late nineteenth century modified their tariff systems to combine two or more of the forms noted earlier. Germany, for example, set legislative limits below which its treaty conventions could not set rates. This was similar to what the United States did in section 4 of the Dingley Tariff of 1897, in which reductions of up to 20 percent of the standard rate were authorized in the so-called Kasson treaties. France also modified its legislative tariff autonomy by concluding a number of treaties that fixed specific rates for a definite period. Russia did the same, ultimately to such an extent that it abandoned its maximum-minimum system of tariffs for a general and conventional one; see *RCT*, pp. 461–64.

13. As Alan Milward has argued, the turn toward protection may be seen not as a breakdown of an idealized free trade but as a resystematizing response to the evolution of European capitalism—the loss of British manufacturing dominance and the developing redundancies of metropolitan productive capacity. See Milward, "Tariffs as Constitutions," pp. 57–66. Cf. John Gallagher and Ronald Robinson, "The Imperialism of Free Trade," *Economic History Review*, 2d ser., 1 (1953): 1–15, esp. 11–12. Milward's argument is similar to Wehler's concept of German "social imperialism," in the sense that Milward sees the increasing "enfranchisement" of domestic European groups, especially in Germany, through the granting of protectionist tariffs by autocratic state systems as a form of compensation for a lack of an *echt* constitutionalism.

14. See, for example, D. C. M. Platt, "Economic Factors in the New Imperialism," *Past and Present* 39 (1968): 120–38, esp. 122–26, 134, on the concern of British officials over the rise of tariffs and intercapitalist economic tensions in the twenty-five years before 1914. See also Jeremiah W. Jenks, "The Economic Outlook," *Dial* 10 (January 1890): 252, a review of David Wells's book, *Recent Economic Changes*, in which Jenks described the rise of protectionism as a response to changing European economic conditions, in particular to recurrent depression.

15. The assimilated French colonies were the main trading colonies of Indochina, New Caledonia, Guiana, and later Madagascar; they excluded the entrepôt colonies.

See Stephen H. Roberts, *The History of French Colonial Policy, 1870–1925* (1929; reprint, Hamden, Conn.: Archon, 1963), p. 23.

16. French exports to the colonies were free of duty. But colonial exports to France were dutied for revenue purposes at half the rate of the maximum tariff until about 1913. French colonies imported, in 1890, goods from foreign nations worth more than 136 million francs, compared with goods from France and the other French colonies totaling only about 74 million francs. Arthur Girault, *The Colonial Tariff Policy of France* (London: Oxford University Press, 1916), p. 94, and chap. 5. See H. H. Powers's comments on the decline of the French empire, "The War as a Suggestion of Manifest Destiny," *Annals* 12 (September 1898): 185–86. For a similar perspective, see Paul S. Reinsch, *World Politics at the End of the Nineteenth Century* (New York: Macmillan, 1900).

17. By the mid-1880s, Germany controlled colonies in Africa, the Pacific, and an outpost in China. *CTP*, pp. 227–30. See also Wehler, "Bismarck's Imperialism," pp. 125, 128–29. With regard to their own colonies, the Germans imposed a generally light tariff, including some export duties, broadly exempting goods imported for German settlement purposes; *CTP*, pp. 239–49.

18. One reason for the assertiveness of German expansion was the extremely rapid growth of German industry and the social tensions that accompanied it—most notably, the rise of social democracy. Bismarck sought to counter the appeal of working-class political and labor organizations in part by a policy of "social imperialism," which used foreign trade and colonial expansion to finance conservative reforms from above. See Wehler, "Bismarck's Imperialism," pp. 131–32; and Wehler, "Industrial Growth and Early German Imperialism," pp. 81–82.

19. See Fritz Fischer, *Germany's Aims in the First World War* (New York: W. W. Norton, 1967), pp. 13, 15. Germany also expanded its merchant marine and navy; advanced its commercial and linguistic education efforts; established large colonies of foreign-based German merchants and an effective foreign banking network closely tied to German industrial interests; and pursued innovative and aggressive selling techniques that British custom forswore. On British-German trade frictions, see Ross J. S. Hoffman, *Great Britain and the German Trade Rivalry, 1875–1914* (Philadelphia: University of Pennsylvania Press, 1933), esp. pp. 73–93 and 201–9. On the influence of German technique on U.S. policymaking, see Burton I. Kaufman, "The Organizational Dimension of United States Economic Foreign Policy, 1900–1920," *Business History Review* 46 (Spring 1972): 17–44, esp. 22–29. Many U.S. reports of German commercial activity can be found in the Department of Commerce Consular reports, but in particular, see O. P. Austin, "Report of Trip around the World, 1905," in RG 40, which clearly singles out German activities as models for emulation. Expansionist American capitalists were interested in German trade techniques no less than the bureaucrats. See also in RG 40, "Report of the Foreign Commerce Committee of the National Council of Commerce," December 1909, written by H. E. Miles, an agricultural implement manufacturer who figured

importantly—as detailed in subsequent chapters—in the movement for tariff revision in the United States.

20. Iron and steel exports represented 13.6 percent, 25.2 percent, and 22.1 percent of the total manufactured exports in 1880, 1900, and 1905, respectively. Export proportions of manufactures for 1890 and 1900 are taken from Emory R. Johnson, T. W. Van Metre, G. G. Huebner, and D. S. Hanchett, *History of Domestic and Foreign Commerce* (Washington, D.C.: Carnegie Institute of Washington, 1915), 2:69, table 56; figures for 1905 are computed from U.S. Department of Commerce and Labor, Bureau of Statistics, *Exports of Manufactures, 1800–1906* (Washington, D.C.: GPO, 1907), p. 8 (table); iron and steel figures are calculated from data on total exports (p. 8) and iron and steel exports (p. 11).

21. Percentages of U.S. exports to Europe in the nineteenth century are taken from Johnson et al., *History of Domestic and Foreign Commerce*, 2:72. See also David E. Novack and Matthew Simon, "Commercial Responses to the American Export Invasion, 1871–1914: An Essay in Attitudinal History," *Explorations in Entrepreneurial History*, 2d ser., 3 (Winter 1966): 126, table 1. Figures for the composition of U.S. exports to Europe are taken by adding crude foodstuffs to crude materials (columns 1 and 3) to get "raw products," and by adding semimanufactures to finished manufactures (columns 7 and 9) to get percentages of industrial manufactures. Column 5, manufactured foodstuffs, was added to columns 7 and 9 to get totals listed for all manufactures as percentages. Cf. O. P. Austin, *Modern Export Trade* (New York: Business Training Corporation, 1916).

22. The development of an international competition for markets and territories is perhaps best known from analyses made by early twentieth-century anti-imperialists, such as the British liberal John A. Hobson, and by socialists in Germany and Russia. The leftists, focusing mostly on England and Germany, broadly associated heightened international tension with the passage of capitalism into a distinct period dominated by monopolies, trusts, and cartels. They also noted the rise of systems of protectionist and discriminatory trade practices as challenging the hitherto dominant British system of free trade. See particularly Rudolf Hilferding, *Finance Capital* (1910; reprint and translation from the German, London: Routledge and Kegan Paul, 1981), p. 310. Hilferding described the rise of cartels as associated with the phenomenon of export pricing. This is, in essence, a theory of "dumping" (see my chapter 5). Cf. Anthony Brewer, *Marxist Theories of Imperialism* (London: Routledge and Kegan Paul, 1980), pp. 86–91.

23. Schmoller is quoted by Fischer, *Germany's Aims in the First World War*, p. 9. Brentano's ideas are paraphrased from George M. Fisk, *Continental Opinion regarding a Proposed Middle European Tariff Union* (Baltimore: Johns Hopkins University Press, 1902), p. 589. Dietzel's article appeared in *Die Nation* of April 1900; it is described in Walter Bennett Harvey, "Tariffs and International Relations in Europe, 1860–1914" (Ph.D. dissertation, University of Chicago, 1938), p. 251. See also Fritz Ringer, *The Decline of the German Mandarins: The German Academic Commu-*

nity, 1890–1933 (Cambridge, Mass.: Harvard University Press, 1969), pp. 143–50.

24. Roberts, *French Colonial Policy,* p. 17. Ringer, *German Mandarins,* p. 144. See also Fisk, *Continental Opinion,* pp. 609–10. On Leroy-Beaulieu's background, see esp. Agnes Murphy, *The Ideology of French Imperialism* (Washington, D.C.: Catholic University of America, 1948), pp. 103–75.

25. Paul Leroy-Beaulieu, "Conditions for American Commercial and Financial Supremacy," *Forum* 20 (December 1895): 385–400; quotation from p. 392.

26. Chauncey M. Depew, ed., *One Hundred Years of American Commerce* (New York: D. O. Haynes, 1895). Contributors included Worthington C. Ford; Carroll D. Wright, the U.S. commissioner of labor; Stuyvesant Fish, of the Illinois Central Railroad; Charles H. Cramp, of the Philadelphia shipbuilding firm; Richard Rothwell, of the *Engineering and Mining Journal*; Francis G. Du Pont, of the Delaware chemical firm; Bernhard Fernow, the pioneering forestry expert of the U.S. Department of Agriculture; Alba B. Johnson, of the Baldwin Locomotive Works of Philadelphia; Philip D. Armour, of the Chicago meatpacking company; Pierre Lorillard, the tobacco entrepreneur; and S. N. D. North, representing the American wool interests.

27. Atkinson reassured his friend that their ideas would be vindicated "after we are dead." Edward Atkinson to David A. Wells, July 8, 1898, David A. Wells Papers, Library of Congress, Washington, D.C. Cf. Harold F. Williamson, *Edward Atkinson: Biography of an American Liberal, 1827–1905* (Cambridge, Mass.: Riverside Press, 1934; reprint, New York: Arno, 1972), pp. 178–91.

28. Worthington C. Ford, "Commercial Superiority of the United States," *North American Review* 166 (January 1898): 76–84. See also his "The Turning of the Tide," *North American Review* 161 (August 1895): 187–95.

29. Powers, "The War as a Suggestion of Manifest Destiny," pp. 173–92; Austin, "Modern Tariff Systems," esp. pp. 3167–68. W. C. Ford's colleague, Oscar Phelps Austin, became head of the Treasury Department's Bureau of Statistics (within the Commerce and Labor Department after 1903). He later became the chief statistician under Frank Vanderlip of the National City Bank of New York. In a much-reprinted address given to the American Association for the Advancement of Science, Austin celebrated the United States' rise to first rank as an exporting nation. Austin, *Expansion of American Commerce: Past, Present, and Prospective* (Washington, D.C.: American Association for the Advancement of Science, 1902). On the influence of German economists on their American counterparts, see also Mary O. Furner, *Advocacy and Objectivity* (Lexington: University of Kentucky Press, 1975).

30. Brooks Adams, "The Spanish War and the Equilibrium of the World," *Forum* 26 (August 1898): 641–51. See also "Commercial Future: New Struggle for Life among Nations," *Fortnightly Review* 71 (February 1899): 274–83. On the importance of Adams as a thinker, see William Appleman Williams, "Brooks Adams and American Expansion," *New England Quarterly* 25 (June 1952): 217–32.

31. Conant later worked with William H. Taft in the Philippines and also in China and several Latin American nations as consultant on gold-standard currency reform. Conant also served as an adviser and publicist for "sound money" and central banking groups, including Nelson Aldrich's National Monetary Commission. The work of Conant, though mentioned occasionally in the historical literature since his death in 1915, has been explicated during the past twenty years largely by Carl P. Parrini and Martin J. Sklar; see their "New Thinking about the Market, 1896–1904: Some American Economists on Investment and the Theory of Surplus Capital," *Journal of Economic History* 48 (June 1983): 559–78; Parrini, "Theories of Imperialism," in *Redefining the Past: Essays in Diplomatic History in Honor of William Appleman Williams*, ed. Lloyd C. Gardner (Corvallis: Oregon State University Press, 1986), pp. 65–84; and Sklar, *The Corporate Reconstruction of American Capitalism, 1890–1916: The Market, the Law, and Politics* (New York: Cambridge University Press, 1988), pp. 78–85. See also Norman Etherington, *Theories of Imperialism: War, Conquest, and Capital* (London: Croom Helm, 1984). On Conant's work in the Philippines, see Emily S. Rosenberg, "Foundations of United States International Financial Power: Gold Standard Diplomacy, 1900–1905," *Business History Review* 59 (Summer 1985): 169–202.

32. See, for example, Conant's essays "The Economic Basis of Imperialism," *North American Review* 167 (September 1898): 326–40; "The Struggle for Commercial Empire," *Forum* 27 (July 1899): 427–40; and "The United States as a World Power: II. Her Advantages in the Competition for Commercial Empire," *Forum* 29 (August 1900): 673–87. With regard to these potentials, Conant held the integrated corporation as the model for effective world market conquest. Conant approved of Johns Hopkins economist Sidney Sherwood's formulation of the importance of corporate-led expansion as expressed in Sherwood's "Influence of the Trust in the Development of Undertaking Genius," *Yale Review* 8 (February 1900): 362–72. See also W. T. Stead's call for an Anglo-American union, *The Americanization of the World* (London: H. Markley, 1902), and particularly commercial banker and former Treasury Department official Frank Vanderlip's commentary on and extension of Stead, calling for alliance and expansion under the aegis of the "great corporation"; *The Americanization of the World: An Address Delivered before the Commercial Club of Chicago, February 22, 1902* (Chicago: Rand, McNally and Company, 1902); copy in Frank A. Vanderlip Papers, Butler Library, Columbia University, New York, Box D-13. Cf. Sklar, *Corporate Reconstruction*, p. 67n, and Parrini and Sklar, "New Thinking about the Market."

In the 1890s, Conant occasionally wrote explicitly on tariff matters, as in his "Anatomy of the New Tariff," *Review of Reviews* 16 (July–December 1897): 167–74, in which he judiciously compared the free raw materials and reciprocity viewpoints. But as he concentrated on monetary and banking methods and developed his association with protectionist Republican Senator Nelson Aldrich in the monetary and banking movement, he became more reticent on specific tariff matters.

33. Emory, introduction to "Review of the World's Commerce," in U.S. Depart-

ment of State, *Commercial Relations of the United States for 1898* (Washington, D.C.: GPO, 1899), pp. 19–24. Cf. Charles Jesse Bullock, "Our Foreign Commerce for the Year 1897," *New York Times*, August 17, 1898. Emory, introduction to "Review of the World's Commerce," in U.S. Department of State, *Commercial Relations of the United States for 1899* (Washington, D.C.: GPO, 1900), pp. 28–29.

34. The Austrian foreign minister, Goluchowski, and the German treasury secretary, Von Theilmann, who urged European "carp" to combine against the American "pike," are quoted in Charles S. Campbell, Jr., *Special Business Interests and the Open Door Policy* (1951; reprint, Hamden, Conn.: Archon Books, 1968), pp. 6, 7. See also Fred A. McKenzie, *The American Invaders* (London: G. Richards, 1902); and B. H. Thwaite, *The American Invasion* (London: S. Sonnenschein, 1902). For American perspectives, see Frank A. Vanderlip, *The American Commercial Invasion of Europe* (New York: National City Bank, 1902), and O. P. Austin, "Has the Threatened War against American Manufacturers Begun?," *North American Review* 173 (November 1901): 684–93. Citing a Hamburg foreign-trade newspaper, Frederic Emory warned of the Europeans' belief in the "imminent danger" of U.S. industrial exports. Introduction to "Review of the World's Commerce" for 1899, pp. 21, 25.

35. The term "preclusive imperialism" is borrowed from Wehler, "Bismarck's Imperialism," pp. 128–33.

36. William Appleman Williams and other historians have stressed that the open door was the touchstone of American conceptions of international economic order, embodying a concept of developmental hierarchy in which rights to invest, trade, and develop were to be based principally on the productive and investment capacity of the metropolitan states rather than on their political, historic, or military dominance, territorial propinquity, or supposed cultural preeminence. Like the British nineteenth-century "imperialism of free trade," the open door universalized particular national objectives as an organizing system for the international economic activity, a fact Americans and Europeans clearly recognized. Its concepts were pursued explicitly by American leaders such as Richard Olney, Theodore Roosevelt, William H. Taft, Woodrow Wilson, Elihu Root, Alfred T. Mahan, Charles A. Conant, and Philander Knox. See William Appleman Williams, *The Tragedy of American Diplomacy* (New York: Delta, 1962), pp. 37–50, esp. 44–45; Williams, *The Contours of American History* (New York: Quadrangle, 1961), pp. 368–69. Key documents in the development of this interpretation include Martin J. Sklar, "Woodrow Wilson and the Political Economy of Modern United States Liberalism," *Studies on the Left* 1 (Fall 1960): 17–47; Carl P. Parrini, *Heir to Empire: United States Economic Diplomacy, 1916–1923* (Pittsburgh: University of Pittsburgh Press, 1969); and Walter LaFeber, *The New Empire: An Interpretation of American Expansion, 1860–1898* (Ithaca, N.Y.: Cornell University Press, 1963), esp. pp. 316–18.

37. The U.S. conditional interpretation dated from America's first independent commercial treaty, with France, in 1778. Treaties involving the German *Zollverein*

and with Mexico were rejected by Congress, and Canadian reciprocity of 1855–66 was canceled by the Radical Republicans. See Guy Shirk Claire, "Reciprocity as a Trade Policy of the United States," *Annals* 141 (January 1929): 36. The United States approved a reciprocity treaty with Hawaii in 1876, helping to preclude the consolidation of British influence there; see LaFeber, *New Empire*, pp. 141–42. Blaine's Pan-American reciprocity proposals of the 1880s also fit into the limited structure of reciprocity as defined by the conditional most-favored-nation clause.

Although subjected to varying interpretations and implementations, the conditional interpretation remained in force until the 1922 Fordney-McCumber Tariff. See William S. Culbertson, "Equality of Treatment among Nations and a Bargaining Tariff," *Annals* 94 (March 1921): 160. In good part, the persistence of the conditional interpretation may be attributable to the strength of protectionism in Congress, which undoubtedly inhibited the State Department from making a direct challenge to legislative prerogatives. Moreover, the conditional interpretation was defended even by Americans who favored the principles of the open door, as giving the United States the flexibility to pursue differential tariff policies toward semicolonial dependencies such as Cuba; see, for example, Chester Lloyd Jones, "The American Interpretation of the 'Most Favored Nation' Clause," *Annals* 32 (September 1908): 119–29. Still, some revision-minded Democrats, such as Henry Parker Willis, argued as early as 1907 that adopting the unconditional, European, interpretation would greatly simplify and harmonize U.S. international commercial relations. See his "Reciprocity with Germany, II," *Journal of Political Economy* 15 (July 1907): 385–97. In practice, then, before World War I, U.S. most-favored-nation tariff treaties were supposed to be passed on individually by a two-thirds majority in the Senate.

38. Powers, "Expansion and Protection," *Quarterly Journal of Economics* 13 (July 1899): 361–78; quotations from pp. 361 and 372; comments on Britain and Canada from pp. 374–75; Atkinson to Wells, July 8, 1898, Wells Papers.

39. Miller warned that continued foreign expansion in conditions of increasing world industrialization would be dependent on tariff reductions; unless increasing numbers of businessmen recognized this fact, overproduction would dog the economy. Miller, "The Next Steps in Tariff Reform," in *Corporations and Public Welfare*, Supplement to *Annals* 15 (May 1900): 187–99.

40. Commented Robert P. Porter, McKinley's commissioner to Guam and Puerto Rico, "The tariff policy of our new possessions must first of all be framed to fit the country and the condition of the people for which it is intended"; "The Tariff Policy of Our New Possessions," in *Corporations and Public Welfare*, Supplement to *Annals* 15 (May 1900): 171–84. In the Insular Cases, U.S. colonies or territories were declared "appurtenant to" the United States and therefore not necessarily subject to complete assimilation within the U.S. tariff wall. *CTP*, pp. 577–78, 580–87.

41. On U.S.-German conflicts over Cuban reciprocity, see my chapter 4; see also *RCT*, p. 428; *CTP*, p. 699.

42. Aldrich, "Industrial Ascendancy of the United States," in *Corporations and Public Welfare*, Supplement to *Annals* 15 (May 1900): 155–68.

Chapter 2

1. See U.S. Congress, House, *Congressional Record*, 55th Cong., 1st sess., 1897, pp. 132–33. The background of the reciprocity provisions is well described in Walter LaFeber, *The New Empire: An Interpretation of American Expansion, 1860–1898* (Ithaca, N.Y.: Cornell University Press, 1963), pp. 374–76; Thomas J. McCormick, *China Market: America's Quest for Informal Empire, 1893–1901* (Chicago: Quadrangle, 1967), pp. 42–51; and Tom E. Terrell, *The Tariff, Politics, and American Foreign Policy, 1874–1901* (Westport, Conn.: Greenwood Press, 1973), pp. 204–5.

2. For Commissioner Kasson's testimony, see U.S. Congress, Senate, 56th Cong., 1st sess., Doc. 225, *Reciprocity Convention with France*, John A. Kasson, "Statement Made on Wednesday, January 10, 1900 . . ." (Washington, D.C.: GPO, 1900), p. 69. Kasson also told the Senate Foreign Relations Committee that if the French treaty could not be approved, it was "vain to attempt any others in Europe. . . . So far as Europe is concerned, it is vain for me to attempt to do better than I have done with France" (p. 80). Lewis L. Gould has argued that French lobbying efforts and U.S. concern for establishing international bimetallism and thus undermining domestic proponents of free silver had more to do with the shaping of the reciprocity provisions of the Dingley Tariff in the House Ways and Means Committee than did interest in foreign trade; see "Diplomats in the Lobby: Franco-American Relations and the Dingley Tariff of 1897," *Historian* 39 (August 1977): 659–80. Gould allows, however, that McKinley and Kasson may have seen "the implications of where reciprocity in the Dingley law would lead after 1897" (p. 680).

3. "The Story of a Great National Organization," *Farm Machinery* 638 (December 29, 1903), n.p. NAAIVM and NAM policies were sometimes so close that the groups were accused of intending to merge. See NAAIVM *Convention*, 1903, ibid., speech of President Martin Kingman, n.p.

4. These materials consisted, for the implement makers, mostly of steel; for the wagon makers, steel and hardwoods; and for the carriage makers, including many of the early automobile and truck shops, steel, hardwoods, and leather. On the needs of implement and vehicle manufacturers for raw materials, see H. E. Miles et al., "Report of the Special Tariff Committee of the National Association of Agricultural Implement and Vehicle Manufacturers to the Executive Committee, 1906," copy in the Theodore Roosevelt Papers, Library of Congress, Washington, D.C. A version of this report is reproduced in N. I. Stone, *One Man's Crusade for an Honest Tariff: The Story of H. E. Miles, Father of the Tariff Commission* (Appleton, Wis.: Lawrence College Press, 1952), pp. 11–20.

5. NAAIVM *Convention*, 1901, in *Farm Machinery* 526 (November 5, 1901), speech of President James Carr, Report of the Committee on National Legislation, n.p. The pages of *Farm Machinery* and *Farm Implement News* can be compared, for their relative stress on trusts, with the position of the *Implement Age*, published in Philadelphia and Chicago. This last-named farm machinery newspaper frequently published material oriented to the Democratic party, such as speeches by William Jennings Bryan. See, for example, the speech of Bryan, "The Real Defenders of Property," *Implement Age*, August 24, 1905, pp. 16–18, a defense of small property owners. See also "The Implement Industry and Monopoly Methods," *Implement Age*, May 4, 1905, p. 24, for a straightforward attack on trusts from the perspective of small property owners that was uncharacteristic of *Farm Machinery* and *Farm Implement News*.

6. On the merger, see, for example, Helen M. Kramer, "Harvesters and High Finance: Formation of the International Harvester Company," *Business History Review* 38 (Autumn 1964): 283–301; see also "Story of a Great Organization," *Farm Machinery* 638 (December 29, 1903), n.p.

7. "Medium-sized" businesses might be those such as H. E. Miles's Racine-Sattley company, which had about 1,500 employees. By contrast, one of the smaller units of Harvester, D. M. Osborne, had upward of 3,000 employees. The composition of the Committee on National Legislation, which was in charge of the lobbying in Washington for the Kasson treaties, was as follows for 1901–2: Chairman James Deering, Deering Harvester/International Harvester; Martin Kingman, Kingman Plow Company; C. H. Deere, John Deere and Company; C. E. Whitman, Whitman Agricultural Company; J. W. Stoddard, Stoddard Manufacturing Company; G. Watson French, Bettendorf Metal Wheel Company; Edwin D. Metcalf, D. M. Osborne and Company (a large harvester manufacturer in upstate New York secretly absorbed by International Harvester in 1903); A. C. Chase, Syracuse Chilled Plow Company; W. C. Barker, Barker Implements, Troy, New York; S. J. Llewellyn, Plano Manufacturing Company/International Harvester; Frederick S. Fish (general counsel for Studebaker Brothers); James C. McMath (general counsel for the Deerings). See NAAIVM *Convention*, 1902, in *Farm Machinery* 576 (October 21, 1902), n.p.

8. NAM *Proceedings*, 1895, p. 33; 1896, pp. 66, 75. See Martin J. Sklar, "The N.A.M. and Foreign Markets on the Eve of the Spanish-American War," *Science and Society* 23 (1959): 133–62. See also Albert K. Steigerwalt, *The National Association of Manufacturers, 1895–1914: A Study in Business Leadership* (Ann Arbor: University of Michigan Press, 1964), pp. 67–82; and Philip H. Burch, Jr., "The NAM as an Interest Group," *Politics and Society* 4 (Fall 1973): 97–130.

9. The comments of Charles Heber Clark on reciprocity are in NAM *Proceedings*, 1895, p. 20. See also Terrill, *Tariff*, p. 214. On the Republican promotion of reciprocity as an alternative to the views of the Democrats favoring free raw materials, see the speech of Sereno Payne of New York in the House, August 13, 1894, cited in *RCT*, pp. 158–59, in which he argues that reciprocity is a more

effective means to achieve a policy of free raw materials because it would give the United States more leverage to force concessions from foreign nations. McKinley also argued that foreign markets would help regain the "ground we have lost in the last two years" of depression. William McKinley, "We Will Recover," Speech at the National Convention of Manufacturers, Cincinnati, NAM *Proceedings*, 1895, pp. 10–13.

10. A few Democrats within the NAM played an important role in promoting tariff revision and the identification of reciprocity and free raw materials ideas. Arthur B. Farquhar, an agricultural implement manufacturer and self-made millionaire from York, Pennsylvania, was a vocal participant in the organization. A Gold Democrat and prolific writer on political economy, Farquhar maintained friendly relations not only with conservative Democrats but with protectionists such as Andrew Carnegie and midwestern Republicans such as Hugh Henry Hanna, head of the Atlas Machine Works of Indianapolis and a leading figure in the Indianapolis Monetary Convention. Participation in the "sound money" movement, which anticipated the creation of central banking in the United States and drafted the basis of the Gold Standard Act of 1900, was a crucial feature of coherence for the capitalist class in this period, as James Livingston has argued in *Origins of the Federal Reserve System: Money, Class, and Corporate Capitalism* (Ithaca, N.Y.: Cornell University Press, 1986). Another important "sound money" and low-tariff advocate was Gustav Schwab, American representative of German steamship lines and member of New York commercial organizations such as the Merchants Association of New York (MANY). On Farquhar and Hanna, see *LHA*, 1:110–11.

11. Of course, there is no necessary connection between government requirements for revenue and the flow of revenue-producing imports. Search, a long-time proprietary capitalist activist, was seeking to undermine the concept of absolute protection of the home market and to replace it with the idea of equalizing American and European competitive conditions. Thus, if, in the interest of "businesslike conduct," manufacturers admitted that they could tolerate substantially lower rates, divisive debates and outmoded party dogmas could be cast aside, and sweeping and profitable alterations of the American tariff system could then be made. On the background of Search and his predecessor, Thomas Dolan, see Philip Scranton, *Proprietary Capitalism: The Textile Manufacturers of Philadelphia, 1800–1885* (New York: Cambridge University Press, 1983). Search's initial statements on reciprocity are from NAM *Proceedings*, 1896, pp. 17–18.

12. NAM *Proceedings*, 1897, pp. 17–18.

13. NAM *Proceedings*, 1898, pp. 3, 15, 60; see also ibid., 1899, pp. 9–10.

14. NAM *Proceedings*, 1900, pp. 3–5.

15. Despite the problems of the French treaty, Search could still enthuse that "American manufacturers no longer measure their productive capacity by the consuming power of the home markets; for the world is their market and all people of the earth are their customers"; ibid., pp. 17–19.

16. Ibid., pp. 137–39, 142–46. See also Edward L. Younger, *John A. Kasson: Politics and Diplomacy from Lincoln to McKinley* (Iowa City: State Historical Society of Iowa, 1955), pp. 367, 374–75.

17. NAM *Proceedings*, 1900, pp. 139–42, 147–51.

18. Kasson's testimony is in U.S. Congress, Senate, Committee on Foreign Relations, *Hearings on Treaty with France*, 56th Cong., 1st sess., Doc. 225 (Washington, D.C.: GPO, 1900), p. 66.

19. NAM *Proceedings*, 1901, pp. 5–9.

20. Ibid., p. 106.

21. The "money center," Taylor argued, had "leaped across the water into New York and is no longer in the old eastern countries." Perhaps consciously here, Taylor was echoing the imperial ideas of intellectuals such as Charles A. Conant and Brooks Adams. Ibid., p. 83.

22. Ibid., pp. 47–50.

23. Ibid., pp. 78–79.

24. Ibid.

25. Ibid., pp. 80, 82.

26. Copy of the call in NAAIVM *Convention*, 1901, in *Farm Machinery* 526 (November 5, 1901): n.p., as letter from Theodore C. Search under date October 25, 1901. Search said, in part, "The object of this convention is to ascertain accurately the views of representative manufacturers on this subject [reciprocity] and to formulate, if possible, some practical suggestions for such legislation or diplomatic negotiations as may be necessary to establish more intimate commercial relations between the United States and other nations."

27. Brooks Adams, "Reciprocity or the Alternative," *Atlantic Monthly* 88 (August 1901): 145–55.

28. Ibid. Adams's comments on U.S. mineral resources are on p. 150. Adams's conception of natural progression is fleshed out in his works *The Law of Civilization* (London, 1895) and *The New Empire* (New York, 1901). The characterization of Brooks Adams as an "imperialist intellectual" is that of William Appleman Williams in *The Roots of the Modern American Empire: A Study of the Growth and Shaping of Social Consciousness in a Marketplace Society* (New York: Random House, 1969), p. 345. See especially Williams's essay, "Brooks Adams and American Expansion," *New England Quarterly* 25 (June 1952): 217–32.

29. Quotations from "Reciprocity or the Alternative," pp. 148, 149.

30. William McKinley, "Last Public Address," reprinted in *National Reciprocity* 1 (September 1902): 4–10. See pp. 8–10 for quotations. McKinley's tour had been interrupted by his wife's illness. The confluence of Adams's and McKinley's ideas on American expansion and commerce is highlighted by John Hay's eulogy of McKinley, delivered before the House of Representatives on February 27, 1902 (*Congressional Record*, 57th Cong., 1st sess., vol. 35, pt. 3, pp. 2197–2202). Hay identified McKinley as one of the "captains" of the transition of the United States to world power as an exporting nation. Moreover, the poetic Hay intoned, in an echo

of Adams, "The financial center of the world, which required thousands of years to journey from the Euphrates to the Thames and the Seine, seems passing to the Hudson between daybreak and dark" (p. 2201). Hay identified McKinley as "an ardent protectionist," yet he singled out McKinley's last speech on reciprocity as "his testament to the nation" (p. 2201).

31. On Republican-Democratic cooperation in "sound money" legislation, see Livingston, *Origins of Federal Reserve*, esp. part 2, "From Market Power to Cultural Authority: The Resolution of the Money Question, 1894–1900," pp. 71–128. Gustav Schwab of the MANY and the New York Chamber of Commerce and Henry R. Towne of the MANY were closely associated with the "sound money" and Federal Reserve movements.

32. NAAIVM, *Commercial Reciprocity* (Chicago: National Association of Agricultural Implement and Vehicle Manufacturers, 1901), pp. 3–5.

33. Ibid., p. 6.

34. See NAAIVM, *Convention*, 1901, "The French Reciprocity Treaty," n.p.; see also Frank E. Lukens to Hon. George Turner, December 19, 1901, cover letter attached to Library of Congress copy of *Commercial Reciprocity*; quotations from *Commercial Reciprocity*, p. 5. From its language, this pamphlet appears to have been written largely by James Deering.

35. Ibid., pp. 5, 6.

36. For example, Owen Osborne, a Philadelphia hosiery manufacturer, renewed the warning he had delivered at the June NAM convention against the French treaty's discrimination against American knit goods. An upstate New York knit goods manufacturer assailed James Deering's proreciprocity testimony before the Senate Foreign Relations Committee and complained that it was not so that implement makers' gains offset the knit manufacturers' losses. A representative of the New England Manufacturing Jewelers' and Silversmiths' Association argued along similar lines, as did a New York perfume manufacturer. See NRC *Proceedings*, 1901. For Osborne's remarks, see pp. 100–105; the criticism of Deering was made by Titus Sheard, p. 93. The jewelry representative was S. O. Bigney, whose remarks appear on pp. 46–47.

37. Ibid., p. 26.

38. Ibid.

39. Ibid., p. 59.

40. Ibid.: Seabury, p. 51; Dalley, p. 44; Schieren, p. 67; Schieren, of the New York Board of Trade, was the manufacturer of "Duxbak" waterproof industrial leather belting, which was discriminated against in the French reciprocity agreement.

41. Material on the National Reciprocity League is drawn from *National Reciprocity* issues from September 1902 through January 1903.

42. The withdrawal of James Deering, now heavily occupied with management at Harvester, probably had other motives than the growing hostility between Har-

vester and the independents in the farm equipment business. Other Harvester-related individuals continued to play important roles in the NAAIVM, as subsequent chapters in the present work will note. These included Edwin D. Metcalf, former co-owner of the Osborne Harvester Company, based in Auburn, New York, who became a manager and silent partner in Harvester when the corporation absorbed Osborne in 1903, and C. S. Funk, the director of Harvester's export operations, who served as an adviser and spokesman for the NAAIVM's Committee on Foreign Commerce. Nonetheless, Harvester generally appears to have sought a low profile in industry affairs during this period of tension.

43. Henry R. Towne, W. A. Marble, and Charles R. Lamb, "Report of the Merchants Association Delegates to the Reciprocity Convention," *Merchants Association Bulletin* 1 (December 1901): 2–3. Towne, the president of the Yale and Towne Lock Company, of Stamford, Connecticut, was a noted industrial engineer who had pioneered the production and marketing of the pin-tumbler lock invented by his partner, Linus Yale, who had died in 1868. Towne would later become a major figure in the tariff commission movement, as would MANY alternate delegate William R. Corwine (see subsequent chapters). Towne offered the tentative suggestions of voluntary reductions by foreign-trade proponents and suggested that the demand for a cabinet-level Department of Commerce and Industry might be bent to create an information-gathering body—in effect, a proto–tariff commission.

Chapter 3

1. Quoted in *RCT*, p. 226. See also Theodore Roosevelt, "First Annual Message," December 3, 1901, *MPP*, 14:6641–80. In his first address, Roosevelt cautiously endorsed reciprocity as the "handmaiden" of protection, but he added that foreign abilities to purchase U.S. goods were dependent on foreign sales of goods in the United States. "The phenomenal growth of our export trade," Roosevelt stressed in his tariff remarks, "emphasizes the urgency of the need for wider markets and for a liberal policy in dealing with foreign nations." See *MPP*, 14:6652. In his "Second Annual Message" of December 2, 1902, Roosevelt also supported reciprocity and seemed to suggest the feasibility of appointing "a commission of business experts . . . to recommend action by the Congress" (*MPP*, 14:6714). On Roosevelt's tariff policies, see also Richard Cleveland Baker, *The Tariff under Roosevelt and Taft* (Hastings, Neb.: Democrat Printing Company, 1941), p. 63; Roosevelt even wrote to Cannon and Aldrich that he specifically followed their advice on the tariff question. William Rea Gwinn, *Uncle Joe Cannon, Archfoe of Insurgency* (n.p.: Bookman Associates, 1957), pp. 74–76, 92–94; Nathaniel Stephenson, *Nelson W. Aldrich* (New York: Scribner's, 1930), pp. 180–81.

2. Gwinn, *Uncle Joe Cannon*, pp. 92–94; Baker, *Tariff under Roosevelt and Taft*, pp. 47, 61–63.

3. Baker, *Tariff under Roosevelt and Taft*, p. 22; Roosevelt, "First Annual Message." See also Roosevelt, "Second Annual Message," December 1902, in which he argued, similarly, that "the cases in which the tariff can produce a monopoly are so few as to constitute an inconsiderable factor in the question"(*MPP*, 14:6714). Roosevelt was specifically guided in preparing his second message by procorporate academics such as Arthur Twining Hadley of Yale, Jeremiah W. Jenks of Cornell, and E. R. A. Seligman of Columbia. See Martin J. Sklar, *The Corporate Reconstruction of American Capitalism, 1890–1916: The Market, the Law, and Politics* (New York: Cambridge University Press, 1988), esp. p. 335. A representative example of the academics' thinking is Arthur T. Hadley, "The Good and the Evil of Industrial Combination," *Atlantic Monthly* 79 (March 1897): 377–85.

4. Roosevelt to Root, September 4, 1906, Elihu Root Papers, Library of Congress, Washington, D.C. Roosevelt's view of Bryan as his imitator perhaps says more about Roosevelt than about Bryan. On Roosevelt's views of the market and the state, see especially Sklar, *Corporate Reconstruction*, pp. 334–64.

5. On New England tariff revisionism, see Baker, *Tariff under Roosevelt and Taft*, pp. 56–57.

6. Roosevelt to Root, August 18, 1906, Root Papers. Beveridge to Roosevelt, August 21, 1906, Theodore Roosevelt Papers, Library of Congress, Washington, D.C. Beveridge said in part, "There are a large number of business men at this hotel from all over the country—many from Massachusetts, several from New York and several from Philadelphia. I have talked with them all and not one . . . does not say that *some* schedules of the tariff ought to be changed—and all of them are protectionist Republicans." Cf. John Braeman, *Albert J. Beveridge: American Nationalist* (Chicago: University of Chicago Press, 1971), pp. 123–25. Beveridge concluded, with Parry, that the drop in Republican votes in the 1906 election was caused by Democratic agitation against the abuses of the tariff by trusts.

7. Root's view was prophetic inasmuch as it was the Democratic Wilson administration that finally established a permanent tariff commission (see chapter 11). Root to Roosevelt, November 16, 1904, Root Papers. Root argued for maximum-minimum tariffs again in 1906, after his return from the Rio conference on trade expansion in Latin America, and it suggests that he was thinking of U.S. commercial expansion in South America as a potential safety valve that would help the administration sell timid manufacturers on the benefits of tariff revisions, because they presumably had less to lose from competition from the mainly agrarian countries to the south. See Elihu Root, "Development of the Foreign Trade of the United States," *Annals* 29 (May 1907): 1–9.

8. Henry F. Pringle, *The Life and Times of William Howard Taft* (New York: Farrar and Rinehart, 1939), 1:261, for Taft's view on Philippine reciprocity. Baker, *Tariff under Roosevelt and Taft*, p. 56, for Taft's views on the tariff and revenue; Taft's Maine and Ohio speeches and his resolution to support tariff revision are noted in Pringle, *Taft*, 1:288–89, 329.

9. Parry's allies and successors were James W. Van Cleave, a St. Louis stove maker, who took over in 1906; and John Kirby, Jr., a Dayton railroad equipment manufacturer, who took charge in 1909.

Historians have generally viewed the Parry, Van Cleave, and Kirby years of the NAM as primarily preoccupied with anti-union activities. Typical in this respect are Robert H. Wiebe, *Businessmen and Reform: A Study of the Progressive Movement* (Cambridge, Mass.: Harvard University Press, 1962), p. 109, and William H. Becker, *The Dynamics of Business-Government Relations: Industry and Exports, 1893–1921* (Chicago: University of Chicago Press, 1982), p. 46. To some extent, the employers' activities sponsored by the three leaders did overshadow the commercial interests that had preoccupied the NAM in earlier years, and they were at variance with the policies of the previous NAM leaders such as Search and Charles Schieren, Search's candidate for the NAM presidency. Search and Schieren were members of the National Civic Federation, for example, whose activities the Parry faction vehemently opposed as compromising with the labor movement. On the other hand, Schieren had become lukewarm about reciprocity even by 1901. As his contributions to the NAM's reciprocity convention suggested, his position was closer to the New York "free raw materials" advocates.

It is important to recognize the NAM's continued support of commercial expansion and tariff revision. For the new leaders, the two issues, labor and tariff, were not antithetical: Both reflected a concern by proprietary businesses to preserve their influence within the political economy. The continued interest of the NAM in foreign commerce can be traced in the pages of its newspaper, *American Industries*. See also Alfred K. Steigerwalt, *The National Association of Manufacturers, 1895–1914: A Study in Business Leadership* (Ann Arbor: University of Michigan Press, 1964), pp. 44–63, 67–86. The connections between the labor and tariff issues in the NAM emerge most clearly in the period around the promulgation of the Payne-Aldrich Tariff and are discussed in greater detail in subsequent chapters.

10. The manufacturers, on behalf of the importer, Gustave A. Jahn, claimed that Russia had merely remitted what would be the payment by Russian sugar producers of double duties (that is, their own excise taxes and foreign tariffs). Hence, they argued, the Russian system was like U.S. "drawbacks," the traditional remission of tariff duties on material being manufactured in the United States for reexport. This was a highly generous interpretation of drawback clauses, it should be noted. Most, if not all, of the Russian sugar was domestically produced beet sugar. The case thus suggests that the NAM was willing to go quite far on behalf of manufacturers who exported to Russia to avoid escalation of trade animosities. See William L. Saunders, "Status of the Russian Sugar Cases," *American Industries* 1 (August 15, 1902): 7–8. Saunders, then a vice-president of the Ingersoll-Sergeant Drill Company, was active later in the National Foreign Trade Council as the chairman of Ingersoll-Rand Corporation. The German tariff was also the subject of intensive negotiation and contention, as is discussed later. See also "New German

Tariff Considerations and Their Relation to American Commerce," *American Industries* 4 (December 15, 1905): 1–3; cf. NAM *Proceedings*, 1905, pp. 60–61, 163–64.

11. These increases did not apply to American agricultural equipment, which the Russians needed badly; see Saunders, "Russian Sugar Cases." In 1905, the Russian chief minister, Sergei Witte, revoked the Russian discriminatory duties on American iron and steel. See "Russia Abolishes Discriminatory Duties against American Goods," *American Industries* 4 (September 15, 1905): 3.

12. NAM *Proceedings*, 1903, pp. 69–73; for NAM support of other measures, see pp. 64–69, 73–78. See also Becker, *Dynamics of Business-Government Relations*, p. 78.

13. On the European boycotts, see John L. Gignilliat, "Pigs, Politics, and Protection: The European Boycott of American Pork, 1879–1891," *Agricultural History* 35 (January 1961): 3–12; Louis L. Snyder, "The German-American Pork Dispute, 1879–1891," *Journal of Modern History* 17 (March 1945): 16–28. For the status of meat exports, see Harold U. Faulkner, *American Economic History*, 8th ed. (New York: Harper Bros., 1960), pp. 391, 412. See also the table on p. 395, "Rank of Leading Industries, 1860, 1914, and 1929." See also *Twelfth Census of the United States, 1900*, vol. 7, *Manufactures* (Washington, D.C.: GPO, 1902), part 1, table LXVIII, p. clxx.

14. The group's immediate goal was to organize for recovery from the depression of the 1890s and to prepare the industry for the expansion of land cultivation westward into former rangeland, the opening of arid lands to grazing through the use of irrigation, and the rise of the "finishing system" whereby western-grown (or even sometimes foreign-grown) animals were fattened for slaughter at feedlots close to the midwestern packinghouses.

15. See NLSA *Proceedings*, 1898.

16. On export considerations as they affected packers and growers, see, for example, the speech of Edward Tilden of the National Packing Company, in NLSA *Proceedings*, 1906, pp. 87–93.

17. NLSA *Proceedings*, 1904, pp. 30–31. For the elder Springer's tariff views, see, for example, William M. Springer, *Tariff Reform the Paramount Issue: Speeches and Writings on the Question Involved in the Presidential Contest of 1892* (New York: C. L. Webster and Co., 1892). In general, the NLSA endorsed Theodore Roosevelt's general approach to corporations, which was to see them as a "natural business evolution" not to be discriminated against for size but to be restrained in the interests of the industry as a whole.

18. NLSA *Proceedings*, 1905, pp. 180–85. The proposed bylaws called for representation by five grower interests (sheep, cattle, horses, swine, and stock feeders) and two packinghouse interests (the packers and the livestock exchanges, most of which were financially associated with the packers).

19. Ibid. Harris specifically justified his argument for associating publicly with

the meatpackers as paralleling Roosevelt's call for trusts to be "reasonable" and "amenable to the public."

20. Ibid., p. 180. See also "Report of the Executive Committee of the American Stock Growers' Association, Denver, Colorado, January 30, 1906," NLSA *Proceedings*, 1906, pp. 101–5, and see the constitution adopted by the rump NLSA group in 1905, *Constitution and Bylaws of the National Live Stock Association as Finally Adopted* (Denver: National Live Stock Association, 1905). Samuel Cowan was president of the Texas Cattlemen's Association; he worked with Iowa Governor Albert Cummins to curb rail rates through the Interstate Commerce Commission. See Thomas James Bray, *The Rebirth of Freedom* (Indianola, Iowa: Record and Tribune Press, 1957).

21. NLSA *Proceedings*, 1905, pp. 180–85.

22. On the new German tariff, see N. I. Stone, "The New German Customs Tariff," *North American Review* 181 (September 1905): 392–406; see also Stone, "The International Aspect of Our Tariff Situation," *North American Review* 180 (March 1905): 381–93. Tom Terrill notes the proposal of an American "zollverein" by Stephen Douglas in 1861 and by William Evarts in the late 1870s as a counter-measure to the European tariff and commercial challenges; see Tom E. Terrill, *The Tariff, Politics, and American Foreign Policy, 1874–1901* (Westport, Conn.: Greenwood Press, 1973), p. 22. American politicians had attempted to deal with German commercial consolidations since the 1840s. See Guy Shirk Claire, "Reciprocity as a Trade Policy of the United States," *Annals* 141 (January 1929): 159.

23. See NLSA *Proceedings*, 1908, for Sanders's recollections on the origins of the conference. On the charges that the reciprocity convention was trust-inspired, see *Protectionist*, August 1905, p. 161. A list of the sponsors and copy of the calls to the convention are in *American Economist*, July 28, 1905, p. 38. The groups sponsoring the conference included the NLSA, various cattle breeders' associations, the Corn Belt Meat Producers Association, the Millers National Federation, the Chicago Board of Trade, the Commercial Association of Chicago, and the National Association of Agricultural Implement and Vehicle Manufacturers.

24. Conference goals are noted in the *Chicago Daily Tribune*, August 17, 1905, p. 2. By keeping the discussion at a general level, organizers hoped to transcend the sectional claims of the various groups. The *Tribune* (p. 1) summarized these claims as follows: "New England was represented as a territory almost denuded of natural resources and demanding free access to markets where raw material could be purchased. The West came as a great agricultural territory which was about to suffer because of foreign retaliatory measures. The South presented its claims for a market for its cotton."

25. On the extension of section 4 of the Dingley Tariff, see, for example, National Board of Trade, *Proceedings of the 36th Annual Meeting, Washington, D.C., January 1906* (Philadelphia: McFedridge, 1906), p. 266. On the reciprocity conference goals, see the speech of Senator Shelby Cullom, reprinted in *Protectionist*, Septem-

ber 1905, p. 223; *American Economist*, August 25, 1905, pp. 92–93. *Chicago Daily Tribune*, August 17, 1905, p. 1. See also N. I. Stone, *One Man's Crusade for an Honest Tariff: The Story of H. E. Miles, Father of the Tariff Commission* (Appleton, Wis.: Lawrence College Press, 1952), pp. 7–9.

26. *Protectionist*, August 1905, p. 220; see also the *Chicago Daily Tribune*, August 17, 1905, p. 1. The *Protectionist* scoffed that "the demand for free raw materials which the Massachusetts delegates carried with them to Chicago was not favorably received, and it dropped with a dull thud." That the conference represented a failure of the midwestern and agricultural and commercial interests to "win significant backing in the East" is the view taken by Wiebe, *Businessmen and Reform*, p. 60.

27. A tariff with the general rates as a minimum would have been more like the McKinley Tariff of 1890 than section 4 of the Dingley Tariff of 1897. Given the high rates of the Dingley Tariff, this certainly would have escalated tariff conflict. Whether Cullom had not yet fully understood the intention of the conference organizers to use the Dingley rates as a maximum, or whether he was hedging his tariff position because he was up for reelection to the Senate is not clear. But as a supporter of tariff reduction—as opposed to "revision"—he cannot have been of great material assistance. *American Economist*, August 25, 1905, pp. 92–93. See the protectionist critique of the speech in an editorial, "Cullomism-Cumminsism," p. 90. A "minimum and maximum" tariff that set the Dingley rates as a *minimum* was actually the suggestion of an editorial in the protectionist *American Economist* (September 8, 1905), "The Only Safe Kind of Dual Tariff." Its reasoning, of course, was casuistic: Protectionists were open to "revision," as long as revision did not mean downward revision of the tariff.

28. Cummins criticized the standpat Republicans for rebuffing reciprocity in competitive products, averring that it was consonant with genuine protectionism and the creed of the Republican forefathers—Blaine, Garfield, Sherman, and Mc-Kinley. *American Economist*, August 25, 1905, pp. 93–94. Cf. Bray, *Rebirth of Freedom*, pp. 53–62.

29. National Boot and Shoe Manufacturers' Association, *Proceedings of the Second Annual Convention* (February 1906), pp. 28–32.

30. Editorial, "Organizing for Reciprocity," in *Cotton* 12 (October 15, 1905): 4–5. H. C. Staver was the former president of the National Association of Agricultural Implement and Vehicle Manufacturers and had been the board chairman of the failed National Reciprocity League of 1902–3. See "Report of the Committee on Reciprocity," *Carriage Monthly* 41 (October 1905): 222–23.

31. *Chicago Daily Tribune*, August 18, 1905, p. 1. Cf. *Protectionist*, August 1905. Wiebe, *Businessmen and Reform*, pp. 59–60, stresses the disharmony and lack of success in the convention as exemplified by the boot and shoe manufacturers' quarrels with the meatpackers. Implicitly, he follows the protectionists' critique. But given the lack of power of a convention to arrange an effective compromise between the interests on the issue of specific rates—a necessary consequence of the

absence of current legislation—this particular form of disunity is not surprising. Moreover, the tentative consensus around the new strategies of a maximum-minimum tariff and a tariff commission should not be disregarded.

32. The composition of the ARTL executive board is taken from the ARTL letterhead, for example, W. E. Skinner, Circular Letter of the American Reciprocal Tariff League (probably early 1906) in J. C. Spooner Papers, Library of Congress, Washington, D.C.

33. The new title mirrored that of the American Protective Tariff League, its antagonist. On the alternative titles, see Sanders to Roosevelt, August 5, 1905, Roosevelt Papers. Roosevelt was especially skeptical of passages Sanders had sent him from reductionist economist and sound money advocate J. L. Laughlin's book on reciprocity; Roosevelt to Sanders, August 9, 1905, ibid. See also the account in Richard Bryan Helmer, *James and Alvin Sanders: Livestock Journalists of the Midwest* (Bryn Mawr, Penn.: Dorrance, 1985).

34. See ANLSA *Proceedings*, 1906.

35. Lest his listeners misunderstand his vision of the new livestock industry, John concluded with this rhetorical question: "Shall we place the live stock industry of this country upon a solid and stable basis in accord with the tendency of the times for the combination of business interests, or shall we remain content to gamble in a game in which the chances are against us?" Instrumental to livestock producers' attempts to regulate production was a need for the federal government to "make a complete and reliable canvass of the live stock of the country which will enable us to form some intelligent conception as to the supply and demand." Ibid., p. 53.

36. ARTL Circular Letter, p. 2.

Chapter 4

1. John L. Gignilliat, "Pigs, Politics, and Protection: The European Boycott of American Pork, 1879–1901," *Agricultural History* 35 (January 1961): 3–12; *RCT*, pp. 422–28.

2. The Saratoga Convention was one of the treaties signed by the Harrison administration under the reciprocity provisions of the McKinley Tariff. Germany's Caprivi government regarded the treaty as part of the system of general and conventional tariffs it was constructing. The United States applied similar discriminations to Russian beet sugar exports, which enjoyed the recision of domestic excise taxes; this was considered akin to a direct bounty under the Dingley Tariff until Russian retaliation against American machine and steel exports forced reinterpretation of the ruling. The legitimation of countervailing duties by the British in 1889 (done within Britain's free-trade context to protect colonial sugar exports to Britain) illustrated the general trend away from liberal interpretations of the most-favored-nation clause and may have contributed to the difficulty of reversing the

trend during the Cleveland administration. See *FRUS* 1898, 1:178; William L. Saunders, "Status of the Russian Sugar Cases," *American Industries* 1 (August 15, 1902): 7–8; and *RCT*, pp. 426, 433.

3. In describing the proposed Cuban reciprocity treaty in 1902, Roosevelt argued that in the Platt amendment the United States had made Cuba "a part of our international political system" and that this should be extended to "becoming part of our economic system" via "the adoption of reciprocity." Roosevelt, "Second Annual Message," 1902, *MPP*, 14:6717. The phrase "relations of proximity" was used by Congressman Samuel McCall (R.-Mass.) of the Ways and Means Committee in debate over Canadian reciprocity in 1912, and by Secretary of State Philander Knox, but the justification dated at least to the U.S.-Hawaiian treaty of 1875; see *RCT*, p. 428.

Legally, the 1900 U.S.-German Argol Agreement ignored the 1828 treaty and implicitly voided it. By early 1903, Count Posadowsky, the German interior minister, had declared most-favored-nation relations between the two nations irrelevant. German academics appeared to agree. A German legal scholar, Professor Glier, published *Die Meistbegungsklausel* in 1905; he claimed that the American-Prussian treaty had always been invalid under the new German empire. Nonetheless, the German Foreign Office continued to press U.S. adoption of European most-favored-relations policies; see *RCT*, p. 430. See also N. I. Stone, "Most-Favored-Nation Relations between Germany and the United States," *North American Review* 182 (March 1906): 433–45.

4. See N. I. Stone, "The New German Customs Tariff," *North American Review* 181 (September 1905): 392–406.

5. Ibid.

6. Charlemagne Tower (U.S. ambassador to Germany) to John Hay (U.S. secretary of state), May 5, 1905, discussing German "tariff war" talk, RG 40/49436. For 1906, see, for example, the editorials in the *New York Times* on January 14, "A Tariff War"; February 3, "The Impending Tariff War"; and February 4, "Germans Fear Tariff War."

7. Of an overall U.S. export total to Germany of about $220 million in 1904, about $125 million was in raw materials (cotton exports were $82 million; copper, $28 million; mineral oil, $15 million). In contrast, most of Germany's approximately $109 million in 1904 exports comprised manufactures, except for potash and beet sugar. See Wolf Von Schierbrand, "Our Tariff Differences with Germany," *Review of Reviews* 32 (August 1905): 205–7; N. I. Stone, "The International Aspect of Our Tariff Situation," *North American Review* 180 (March 1905): 381–93, and Stone, "The New German Customs Tariff." U.S. trade to Germany also included wheat, corn, tobacco, flour, lard, leather, lumber, and fertilizers. But manufactures increased steadily in proportion during the 1890s and early 1900s.

8. German exports to the United States as a share of total German exports declined between 1891 and 1900, from 10.7 percent to 9.3 percent. Editorial, "Can

We Grant the Most-Favored-Nation Treatment to the United States of America?,"
Kölnische Volkszeitung, May 4, 1905. This newspaper was associated with the Center
party and with German manufacturing interests. See also the editorial of May 4,
1905, from *Magdeburgische Zeitung* (national-liberal newspaper). Translations enclosed in Tower to Hay, May 5, 1905, RG 40/49436.

9. "Address of Mr. Eugene N. Foss," NAM *Proceedings*, 1905, pp. 152–71; esp.
163–64. For text of the *Kampfzoll* paragraph, see U.S. Department of Commerce
and Labor, *Customs Tariff of the German Customs Union*, Tariff Series, no. 7 (Washington, D.C.: GPO, 1908), p. 9. Animal products, lard in particular, already
cramped by German health regulations, represented a $25-million export item;
manufactures in general amounted to about $15 million, of which machinery
constituted $3 million, but they represented a rapidly growing sector composed of a
large number of well-organized exporters. See Von Schierbrand, "Our Tariff Differences with Germany," pp. 205–7; Stone, "International Aspect of Our Tariff
Situation," pp. 381–93, and "The New German Customs Tariff," pp. 392–406.
For official discussion, see, for example, Tower to Hay, May 5, 1905, RG 40/
49436.

10. Frank H. Mason (consul general in Paris) to Secretary of State, March 15,
1905, *FRUS* 1905, pp. 453–58. The other members of the German treaty convention were Italy, Belgium, Romania, Switzerland, Servia, and Austria-Hungary.
Stone noted, for example, that the disparity between the general and the conventional tariffs was for bicycles, 50 percent; for flour, 84 percent; for corn, 63 percent;
and for some shoes, 100 percent; see his analysis in "International Aspect," p. 382,
and "The New German Customs Tariff," p. 406.

11. Tower summarized the restiveness of Germany on the trade question for
Secretary of State John Hay in a letter of May 1905, in which he maintained that
German public opinion "not only amongst the . . . agrarians but also amongst the
manufacturers and traders, as well as . . . in the Reichstag" resents that "whilst
America enjoys the privileges of the 'most-favored-nation,' . . . 90 percent of the
German goods imported into the United States are subjected to . . . our general
tariff law." Tower to Hay, May 5, 1905, RG 40/49436; Mason to Hay, March 15,
1905, *FRUS* 1905, pp. 456–57. On moderate trade views, see the editorial in
Magdeburgische Zeitung (enclosed in Tower to Hay, May 5, 1905), for quotation on
readjustment of commercial relations. Later, the American consul in Frankfurt
forwarded a document of a local German Chamber of Commerce that urged
exporters to "make front against those who incline toward forcible measures in
shaping our trade relations with the United States." The American consul was
forwarding a report by the Chamber of Commerce of Sonneburg, a center of toy,
china, and glassware manufacturing. The Chamber of Commerce report continued
by suggesting that Germany "must make most strenuous efforts to conquer foreign
markets. . . . Whoever advocates a tariff war forgets that the 500 million marks of
goods we annually sell to the United States come into question; that the relations

with our third largest customer will be interrupted for an indefinite time, that once the threads of intercourse are torn it will be a hard task to tie them together again." See [Richard] Guenther, "Report of Consul-General Guenther of Chamber of Commerce at Sonneburg," *Monthly Consular and Trade Reports*, no. 305 (February 1906): 171–78.

12. German demands regarding the most-favored-nation clause were ambiguous; the implication was that Germany wished the United States to adopt unconditional most-favored-nation status as a means of repudiating colonial preference tariff arrangements such as the U.S.-Cuban treaty. See H. Parker Willis, "Reciprocity with Germany, I," *Journal of Political Economy* 15 (June 1907): 321–44, esp. pp. 328–29; Von Schierbrand, "Our Tariff Differences with Germany," p. 206. On the proclamation of maximum tariff, see Sternberg to Root, January 29, 1905, *FRUS* 1906, 1:640.

13. Consignees did not yet own the goods being shipped to them. These terms were outlined in an exchange of correspondence between Secretary of State Root and Baron Hermann Speck Von Sternberg, the German ambassador; it is reprinted in *Congressional Record*, 59th Cong., 1st sess., vol. 40, pp. 9697–99. Cf. *FRUS* 1906, 1:640. See especially Root to Sternberg, February 16, 1906, noting German terms and Sternberg to Root, February 18, 1906.

The customs process was a complex one, involving several steps. American importers who went abroad to purchase goods for sale in the United States had to have these goods evaluated for customs purposes. Before 1906, American businesses collected purchase invoices as documentation of transactions. These were presented to American consuls in the foreign country, who confirmed their veracity against their own knowledge of the prevailing foreign market conditions. Then, at the port of entry, a domestic or "local" Treasury Department official appraised the goods in light of U.S. market conditions. If the importer believed that the valuation given by the U.S. local appraiser was too high, the importer could appeal to the Board of General Appraisers, created by the Customs Administrative Act of 1890 as a part of the Treasury Department. Importers could bring counsel and present evidence on the value of goods abroad and the "true entry value of the material." The local appraiser would then hold separate closed hearings—excluding the importer—with expert witnesses, business competitors, and others who might provide information relevant to a judgment on the market value of the items in question. The General Appraisers then rendered a judgment. If this judgment was against the importer, the importer had to pay the duty as determined on the goods, plus 1 percent penalty for each percentage point of difference between the claimed and judged valuations. This penalty, it may be added, pertained not only to the goods that occasioned the protest, but to all goods of like type imported between the original hearing and the decision. See Carl W[ilhelm] Stern, *Importing: With Special Attention to Customs Requirements* (New York: Business Training Corporation, 1916), pp. 55–58, 71–78. Cf. Willis, "Reciprocity with Germany, I," pp.

331–32. Importers had one final appeal, this time to a board of three general appraisers. Some appeals had been carried beyond this point, to federal courts and to the Supreme Court, but the Court had rejected both the suit and the right to bring it in a decision of 1903. See U.S. Customs Court, *The U.S. Customs Court: Its Origin and Jurisdiction* (New York: U.S. Customs Court, 1970). See also testimony of Wickham Smith, attorney for the New York Merchants Association, in U.S. Congress, House, Committee on Ways and Means, 59th Cong., 1st sess., *Customs Administrative Act—Licensing of Custom-House Brokers*, Report of Hearings before the Committee on Ways and Means, February 23–March 2, 1906 (Washington, D.C.: GPO, 1906).

14. The first of McCleary's bills would have made the rates of the Dingley Tariff a minimum and enacted a new maximum tariff rate 25 percent above it. The second bill extended retaliation to colonial tariff discriminations and sought to impose a 25 percent ad valorem duty on American free-list items as a further counterdiscrimination—essentially an American version of the German *Kampfzoll* clauses. The bills were HR 9004 and HR 9752; see *Congressional Record*, 59th Cong., 1st sess., Bill Index, pp. 558, 663; *House Bills*, 59th Cong., 1st sess. The Lodge bill did not specify exact punitive percentages and seemed to offer the possibility of reductions as well. The Lodge bill was S 688; *Senate Bills*, 59th Cong., 1st sess. See also *Congressional Record*, 59th Cong., 1st sess., vol. 40, app., House, pp. 176–211 (June 25, 1906) for McCleary's speech on the tariff, in which he attacked importing and shipping interests with arguments the exporters had often used to justify increased support for manufacturing efforts to build foreign trade. That is, McCleary charged that importers sought to build up German manufacturing and shipping at the expense of American industry while leaving the United States as a source of raw materials for foreign industry.

15. Shaw to Roosevelt, September 16, 1905 (copy in the Nelson W. Aldrich Papers, Library of Congress, Washington, D.C.). See also Leslie Mortier Shaw, *Current Issues* (New York: D. Appleton Co., 1908), pp. 169–71; and Shaw to W. R. Boyd ([editor?] of Cedar Rapids [Iowa] *Republican*), [October] 1905, ibid., pp. 171–77, and the somewhat later statement, Shaw to "New England Banker," September 10, 1907, ibid., pp. 177–85.

16. See Shaw to "New England Banker," in *Current Issues*, pp. 177–85. Shaw ridiculed the German customs process in hearings before the Ways and Means Committee: "In Europe, they have no reappraisement proceedings. It is a military system. A little company of soldiers, with side arms, stands on the dock. They look at your merchandise and don't tell you what it is worth, but mark what it is worth, pass it over to the cashier, and you pay it. . . . If you complain enough they will go inside, see a man there, and talk with him. They come out, write their decision, pass it over and that settles it. There is no appeal and there is no reappraisement." See Shaw testimony in Committee on Ways and Means, *Customs Administrative Act*, p. 31.

17. On the resistance of New England textile interests to alienating German exporters, see Ebenezer J. Hill (Republican member of the Ways and Means Committee from Connecticut) to Roosevelt, September 4, 1906, Theodore Roosevelt Papers, Library of Congress, Washington, D.C. Cf. *Washington Post*, March 2, 1906, 2:5; See also *New York Times*, February 4, 1906, 4:2, for German attitudes on tariff war possibilities, and *New York Times*, February 22, 1906, 1:3, "Reichstag Sanctions the Concession to U.S.," which relates Von Bulow's regret at the incomplete character of the accord and the influence of German manufacturing exporters in pressing for the compromise. The proclamations of the two nations are printed in *FRUS* 1906, 1:645–47.

18. For the original MANY proposal, see *Revision of Customs Laws, General Committee Report to His Excellency William McKinley* (New York: Merchants Association of New York, 1900), in New York Public Library Pamphlet Collection. The original committee included Thomas H. Downing, of R. F. Downing and Company, Customs Brokers; S. N. D. North, representing the National Wool Manufacturers Association; and J. T. Pirie, of Carson, Pirie, Scott Company of Chicago. It was chaired by John Gibb, of Mills and Gibb, of New York, although Thomas Downing soon took over the chairmanship of the committee. Cf. "A Review of the Association's Past Work," *Bulletin of the Merchants Association of New York* 1 (November 1901): 21. The Olcott bill was HR 15267, the Payne bill, HR 7113; see Committee on Ways and Means, *Customs Administrative Act*; comment is from Willis, "Reciprocity with Germany, I," p. 332.

19. See, for the updated text of revisions, MANY, *Revision of the Customs Laws: Report of the Committee on Customs Service and the Revenue Laws* (New York: Merchants Association of New York, 1906), and Thomas H. Downing to L. M. Shaw, January 27, 1906, reproduced in the report, in New York Public Library Pamphlet Collection. Smith's and Downing's presentations are in Committee on Ways and Means, *Customs Administrative Act*, pp. 5–12, 13–19, respectively.

20. Committee on Ways and Means, *Customs Administrative Act*, pp. 106–10.

21. Ibid., p. 10; the Supreme Court decision had denied this right on the basis of existing legislation.

22. Ibid., pp. 25, 94–97; cf. Willis, "Reciprocity with Germany, I," p. 339.

23. Willis, "Reciprocity with Germany, I," p. 339.

24. Hill to Roosevelt, September 4, 1906, Roosevelt Papers. See also "No Danger From the Philippines at All," *American Industries* 4 (March 1, 1906).

25. Hill to Roosevelt, September 4, 1906, Roosevelt Papers.

26. Ibid.

27. Ibid. Both Root and Hill had thus anticipated the arguments made by Hilferding in 1910 in relation to the shift in the nature of protection caused by export pricing (see chapter 1).

28. Shaw to Roosevelt, September 9, 1906, Roosevelt Papers.

29. Ibid.

30. Roosevelt to Shaw, September 11, 1906, in *Letters of Theodore Roosevelt*, vol. 5, *1905–1907*, ed. E. E. Morison (Cambridge, Mass.: Harvard University Press, 1952), p. 405; Roosevelt to Root, September 4, 1906, August 18, 1906, Elihu Root Papers, Library of Congress, Washington, D.C.

31. On Algeciras, see Fritz Fischer, *Germany's Aims in the First World War* (New York: Norton, 1967; originally published in German, 1961), p. 22. On Roosevelt's relations with the meatpackers, see John Braeman, *Albert J. Beveridge: American Nationalist* (Chicago: University of Chicago Press, 1971), pp. 104–9.

32. Like his friend Elihu Root, North was a committed expansionist, although as late as 1904 he had dismissed the dangers of European commercial alliances against the United States, reasoning that U.S. raw materials and markets were too essential for Europeans to forgo at any price; see S. N. D. North, "The Tariff and the Export Trade of the United States," *Annals* 23 (January 1904): 1–11. See MANY, *Revision of the Customs Laws*. Fluent in German, Stone had translated Marx's *Contribution to the Critique of Political Economy* into English and defended Seligman's attempt to view Marx through the lens of marginal utility theory; his views are noted in his translator's preface to the work (New York, 1904); on Seligman and Marx, see Joseph Dorfman, *The Economic Mind In American Civilization* (New York: Viking, 1949), 3:237–38, 253, 254. Stone's relationship with Sanders and with Herbert E. Miles of the NAM Tariff Committee is noted in Stone's commemorative biography, *One Man's Crusade for an Honest Tariff: The Story of H. E. Miles, Father of the Tariff Commission* (Appleton, Wis.: Lawrence College Press, 1952). See also Stone's memorandum in the William H. Taft Papers, Library of Congress, Washington, D.C., "Dual Tariff System."

33. Tower to Root, September 27, 1906, Personal and Confidential, no. 1028, RG 59/321.0. Tower also noted that a tariff war would cripple the North German Lloyd and Hamburg-American shipping lines and that they among the German commercial interests were most bent on avoiding a tariff conflict. In fact, North German Lloyd offered free transportation for the North Commission, which Assistant Secretary of State Robert Bacon ordered the commission to decline because of German Lloyd's status as an "interested party" to the discussions. See Bacon to A. A. Adee, January 1, 1906, RG 59/321a.

34. The North Commission's work began on November 17, 1906, and ended on January 23, 1907. On the commission's discussions with German trade representatives, see RG 59/321/87–88. The Germans included Dr. Lehmann, trade counselor in the Foreign Office; G. D. Waetzoldt, trade adviser in the German consulate in New York; and Government Confidential Counselor Delbrueck (possibly Clemens von Delbrueck, who was German minister of the interior, 1909–16). See S. N. D. North to Secretary of State (Root), March 14, 1907, RG 59/321/87. Frank Mason participated in discussions from about November 26 to December 23, 1906. On the addition of Mason to conference, see (Ambassador Charlemagne) Tower to Root, November 20, 1906, (Assistant Secretary of State Robert) Bacon

to Tower, November 20, 1906, Tower to Root, November 21, 1906, all in RG 59/321/26, and Root to American Embassy Berlin, November 26, 1906, RG 59/321/28 and Mason to Root, December 24, 1906, RG 59/321/56. It would appear that North and Gerry wanted Mason on their commission to add diplomatic stature to the American side, and possibly to deemphasize the prominence of Stone, who was Jewish, in the discussions.

35. Sanders had a particular expert in mind, a Dr. Stiles; see Sanders to Root, December 1, 1906, RG 59/321/34, and Sanders to Root, November 10, 1906, RG 321/26.

36. See Sanders to Root, December 1, 1906, RG 59/321/34, Sanders to Root, December 22, 1906, RG 59/321/48, and Root to Sanders December 29, 1906, ibid. On the western cattlemen's position on the reciprocity question, see Ike T. Pryor to Root, April 27, 1907, RG 59/5727/3–4, and enclosure, "Address of Ike T. Pryor at Kansas City," November 23, 1906. On support of agricultural interests for a treaty, see Sanders to Root, December 19, 1906, RG 59/Minor Files.

37. Thomas H. Downing to Robert Bacon, August 20, 1906, A. A. Adee to Merchants Association of New York, August 24, 1906, Merchants Association of New York to President Theodore Roosevelt, September 19, 1906, S. C[hristy] Mead (secretary of MANY) to A. A. Adee, September 28, 1906, all in RG 59/321/2 and T. H. Downing to Robert Bacon, November 19, 1906, RG 59/321/47.

38. See William R. Corwine to Elihu Root, October 26, 1906, RG 59/321; A. A. Adee to John Ball Osborne (State Department Bureau of Trade Relations), October 27, 1906; and W. R. Corwine to Robert Bacon, November 5, 1906, RG 59/321.12 (two letters).

39. Papers of Conference for November 19, 1906, in RG 59/321/87–88; remarks of N. I. Stone, p. 18. See also the letter from Secretary Shaw to Congress, February 28, 1906, 59th Cong., 1st sess., Doc. 576, urging liberalization of consignee valuation procedures. See also North to Root, December 29, 1906, RG 59/321/38, on U.S. satisfaction with the progress of the conference, and Papers of Conference, RG 59/321/87–88, passim. That the North Mission was an effort to bypass the protectionists and Secretary Shaw may be seen in North's request for Root to intercede with Roosevelt on behalf of James Gerry, urging that "it would be most unfortunate if Mr. Gerry shall be obliged to report to Mr. Shaw what has been done here, and his own important part in it." North suggested to Root that Gerry be allowed to delay reporting back to his official post until "a Secretary of the Treasury more fully in sympathy with the President and yourself is installed." North to Root, December 23, 1906, Root Papers. For scheduled appointment of Cortelyou to the Treasury Department, see *Washington Post*, October 24, 1906.

40. See Collector of the Port of New York to J. B. Reynolds (assistant secretary of the treasury), March 27, 1907: "I think it can be safely said that such an arrangement would probably result in increased importations from Germany and payment of less duty per importation than at present, but that the revenue would not be reduced owing to the increased amount of the importations"; RG 59/5727.

41. See North to Root, December 6, 1906 (telegram), asking for instructions on how far to press for concessions on meat imports, RG 59/321/37, and Root to North, December 6, 1906, saying "you are hardly in a position to demand concessions . . . because you are not negotiating a treaty," RG 59/321/38. See also E. Root, "Reply to Memorandum of the German Commissioners," December 10, 1906, authorizing negotiation of a Dingley Tariff "section 4" treaty with Germany, RG 59/321/87; for the German replies, see Sternberg to Root, April 4, 1907, RG 59/5727.

42. On the agreement, see Baron [Hermann] Speck von Sternberg to Secretary of State Root, April 4, 1907, RG 59/5727. For the treaty text, see U.S. Department of Commerce and Labor, Bureau of Manufactures, *Commercial Agreement between the United States and Germany, June, 1907*, Tariff Series no. 5 (Washington, D.C.: GPO, 1907).

43. Letter of Samuel S. Dale to S. N. D. North, circa August 1, 1907, in *Protectionist*, September 1907, pp. 236–44. John Bruce McPherson (secretary of the National Association of Wool Manufacturers), *The German Agreement and Its Defence by the Chairman of the Commission to Germany: Some Points Involved*, reprint from the *Bulletin* (of the National Association of Wool Manufacturers for March 1908) (Boston: Rockwell and Churchill, 1908).

44. S. N. D. North, "What the German Tariff Agreement Means," letter of July 2, 1907, printed in *American Industries* 5 (July 15, 1907): 1–3.

45. John Ball Osborne, "Our New Commercial Pact with Germany," *Harper's Weekly* 51 (September 14, 1907): 1338, 1358.

46. Roosevelt to Root, July 2, 1907, Root Papers.

47. Low-tariff Democrat Henry Parker Willis ("Reciprocity with Germany, I," p. 321) described its potential for catalyzing an "entire change" in U.S. tariff policy and argued for extending reciprocity to unconditional most-favored-nation relations ("Reciprocity with Germany, II," *Journal of Political Economy* 15 [July 1907]: 394–95). "Radical" was used by the ultraprotectionist *American Economist*; see article, "Remarkable Concessions," May 10, 1907, p. 218.

48. These last criticisms were made by Henry Parker Willis. Corporate-oriented academics such as Willis thus held Roosevelt to a reductionist standard from the Democratic viewpoint. See "Reciprocity with Germany, I," p. 344, and "Reciprocity with Germany, II," pp. 394–95.

49. On German complaints of "one-sidedness," see editorial, "Have We Been Unfair to German Commerce," *Review of Reviews* 37 (January 1908), quoting Dr. Ludwig Max Goldberger's remarks in the New York–based German-American commercial monthly *Deutsche Vorkaempfer*. The U.S. Tariff Commission study (*RCT*, pp. 214–15) concluded that actual "American concessions were nominal in character" and that the Europeans "were not, as a rule seeking special favors, but used their bargaining tariffs as a means of protecting their exports against unfair discrimination. As soon as American negotiators succeeded in convincing the European governments that the reductions . . . they offered were not exceeded in

the commercial agreements of the United States with other countries, they were able [except in the case of an attempted agreement with France] to secure most-favored-nation treatment for American products."

50. Willis, "Reciprocity with Germany, I," p. 321. As one of Taft's advisers wrote him shortly before Taft assumed the presidency, "There is no means of getting away from the fact that our present schedules are high as compared with other countries. . . . We have pretty near reached the limit and the efforts of these countries to approximate to our level cannot justly be regarded as a declaration of tariff war against us." See Charles M. Pepper (agent of the Bureau of Manufactures of the Department of Commerce and Labor) to Taft, March 2, 1909, copy in Aldrich Papers.

Chapter 5

1. Havemeyer's statement is in U.S. Industrial Commission, *Preliminary Report on Trusts and Industrial Combinations*, vol. 1, *Testimony* (Washington, D.C.: GPO, 1900), p. 100.

2. On the positions of the Democrats and Republicans on the tariff, see Kirk H. Porter and Donald Bruce Johnson, *National Party Platforms, 1840–1968* (Urbana: University of Illinois Press, 1970), pp. 98, 114. The Republican "Iowa idea" plank actually was written by "sound money" advocate George E. Roberts, an Iowa printer who was later director of the U.S. Mint and a Chicago commercial bank executive and who soon sought to dissociate himself from its radical implications. See Roberts, "The Origin and History of the Iowa Idea," *Iowa Journal of History and Politics* 2 (January 1904): 69–82. Thus, Cummins and other Iowa proto-Progressives were the notion's chief defenders and "radical" exponents. For a contemporary Iowa Progressive's account, see Thomas James Bray, *The Rebirth of Freedom* (Indianola, Iowa: Record and Tribune Press, 1957), esp. pp. 55–60, 63 (quotation from inaugural address), and 78–80. See also David P. Thelen, "Patterns of Consumer Consciousness in the Progressive Movement: Robert M. La Follette, the Antitrust Persuasion, and Labor Legislation," in *The Quest for Social Justice: The Morris Fromkin Memorial Lectures, 1970–80*, ed. Ralph M. Aderman (Madison: University of Wisconsin Press, 1983), pp. 19–50.

3. Under Parry (1902–6), the NAM created a national lobby for antilabor employers' associations—the Citizens' Industrial Association of America. Under Van Cleave (1906–9), the NAM formed another such federation, the National Council for Industrial Defense. Through these groups, the NAM fought the extension of the eight-hour day to government work. For details on the development of the NAM in the period after 1903, see Albert K. Steigerwalt, *The National Association of Manufacturers, 1895–1914: A Study in Business Leadership* (Ann Arbor: University of Michigan Press, 1964), esp. pp. 110, 115, 124, 126–27. Search's candidate as his successor was Charles Schieren, the New York leather manufacturer

and banker, who favored the eight-hour day in government contracts. See also James Weinstein, *The Corporate Ideal in the Liberal State, 1900–1918* (Boston: Beacon Press, 1968), esp. chap. 2; Robert H. Wiebe, *Businessmen and Reform: A Study of the Progressive Movement* (Cambridge, Mass.: Harvard University Press, 1962), esp. pp. 164–75; and Philip Burch, "The NAM as an Interest Group," *Politics and Society* 4 (Fall 1973): esp. 100n–101n. See also J. W. Van Cleave, "Address," NAM *Proceedings*, 1907, pp. 31–47; and John Kirby, Jr., "Mob Rule and the Anti-Injunction Bill," *American Industries* 1 (January 15, 1903). The revolutionary character of the NAM leaders' assumption of power was expressed in a deathbed letter by James W. Van Cleave, who recalled the times as "like those of Washington at Valley Forge"; Van Cleave to Kirby, May 11, 1910, in NAM *Proceedings*, 1910, pp. 5–6.

4. Weinstein, *Corporate Ideal*, pp. 16–17; see also NAM resolutions on the Buck's Stove and Range case and Van Cleave's résumé, *LHA*, 3:2863–65.

5. "Go into Politics" was Van Cleave's theme; see the cover of the NAM newspaper, *American Industries* 7 (March 1, 1908), and Van Cleave, "Politics and the Employing Interests," ibid., p. 18. In particular, the NAM portrayed its tariff politics as "nonpartisan."

6. David M. Parry, "Reciprocity and the Middle West," *Annals* 29 (May 1907): 22–25.

7. Tom E. Terrill, *The Tariff, Politics, and American Foreign Policy, 1874–1901* (Westport, Conn.: Greenwood Press, 1973), pp. 48–49, describes the ideological parallels of the protectionist Republican Blaine's reciprocity ideas and those of the free-trade Democrat Wells: "Both argued that American prosperity depended on the immediate expansion of American exports, and both emphasized industrial exports" (p. 49). Terrill continues: "Only tactics . . . separated them" (ibid.).

8. See A. B. Farquhar, "Reciprocity and Tariff Revision," *American Industries* 1 (October 1, 1902): 1–2; and A. B. Farquhar, "Dangers in the Trusts," *American Industries* 1 (May 15, 1903): 5–6, quotation, p. 6.

9. Memorandum, unsigned (probably by Ferdinand Schwedtman, the NAM president's secretary), "Suggestions for President's Report, 1907," *LHA*, 1:940.

10. Towne's commentary is noted at the end of chapter 2. For Parry's views, see "President's Address," NAM *Proceedings*, 1905, pp. 61–62. On "reciprocity fever," see George Seabury, "Tariff Revision and the Remedy," NAM *Proceedings*, 1905, p. 221. An internal NAM memorandum summarized the dismal state of tariff affairs: "Under the Search administration of our affairs [1896–1902] stand-pat members thought the Association was stand pat and revision members thought it was revision. For the first two or three years of the Parry administration the subject was not active, and the executive officers did not need to get into it. In the last year of Mr. Parry's administration [1905–6], a committee was appointed but nothing was done because no means was adopted to keep the two factions together." "Suggestions for President's Report, 1907," *LHA*, 1:940.

11. See U.S. Industrial Commission, in *Report of the Industrial Commission on Trusts and Industrial Combinations*, vol. 13, *Testimony Taken since March 1, 1900* (Washington, D.C.: GPO, 1900); see particularly in the chapter entitled "Review of Evidence," pp. xv–xxv, the sections "Prices—Raw Material," and "Control of Product." See also Testimony of Edward Atkinson, pp. cxlv–cxlvi. The bulk of testimony denied a relation between tariffs and trusts, although the choice of witnesses may have reflected the fact that Albert B. Clarke, longtime secretary of the protectionist Boston Home Market Club, was chairman of the commission.

12. See Testimony of Byron W. Holt, secretary of the New York Reform Club, before U.S. Industrial Commission, in ibid., pp. xxvi–xxvii, 553–68, and Testimony of Edward Atkinson, pp. cxlv–cxlvi. On dumping practices, see, in particular, Byron W. Holt, *Export Prices to Date* (New York: Tariff Reform Committee, 1906). Dumping or export pricing is "price discrimination between national markets," in general, disposing of surplus abroad at low prices or at cost with the objective of acquiring liquid capital, reducing storage costs, and keeping up payments on fixed assets. See Jacob Viner, *Dumping: A Problem in International Trade* (1929; reprint, New York: A. M. Kelly, 1966), p. 3. The marginal profits of foreign trade so secured were of greater utility to the steel companies than the returns on sales alone; the export of goods prevented the saturation of domestic demand and consequent price depression. As Viner noted, dumping sometimes was pursued to capture foreign markets later to be more profitably exploited or to inhibit the growth of foreign industries (so-called predatory dumping; see p. 64).

13. By 1896, U.S. exports of steel exceeded imports, and from that point onward, the United States was a dominant influence in world markets for steel rails and tonnage products. In part, this early export growth was spurred by the flaccidity of domestic demand for steel products during the depression of the 1890s and by the broad influence of reciprocity and the sentiment for foreign trade expansion within the Republican party, which generalized concern about overproduction and saturation of American markets in the future and stressed the countercyclical value of foreign sales. For background on the status of the steel industry, see William T. Hogan, *The Economic History of the Iron and Steel Industry in the United States* (Lexington, Mass.: D. C. Heath, 1971), vol. 2, part 3, esp. chap. 23.

14. The SPEC's operations can for most purposes be considered definitive in the basic steel export market for this period (1904–10); they accounted for between 80 and 90 percent of all steel exports, including materials purchased from independent steel companies and marketed by U.S. Steel abroad; see Hogan, *Economic History of Iron and Steel*, 2:781.

15. See testimony of Charles Schwab, *Report of the Industrial Commission*, 13:xxv, 454–55, 564. *Report and Hearings of the Merchant Marine Commission, 1905*, 58th Cong., 3d sess., Sen. Rep. 2755 (Washington, D.C.: GPO, 1905), pp. 813–14; cf. Viner, *Dumping*, p. 87.

16. U.S. Congress, House, Committee on Investigation of U.S. Steel Corpora-

tion (Stanley Committee), *Hearings*, vol. 6, part 2, *Extracts from the Minutes of the U.S. Steel Corporation and Subsidiary Companies* (Washington, D.C.: GPO, 1913), pp. 3938–39. The U.S. Steel Corporation decided, thus, to try to export cruder forms of its semimanufacture only at times when it could "be done to advantage in order to keep certain of the plants running" (ibid.). E. H. Gary testimony, in U.S. Congress, Senate, Committee on Interstate Commerce, *Hearings: Regulation of Railway Rates* (Washington, D.C.: GPO, 1905), 4:3084. See testimony of Schwab, *Report of the Industrial Commission*, 13:xxv, 454–55, 564. On allegations of U.S. Steel's wage cuts in tin-plate operations for foreign production, see Byron W. Holt, *Home and Foreign Prices of American-Made Goods, 1906* (New York: Tariff Reform Club, 1906), reprinted in *Congressional Record*, 1906, vol. 40, part 8, p. 8029.

17. On the tariff and the steel industry in this period, see Abraham Berglund and Philip G. Wright, *The Tariff on Iron and Steel* (Washington, D.C.: Brookings Institution, 1929), p. 56, noting the vertical combination strength of the U.S. steel industry, and pp. 116–17, 122–23, and 130, on export pricing and stabilization of domestic rail prices. Berglund and Wright indicate that by 1896, for the U.S. steel market as a whole, productive efficiency would have inhibited large-scale imports of foreign steel. But, they note, if the industry as a whole was independent of the tariff for tonnage products, with perhaps the exception of "establishments located near the seaboard," the tariff "in times of strong demand assist[ed] producers to obtain higher prices than would have been possible without its aid, and in some instances to control prices" (p. 130).

18. On the steel policy vis-à-vis countervailing duties, see J. A. Farrell to T. Guilford Smith (manager of sales, U.S. Steel Products Export Company), "United States Maximum and Minimum Tariff," October 27, 1909, enclosed in John Hughes (general agent, U.S. Steel) to Henry C. Emery, RG 81/185.83. See also Viner, *Dumping*, pp. 201–2.

19. Testimony of H. E. Miles, U.S. Congress, House, Committee on Ways and Means, *Tariff Hearings, 1908–1909; Free List and Miscellaneous*, vol. 7 (Washington, D.C.: GPO, 1909), pp. 7610, 7645.

20. See James G. Parsons, *Protection's Favors to Foreigners*, 61st Cong., 1st sess., Sen. Doc. 54 (Washington, D.C.: GPO, 1909), pp. 7–8, 12; Senate Committee on Interstate Commerce, *Hearings: Regulation of Railway Rates*, 4:3084. United States Congress, House, Committee on Marine and Fisheries, *Hearings: Development of the American Merchant Marine* (Washington, D.C.: GPO, 1906); James H. Bridge, *History of the Carnegie Steel Company* (New York: Aldine, 1903), pp. 312–14. See also U.S. Congress, House, Committee on Ways and Means, *Tariff Hearings, 1908–1909; Schedule C, Metals*, part 1 (Washington, D.C.: GPO, 1909), p. 1628.

21. On the shift in Republican Congressional treatment of export pricing, the Republican *Campaign Text-Book* of 1906 said with regard to export dumping that "it is to the glory and honor of every American manufacturer who does it," because it sustained domestic employment and expanded U.S. trade; cited in Parsons,

Protection's Favors, p. 13. On Schwab's and Gary's view on export pricing, see Hogan, *Economic History of Iron and Steel*, 2:783–84.

22. The official German inquest was the so-called *Kartellenquete*; see Viner, *Dumping*, pp. 56–57. See Federal Trade Commission, *Cooperation in American Export Trade* (Washington, D.C.: GPO, 1916), part 1, pp. 207–15, on the operation of the German steel cartel.

23. On the problem of export combination, see, for example, John D. Ryan, "The Sherman Law and Its Effect on Export Trade," in *Official Report of the National Foreign Trade Convention* (Washington, D.C.: National Foreign Trade Council, 1914), pp. 161–78; see also William L. Saunders (chairman, Ingersoll-Rand Corporation), "Government Regulation of Commerce as Affecting Foreign Trade," in *Official Proceedings of the Second National Foreign Trade Convention* (St. Louis: National Foreign Trade Council, 1915), pp. 57–69, and "Address of Mr. [John D.] Ryan" (Amalgamated Copper Company), ibid., pp. 69–73. See also Federal Trade Commission, *Cooperation in Export Trade*, part 1, esp. pp. 201–2. Here, the FTC declares itself "strongly impressed with the effect that the doubt as to the application of the antitrust law has had in the formation of cooperative export organizations . . . even of those who believe such organizations legal for export trade" (p. 201). This investigation was a precursor to the legalization of export cooperation agreements in the Webb-Pomerene Act of 1918 (see chapter 11).

24. On drawback commissions, see "Address of Mr. Leonard Hall Jerome," *American Manufacturers' Export Association, Fourth Annual Convention*, 1913, pp. 14–16.

25. See the speeches of George Seabury and William McCarroll regarding the Lovering bill, NAM *Proceedings*, 1904, pp. 177–79. Seabury was a medicinal goods exporter interested in reduction of costs on imported medicinal alcohol, McCarroll a leather manufacturer. On problems of exporters with drawback legislation, see "Tariff and the Canning Industry," *American Industries* 7 (February 15, 1908); see also the complaints of hardware and machinery manufacturers (the Stanley Works of New Britain, Connecticut, and Merchant and Evans of Philadelphia, respectively), who favored liberalized drawback accounting; see Committee on Ways and Means, *Tariff Hearings, 1908–1909; Free List and Miscellaneous*, vol. 7, pp. 7385–7412. Shipbuilders such as Cramp and Sons of Philadelphia who were manufacturing for export had been supporters of liberalized drawback provisions since the late 1890s; see "Statement Made by Hon. William C. Lovering Relative to the Drawback Law," ibid., pp. 7412–17.

26. See *United States* v. *United States Steel Corporation et al.*, District Court of New Jersey, Opinions, June 3, 1915, 223 *Federal Reporter* 101–9, and *U.S.* v. *U.S. Steel Corporation, Transcript of Record in the District Court of the U.S. for New Jersey*, vol. 10, pp. 3848, 3885, and vol. 11, pp. 4471–72.

27. At the 1901 NAAIVM convention, President James A. Carr of the Hoosier Drill Company of Richmond, Indiana, opined that there were "good and bad

combinations," but hoped that the process would not extend to implements and would be a "transitory phase." NAAIVM *Convention*, 1901, in *Farm Machinery* 526 (November 5, 1901), n.p. Kingman, a Peoria manufacturer, suggested "free trade" for iron and steel in 1902, and as NAAIVM president in 1903 characterized the trust and inflated price issues as central; see NAAIVM *Convention*, 1902, in *Farm Machinery* 576 (October 21, 1902), and NAAIVM *Convention*, 1903, in *Farm Machinery* 629 (October 27, 1903). For Munn's comments, see "Procuring Materials," *Farm Machinery* 576 (October 21, 1902); the quotations are from "Petition to Roosevelt against the International Harvester Co.," *Implement Age* 26 (September 21, 1905).

28. H. E. Miles, "How the Tariff Affects My Business," *American Industries* 6 (November 15, 1907): 14–15; see also N. I. Stone, *One Man's Crusade for an Honest Tariff: The Story of H. E. Miles, Father of the Tariff Commission* (Appleton, Wis.: Lawrence College Press, 1952).

29. Miles later testified that he accounted his raw materials costs at 60 to 70 percent of his total cost of manufacture, even considering hidden labor costs in the raw materials production. Miles, "How the Tariff Affects My Business"; see also testimony in Committee on Ways and Means, *Tariff Hearings, 1908–1909; Free List and Miscellaneous*, vol. 7, pp. 7694–95. Miles claimed that this trust-created raw material inflation was broadly the case in many trust-dominated industries. Although he drew most of his examples from steel, he included lumber, leather, sugar, and others. Miles tended to downplay the sources of his information. In part this may have been because he used information from the Free Hides League and the New York Reform Club; the latter group was a Democratic organization, and, as a midwestern Republican, Miles may have wanted to avoid giving protectionists an opportunity to question his party loyalty.

30. For notes on the meeting, see House Committee on Investigation of United States Steel Corporation, *Hearings*, vol. 6, part 2, p. 3952, extracts from minutes of general sales managers' meeting of April 18, 1906. See also ibid., p. 4078, extracts from minutes of Carnegie Steel Company meeting of April 2, 1906. The implement makers claimed, for example, that Harvester had produced 20,000 farm wagons in 1905 and expected to turn out 40,000 and 100,000 wagons in 1906 and 1907, respectively. Actually, Harvester would produce only 55,000 wagons in 1910 and 65,000 in 1911, constituting 13 percent and 15 percent of the market at that time. However, Harvester's market share of other lines—harrows, for example—did rise rapidly, to 43 percent in 1911, and of course Harvester already dominated in large implements such as harvesters, binders, and reapers, with over 80 percent of the market. Possibly disquieting to the implement manufacturers was the fact that Harvester was entering into retail selling arrangements with various independent lines. For example, in 1904 Harvester signed a marketing agreement with Weber Wagon Company of Illinois, then bought its stock of equipment (in 1904 and 1905), and finally absorbed the company entirely. Harvester also signed contracts

with the Bettendorf Axle Company of Davenport, Iowa, in 1905. Here, Harvester would sell Bettendorf's output of steel gears, frames, and wheels and, in this manner, assure its own supply of equipment and position itself to influence the trade. See U.S. Department of Commerce and Labor, Bureau of Corporations, *The International Harvester Company* (Washington, D.C.: GPO, 1913), pp. 142, 167. See also *Farm Implement News* 25 (November 17, 1904). On the NAAIVM committee's role as a buying combination, see H. E. Miles, "A Plain Talk on Pertinent Topics," Address at Illinois Dealers' Convention, Peoria, December 6, 1906, *Farm Implement News* 27 (December 27, 1906): 21–22.

31. House Committee on Investigation of United States Steel Corporation, *Hearings*, vol. 6, p. 3952, sales managers' minutes, April 18, 1906. The show of flexibility on the part of the steel corporation may have owed something to the fact that Harvester at the time was buying little or no steel from the U.S. Steel Corporation and so would not be alienated. Of Harvester, Carnegie Vice-President Henry B. Bope commented that "they make all their own steel, and all this tonnage has been taken away from the steel manufacturers." See ibid., p. 4078, minutes of Carnegie Steel Company, April 2, 1906, for Bope quotation.

32. For Miles's comments on buying combination, see "A Plain Talk on Pertinent Topics," p. 21. The steel company representative was Henry B. Bope, vice-president and sales manager of Carnegie Steel Company; his comment is in House Committee on Investigation of United States Steel Corporation, *Hearings*, vol. 6, p. 4078, minutes of Carnegie Steel Company, April 2, 1906. In fact, the steelmakers had decided not to offer further rebates to the independent implement materials buyers; ibid.

33. On the accusation that the independents engaged in dumping, see, for example, the exchange between N. I. Batchelder of the National Grange and G. A. Stephens (NAAIVM president, 1908–9), of the Moline Plow Company of Moline, Illinois, makers of the widely advertised "Flying Dutchman" line of plows and implements, in U.S. Congress, House, *A Permanent Tariff Commission: Hearings before the Speaker of the House of Representatives and the Chairman of the Committee on Ways and Means*, 60th Cong., 1st sess., February 4, 1908 (Washington, D.C.: GPO, 1908).

34. Also on the committee were G. A. Stephens of Moline Plow; W. H. Parlin, a former NAAIVM president (1897–98), of Parlin and Ohrendorff, of Canton, Illinois, makers of plows, harrows, and cultivators, with factories scattered across the Midwest; J. B. Bartholomew, of the Avery Manufacturing Company of Peoria, Illinois, a $2.5 million company with a strong interest in foreign trade; William Butterworth, vice-president (and after November 1907, president) of the John Deere Company of Moline, Illinois, and the son-in-law of company president C. H. Deere; and C. A. Carlisle of the Studebaker Brothers Manufacturing Company of South Bend, Indiana, a large maker of wagons and an early automobile manufacturer. Later in the year, Newell Sanders, who would be president of the NAAIVM

in the following year (1907–8), was appointed to the committee; his concern was the Newell Sanders Plow Company of Chattanooga, Tennessee. Supervising the work of the committee was the current NAAIVM president, C. F. Huhlein, of B. F. Avery and Sons, implement makers of Louisville, Kentucky. Information on the various committee members was gleaned from convention issues of *Farm Implement News* and *Farm Machinery*.

35. The report text is in "H. E. Miles et al. to Executive Committee" (of the NAAIVM), July 12, 1906, copy in Theodore Roosevelt Papers, Library of Congress, Washington, D.C. Portions of a similar version of the report are reproduced in N. I. Stone, *One Man's Crusade*, pp. 11–20. This appears to be the report cited in Parsons, *Protection's Favors to Foreigners*, p. 46.

36. "H. E. Miles et al. to Executive Committee," Roosevelt Papers.

37. On the interest of the Harvester group in deflecting attention from its activity as a "trust" and the response of the Republican administration, see Roosevelt to (Attorney General) Charles J. Bonaparte, August 22, 1907, and (Commissioner of Corporations) Herbert Knox Smith to Roosevelt, September 21, 1907, in U.S. Congress, Senate, 62d Cong., 2d sess., Sen. Doc. 604, *Prosecution of the Harvester Trust* (Washington, D.C.: GPO, 1907). On Harvester's position on the trust question within the agricultural implement industry, see NAAIVM committee member and Harvester General Manager C. S. Funk's comments in "Urges Law for Bad Trusts," in *Farm Implement News* 28 (December 12, 1907): 13. Funk was also one of the principals in Harvester's Russian building policy, which he defended to Secretary of State Knox in 1910 as defensive, to protect Harvester's $6.4-million Russian export trade from inevitable Russian protectionist legislation; see C. S. Funk to Philander Knox, April 22, 1910, cited in George W. Queen, "The United States and the Material Advance in Russia, 1881–1906" (Ph.D. dissertation, University of Illinois, 1941). On Harvester executives' views of the tariff issue, see "Conference, Russian Situation," November 1, 1909, also cited by Queen. Edwin Metcalf would become NAAIVM president in 1910.

38. For quotation on Harvester and Canadian reciprocity, see "H. E. Miles et al. to Executive Committee," Roosevelt Papers. Harvester owned one of several American-built plants in Hamilton, Ontario. On the association's views of tariff reform, see C. F. Huhlein, "Address of President C. F. Huhlein" at the NAAIVM convention, Chicago, 1906, in *Farm Implement News* 27 (October 11, 1906): 32–33, and H. E. Miles, "Report of the Chairman of the Executive Committee," ibid., pp. 33–34. Comments on manufacturers' desire to join trusts were made, for example, by NAAIVM President Kingman; see "President's Address," *Farm Machinery* 629 (October 27, 1903).

39. For quotation on profits, see H. E. Miles to Albert J. Beveridge, March 18, 1908, Albert J. Beveridge Papers, Library of Congress, Washington, D.C. On the role of the steel corporation in maintaining stable prices and profits in the industry as a whole, see comments of H. E. Miles on the panic of 1907, "Remarks of H. E.

Miles on Credits and Prices," at Dealers' Meeting, Milwaukee, *Farm Implement News* 28 (December 19, 1907): 23–24.

40. See Miles to Roosevelt, August 8, 1906; Cannon to (Treasury Secretary) Leslie M. Shaw, August 20, 1906, Roosevelt Papers.

41. Cannon to Shaw, August 20, 1906, Roosevelt Papers.

42. Roosevelt to Miles, August 11, 1906, Roosevelt Papers.

43. Roosevelt to Leslie M. Shaw, September 11, 1906, in *Letters of Theodore Roosevelt*, vol. 5, *1905–1907*, ed. E. E. Morison (Cambridge: Harvard University Press, 1952), p. 405. Shaw was then still mentioned as a possible presidential candidate for 1908, so it may be that Roosevelt was telling Shaw that although a refusal to deal with the tariff at the point of the 1906 elections was appropriate, the revisionists would have to be taken more seriously by politicians who hoped to gain Roosevelt's endorsement in future national campaigns.

Chapter 6

1. For a brief biography of Van Cleave, see "James Wallace Van Cleave, New President of the Manufacturers," *American Industries* 4 (June 15, 1906): 12–13, and Albert K. Steigerwalt, *The National Association of Manufacturers, 1895–1914: A Study in Business Leadership* (Ann Arbor: University of Michigan Press, 1964), p. 124.

2. The Arthur Commission had been popular but somewhat ineffective because of congressional protectionism; see Tom E. Terrill, *The Tariff, Politics, and American Foreign Policy, 1874–1901* (Westport, Conn.: Greenwood Press, 1973), pp. 52–54. Van Cleave specifically invoked the Arthur Commission in a speech before the Home Market Club in Boston in November 1906. See Van Cleave, "What to Do about the Tariff," *American Industries* 5 (December 1, 1906): 1–3, the text of a speech of November 20, 1906.

3. In Seabury's plan, the secretary of the Department of Commerce and Labor would serve as chairman, with ex-officio participation of the Board of General Appraisers, the Bureaus of Statistics and Manufactures of the Commerce and Labor Department, and other departments' midlevel officials. Seabury, "Revision and Remedy," NAM *Proceedings*, 1905, pp. 220–34.

4. Van Cleave, "What to Do about the Tariff"; Colonel Albert Clarke, in "Two Opinions on Tariff," *American Industries* 5 (June 15, 1907): 1–2 (the second opinion was that of tariff revisionist William R. Corwine, "Tariff Should Be Readjusted in a Businesslike Way," ibid., p. 2). Cf. Albert B. Cummins, "Tariffs, Reciprocity, Combinations," *American Industries* 2 (November 2, 1903): 1–2. It is also possible that the new tack taken by NAM and other groups (the American Reciprocal Tariff League, for example) on the tariff was facilitated by the general rise of antitrust sentiment within the Republican party after 1906. The NAM had fol-

lowed the rise of Cummins and the "Iowa idea" and other antitrust tariff viewpoints that had passed midwestern state Republican party platforms during the reciprocity boom earlier in the decade. But many held back for fear of associating themselves with Democratic themes. By 1905, however, the tariff commission idea, linked to trust regulation, had made the issue less partisan and a safer one for Republicans to endorse, because it now explicitly was linked to the continuation of protection and national Republican politics.

5. See, in general, N. I. Stone, *One Man's Crusade for an Honest Tariff: The Story of H. E. Miles, Father of the Tariff Commission* (Appleton, Wis.: Lawrence College Press, 1952), for an account of and tribute to Miles's role in the tariff commission movement.

6. "Report of the Tariff Committee," NAM *Proceedings*, 1907, pp. 163–68.

7. Ibid.

8. See, for example, H. E. Miles, "Tariff Inequalities and the Remedy," *American Industries* 6 (November 1, 1907): 21–24; J. W. Van Cleave, "Why Manufacturers Desire a Tariff Commission," an article from *Circle* magazine for November 1907, reprinted in *American Industries* 6 (November 1, 1907): 13–16. See also the special issues of *Annals*, "Tariffs, Reciprocity, and Foreign Trade," *Annals* 29 (May 1907), and "Tariff Revision," *Annals* 32 (September 1908). See also the comments of the president of Columbia University, Nicholas Murray Butler, "Why a Tariff Commission Is Demanded," *American Industries* 6 (October 1, 1907): 1–2.

9. See "Congress and the Tariff Commission," *American Industries* 6 (September 1, 1907): 9–10, citing the call by former treasurer Ellis H. Roberts for a 13 percent across-the-board reduction. Cf. J. W. Van Cleave, "President's Page," *American Industries* 6 (January 15, 1908): 17, and H. E. Miles, "Old Style Revision Would Be a Menace," *American Industries* 5 (August 1, 1907): 1–2, a reprint of an interview with the *New York Herald*.

10. H. E. Miles to Franklin Pierce, January 10, 1908, *LHA*, 1:1270–71. Miles recommended Pierce's book to Senator Robert M. La Follette in December 1907; Miles to Senator Albert J. Beveridge, December 12–13, 1907, Albert J. Beveridge Papers, Library of Congress, Washington, D.C.

11. H. E. Miles to Franklin Pierce, January 10, 1908, *LHA*, 1:1271. Cf. Miles to Beveridge, *LHA*, 1:1270.

12. Editorial, *American Economist*, October 18, 1907, p. 181. *American Economist* editors also tried to sow dissension within the NAM by publicizing opposition to the activities of its Tariff Committee chairman, suggesting that "although half-way Protectionists and all the way Free Traders held the reins" in the organization, the membership did not really "subscribe to the views of the Miles faction." See *American Economist*, August 2, 1907, p. 54.

13. *New York Times*, January 15, 1907; see also "Features of the Real Work Done at the Foreign Commerce Convention," and the text of a speech by J. W. Van Cleave, "What Americans Must Do to Make an Export Business," both in *American*

Industries 5 (February 1, 1907): 1–3, 14–15; and "Resolutions of the National Foreign Commerce Convention, Washington D.C., January 14–15, 1907," in *Foreign Trade Expansion: Bulletin of the ARTL* 1 (November 1907): 1.

14. Stone, *One Man's Crusade*, p. 9; see also Stone, "How the Germans Revised Their Tariff," *Review of Reviews* 32 (December 1905): 719–21; and Stone, "The New German Customs Tariff," *North American Review* 181 (September 1905): 405. Stone had been cautious about raw material exports, however, warning that as less developed areas of the globe were opened to agricultural and mineral production, U.S. advantages would diminish, so that overreliance on the power of raw material exports was unwise.

15. William R. Corwine, "Tariff Should Be Readjusted in a Businesslike Way," *American Industries* 5 (June 15, 1907): 2. See also his "Why the Country Wants Tariff Readjustment," in *Foreign Trade Expansion* 1 (November 1907): 15–16, giving publicity to H. E. Miles's poll of the NAM membership indicating vast majority support for a tariff commission. The ARTL secretary, William Rossel Corwine, was a longtime member of the MANY who had also held staff positions with the National Civic Federation and with the National Council of Commerce, a government advisory group organized in late 1907 by MANY executive Gustav Schwab and Commerce and Labor Secretary Oscar Straus (see chapter 8).

16. H. E. Miles to Hon. Joseph Benson Foraker, August 28, 1907, quoted in *American Economist*, September 13, 1907, p. 130; cf. copy in Beveridge Papers.

17. See H. E. Miles to Beveridge, October 2, 1907, and Beveridge to Miles, October 9, 1907. Beveridge Papers.

18. Parry, who hoped to promote Beveridge's political ambitions for the presidency (see Parry to Beveridge, November 8, 1907), played a key role in bringing Miles and Beveridge together, recommending Miles to the Indiana senator as a "very well posted chap" (Parry to Beveridge, October 16, 1907) and mediating between the sometimes overenthusiastic Miles and Beveridge (see Parry to Beveridge, December 2, 1907). See A. H. Sanders to Beveridge, October 2, 1907, and Beveridge to Sanders, October 13, 1907. Beveridge Papers.

19. See Miles to Beveridge, November 27, 1907, and Beveridge to Parry, November 29 and 30, 1907; Beveridge to Van Cleave, October 22, 1907; Beveridge to Dalzell, November 1, 1907; and Beveridge to Roosevelt, November 4, 1907. Beveridge Papers.

20. Beveridge to Dalzell, November 1, 1907, Beveridge Papers; Albert J. Beveridge, "Revision Necessary—By Commission," *Reader* 10 (November 1907): 618–20, and 11 (December 1907): 73–81; on the panic, see Robert H. Wiebe, *Businessmen and Reform: A Study of the Progressive Movement* (Cambridge Mass.: Harvard University Press, 1962), p. 90.

21. On the NAM's attempts to involve Beveridge in the commission movement, see Parry to Beveridge, October 16, 1907; Beveridge to Parry, November 30, 1907, December 4, 1907; Beveridge to Miles, October 9, 1907; Miles to Beveridge,

November 27, 1907; Beveridge to Parry, November 29, 1907, November 30, 1907; Parry to Beveridge, December 2, 1907; quotations on manufacturers' sentiments from Beveridge to Dalzell, November 1, 1907. Beveridge Papers.

22. See "The Beveridge Tariff Commission Bill," *American Industries* 6 (January 15, 1908): 20; and "The Beveridge Bill," *American Industries* 6 (February 1, 1908): 16. Groups that endorsed Beveridge's bill included the NAM, National Grange, American National Live Stock Association, NAAIVM, Indiana Republican Editorial Association (interested in imports of Canadian wood pulp), Massachusetts State Board of Trade, MANY, Chicago Association of Commerce, ARTL and its "200 constituent organizations," American Hardware Manufacturers Association, Baltimore Chamber of Commerce, Millers National Federation, Merchants Exchange of St. Louis, Boston Chamber of Commerce, and many local chambers of commerce. Beveridge's speech on the bill is in *Congressional Record*, Senate, 60th Cong., 1st sess., vol. 42, pt. 2, pp. 1576–82, February 5, 1908. See also his remarks in *Congressional Record*, vol. 42, pt. 4, pp. 3778–82, March 24, 1908. On Miles's plans to organize the delegation, see Miles to Beveridge, January 6 and 24, 1908, January 25, 1908, Beveridge Papers. On Moline Plow and reciprocity, see Walter LaFeber, *The New Empire: An Interpretation of American Expansion* (Ithaca, N.Y.: Cornell University Press, 1963), p. 375. Originally scheduled to meet in Washington in January, some days after Beveridge's introduction of the bill, the group recoordinated its lobbying efforts with Beveridge's speech, which he pushed back to early February.

23. Of Roosevelt, Miles commented that "if he will shut the door and have two or three of his Cabinet with him, we will end the conference with a complete plan." Miles to Beveridge, January 24, 1908; see also Miles to Beveridge, January 12 and 25, 1908; Beveridge to Miles, January 29, 1908. J. W. Van Cleave, "The Real Opposition to Tariff Adjustment, *American Industries* 6 (February 1, 1908): 5–6. For Van Cleave's cautions, see Ferdinand Schwedtman (Van Cleave's secretary) to Miles, January 11, 1908, *LHA*, 2:1273.

24. Aldrich's remark is quoted from the *Congressional Record*, May 17, 1909, p. 2182, in Frank W. Taussig, *Free Trade, the Tariff and Reciprocity* (New York: Macmillan, 1927), pp. 136–37.

25. The cost-of-production idea had been mentioned specifically in the instructions of Congress to the Department of Labor under Carroll D. Wright in 1888, and his committee report declared in favor of the principle, although it was not invoked in the formulation of the McKinley Tariff. See John Cummings, "Cost of Production as a Basis for Tariff Revision," *Journal of Political Economy* 17 (March 1909): 153.

26. The expansionist proprietary ideology was well expressed by H. E. Miles in his initial letter to Beveridge: "Too much cannot be made of the fact that the manufacturers themselves in whose interest the tariff is made, are in very great numbers bitterly opposed to it, because the practical use now made of unjust

schedules is favoring some manufacturers almost to the ruin of others. . . . For instance, it is the cause of the excessive profits in the steel industry, and that same steel tariff is the cause of the very small profits made in almost all industries who use that steel as their raw material. It is limiting export business most unfortunately with this latter class though the steel companies themselves go abroad and sell against European competition at a splendid profit and at prices which, if granted to our home manufacturers, would enable a great increase in export business on steel, not as it leaves the steel makers little advanced beyond the raw material, but in much more highly finished products, containing several times the amount of American wages." Miles to Beveridge, October 2, 1907, Beveridge Papers. See also Miles to Beveridge, March 18, 1908, Beveridge Papers. Cf. H. E. Miles, "Why Manufacturers Want Tariff Revision," *North American Review* 187 (January 1908): 34–45, esp. 44; also Miles, "Tariff Revision from the Manufacturer's Standpoint," *Popular Science Monthly* 74 (May 1909): 450–56. Cf. Stone, *One Man's Crusade*, p. 32.

27. See U.S. Congress, House, *A Permanent Tariff Commission: Hearings before the Speaker of the House of Representatives and the Chairman of the Committee on Ways and Means*, 60th Cong., 1st sess., February 4, 1908 (Washington, D.C.: GPO, 1908). G. A. Stephens maintained that his company did not dump implements at lower prices abroad, but rather produced specialized implements for differing conditions abroad.

28. Remarks of Sereno E. Payne and Joseph G. Cannon, in *Permanent Tariff Commission*, pp. 54–59, 59–61, respectively.

29. H. E. Miles, "Tariff Making, The Old and the New," *American Industries* 7 (March 15, 1908): 20–22, and "The Demand for a Tariff Commission," *American Industries* 7 (April 1, 1908): 1–3; Van Cleave, "Growth of the Tariff Movement," ibid., 14–15; and H. H. Lewis, "Tariff Making a Fine Art," ibid., 8–13.

30. Beveridge to Miles, March 2 and 3, 1908, Beveridge Papers.

31. Van Cleave expressed his position with a "President's Page" column promising that the NAM did not seek to prejudge tariff rates—just that a commission would give manufacturers "A Square Deal for Tariff Adjustment," *American Industries* 7 (February 15, 1908): 18. Beveridge also promoted the commission in less specific terms, see "Tariff for Trade; Trade for Prosperity," *American Industries* 7 (February 15, 1908): 8–9. For Miles's views, see Miles to Beveridge, March 12, 1908, Beveridge Papers.

32. The notion that the lack of prestige of a commission was Miles's and Beveridge's reason for opposing it is advanced by John Braeman, *Albert J. Beveridge: American Nationalist* (Chicago: University of Chicago Press, 1971), p. 130. This was undoubtedly one reason, as Miles suggested: "The great objection to department experts exclusively constituting the proposed Body is that Congress treats them like servants and effects a superior wisdom and ignores them and the truth of the fact as presented by them"; Miles to Beveridge, March 12, 1908, Beveridge

Papers. But early on, Miles had advised Beveridge that the commission must not represent "every section and every interest" but must be "relatively small," and consist of "one technical expert, like Mr. N. I. Stone, . . . one Jurist, who is also in a large measure a practical man of affairs, . . . one businessman who has had large and varied experience in manufacturing and selling, and . . . one farmer or ex-farmer, [and finally] one Legislator." Miles to Beveridge, January 27, 1907, ibid.; see also Miles, "Why Manufacturers Want Tariff Revision," p. 44. For views of North and Stone, see S. N. D. North, *The Need for a Permanent Tariff Commission* (Boston: Rockwell and Churchill, 1902), and N. I. Stone, "Is a Tariff Commission Necessary?," *American Industries* 6 (December 1, 1907): 29–30.

33. Miles to Van Cleave and Agar, March 13, 1908, *LHA*, 2:1441–43; cf. Wiebe, *Businessmen and Reform*, pp. 90–91.

34. Albert J. Beveridge to *American Industries*, n.d., in "No Usurpation of Congressional Power," *American Industries* 7 (April 1, 1908): 18. See "The La Follette Tariff Commission Bill," ibid. See also Halvor Steenerson, "A Tariff Commission Means Real Protection," *American Industries* 6 (November 15, 1907): 19–20.

35. Miles to Beveridge (telegrams) March 13 and 14, 1908, Beveridge Papers.

36. Beveridge to Miles, March 16, 1908; see also second letter, same date, for further detail. Beveridge Papers.

37. Sanders to Beveridge, May 20, 1908, Beveridge Papers. See also Braeman, *Beveridge*, pp. 131–32.

38. Miles to Schwedtman, May 1, 1908, in U.S. Congress, House, Select Committee on Lobby Investigation, *Charges against Members of the House and Lobby Activities of the National Association of Manufacturers: Hearings*, 63d Cong., 1st sess. (Washington, D.C.: GPO, 1913), 1:160–62. See also Report of the Tariff Committee, NAM *Proceedings*, 1908, pp. 193–98, and Van Cleave's "Growth of the Tariff Movement," *American Industries* 7 (March 15, 1908): 14–15, for complete list of individuals and organizations supporting the tariff commission movement. Prominent individuals included Miles, Sanders, Batchelder, and others who had traveled with Miles to Washington in February, such as Murdo Mackenzie and Samuel H. Cowan of the livestock association, and G. A. Stephens of Moline Plow. In addition, the committee included William McCarroll of the New York Board of Trade and Transportation, S. Christy Mead, secretary of the Merchants Association of New York; H. W. Ackhoff of the Chicago Association of Commerce and the National Businessmen's League of America; J. S. Agar, president of the American Meat Packers Association; Daniel A. Tompkins of the National Cotton Manufacturers Association (also of NAM); George F. Stone of the Chicago Board of Trade; and H. T. Clinton, the New York auto manufacturer.

39. See Kirk H. Porter and Donald Bruce Johnson, *National Party Platforms, 1840–1968* (Urbana: University of Illinois Press, 1970).

Chapter 7

1. Taft's speeches of September 22, 1908, in Cincinnati, and September 24, 1908, in Milwaukee, are quoted by George M. Fisk, "The Payne-Aldrich Tariff," *Political Science Quarterly* 25 (March 1910): 38–39; on Taft's domestic tariff perspective, see Stanley R. Solvick, "William Howard Taft and the Payne-Aldrich Tariff," *Mississippi Valley Historical Review* 50 (December 1963): 424–25. Taft's comment on the possibility of a party split is in Taft to Colonel W. R. Nelson (of the *Kansas City Star*), January 5, 1909, William H. Taft Papers, Library of Congress, Washington, D.C.

2. Fisk, "Payne-Aldrich Tariff," p. 37.

3. On the NAM and the Spanish-American War, see Martin J. Sklar, "The N. A. M. and Foreign Markets on the Eve of the Spanish-American War," *Science and Society* 23 (1959): 133–62. See also Albert K. Steigerwalt, *The National Association of Manufacturers, 1896–1914: A Study in Business Leadership* (Ann Arbor: University of Michigan Press, 1964).

4. See NAM *Proceedings*, for speeches by McKinley, Root, Taft, Straus, and other Republican officials.

5. Thomas Ferguson, "Party Realignment and American Industrial Structure: The Investment Theory of Political Parties in Historical Perspective," *Research in Political Economy* 6 (1985): 1–82, see esp. 52–54; on commercial bankers' renewed interest in reduction, see "A Straw from Wall Street," and "Bankers Endorse Commission," in *Foreign Trade Expansion: Bulletin of the American Reciprocal Tariff League* 1 (November 1907): 1, 7. A major group of revisionists comprised manufacturers from New England, the mid-Atlantic states, and the Midwest, generally prosperous proprietary finishing manufacturers whose products incorporated significant amounts of steel or other raw material products of integrated corporate producers. They included agricultural implements, vehicles, machine tools, hardware, pharmaceuticals, and other products. Most of these businesses were threatened by the expansion of corporations into finished manufacture through their use of controlled pricing of raw material supplies.

6. Franklin MacVeagh, the new Treasury secretary, was a banker and former Gold Democrat. Taft to Roosevelt, November 7, 1908, Taft Papers.

7. Taft told Elihu Root that "I am not . . . particularly averse to having Mr. Payne, and Mr. Dalzell, and Mr. Cannon understand that they cannot go ahead and fool the public without a protest from somebody, and that protest seems to fall to me. If they do not pass a bill that is a genuine revision bill I will veto it." Taft to Root, November 25, 1908. See also Taft to Colonel W. R. Nelson, January 5, 1909; here he states his ambition to have controlled Cannon and Aldrich by the end of the tariff struggle, "or else [to] have broken up the party and turned the matter over to the Democrats to make fools of themselves." Taft to E. J. Hill, May 1, 1909, is an example of Taft's cooperation with Hill, who had been particularly helpful to

Roosevelt during the German tariff negotiations (see chapter 4). All citations, Taft Papers.

8. Between May and November 1908, two volumes were prepared, the first a compilation of tariff material that covered the Dingley Act and all amendatory treaty and court cases, and the second a preliminary study of comparative prices. See, respectively, U.S. Congress, House, Committee on Ways and Means, *Notes on Tariff Revision* (Washington, D.C.: GPO, 1908); U.S. Congress, House, Committee on Ways and Means, *Imports and Duties* (Washington, D.C.: GPO, 1908). For Payne's view of the volumes and the committee's preparations, see his speech introducing the bill in *Congressional Record*, 61st Cong., 1st sess., pp. 138ff.

9. See John Braeman, *Albert J. Beveridge: American Nationalist* (Chicago: University of Chicago Press, 1971), pp. 131–32; Fisk, "Payne-Aldrich Tariff," pp. 39–40.

10. A railroad trustee, merchant, and shipper involved in the Asian trade, Cobb had been active in Republican politics since the 1890s. Cobb had also become involved in the NAM's tariff commission movement. Fred W. Carpenter (Taft's secretary) to J. C. Cobb, November 23, 1908; Cobb to Taft, December 3 and 9, 1908; Taft to Cobb, December 12, 1908, Taft Papers. For the resolution of the Boston Merchants Association, see Boston Merchants Association, *Bulletin* no. 71 (December 14, 1908): 6.

11. Cobb to Taft, December 23, 1908, Taft Papers.

12. Taft to Cobb, December 12, 1908; Taft to Cobb, December 28, 1908. On Taft's approval of the commission, see Taft to Riesenberg, January 5, 1909, *LHA*, 3:2484. But see his skeptical comment of same date to W. R. Nelson, "I am very much afraid that the proposition to put in a tariff commission would utterly fail. What I am hopeful of is that we may get a bill which will contain within itself a provision for a permanent tariff commission which could make its investigations and report each year the facts in respect to the matter." Taft Papers.

13. *Breeder's Gazette* 54 (December 2, 1908).

14. Swank's testimony is in U.S. Congress, House, Committee on Ways and Means, *Tariff Hearings, 1908–1909; Schedule C, Metals,* part 1 (Washington, D.C.: GPO, 1909), pp. 1882–90.

15. *Breeder's Gazette* 54 (December 2, 1908); N. I. Stone, "Dual Tariff System," memorandum enclosed in Sanders to Payne, January 12, 1909, copy in Taft Papers. This is a typescript of a paper Stone delivered before the American Economic Association in December 1908, later published as "Dual Tariff Systems," *American Economic Association Quarterly*, 3d ser., 10 (April 1909): 301–13.

16. Stone, "Dual Tariff Systems," pp. 301–8, 310.

17. Ibid.

18. Ibid., p. 312. Note that the notion of a punitive maximum was similar to the McCleary and Lodge bills of 1907; it was also the form of the maximum provision of the McKinley Tariff of 1890. See chapter 4.

19. A U.S. Tariff Commission study of 1919 concluded that during this period,

"the European countries were not, as a rule, seeking special favors, but used their bargaining tariffs as a means of protecting their exports against unfair discrimination"; *RCT*, p. 213.

20. Pepper to Taft, March 2, 1909. See also Taft to Pepper, March 12, 1909, in which Taft notes that he forwarded Pepper's comments to Payne and Aldrich. Both appear in Taft Papers. After Taft took office, Pepper, who as a reporter had covered American business expansion in Latin America, was transferred and promoted to assistant chief of the State Department's Bureau of Trade Relations, where he was one of the principals in the 1910–11 Canadian reciprocity negotiations.

21. J. W. Van Cleave, "The Tariff Hearings at Washington," *American Industries* 7 (December 1, 1908): 5–7; cf. N. I. Stone, *One Man's Crusade for an Honest Tariff: The Story of H. E. Miles, Father of the Tariff Commission* (Appleton, Wis.: Lawrence College Press, 1952), p. 49.

22. For Van Cleave's defense of Miles, see Ferdinand C. Schwedtman (the NAM president's secretary) to Charles H. Becker (assistant to the president), January 11, 1908, in *LHA*, 2:1276–77. Van Cleave's criticism of Miles is in Schwedtman to Miles, January 11, 1908, *LHA*, 2:1273–74. Van Cleave had telegrammed Miles, in reference to an article on the tariff, "earnestly urge you to eliminate all specific reference to schedule wool, steel, etc. Round out your forceful argument for the commission only." Van Cleave to Miles, January 11, 1908, *LHA*, 2:1273.

23. Ferdinand Schwedtman to J. P. Bird, November 10, 1908, *LHA*, 2:2362. Van Cleave and his associates may have been influenced in their attitude toward the tariff-making process by Edwin D. Metcalf, of International Harvester's Osborne Harvester division of Auburn, New York. Metcalf was generally friendly with H. E. Miles, with whom he had served on several committees in the National Association of Agricultural Implement and Vehicle Manufacturers (NAAIVM). But Metcalf was apparently irked by Miles's attack in 1908 on "Old Schedules" Payne. Payne, the upstate New York congressman, was from Auburn and was Metcalf's personal friend, and Metcalf had pressed Van Cleave since the 1908 NAM convention to "be on friendly terms" with "the old leaders, . . . Cannon, Payne, and Dalzell." Van Cleave replied in full accord, assuring Metcalf that "I feel that no matter what our convictions may be on any subject we must never and under no circumstances hurt Uncle Joe, and I shall stick to this position as long as I have a voice in the management of [NAM] affairs." See Metcalf to Van Cleave, November 4, 1908, and Van Cleave to Metcalf, November 7, 1908, *LHA*, 2:2338, 2356.

24. Miles to Taft, November 12, 1908; see also Taft to Miles, November 20, 1908, and Miles to Taft, November 27, 1908. Taft Papers.

25. Miles alluded to the nature of his meeting with Taft, suggesting that the president guided his testimony, in Miles to Charles M. Jarvis (a member of the NAM tariff committee), December 3, 1908, *LHA*, 3:2421. On the extension of the hearings, see unidentified news clipping, "Tariff Committee to Ask for More Witnesses," reproduced in *LHA*, 3:2411.

26. See Miles to Van Cleave and Members of the (NAM) Tariff Committee, November 13, 1908, *LHA*, 3:2370–71; see also Miles to Taft, November 14, 1908, Taft Papers.

27. U.S. Congress, House, Committee on Ways and Means, 60th Cong., 2d sess., *Tariff Hearings, 1908–1909; Free List and Miscellaneous*, vol. 7 (Washington, D.C.: GPO, 1909), pp. 7589–7710. Miles suggested that the ultimate consumer was also hurt by the trust system, but most of his indignation was evinced on behalf of his constituencies within the NAM and the NAAIVM. Quotation from p. 7590. See also Martin M. Mulhall (NAM lobbyist in Washington) to Ferdinand C. Schwedtman, December 2, 1908, *LHA*, 3:2414–15; cf. Stone, *One Man's Crusade*, pp. 50–51.

28. For example, he noted labor cost for plate glass at 48 percent of selling price, tariff at 80 percent; cost of brass production at 17 percent of selling price, tariff at 45 percent; cost of lead refining at 4 percent, tariff at 50 to 79 percent; labor cost of tobacco at 19 percent, tariff at about 150 percent. See Stone, *One Man's Crusade*, pp. 51–52; also *Tariff Hearings, 1908–1909; Free List and Miscellaneous*, vol. 7, pp. 7592–94, "Table Showing the Relation of the Dingley Law to American Trusts."

29. Pig iron wage costs were about 90 cents per ton, but the tariff was $4 per ton; on a percentage basis, rail costs were about 15 percent of the selling price, but the tariff was 29 percent. Similarly, the tariffs were 28 percent on bars, 14 to 35 percent on ingots, 8 to 65 percent on sheet iron, and so on, compared with the general labor cost of about 15 percent. The Schwab letter to Frick is reprinted in full in Committee on Ways and Means, *Tariff Hearings, 1908–1909; Schedule C,* part 1, p. 1628. Miles cited information on steel tariffs and wages from the U.S. *Statistical Abstract* for 1907; see *Tariff Hearings, 1908–1909; Free List and Miscellaneous*, vol. 7, p. 7604.

30. As another example of the effects of trust expansion, Miles quoted a letter of a wire mill operator—"the cry of a man in distress"—who related that the steel corporations charged him high prices for rods, essentially adding the duties of the current Dingley Tariff to their "export price." The corporation sold at its export price to its developing domestic wire-making subsidiaries and by this control of raw material could afford to undersell the long-established independent wire firm. But the tariff prevented the independents from countering by importing foreign rods, and thus even with all other costs equal, they were being slowly driven out of business. Some manufacturers, Miles warned, were building plants in Canada to secure export or "international" prices, but most could not afford to do so; *Tariff Hearings, 1908–1909; Free List and Miscellaneous*, vol. 7, pp. 7628, 7638–39.

Miles's argument—that is, linking increasing raw material costs to a general inflation—was made by Democrats in the 1890s and by procorporate observers such as Charles A. Conant in criticism of the Dingley Tariff's high materials duties at the time of its passage in 1897. See Charles A. Conant, "The Anatomy of the New Tariff," *Review of Reviews* 16 (July-December 1897): 167–74.

31. Miles's testimony on these points is in *Tariff Hearings, 1908–1909; Free List and Miscellaneous*, vol. 7, pp. 7610, 7645.

32. Miles said, "One half of all our manufactured goods we send abroad are crude and semicrude . . . trust-made goods with the minimum of labor in them. We people who go on to the highly finished goods want to get the raw material and the low-finished stuff at as near the international price as will justify under . . . protection, and . . . send abroad twenty times more wages in the stuff." Ibid., 7632. He went on to suggest that if an "international trust" was formed to hold up prices, independents would be rendered powerless: "It is a great question whether you can save the manufacturers—the independent manufacturers—of the higher product or not from absolute trust domination. But you ought to try it." Ibid., 7646.

33. Ibid. Miles clarified the ideological character of his position in a letter to Senator Beveridge the previous March; Miles had claimed that he had no immediate pecuniary interest in the tariff fight because he was still profiting by passing his costs along to the consumer. It was, rather, the *system* of combination that the radical reductionists sought to combat in resisting becoming "cats' paws" of the corporations. Miles to Beveridge, March 18, 1908, Albert J. Beveridge Papers, Library of Congress, Washington, D.C. Miles, however, had not complained about such combinations when the steel company had been responsive to price pressures by the implement makers (see chapter 5).

34. *Tariff Hearings, 1908–1909; Free List and Miscellaneous*, vol. 7, p. 7612. Charles Schwab, head of Bethlehem Steel, did testify for reduction of ore schedules; see *Tariff Hearings, 1908–1909; Schedule C*, part 1, pp. 1627–79.

35. *Tariff Hearings, 1908–1909; Free List and Miscellaneous*, vol. 7, pp. 7648–49; cf. Stone, *One Man's Crusade*, pp. 49–57.

36. *Tariff Hearings, 1908–1909; Free List and Miscellaneous*, vol. 7, p. 7666.

37. Schwab claimed that German costs were $9.50 to $12.00 per ton for pig iron, which with the $2.30 per ton transportation rate made the Germans potentially able to deliver pig iron at a price roughly equivalent to the selling price of the U.S. product. Robert Hessen, *Steel Titan: The Life of Charles M. Schwab* (New York: Oxford University Press, 1975), pp. 190–94. See also *Tariff Hearings, 1908–1909; Schedule C*, part 1, pp. 1627–79.

38. *Tariff Hearings, 1908–1909; Schedule C*, part 1, esp. pp. 1629, 1640–41, 1648, 1666, 1658–59, 1662. At the same time as he argued for the continuation of tariffs to protect his mostly East Coast steel works from foreign inroads, Schwab argued for free ores, because Bethlehem was developing its ore holdings in Cuba as a counterweight to U.S. Steel's control of the Lake Superior fields. Attentive listeners at the hearings could thus perceive that the interest of Bethlehem in playing a greater role in the corporate order of steel, rather than the advancement of a consistent tariff rationale, was Schwab's principal objective.

39. *Tariff Hearings, 1908–1909; Schedule C*, part 1, Gary testimony; see esp. p. 1715. Cf. Abraham Berglund and Philip G. Wright, *The Tariff on Iron and Steel*

(Washington, D.C.: Brookings Institution, 1929), pp. 128–30, who note the obsolescence of the steel tariff by this period. The steel companies had already decided not to accommodate the price demands of the agricultural implement industry, whose consumption by early 1908 they had already characterized as "insignificant compared with the total." The speaker was Carnegie Vice-President Henry Bope; see Minutes of the Carnegie Steel Company, February 17, 1908, in U.S. Congress, House, Committee on Investigation of United States Steel Corporation (Stanley Committee), *Hearings*, vol. 6, part 2, *Extracts, Minutes of United States Steel Corporation and Subsidiary Companies* (Washington, D.C.: GPO, 1913), p. 4082.

40. Federal Trade Commission, *Report on the Meat-Packing Industry, 1919*, part 1 (Washington, D.C.: GPO, 1919), p. 88. Cf. Mira Wilkins, *The Emergence of Multinational Enterprise: American Business Abroad from the Colonial Era to 1914* (Cambridge, Mass.: Harvard University Press, 1970), p. 189. On packer-cattleman cooperation in inspection legislation, see Mary Yeager, *Competition and Regulation: The Development of Oligopoly in the Meat Packing Industry* (Greenwich, Conn.: JAI Press, 1981), p. 203.

41. Federal Trade Commission, *Food Investigation, Summary* (Washington D.C.: GPO, 1918), see chart following p. 22 for list of packer-associated banks. See also Forrest M. Larmer, *Financing the Livestock Industry* (New York: Macmillan, 1926), pp. 49–53.

42. On the flywheel or "governor" effect, see the speech of W. A. Harris, ANLSA *Proceedings*, 1909, pp. 37–38; Mackenzie's remarks are in ANLSA *Proceedings*, 1908, p. 19. Compare with the parallel analysis presented by packer J. Ogden Armour, "The Tariff and Our Foreign Trade in Meats," *Annals* 29 (May 1907): 537–38, 540.

43. Domestic production of beef declined as part of a secular trend away from grazing and toward more intensive use of tillable land. Although this raised beef prices initially, to the benefit of grower and packer, it also was a factor in pushing the packers to invest in foreign operations that took advantage of the extensive South American grazing lands and cheaper production costs. By 1911, the packers had entered into an international meat pool with British and South American companies, and by 1913, they were pushing to advance imports of foreign-grown beef to supply their domestic packing operations. The livestock interests, on the other hand, continued to demand tariff protection, and they were instrumental in sparking a Federal Trade Commission investigation in 1916. Problems between cattlemen and packers were partly resolved by government investigations, by the dispersion of markets for livestock away from the big packers and toward more western and local operations, and by the development of cooperatives and producer-managed selling operations that sought to negotiate stable price relations with the packers. See, on the secular decline in production, Lynn R. Edminster, *The Cattle Industry and the Tariff* (New York: Macmillan, 1926), esp. pp. 49–53. See also

Edwin G. Nourse and Joseph G. Knapp, *The Cooperative Marketing of Livestock* (Washington, D.C.: Brookings Institution, 1931), pp. 15–18, and Rudolf A. Clemen, *The American Livestock and Meat Industry* (New York: Ronald Press, 1923), esp. pp. 667–77, on cooperation between growers and packers in the 1920s, and chaps. 33 and 34, on monopoly and the Federal Trade Commission investigations.

44. ANLSA *Proceedings*, 1908, p. 19.

45. See the testimony, for example, of Elisha W. Cobb, Boston leather manufacturer, *Tariff Hearings, 1908–1909; Free List and Miscellaneous*, vol. 7, pp. 6817–31. See also letter of the Standard Leather Company of Pittsburgh, "Packers the Only Beneficiaries from the Duties on Hides," ibid., pp. 6907–10. Cf. Augustus Healy (vice-president of the U.S. Leather Company), "The Leather Industry and the Tariff," *Annals* 29 (May 1907): 553–55.

46. Testimony of Samuel H. Cowan, *Tariff Hearings, 1908–1909; Free List and Miscellaneous*, vol. 7, pp. 6915, 6978; see also 6993–97.

47. Jastro reported that "it developed at the meeting of all those interests that, while the manufacturers desired a revision, they wanted it at the expense of the live stock men and other producers; they demanded free hides and wool, and were willing to concede but scanty reductions in duties on articles competitive with what they manufactured. . . . Your committee felt that our interest would be better protected by continuing to urge such a change in the tariff laws as would permit of reciprocal arrangements." President's Speech, ANLSA *Proceedings*, 1909, p. 20.

48. Metcalf testimony, *Tariff Hearings, 1908–1909; Free List and Miscellaneous*, vol. 7, pp. 7314–34; Metcalf also wanted to delay enforcement of the new tariff for a year to dissociate it from Miles and others who sought to make it a lever against corporations. "You are now considered somewhat radical," Metcalf told Taft, but a delay would reassure the nation of the president's fundamentally "conservative" course; Metcalf to Taft, December 10, 1908, ibid., pp. 7566–67.

49. Metcalf testimony, ibid., p. 7334; see also chapter 2.

50. On Harvester's expansion, see Wilkins, *Emergence of Multinational Enterprise*, pp. 102–3, 146. See also Metcalf testimony, *Tariff Hearings, 1908–1909; Free List and Miscellaneous*, vol. 7, pp. 7318–19.

Chapter 8

1. On Miles's belief in Taft's intentions, see Miles to Van Cleave, December 14, 1908, *LHA*, 3:2438–40. "Mr. Taft is . . . determine[d] . . . to have the next tariff fair and just, and in accord with the principles which the National Association of Manufacturers has all along held, and he will insist upon a Bill substantially in accord with these principles." "Mr. Taft," Miles believed, had urged him to testify and had said, "as it were, 'Go and tell them I sent you.'" See also Stone to Van Cleave,

December 22, 1908, *LHA*, 3:2471–72, supporting Miles's candidacy. On Miles's appointment to the advisory commerce committee of the National Council of Commerce, see "Minutes of the Meeting of the Advisory Committee of the National Council of Commerce Held at Washington, D.C., May 12, 1908," RG 40/66419. The council largely comprised manufacturers' associations and chambers of commerce, and in 1908 its advisory committee included chamber of commerce members from Atlanta, Galveston, San Francisco, Boston, Cincinnati, New York, and the NAM and American Meat Packers' Association; ibid. By the latter part of the Taft administration, the council was divorced from its quasi-governmental role and became the U.S. Chamber of Commerce.

2. Van Cleave's recommendation to Taft is in Van Cleave to Taft, December 26, 1908, *LHA*, 3:2474–76. On organizing for Watson, see M. M. Mulhall to Captain John Gowdy, January 23, 1909, *LHA*, 3:2564–65; Mulhall to Hon. Frederick Sims, January 22, 1909, and Mulhall to Schwedtman, January 22, 1909 (two letters), *LHA*, 3:2566–68; Parry to Mulhall, January 25, 1909, *LHA*, 3:2572–73. See especially Schwedtman to Mulhall, January 28, 1909, *LHA*, 3:2583–85, suggesting that the need to nominate Miles was a political obligation but that it would not interfere with the NAM's promotion of Watson. Mulhall would later become the chief witness in the 1913 congressional investigation of the NAM's lobbying activities.

3. Van Cleave to Miles, January 11, 1909, *LHA*, 3:2497–2501.

4. Van Cleave to Miles, January 11, 1909, *LHA*, 3:2497–2501; see also Metcalf to Van Cleave, November 4, 1908, *LHA*, 2:2338, and Van Cleave to Metcalf, November 7, 1908, *LHA*, 2:2356.

5. Schwedtman to Miles, January 16, 1909, *LHA*, 3:2522–24.

6. Miles to Schwedtman, January 19, 1909, *LHA*, 3:2443–44.

7. Miles to Taft, January 18, 1909; Taft to Miles, January 22, 1909, William H. Taft Papers, Library of Congress, Washington, D.C. "I am fairly sickened by the way people give me proof that I am right and then beg me not to make disclosures," Miles complained. "Such men are like habitual inebriates. When they get before the tariff-making committee they . . . make a hurtful impression, and then come back . . . with poultices on their consciences."

8. See Sanders to Aldrich, January 12, 1909, Nelson W. Aldrich Papers, Library of Congress, Washington, D.C. Sanders was one of three initial appointees to the Tariff Board.

9. But eastern Republicans William Lovering of Massachusetts, who had championed expanded drawback legislation, and Jacob Van Vechten Olcott, associated with the MANY, also supported the commission. See F. C. Schwedtman to Miles, Boudinot, and Mulhall, February 3, 1909, *LHA*, 3:2628–29; Mulhall to Schwedtman, January 16, 1909, *LHA*, 3:2527–30. See Mulhall to Schwedtman, January 28, 1909, *LHA*, 3:2586–89, citing Hill's opposition on the ground that "the fellows" who wanted it didn't "really know what they wanted." On Lovering and drawbacks and on Olcott's association with the MANY, see chapter 4.

10. Henry Tarleton Wills, *Scientific Tariff Making: A History of the Movement to Create a Tariff Commission* (New York: Blanchard Press, 1913), pp. 24–26; Joseph F. Kenkel, *Progressives and Protection* (Washington, D.C.: University Press of America, 1983), p. 56.

11. The gathering opened in Indianapolis a day late, on February 16, in the wake of a sleet storm that was pelting Indiana. Also on the list of supporters of the convention were many urban chambers of commerce and boards of exchange and individual industry associations such as those in the shoe, piano, and vehicle industries, the American Meat Packers' Association, and the American National Live Stock Association. See C. C. Arbuthnot, "The National Tariff Commission Convention," *Journal of Political Economy* 7 (April 1909): 220–27. Cf. Indianapolis *Star*, February 17, 1909.

12. Wills, *Scientific Tariff Making*, pp. 23–24, 27–29, 31–32.

13. Henry R. Towne, "The Neutral Line," reproduced in Wills, *Scientific Tariff Making*, pp. 39–60. An addendum to Towne's paper specifically endorsed a commission over a less influential "board." Towne, president and chief engineer of the Yale and Towne Lock Company, would later take an important role as an adviser to the Tariff Board; see chapter 10.

14. Ibid., p. 46. Towne's essay went through several printings in quick succession.

15. Ibid., p. 22.

16. *Congressional Record*, 61st Cong., Special Session of the Senate, March 4, 1909, p. 2.

17. Taft observed that "the scope of a modern government . . . has been widened far beyond the principles laid down by the old laissez faire school of political writers, and this widening has met popular approval." On the expanded role of the state, Taft said that domestically, the state's role encompassed involvement in agricultural science, railroad regulation, internal waterway improvements, and conservation. In foreign commerce, it involved building the Panama Canal and modernizing the armed forces to defend U.S. trade and to enforce the Monroe Doctrine against "colonization of European monarchies in this hemisphere"; ibid., p. 3.

18. For examples, see Taft to Payne, December 21 and 28, 1908, January 7, 1909, February 11, 1909, and March 10, 1909, Taft Papers. Among other activities, Taft sent to Payne the Philippine tax and customs commissioners to press his arguments for U.S.-Philippine free trade. See Taft to Payne, January 18, 1909, ibid., on maximum-minimum tariffs and Taft's opposition to a rate-making commission.

19. *Congressional Record*, 61st Cong., 1st sess., March 16, 1909, p. 140. For Payne's 1894 criticism of the Wilson Tariff, see *RCT*, p. 158.

20. *Congressional Record*, 61st Cong., 1st sess., p. 143.

21. Ibid.

22. The case for retaining U.S. protectionism was also viable, Payne believed, as long as Britain retained domestic free trade. Such policies limited the capacity of

other nations to retaliate against U.S. protectionism because of the risk of polarizing U.S. trade into exclusive Anglo-American channels. Britain's leadership in international economic finance gave further weight to the threat of Anglo-American trade alliances. Ibid., pp. 143–44.

23. Ibid., p. 145. It is interesting to note as well that the not unbiased Frank W. Taussig, the Democrat and free-trade Harvard economist who would head the Tariff Commission under Wilson, singled out Payne's speech as, to his credit, "a very careful one" and complimented its "fullness of detail" as contrasted with the rhetorical speeches of McKinley and Dingley in 1890 and 1897. Taussig, *Tariff History of the United States*, 6th ed. (New York: G. P. Putnam's Sons, 1914), pp. 368n–69n. Taussig had recently clashed with Payne during the tariff hearings of 1908. Taussig's testimony is in U.S. Congress, House, Committee on Ways and Means, *Tariff Hearings, 1908–1909; Free List and Miscellaneous*, vol. 7 (Washington, D.C.: GPO, 1909), pp. 7711–32. Even Miles, who had earlier attacked "Old Schedules" Payne, also apparently admitted that Payne had done a "splendid" job in framing the tariff, as alluded to in the comments of E. D. Metcalf, NAM *Proceedings*, 1909, p. 150.

24. *Congressional Record*, 61st Cong., 1st sess., p. 145.

25. Ibid., pp. 145–56.

26. Ibid.

27. Ibid., p. 285.

28. Lowden's comments are in ibid., p. 611. For other Republican defenses of the Payne bill, see the speeches of Gaines of West Virginia, ibid., p. 737, and Sturgiss of West Virginia, p. 1032.

29. See speech of Martin Dies of Texas, ibid., pp. 195–300. The Democratic position was officially expressed by Champ Clark, the minority leader; ibid., pp. 209–32. Cf. *RCT*, p. 267. It called for a maximum based on the current minimum and a new minimum at a reduction below that. But, as Clark later admitted, the Democrats really were unprepared for a systematic tariff initiative, which historically had been undertaken only by the majority members of the Ways and Means Committee, and their own effort was largely based on an ad hoc survey of Democratic views; Champ Clark, *My Quarter Century of American Politics* (New York: Scribner's, 1920), 1:381–83. The failure of the Democrats' appeal to the Insurgents is noted in Kenneth Hechler, *Insurgency: Personalities and Politics of the Taft Era* (1940; reprint, New York: AMS Press, 1970), p. 98; cf. Richard Cleveland Baker, *The Tariff under Roosevelt and Taft* (Hastings, Neb.: Democrat Printing Company, 1941), pp. 78–79.

30. Taft to John V. Farwell (Chicago dry goods merchant and "sound currency" advocate), April 13, 1909; Taft to Horace Taft, June 27, 1909; Taft also told T. J. Akins, a St. Louis postmaster, that he meant to make the Senate version of the bill "as near like the House bill as I can." Taft to Akins, June 24, 1909. All in Taft Papers.

31. See *Congressional Record*, 61st Cong., 1st sess., May 17, 1909, p. 2182. Cf. Nathaniel W. Stephenson, *Nelson W. Aldrich* (New York: Scribner's, 1930); Taus-

sig, *Tariff History*, pp. 364n–65n, and George M. Fisk, "The Payne-Aldrich Tariff," *Political Science Quarterly* 25 (March 1910): 37–38.

32. An example of the Insurgents' inconsistency was La Follette's opposition to the print paper reductions, which were unpopular in Wisconsin; see Baker, *Tariff under Roosevelt and Taft*, p. 85. *La Follette's Autobiography* (Madison, Wis.: privately printed, 1913), p. 187, suggests the tariff issue as "formative" for the Progressive bloc. Cf. James Weinstein, *The Corporate Ideal in the Liberal State* (Boston: Beacon Press, 1968), pp. 140–41. See also John Braeman, *Albert J. Beveridge: American Nationalist* (Chicago: University of Chicago Press, 1971), pp. 154–55.

33. Taft was not without misgivings about his dealings with "these very acute and expert politicians," but he felt that, like Payne, Aldrich would work in good faith and knew that as president he could veto the bill if Aldrich would not compromise. Taft to Helen Taft, July 18, 1909; Taft to Horace Taft, June 27, 1909; Taft to Edward Colston (a Cincinnati attorney), June 24, 1909; Taft Papers. Cf. Henry F. Pringle, *The Life and Times of William Howard Taft* (New York: Farrar and Rinehart, 1939), 1:429.

34. Taft to Helen Taft, July 11, 1909; Taft to Charles Taft, July 13, 1909; Taft Papers. See also Stephenson, *Aldrich*, pp. 351–52.

35. Taussig, *Tariff History*, pp. 376–87; Fisk, "Payne-Aldrich Tariff," pp. 55–57; William T. Hogan, *The Economic History of the Iron and Steel Industry in the United States* (Lexington, Mass.: D. C. Heath, 1971), 2:791. On other schedules, rates were essentially retained from the previous tariff: cottons, silks, sugar, and most woolens; Taussig, *Tariff History*, pp. 387–403.

36. See Taussig, *Tariff History*, pp. 403–5.

37. On Beveridge's role in the origins of the Tariff Board see Braeman, *Beveridge*, pp. 163–65.

38. Ibid. On NAM lobbying efforts, see, for example, Executive Committee of the General Committee of One Hundred, Circular Letter, July 13, 1909, *LHA*, 3:3000–3001; on Taft and the Tariff Board appropriation, see H. E. Miles to Executive Committee of the Committee of One Hundred, August 2, 1909, *LHA*, 3:3046–47. As for the NAM's hiring of the standpat Speaker Cannon's former chief deputy Watson to work for a reductionist tariff commission, the following anecdote is instructive on the reform process. Hearing at a meeting with the revisionist lobby about the NAM's effort to raise $25,000 to press Congress for an independent tariff commission, "Cannon got mad . . . and after a few minutes of anger he looked up and said, 'By ——, Watson I guess you got some of this money,' and Watson replied, 'I guess I got my share,' and then both laughed and the incident ended." Miles to Schwedtman, August 9, 1909, *LHA*, 3:3073.

39. Taussig, *Tariff History*, p. 408.

40. Taft had developed two instruments of policymaking: the Bureau of Trade Relations, under strong executive control, and the Tariff Board, which was charged with developing the cost-of-production data and providing an outlet for the revi-

sionist movement's aspirations to influence tariff policy. On the split in functions between the Department of State and the Tariff Board, see chapter 9; cf. H. E. Miles to A. H. Sanders, November 16, 1909, RG 81/100.03.

41. The attitude of the steelmakers can be seen in the following observations of Henry B. Bope of U.S. Steel, who noted in December 1908 that cuts of even up to 50 percent would not be harmful (though perhaps somewhat so to independent manufacturers) and that in general, "there is really more sentiment than actual loss or gain involved in this matter, and . . . if we can get it out of the way and have it settled for a term of years nothing will interfere with the tremendous swing in business for some considerable time." U.S. Congress, House, Committee on Investigation of United States Steel Corporation (Stanley Committee), *Hearings*, vol. 6, part 2, "Minutes of the Board of Directors of the Carnegie Steel Company," December 7, 1908 (Washington, D.C.: GPO, 1913), p. 4087. After the passage of the act, Bope was more specific and only slightly less sanguine, noting that the steel company business would be markedly affected on the Pacific Coast, and the company would be compelled to "meet the European price" in the Atlantic and Gulf coast markets to keep the business. This was comparatively easy to do, Bope said, because in the short run, European mills were not equipped to shift their output to meet the American market. In the longer run, however, he acknowledged that the effect of the lower tariff would be to restrict somewhat the steel company's ability to raise prices at will. Ibid., Minutes of September 6, 1909, p. 4093. Cf. Abraham Berglund and Philip G. Wright, *The Tariff on Iron and Steel* (Washington, D.C.: Brookings Institution, 1929), p. 130.

42. William H. Taft, *Address of President Taft at Winona, Minn., September 17, 1909* (Washington, D.C.: GPO, 1909), pp. 56–57.

43. Ibid., pp. 56–58.

Chapter 9

1. Franklin MacVeagh, "Memorandum," March 25, 1910, Franklin MacVeagh Papers, Library of Congress, Washington, D.C. Henry C. Emery, "The Best Way to Work for Tariff Revision," speech before the American Economic Association, December 1908, *American Economic Association Quarterly*, 3d ser., 10 (April 1909): 287–99. Cf. Henry C. Emery, "The Tariff and Foreign Trade," in *Official Report of the National Foreign Trade Convention*, May 27 and 28, 1914 (New York: National Foreign Trade Council, 1914), pp. 258–73, esp. 260–61, in which Emery notes that he had "urged . . . economists of the country to put aside . . . the general free trade theory and to work in sympathy with this new [reductionist] element in the business world. . . . I thought that perhaps the time had come when the new interest in foreign markets on the part of American business men might become a genuinely effective force in determining the course of tariff legislation." For background, see

Joshua Bernhardt, *The Tariff Commission: Its History, Activities, and Organization*, Institute for Government Research Service Monographs, no. 5 (New York: D. Appleton, 1922), pp. 10–13.

2. In fact, N. I. Stone later dubbed Miles "The Father of the Tariff Commission." See Stone, *One Man's Crusade for an Honest Tariff: The Story of H. E. Miles, Father of the Tariff Commission* (Appleton, Wis.: Lawrence College Press, 1952).

3. *RCT*, pp. 270–71.

4. U.S. Department of State, *Biographical Register* (Washington, D.C.: GPO, 1909). The BTR was later the Office of Foreign Trade Adviser, then Office of Economic Adviser. Taft was very much pleased with Knox's appointment of "Harry" Hoyt; see Taft to Knox, October 24, 1909, Philander C. Knox Papers, Library of Congress, Washington, D.C.

5. See Charles M. Pepper, "The Open Door to Canada: Memorandum for the President," typescript in Knox Papers, esp. pp. 4–6, 15. This memorandum is noted in L. Ethan Ellis's *Reciprocity 1911* (Washington, D.C.: Carnegie Endowment, 1939), pp. 5–6n, and is discussed more extensively in the context of an American "continentalism" by Robert E. Hannigan, "Reciprocity 1911: Continentalism and American Weltpolitik," *Diplomatic History* 4 (Winter 1980): 1–18.

6. In his detailed analysis, Pepper argued that low U.S. rates on Canadian coal would not hurt U.S. suppliers to the northwest and northeast markets because Nova Scotia coal exporters would have to expend funds on terminal facilities to compete with the West Virginia suppliers of the Boston market, whereas Wyoming producers could not hope to compete effectively with British Columbia coal producers in much of the northwestern market in any case. Canadian wheat imports would benefit the millers of the middle Northwest by providing hard winter wheat for mixing for export purposes. At the same time, the hard wheat would not substantially harm U.S. wheat producers, and the United States would gain the added advantage of forestalling shipment east of Canadian products by Canadian rail lines. The lumber and wood pulp reductions in the House bill, Pepper argued— as a former newspaperman, he may have been biased on this issue—would benefit the print media, whereas reductions on agricultural implements would benefit U.S. manufacturers, who were in general much more efficient producers of such articles than were the Canadians. Pepper, "Open Door to Canada," pp. 4–11, Knox Papers.

7. Ibid.

8. Ibid. On U.S. investments in Canadian resources, see also Stephen Scheinberg, "Invitation to Empire: Tariffs and American Economic Expansion in Canada," *Business History Review* 47 (Summer 1973): 219–38.

9. Pepper, "Open Door to Canada." Cf. Hannigan, "Reciprocity 1911," pp. 11–13; Taft shared this view, as he illustrated in a letter to Roosevelt in which he argued that a reciprocity agreement would "make Canada only an adjunct of the U.S." See Taft to Roosevelt, January 10, 1911, Theodore Roosevelt Papers, Library of Congress, Washington, D.C.; cf. Richard Cleveland Baker, *The Tariff under Roosevelt*

and Taft (Hastings, Neb.: Democrat Printing Company, 1941), pp. 206–7. Ronald Radosh, "American Manufacturers, Canadian Reciprocity, and the Origins of the Branch Factory System," *Canadian Association for American Studies Bulletin* 3 (Spring–Summer 1967): 19–54, also stresses the broad interest among American business interests in an agreement, suggesting that Pepper's conception of the viability of a business constituency for commercial agreement with Canada was reasonable.

10. C. M. Pepper, "Effect of the Iron and Steel Schedules," September 13 [?], 1909. Typescript in Knox Papers. See H. E. Miles to H. H. Lewis, April 11, 1908, in *LHA*, 3:1542–43. Miles was certainly skeptical of Pepper's view that the Payne-Aldrich reductions would have a salubrious effect on the implement industry. For this or for other reasons, he viewed Pepper as an "unfortunate" choice in his position in the BTR. See Miles to Alvin H. Sanders, November 16, 1909, RG 81/100.03.

11. See R. M. Roy (assistant to president, Hamilton Bridge Works) to T. Guilford Smith (export manager, Steel Products Export Company), October 21, 1909, RG 81/320.009. Roy enclosed an article from the *Toronto Globe* that suggested that Canadian buyers of U.S. steel would have to go to Britain exclusively if the United States demanded equality with the British preferential rate, because such a demand inevitably would be met in Canada by the imposition of punitive duties that would assure the unsalability of U.S. goods in Canada. J. A. Farrell to T. Guilford Smith, October 27, 1909, RG 81/485.83, enclosed in John Hughes (general agent, Steel Products Export Company) to H. C. Emery, November 3, 1909, RG 81/485.83.

12. Pepper, "Effect of the Iron and Steel Schedules." William H. Taft, *Address of President Taft at Winona, Minn., September 17, 1909* (Washington, D.C.: GPO, 1909).

13. [John Ball Osborne], "Memorandum on the New Tariff Law," September 16, 1909, Knox Papers; cf. "Memorandum Respecting the Merits of the Payne Tariff Law," September 15, 1909, and "Memorandum Respecting the New Tariff Act of the United States," September 13, 1909, ibid. See Osborne to Knox, September 10, 1909, mentioning his work on "a memorandum relative to the new tariff act," ibid. Earlier versions of the tariff memorandum may have reached Taft in time to influence his Winona speech on the tariff.

14. [Osborne], "Memorandum on New Tariff Law."

15. Ibid. This memo drew on a Pepper memorandum of the previous week; see Pepper, "Memo Respecting Wholesale Valuation Clause," September 14, 1909, Knox Papers. The Merchants Association of New York, which had promoted many of the customs changes, opposed creating a customs court with final decision powers, however, probably because it removed jurisdiction from regular courts in the coastal areas that were more sympathetic to mercantile interests. See Thomas Downing, *Customs Administrative Features of the Aldrich Tariff Bill: A Report to the*

MANY by Its Committee on Customs Service and Revenue Laws, June 8, 1909 (New York: Merchants Association of New York, 1909).

16. Taft gave special notice to Knox's attempts to build up the Bureau of Trade Relations and to implement the maximum-minimum provisions; see "Address of President Taft at the Banquet Given in His Honor by the Americus Club, Pittsburg [*sic*], Pa., May 2, 1910" (N.p., n.d.), pp. 5–10. The Taft policies suggest that American "continentalism" vis-à-vis Canada can be understood within the context of an American "globalism," in the sense that the United States took a similar stance toward the operation of preference tariffs all over the world.

17. See "Memo on File with the [Tariff] Board" (circa November 1909), with Taft's handwritten answers to questions, William H. Taft Papers, Library of Congress, Washington, D.C.

18. In private conversations in England, Nelson Aldrich had assured David Lloyd George (then chancellor of the Exchequer) and Winston Churchill (then head of the British Board of Trade) that Britain would almost certainly qualify for the minimum rates. Aldrich implied that it had been his strategy to create a tariff with high rates and large powers, to be interpreted liberally. This strategy was reflected, for example, in the fact that the Senate had dropped the House exclusion of imperial preferences from the definition of exclusionary laws against which the maximum tariff could be invoked, but had inserted the phrase "undue" discrimination, giving the executive branch discretionary power to ignore such discriminations. See Aldrich to Knox, October 24, 1909, RG 59/18659. U.S. State Department officials differed on the propriety of giving away U.S. intentions not to treat the Canadians' British preference rate as a discrimination, but they basically agreed with that policy. See Pepper to Osborne, November 3, 1909, RG 59/18659. Cf. the later notation of the BTR's assistant chief, Charles M. Pepper, that the United States had never considered treating the Canadians' imperial preference rate as a discrimination, in "Canadian Tariff Negotiations," U.S. Department of State Memo, April 19, 1910, copy in Knox Papers.

19. C. M. Pepper, "Canadian Tariff Negotiations," Memorandum, April 19, 1910, in U.S. Department of State, *Canadian Tariff Negotiations*, Exceptionally Confidential, To Be Filed as a Confidential Document, typeset copy in Knox Papers, pp. 1–19, quotation from p. 2. See also C. M. Pepper and M. H. Davis, "Trade Relations with Canada, Newfoundland, and Mexico," Memorandum, May 23, 1910, ibid., pp. 31–37, esp. 35. See, on Canadian reciprocity, Ellis, *Reciprocity 1911*, and Hannigan, "Reciprocity 1911."

20. Emery to Taft, February 19, 1910; Hoyt to Taft, March 8, 1910, enclosing Pepper to Hoyt, March 5, 1910; Pepper to Taft, March 14, 1910, describing the involvement of Pepper, Knox, and Taft in securing a select list of Canadian concessions; Taft to Emery, February 19, 1910. Perhaps uncomfortable with his earthy metaphor, Taft rephrased his decision in loftier terms: "It sometimes comes to such a situation that nations have to forego what is profitable in order to meet the

demands of dignity and self-respect." Taft to Helen Taft, March 19, 1910. All in Taft Papers.

21. Taft, "Address to the Americus Club," May 2, 1910, pp. 9–10; see also "Second Annual Message," December 6, 1910, *MPP*, 15:7501–2.

22. Quotation is from Taft to Roosevelt, January 10, 1911, Roosevelt Papers. Cited by Baker, *Tariff under Roosevelt and Taft*, pp. 206–7.

23. The characterizations of Canada and Mexico are from Pepper and Davis, "Trade Relations with Canada, Newfoundland, and Mexico," p. 31. See also Pepper, "Open Door to Canada," pp. 12–15.

24. See chapter 4 for U.S.-German commercial relations to 1907. See also "Memorandum on the New Tariff Law," September 16, 1909, Knox Papers. On the complaint of the Germans about abrogation of the commercial agreement of 1907, see Bernstorff to Huntington Wilson, May 16, 1909, RG 59/18775; see also Huntington Wilson, aide mémoire, ibid.

25. On German commercial sentiment, see translated editorials from the daily *Ostsee Zeitung und Neue Stettiner Zeitung*, May 19, 1909, and *Deutsche Export-Revue*, October 22, 1909, RG 59/18775; see also Knox, "Memorandum of Conversation with German Ambassador," November 4, 1909, ibid. For the State Department instructions on commercial intelligence gathering, see "Circular of Department of State of October 18, 1909 re Treatment of American Commerce in Foreign Countries," by Alvey A. Adee, acting secretary of state, in U.S. Department of State, *Tariff Negotiations between the United States and Foreign Governments*, printed as House Document no. 956, 61st Cong., 2d sess. (Washington, D.C.: GPO, 1910), pp. 14–17. On U.S. concern over the reorientation of German raw material purchases—in this case, oil—toward Austria-Hungary and Russia, see William H. Libby (Standard Oil export manager) to Knox, November 19, 1909, RG 59/18775/12, and Huntington Wilson to Libby, November 24, 1909, ibid.

26. MacVeagh, "Memorandum," March 25, 1910. See also H. C. Emery, "Confidential Memorandum for the Secretary of the Treasury from the Tariff Board, in the Matter of German Negotiations," February 5, 1910, RG 81/321.020. Taft's instruction to Knox is in Taft to Knox, December 19, 1909, Knox Papers.

27. Bernstorff to Knox, November 16, 1909; D. J. Hill to Knox, January 3 and 4, 1910, RG 59/18775; Baron Von Schoen was later the German ambassador to France. See J. B. Reynolds to Frank H. Mason (U.S. consul general, Paris), February 8, 1910, on German (and French) attempts to deny that the U.S. minimums were legitimate and on the German desire to exchange minimum rates only on the basis of treaty conventions. Reynolds noted the "very hard struggle over the German situation"; see RG 81/600.1.019. Americans later recognized the inflexibility of the legislatively established minimum, as France had done earlier. See, for example, W. S. Culbertson, "Equality of Treatment among Nations and a Bargaining Tariff," *Annals* 94 (March 1921): 160–75.

28. Bernstorff to Knox, November 16, 1909, RG 59/18775/14–15; Knox to

Bernstorff, ibid., 27–28. Knox argued that for reasons of geography and politics, Cuban-U.S. relations were exceptional. On the first point, Knox argued that Germany had already recognized in the U.S.-Hawaiian reciprocity treaty the existence of "special relations of proximity" that countenanced unusual commercial relations for strategic reasons. On the second point, Knox asserted that by virtue of the U.S.-imposed amendments to the Cuban constitution reserving U.S. rights to approve Cuban loan arrangements and to intervene in Cuban civil affairs, Cuba was obviously not a fully sovereign state and thus not comparable with Germany.

29. J. B. Osborne to H. M. Hoyt, November 30, 1909, RG 59/18775; Hoyt to Osborne, January 19, 1910, ibid.

30. [N. I. Stone], "Memorandum as to the Proposed Agreement with Germany," [December 1909], RG 81/321.020. Other European most-favored-nation signatories that could be affected by the German case included Austria-Hungary, Russia, Switzerland, Italy, and Belgium.

31. U.S. Tariff Board, "Memorandum from Tariff Board Prepared at the Request of Honorable Henry M. Hoyt, in Re Section 2, Tariff Act of August 5, 1909," [December 1909], RG 81/321.020; cf. H. C. Emery, "Confidential Memorandum for the Secretary of the Treasury," ibid. Memo of the Meeting of the Board, December 2, 1909, Chicago, RG 81/190. The meeting included J. Ogden Armour, T. J. Connors, and William Reid of Armour and Company; E. W. Morris and Thomas E. Wilson of Morris; R. Mair, export manager of Swift; W. E. Skinner, president-elect of the International Live Stock Exposition; A. G. Leonard, general manager of the Union Stock Yard Company; former senator W. A. Harris, a current member of the board of the American National Live Stock Association and the National Tariff Commission Association; and John Clay, of Clay, Robinson and Company, a leading U.S. livestock commission firm. The Tariff Board also suggested that because many of the important U.S. exports to Germany fell outside the rates Germany had conventionalized with other European powers, the negotiation of the full conventional rate with Germany should be regarded as merely preliminary to a full commercial agreement between the two countries.

32. H. C. Emery, "Confidential Memo for the Secretary of the Treasury," RG 81/321/020; J. B. Osborne, "Memo," January 18, 1910, noting that Pepper and Davis opposed sending of Sanders's memo on meat discriminations to the Germans. See also Hoyt to Osborne, January 19, 1910, indicating Hoyt's opposition as well, RG 59/18775/14–15. See also H. C. Emery to P. C. Knox, February 15, 1912, RG 81/600.1.020, reviewing events of the conference of January 28, 1910, concerning American promises to adopt a quasi-unconditional most-favored-nation position. In J. B. Osborne and H. C. Emery, "Joint Memorandum," the two bureau heads agreed to drop the live cattle question, but the Tariff Board stipulated that it did not accept German claims that no discrimination on the cattle issue existed. It merely agreed to defer the question because political reasons made it impractical to pursue it at the moment. RG 59/18775. For a résumé of the outcome of the negotiations, see

Knox to Taft, June 6, 1910, in U.S. Department of State, *Tariff Negotiations between the United States and Foreign Governments*, pp. 10–11.

33. Sanders to E. L. Boas (general manager, Hamburg-American Line), February 4, 1910, RG 81/321/020; Reynolds to Mason, February 8, 1910, RG 81/600.1.019.

34. The U.S. reciprocity agreement with Cuba, however, was not impaired by this minimum; thus Cuba continued in effect to receive an American "imperial preference" tariff rate. The Merchants Association of New York may have opposed the customs court with "final decision" because a federal court would be less accessible to influence by coastal import-export groups. See Thomas Downing, *Customs Administrative Features of the Aldrich Tariff Bill: A Report to the MANY by Its Committee on Customs Service and Revenue Laws*, June 8, 1909 (New York: Merchants Association of New York, 1909), New York Public Library Pamphlet Collection.

35. *RCT*, p. 272; Emery to Knox, December 12, RG 81/600.1.020.

36. On U.S.-French commercial relations, 1899–1909, see M. H. Davis and C. M. Pepper, "Memorandum, FRANCE: Analysis of Ten Years' Progress of Trade with the United States," November 11, 1909, RG 59/186591. Cf. *RCT*, pp. 228, 242–44. On the revisionists' call for expanded exports to France, see, for example, NAM *Proceedings*, 1901, pp. 47–50.

37. See H. M. Hoyt to J. B. Osborne, November 14, 1909, RG 59/18659, on the legal basis of U.S. cancellation of the terms of the U.S.-German commercial agreement with France. France later raised its minimum tariff rates and effectively closed out a portion of Canadian and other foreign trade; see *RCT*, p. 364.

38. On this point, see Pepper, "Canadian Tariff Negotiations," April 19, 1910. Canadian negotiations were specifically delayed by the U.S. to allow the French negotiations to proceed.

39. White to Knox, September 30, 1909, giving account of the Aldrich dinner with the French minister of finance and governors of the Bank of France; White to Knox, October 15, 1909; Department of State to French Ambassador, January 7, 1910, all in RG 59/186591. See on State Department reaction, Memo of Messrs. Pepper and Davis re Note of the French Ambassador, November 17, 1909, ibid.

40. See, for terms of agreement, U.S. Department of State, *Tariff Negotiations between the United States and Foreign Governments*, p. 11; cf. *RCT*, p. 272.

41. Taft, "Address to Americus Club," May 2, 1910; Department of State, *Tariff Negotiations between the United States and Foreign Governments*; Emery to Taft, March 23, 1910, Taft Papers.

Chapter 10

1. The provisions were under section 2, article 718 of the Payne-Aldrich Tariff.

2. The phrase "difference in cost of production here and abroad" was repeated by

Taft a number of times and can be found, for example, in the Republicans' 1908 electoral platform; see Kirk H. Porter and Donald Bruce Johnson, *National Party Platforms, 1840–1968* (Urbana: University of Illinois Press, 1970). In the Winona speech, Taft called for the development of a tariff "glossary" that would list such costs; see *Address of President Taft at Winona, Minn., September 17, 1909* (Washington, D.C.: GPO, 1909). In his message of December 7, 1909, he again called for a comprehensive "tariff glossary and encyclopaedia." In his message to Congress of March 28, 1910, Taft, in asking for a $250,000 appropriation for the Tariff Board (its original allocation was $75,000), justified the need for the increase as due to the need to hire a staff of experts to conduct the cost-of-production investigations. See "Message from the President of the United States," 61st Cong., 2d sess., Sen. Doc. 463, March 28, 1910. Cf. Emery's request for such an appropriation, Emery to Taft, February 5, 1910, William H. Taft Papers, Library of Congress, Washington, D.C. For general background on the Tariff Board, see Joshua Bernhardt, *The Tariff Commission: Its History, Activities, and Organization* (New York: D. Appleton, 1922), pp. 10–14; see also Joseph F. Kenkel, *Progressives and Protection* (Washington, D.C.: University Press of America, 1983), pp. 59–90.

3. Emery expressed the notion that the board was freed of "statutory provisions" in Tariff Board Meeting with National Tariff Commission Association (NTCA), February 1910, RG 81/130.1. Present at this meeting were the board; its chief economist, Stone; John Candler Cobb, the president of the NTCA; and Henry R. Towne and H. E. Miles of the NTCA executive committee. On the role of the board vis-à-vis Congress, see also the retrospective assessment by William S. Culbertson, a doctoral student of Emery who worked on the board's wool report and later served on the U.S. Tariff Commission, "The Tariff Board and Wool Legislation," *American Economic Review* 3 (March 1913): 59–84.

4. After meeting with the major livestock groups in Chicago in early December 1909, the board met at the Union League Club in Chicago with members of the Chicago Association of Commerce and others. The group included E. M. Skinner, chairman of the association; George W. Sheldon, a member of the Board of the NTCA and chairman of the Chicago Association's Export Committee; George E. Roberts, author of the "Iowa idea" plank of 1902, gold-standard publicist, former director of the U.S. Mint, and current president of the Commercial National Bank of Chicago; C. S. Funk, the export manager of International Harvester Corporation; A. L. Goetzman, secretary of the Millers National Federation; John E. Wilder, ex-president of the Illinois Manufacturers Association; and Kenneth Barnhart, manager of Marshall Field wholesale operations; see RG 81/100. On the Tariff Board's correspondence with the steel industry, see J. A. Farrell (president, United States Steel Export Products Company) to T. Guilford Smith (sales manager), October 29, 1909, RG 81/485.83.

5. On the Tariff Commission Convention of February 1909, see chapter 8. On the NTCA, see Gustav H. Schwab to Henry C. Emery, January 11, 1909, RG

81/100.5, reporting on the organizing meeting at the offices of the MANY; see also Henry Tarleton Wills (secretary of NTCA), *Scientific Tariff Making: A History of the Movement to Create a Tariff Commission* (New York: Blanchard Press, 1913), esp. pp. 61, 87–91. The NTCA statement is in Tariff Board Meeting with National Tariff Association Executive Committee, February 1910, RG 81/130.1. Cobb conceived of the NTCA's following as strongest in New England and the northern Midwest, weaker along the Pacific coast and in the South. Among organizations represented by delegates were chambers of commerce, boards of trade, or merchants associations of Albany, New York; Bismarck, North Dakota; Dayton, Ohio; Denver, Colorado; Fargo, North Dakota; Portland, Maine; Milwaukee, Wisconsin; Newark, New Jersey; New York City; Oklahoma City; Portland, Oregon; Rochester, New York; Spokane, Washington; Springfield, Massachusetts; St. Paul, Minnesota; Syracuse, New York; Tacoma, Washington; Los Angeles; and Worcester, Massachusetts, as well as many industry exporting associations. List from NTCA letterhead in RG 81/100.03.

6. Stone's comments on the "Wirtschaftlichen Ausschuss," in Meeting with NTCA, February 1910, RG 81/130.1. Emery continued to follow the activities of this commission, especially on a study trip to Europe in 1910. The commission was increased to forty-eight members in July 1910. See George Atwood (American Association of Commerce and Trade, Berlin) to H. C. Emery, July 15, 1910, RG 81/100.

7. Emery comments in Meeting with NTCA, February 1910, RG 81/130.1. Cf. Address of Mr. Henry C. Emery before NTCA Convention, January 11, 1911, cited in Wills, *Scientific Tariff Making*, pp. 140–41.

8. Miles comments in Meeting with NTCA, February 1910, RG 81/130.1. Cf. Miles to H. C. Emery, February 4, 1910, RG 81/100.03, in which Miles elaborates on the U.S. need to emulate German commercial structures and practices as a means of competing with Germany, for example, in South American markets. Miles had been co-opted onto the NCC by Gustav Schwab, the NCC chairman and associate of Oscar Straus. Straus's family, associated with Macy's department store, was well known in New York import-export circles. Schwab represented German shipping interests in the United States and was prominent in the New York Chamber of Commerce and in the MANY, whose current president was Henry R. Towne. In addition, William R. Corwine, who had been the secretary of the American Reciprocal Tariff League (ARTL), and who had connections to the MANY through its association with ARTL, had been appointed secretary of the NCC.

9. See A. B. Farquhar to J. W. Van Cleave, December 7, 1907, *LHA*, 1:1194–95, and D. A. Tompkins to J. W. Van Cleave, December 12, 1907, *LHA*, 2:1208–9. Cf. George B. Cortelyou to Gustav H. Schwab, June 10, 1908, RG 40/56930. See also Miles to Sanders, November 16, 1909, RG 81/100.03, in which Miles expressed the hope that his semiofficial status in the Commerce and Labor Department as chairman of the NCC Committee on Foreign Commerce would give him some entrée

into the Tariff Board. "Report of the [NCC] Committee on Foreign Commerce," December 2, 1909, RG 40/66419, contains a fuller exposition of Miles's views on foreign trade. He praised, for example, the German practice in which "every manufacturer occupies a semi-official relation to the Government, and a stream of information is flowing constantly from the manufacturers to the Government."

10. See George L. McCarthy to H. E. Miles, December 3, 1909, RG 40/66419. On Towne's plans, see Gustav H. Schwab to Henry C. Emery, November 1, 1909, RG 81/100.5. Miles had been greatly encouraged by MacVeagh's and Taft's statements on the tariff in December 1909 (Taft's December 7 message and, presumably, MacVeagh's address to the Massachusetts Bankers' Association of December 8); Miles, echoing MacVeagh, called the statements "almost epocal"; see H. E. Miles to Alvin H. Sanders, December 13, 1909, RG 81/100.03. By February, however, Miles was beginning to abandon his passive faith in Taft and to press for a more activist and expanded board. See Miles to Emery, February 4, 1910, RG 81/100.03, in which he notes that enlarging the board should be a high priority. To match the thirty-two-member German commission's work on a manpower basis alone, Miles complained, would take the Tariff Board until "the blessed year 1962."

11. See R. B. Horton (secretary of Tariff Board) to Charles D. Norton (Taft's secretary), September 12, 1910, enclosing Emery to MacVeagh, n.d., and copy of Emery, Memorandum to the Secretary of the Treasury from the Chairman of the Tariff Board (Report on European Investigation), Taft Papers.

12. MacVeagh to Taft, August 9, 1910, notes that MacVeagh has seen Emery and discussed the trip and plans of the board. MacVeagh advised Taft "to keep in touch too, and I am sending Emery's full report on trip for your perusal. He has learned a lot and you may want to talk with him at greater length." W. Stoddard to C. D. Norton, August 28, 1910, enclosing his summary of Emery's memorandum and extracts from the Emery Report. See also Emery, "Memorandum to the Secretary of the Treasury," in Horton to Norton, September 12, 1910, Taft Papers. Cf. J. B. Reynolds, "The Tariff Commission Plan: Its Facts and Fallacies," *North American Review* 203 (June 1916): 852–66, and Culbertson, "Tariff Board and Wool Legislation," pp. 59–62.

13. Miles to Emery, September 27 and 30, 1910, Emery to Miles, October 3, 1910, RG 81/100.3; see also Emery, "Memorandum to the Secretary," ibid. Cf. Miles to Emery, February 9, 1910, and Emery to Miles, February 14, 1910, ibid., for comments on their differences.

14. H. E. Miles, "Address," at the National Tariff Commission Association Convention, January 1911, in Wills, *Scientific Tariff Making*, pp. 156–63; quotation from p. 162.

15. Emery's remarks are in Tariff Board Meeting with NTCA, February 1910, RG 81/130.1. Emery added that Taft "seems to have the idea of a document that can be prepared, by which anybody who wants to know what it costs to make horseshoe nails can turn to this alphabetical document and find out how much

horseshoe nails ought to be. . . . . The trouble is, by the time you got down to 'B,' what you said about 'A' would be out of date"; ibid.

16. Emery, "Memorandum to the Secretary"; Stoddard to Norton, August 28, 1910, Summary and Extracts of Memo, Taft Papers.

17. Emery, "Memorandum to the Secretary"; Stoddard to Norton, August 28, 1910, Summary and Extracts of Memo, Taft Papers.

18. Tariff Board, Report of Conference of September 22, 1910, RG 81/130.1. Emery told Towne that the board was coming to look on him as its "mentor"; Emery to Towne, September 26, 1910, RG 81/100.03. Henry R. Towne (1844–1924) began his career working in naval engineering with his father and Captain John Ericsson, the designer of Union ironclad ships, during the Civil War. The younger Towne then studied in Europe under the American engineer Robert Briggs and at the Sorbonne. In the late 1860s, H. R. Towne became associated with Linus Yale, Jr., who had produced locks for safes and had invented the small-key pin-tumbler lock. It was Towne who saw the possibilities for mass production in the separate tumbler cylinder of the Yale lock, and Yale's sudden death in 1868 propelled Towne into prominence as an engineer and expert on shop management. His paper, "The Engineer as Economist," published in 1886, was a landmark in the literature of "efficiency," and the Towne-Halsey plan, a modified wage-piecework system, was praised by F. W. Taylor as a "great invention." See, on Towne, obituary, *Transactions of the American Society of Mechanical Engineers* 46 (1924): 1324–26. Cf. Oberlin Smith, "Discussion of an Accurate Cost-Keeping System," *Transactions of the American Society of Mechanical Engineers* 19 (1898), and F. W. Taylor, "Shop Management," *Transactions of the American Society of Mechanical Engineers* 24 (1903): esp. 1354–55.

19. Henry R. Towne, comments in Tariff Board Meeting with NTCA Executive Committee, February 1910, RG 81/130.1; Tariff Board, Report of Conference of September 22, 1910, RG 81/130.1. Quotations from Henry R. Towne to Henry C. Emery, September 26, 1910, RG 81/100.03.

20. Tariff Board, Report of Conference of September 22, 1910, RG 81/130.1. Quotations from Henry R. Towne to Henry C. Emery, September 26, 1910, RG 81/100.03. Compare the earlier criticism by University of Chicago political economist John Cummings, "Cost of Production as a Basis of Tariff Revision," *Journal of Political Economy* 17 (March 1909): 153–57: "Price would seem . . . to be a perfectly good index of the amount of protection required . . . to keep any commodity out of our market, without any analysis of cost in terms of wages and prices of materials in foreign countries."

21. H. E. Miles to H. C. Emery, September 27, 1910, RG 81/100.03. See also Emery to Miles, September 29, 1910, appeasing Miles with the thought that although Miles and Towne "seem to differ somewhat, . . . our work will be of a kind to cover both what you desire and what he desires." On Miles and the Beveridge bill of 1908, see chapter 5.

22. Towne quotation from February 1910 Conference, RG 81/130.1. See Henry C. Emery, Address to Chicago Association of Commerce, December 3, 1910, Taft Papers, published as *The Tariff Board and Its Work* (Washington, D.C.: GPO, 1910). Taft strongly approved Emery's formulations; on his copy of Emery's speech is written, "I like this very much indeed; a little long for popular consumption but it may be intended that it will be read by business men. It epitomizes something of what I have said in my messages. William H. Taft, November 10, 1910." See also, H. C. Emery, "The Plans of the Tariff Board," *New York Times Annual Financial Review*, January 8, 1911, p. 16. Cf. J. B. Reynolds's summation of the Tariff Board's mission in "The Tariff Commission Plan: Its Facts and Fallacies," esp. pp. 856–57.

23. Emery to Taft, February 5, 1910, enclosed in Emery to Carpenter, February 25, 1910, Taft Papers. The experts included C. W. A. Veditz; Lewis Dwight Harvell Weld, on loan from the Census Bureau; and William S. Culbertson, later a member of the Tariff Commission, who was Emery's doctoral student at Yale and who traveled to Europe on Emery's behest and worked on the wool investigation.

24. See Memorandum of Conference of Tariff Board at Waldorf-Astoria, New York, May 9, 1910, and Conference between the Tariff Board and Certain Representatives and Agents of the Board held at U.S. Customs House, New York, November 10, 1910, RG 81/130.1. "Know what you're after; don't bluff or bluster," was the advice of Emery.

25. Testimony of James W. Good, J. C. Cobb, and Irvine Lenroot in U.S. Congress, House, Committee on Ways and Means, *Tariff Commission*, Hearings, 61st Cong., 3d sess., December 13, 1910 (Washington, D.C.: GPO, 1910); speeches of Samuel McCall in *Proceedings of NTCA Convention*, January 1911, in Wills, *Scientific Tariff Making*, pp. 151–56, quotation taken from p. 155, and of Taft, ibid., pp. 250–55.

26. See U.S. Tariff Board, *Reciprocity with Canada*, 61st Cong., 3d sess., Sen. Doc. 849 (Washington, D.C.: GPO, 1911). See also "Memorandum of Investigations of the Work of the Tariff Board by Committee of the NTCA, May 4–5, 1911," RG 81/130.1.

27. A companion tariff commission bill introduced for Taft in the Senate by Henry Cabot Lodge also failed. On Taft's motives in appointing Page and Howard, see E. F. Baldwin (editor, *The Outlook*) to Emery, March 7, 1910, Emery to Baldwin, March 8, 1910, RG 81/100.10. Page would become chairman of the Tariff Commission created during the Wilson administration.

28. La Follette, speech, *Congressional Record*, 62d Cong., 2d sess., June 13, 1911, p. 1963. See also *La Follette's Autobiography* (Madison, Wis.: privately printed, 1913), pp. 504–5, 621–30. Henry F. Pringle, *The Life and Times of William Howard Taft* (New York: Farrar and Rinehart, 1939), 2:724–28; Richard Cleveland Baker, *The Tariff under Roosevelt and Taft* (Hastings, Neb.: Democrat Printing Company, 1941), p. 162; *New York Times*, August 1, 1911. Miles to Taft, August 4, 1911, RG 81/100.03, Miles was shifting toward Progressivism and Roosevelt,

"whose blood is insurgent," as early as 1910; Miles to Sanders, June 28, 1910, ibid. Miles later joined the Progressive party and supported Roosevelt in the 1912 election.

29. Frank W. Taussig, "The Tariff and the Tariff Commission," *Atlantic Monthly* (December 1910): 721–29; James Laurence Laughlin, "The Tariff Commission and Its Problems," *New York Times Annual Financial Review*, January 8, 1911, p. 17; E. V. Robinson, "Tariff Legislation—Discussion," *American Economic Review, Supplement* 2 (March 1912): 37–41. H. Parker Willis, "'Costs' and Tariff Revision," *Journal of Political Economy* 19 (May 1911): 361–84, esp. 375–76, and "Economic Investigation as a Basis for Tariff Legislation," *American Economic Review, Supplement* 2 (March 1912): 26–36, esp. 32–33. Frank W. Taussig, "The Report of the Tariff Board on Wools and Woolens," *American Economic Review* 2 (June 1912): 257–68; Taussig recognized the value of economic inquiry but found the wool report easy to criticize because the drastically varying reasons for wool production—as a by-product of mutton raising and for textile making—made ascertainment of real costs difficult.

30. Henry C. Emery, "Economic Investigation as a Basis for Tariff Legislation," *American Economic Review, Supplement* 2 (March 1912): 19–25; Reynolds, "The Tariff Commission Plan," pp. 864–65; U.S. Tariff Board, *The Pulp and News Print Industry* (Washington, D.C.: GPO, 1911), *Wool and Manufactures of Wool*, 2 vols. (Washington, D.C.: GPO, 1912), and *Cotton Manufactures* (Washington, D.C.: GPO, 1912); cf. Kenkel, *Progressives and Protection*, pp. 84–89; L. D. H. Weld, "'Costs' and the Tariff Board," *Journal of Political Economy* 20 (May 1912): 492–508; quotation from Emery, "Economic Investigation," p. 25. See also W. S. Culbertson, "Tariff Board and Wool Legislation"; Culbertson had defended the wool report, a year after Taussig had criticized it, on the basis that its figures were useful in distinguishing the differences between proposals for a tariff and should not have been expected to define a scientific level of protection; defining a philosophy of protection was a problem that had to be worked out between the political parties, Culbertson maintained (pp. 59–61, 82–84). H. C. Emery, "The Tariff and Foreign Trade," *Official Report of the National Foreign Trade Convention*, May 27 and 28, 1914 (New York: National Foreign Trade Council, 1914), pp. 258–73.

31. Roosevelt, Address to the Progressive Party National Convention, Chicago, August 6, 1912, *New York Times*, August 7, 1912; Reynolds, "Tariff Commission Plan," pp. 864–65; Weld, "'Costs' and the Tariff Board," p. 505.

Chapter 11

1. Franklin MacVeagh, "Address to Massachusetts Bankers' Association," December 8, 1909, quoted in *Bulletin of the American Iron and Steel Association*, January 1, 1910.

2. See William S. Culbertson, "The Tariff Board and Wool Legislation," *American Economic Review* 3 (March 1913): 59–84.

3. Laurence F. Schmeckebier and Gustavus A. Weber, *The Bureau of Foreign and Domestic Commerce*, Institute for Government Research Service Monographs, no. 29 (Baltimore: Johns Hopkins University Press, 1924), pp. 29–30; see also Joshua Bernhardt, *The Tariff Commission: Its History, Activities, and Organization*, Institute for Government Research Service Monographs, no. 5 (New York: D. Appleton, 1922), p. 13.

4. U.S. Bureau of Foreign and Domestic Commerce, *Annual Report of the Chief of the Bureau of Foreign and Domestic Commerce, 1916* (Washington, D.C.: GPO, 1916), pp. 81–95. The specific studies were on the sugar industry; cost of production in the pottery industry (summary and full volume comparing costs in the United States, England, Germany, and Austria); industrial conditions in Montgomery County, Pennsylvania; the women's muslin underwear industry; the hosiery industry; the knit underwear industry; the shirt and collar industry; the cotton-spinning industry; and the men's factory-made clothing industry; ibid., p. 87.

5. On Wilson's tariff views, see, for example, William Diamond, *The Economic Thought of Woodrow Wilson* (Baltimore: Johns Hopkins University Press, 1943), pp. 97–99, and Arthur S. Link, *Wilson: Confusions and Crises, 1915–1916* (Princeton, N.J.: Princeton University Press, 1964), pp. 341–45. The rates of the Underwood Tariff were less than 10 percent on all imports (about equivalent to the European minimum tariff rates), compared with about 20 percent for the equivalent Payne-Aldrich minimum rates, 26 percent for the Dingley rates, and 20 percent for the Wilson-Gorman rates. See Frank W. Taussig, *Tariff History of the United States*, 6th ed. (New York: G. P. Putnam's Sons, 1913), pp. 451–52. The quotation from John Sharp Williams is taken from Joseph F. Kenkel, *Progressives and Protection* (Washington, D.C.: University Press of America, 1983), p. 97. Wilson cited Taussig in 1912; see, for example, "Address on the Tariff to the National Democratic Club in New York, January 3, 1912," in *The Papers of Woodrow Wilson*, ed. Arthur S. Link et al., 59 vols. to date (Princeton, N.J.: Princeton University Press, 1966–), 23:637–50.

6. Chamber of Commerce of the United States of America, *Referendum No. 2: On the Question of a Permanent Tariff Commission* (Washington, D.C., October 30, 1913). The Payne bill was HR 32010. See also Bernhardt, *Tariff Commission*, pp. 14–16. On the NTCA's demise, see H. R. Towne to G. W. Loft, December 7, 1915, Woodrow Wilson Papers, Princeton University, cited by Kenkel, *Progressives and Protection*, p. 261n.

7. On Miles, see N. I. Stone, *One Man's Crusade for an Honest Tariff: The Story of H. E. Miles, Father of the Tariff Commission* (Appleton, Wis.: Lawrence College Press, 1952). On the lobby investigation itself, see the Senate hearings, U.S. Congress, Senate, Subcommittee of Committee on the Judiciary, *Maintenance of a*

Lobby to Influence Legislation: Hearings, 4 vols., 63d Cong., 1st sess. (Washington, D.C.: GPO, 1913); the appendix to the hearings, consisting largely of exhibits of correspondence from the NAM files, U.S. Congress, Senate, Subcommittee of Committee on the Judiciary, *Maintenance of a Lobby to Influence Legislation: Appendix. Exhibits Introduced during the Hearings*, 4 vols., 63d Cong., 1st sess. (Washington, D.C.: GPO, 1913); and the House lobby hearings, in which exhibits are interspersed, U.S. Congress, House, Select Committee on Lobby Investigation, *Charges against Members of the House and Lobby Activities of the National Association of Manufacturers: Hearings*, 4 vols., 63d Cong., 1st sess., (Washington, D.C.: GPO, 1913). See also "National Association of Manufacturers Attacked," *American Industries* 14 (August 1913). Cf. Albert K. Steigerwalt, *The National Association of Manufacturers: A Study in Business Leadership* (Ann Arbor: University of Michigan Press, 1964), pp. 138–47.

8. See the MANY *Yearbook*, 1907–16, for the notable expansion of the financial and corporate exporters in MANY's classified lists of members. On the commission drive, see "Campaign for Tariff Commission Is Launched," *Greater New York: Bulletin of the Merchants Association of New York* 4 (December 13, 1915): 1–8.

9. "To Divorce Tariff and Politics: Prominent Men Back a National Campaign for a Permanent Non-partisan Tariff Commission," *New York Times*, July 25, 1915. Childs was a board member of Crucible Steel and several other corporations; his own company, a $15 million New Jersey corporation (1902), was listed as one of Moody's "lesser" trusts. He was also a member of the MANY. Marshall's American Locomotive Company was a New York–based corporation (1901) with plants from Virginia to New Hampshire to Pittsburgh, controlling about 70 percent of locomotive production. See John Moody, *The Truth About the Trusts* (1904; reprint, Westport, Conn.: Greenwood Press, 1968), pp. 228, 455. The labor support for the TCL came from Warren S. Stone, of the International Brotherhood of Locomotive Engineers. Also supporting the TCL were prominent procorporate academics such as university presidents Arthur Twining Hadley of Yale, David Starr Jordan of Stanford, Frank Goodnow of Johns Hopkins, and Benjamin Ide Wheeler of the University of California. On Farwell, see James Livingston, *Origins of the Federal Reserve System: Money, Class, and Corporate Capitalism* (Ithaca, N.Y.: Cornell University Press, 1986), p. 104. See also "Favors Tariff Commission: H. H. Gross Wants Permanent Body to Fix Imposts after War," *New York Times*, September 26, 1915. Gross had worked with railroad entrepreneurs and with Wilson's secretary of agriculture, David F. Houston, to pass the Smith-Lever Agricultural Education bill.

10. William L. Saunders, chairman of Ingersoll-Rand, told a 1915 FTC hearing in New York, for example, that postwar European dumping in the United States represented "a very great danger." If the FTC did not already have the authority to "prevent a foreign country from enabling a foreign . . . producer, . . . through bounties or otherwise, to sell goods in this country at a lower figure than the American producer, . . . the laws should . . . give them that power; . . . the alternative

being a very high tariff, [which] I do not favor [because foreign governments] would simply pay a bounty that would overcome the high tariff." Testimony of Saunders, Federal Trade Commission, "Hearings in re: Foreign Trade Extension," Third and Fourth Days, New York, New York, June 3–4, 1915, p. 152, RG 122/8519-1-2. Within the Wilson cabinet, Commerce Secretary Redfield was a proponent of the "dumping" threat, whereas Treasury Secretary McAdoo held a broader interpretation of the European trade issue. See, for example, Redfield to Wilson, January 4, 1916, in which he argues that tariffs could not offset German dyestuff dumping effectively if the German cartel and government chose to sell at a loss to regain the markets; see Link et al., *The Papers of Woodrow Wilson*, 35:427–28. McAdoo saw the dumping issue as largely Republican electoral propaganda. Yet he himself had proposed antidumping clauses as part of the Underwood bill and consented to consideration of the issue within the context of a Democratic tariff commission; McAdoo to Wilson, January 14, 1916, ibid., pp. 475–77. The quotation is from Charles A. Conant, "German Trade after the War," *Wall Street Journal*, July 8, 1915; the article, Conant's last, was published shortly after his death in Havana.

11. On the procorporate cast of the Webb-Pomerene Act, see the analysis of Carl P. Parrini, *Heir to Empire: United States Economic Diplomacy, 1916–1923* (Pittsburgh: University of Pittsburgh Press, 1968), esp. pp. 27–31. See also Burton Kaufman, *Efficiency and Expansion: Foreign Trade Organization in the Wilson Administration, 1913–1921* (Westport, Conn.: Greenwood Press, 1974), which stresses the wartime events as stimuli to "organization," esp. chap. 6, "The Growing Specter of European Efficiency, 1915–1916," pp. 143–64.

12. See especially Martin J. Sklar, *The Corporate Reconstruction of American Capitalism, 1890–1916: The Market, the Law, and Politics* (New York: Cambridge University Press, 1988), pp. 228–85. Cf. James Weinstein, *Corporate Ideal in the Liberal State, 1900–1918* (Boston: Beacon Press, 1968), pp. 62–91. The Hepburn measure would have allowed registered corporations to file notices of proposed rate changes, contracts, or mergers with the commissioner. The absence of a bureau declaration of the action as illegal within thirty days would be considered an estoppel to future antitrust proceedings. The Clayton Act sections were 2, 3, 7, and 8; see W. Stull Holt, *The Federal Trade Commission*, Institute for Government Research Service Monographs, no. 7 (New York: D. Appleton, 1922), pp. 1–16.

13. Testimony of Henry R. Towne, in U.S. Congress, House, Committee on Interstate and Foreign Commerce, 63d Cong., 2d sess., *Interstate Trade Commission*, Hearings, January 30 to February 16, 1914 (Washington, D.C.: GPO, 1914), pp. 301–31. See also Chamber of Commerce of the United States of America, *Speeches on Antitrust Legislation Delivered at Second Annual Meeting, February 12, 1914* (Washington, D.C., 1914), for speeches by Henry R. Towne et al. Although critical of aspects of proposed legislation, Towne characterized current antitrust sentiment as the result of a broad business consensus to "restrict and regulate

privilege and monopoly" without hampering the legitimate activities of small business and to promote "efficiency and proper co-operation, especially as to our export trade" (p: 57). Cf. Merchants Association of New York, "Report of the Committee on the Federal Trade Commission," New York, May 20, 1915, in RG 122/8519-1-2, Hearings in New York, June 1915. See also E. N. Hurley to H. R. Towne, June 12, 1915, RG 122/8508-68-1. Members of the MANY's Foreign Trade Committee officially concurred in the Towne Committee's broad cooperation proposals. They included E. A. DeLima, commercial banker; Franklin Johnston, export publisher; William H. Douglas, commission merchant; Silas Webb, of the American Asiatic Association; and Philip B. Kennedy, later a U.S. commercial attaché in London who advised the State Department on international banking affairs.

14. Clyde William Phelps, *The Foreign Expansion of American Banks* (New York: n.p., 1927), chap. 6; Paul Philip Abrahams, "The Foreign Expansion of American Finance and Its Relationship to the Foreign Economic Policies of the United States, 1907–1921" (Ph.D. dissertation, University of Wisconsin, 1967). Parrini, *Heir to Empire*, pp. 7–10, 102–15, esp. 111–12. Livingston, *Origins of Federal Reserve*, pp. 203–4.

15. Federal Trade Commission, *Annual Report, 1915* (Washington, D.C.: GPO, 1915), p. 2. The MANY also supported this drive. In addition, Benjamin Strong, governor of the New York Federal Reserve Bank, joined the merchants' group, and Henry Towne, former president of the MANY, became a board member of the New York Federal Reserve Bank.

16. Federal Trade Commission, "Hearings in re: Foreign Trade Extension," Third and Fourth Days, New York, New York, June 3–4, 1915, transcripts, in RG 122/8519-1-2. See also "Exporters Favor Trade Combine," *New York Times*, June 4, 1915, and "Lift Trust Law Ban, Exporters Demand," *New York Times*, June 5, 1915. See also Gilbert H. Montague to Joseph E. Davies, RG 122/1723-1, cited by Kaufman, *Efficiency and Expansion*, p. 164n. The FTC study itself is *Cooperation in American Export Trade*, part 1 (Washington, D.C.: GPO, 1916). On the relations of Amalgamated (the holding company for Anaconda Copper) with the NCB, the Rockefeller interests, and Guaranty Trust, see F. Ernest Richter, "The Amalgamated Copper Co.: A Closed Chapter in Corporate Finance," *Quarterly Journal of Economics* 30 (February 1916): 387–407.

17. See Vanderlip to Cyrus McCormick, November 20, 1915 and November 27, 1915, Frank A. Vanderlip Papers, Butler Library, Columbia University, New York. See also Austin to Vanderlip, August 30, 1918, and September 17, 1918, ibid. Cf. Parrini, *Heir to Empire*, pp. 62–63; Kaufman, *Efficiency and Expansion*, pp. 145–47.

18. For views of commission merchants, see William Harris Douglas, interview by FTC agent D. Morrow, July 1915, RG 122/8401-5, and Franklin Johnston and B. Olney Hough (editors of *American Exporter*), interview by FTC agent W. Y. Durand, July 1915, RG 122/8401-13. See also testimony of Douglas and Welding

Ring in Federal Trade Commission, "Hearings in New York," RG 122/8519-1-2, pp. 195–200, 206–11. See William L. Saunders, remarks and paper, "Government Regulation of Commerce as Affecting Foreign Trade," *Official Report of the Second National Foreign Trade Convention*, St. Louis, Mo., January 21 and 22, 1915 (New York: National Foreign Trade Council, 1915), pp. 53–68, and "Address of Mr. Ryan," ibid., pp. 69–75. See also testimony of Saunders, Lewis, and Babson before the FTC, in Federal Trade Commission, "Hearings in re: Foreign Trade Extension," pp. 135–71, 183–87, and 77–89, respectively. See also Babson to Joseph E. Davies, June 14, 1915, RG 122/8508-83-1, modifying his testimony. On H. C. Lewis's proposals, see also Lewis to E. N. Hurley, April 15, 1915, and Hurley to Lewis, May 2, 1915, RG 122/8404-282.

19. Ryan, in *Official Report of the First National Foreign Trade Convention* (New York: National Foreign Trade Council, 1914), pp. 161–71. See also Ryan, "Combination in Foreign Trade," *The Americas* 1 (December 1914): 7–10. Quotation from John D. Ryan to James H. Perkins, September 29, 1914, Vanderlip Papers. Cf. comments of Alonzo H. Weed, attorney for Manufacturing Chemists Association, in Federal Trade Commission, *Cooperation in American Export Trade*, part 1 (Washington, D.C.: GPO, 1916), 2:301, and testimony of Weed and Henry H. Howard of Merrimac Chemical Company at FTC Hearings in Boston, June 1–2, RG 122/8519-1-1, and "The Federal Trade Commission at Work," *American Industries* 15 (July 1915): 13–16.

20. Ryan, "Combination in Foreign Trade," pp. 8–9. See also William C. Downs, "Problems of the Smaller Manufacturers and Merchants in Development of Foreign Trade," *Official Report of the Second National Foreign Trade Convention*, St. Louis, Mo., January 21 and 22, 1915 (New York: National Foreign Trade Council, 1915), pp. 75–84, and "The Commission House in Latin American Trade," *Quarterly Journal of Economics* 26 (November 1911): 118–39. Cf. W. S. Kies, *Cooperation in Export Trade: Address before American Academy of Political and Social Science, April 30, 1915* (New York: National City Bank, 1915). Carl Parrini has noted the "ostensible" small-business orientation of the Webb-Pomerene Act; see *Heir to Empire*, pp. 27–31. Parrini suggests that the price of copper was an important factor in balancing U.S. trade deficits; the weight of Ryan's Anaconda Copper Company in the export cooperation movement thus was great. On the history of copper export price problems, see the Federal Trade Commission, *Report on the Copper Industry*, 2 vols. (Washington, D.C.: GPO, 1947), 1:11, and Thomas R. Navin, *Copper Mining and Management* (Tucson: University of Arizona Press, 1978), chaps. 9 and 10.

21. Ryan, "Combination in Foreign Trade," p. 9.

22. Federal Trade Commission, *Cooperation in Export Trade*, 1:200–201. See, for example, Davies to W. S. Kies (vice-president, NCB), November 22, 1915, RG 122/8404-359. The two had been classmates at the University of Wisconsin; cf. Joseph T. Talbert (vice-president, NCB) to E. N. Hurley, November 22, 1915, and Hurley to Talbert, December 3, 1915, ibid.

23. On opposition to the Webb bill, see *Congressional Record*, 64th Cong., 1st sess., 1916, pp. 13676–727; 65th Cong., 1st sess., 1917, pp. 2784–91, 3563–85, 7324–28; cf. William F. Notz and Richard S. Harvey, *American Foreign Trade as Promoted by the Webb Pomerene and Edge Acts* (Indianapolis: n.p., 1920), pp. 149–52. Cf. Kaufman, *Efficiency and Expansion*, pp. 158–59. On Lewis's support of the Webb bill, see U.S. Congress, Senate Committee on Interstate Commerce, 64th Cong., 2d sess., *Promotion of Export Trade: Hearings . . . on HR 17350 . . .* (Washington, D.C.: GPO, 1917), p. 33. U.S. Chamber of Commerce, "Federal Trade Commission Investigation of Foreign Trade," *Bulletin No. 2* (June 10, 1915), p. 8; see also "Federal Trade Commission," *Bulletin No. 1* (May 20, 1915), and "Combination in Export Trade" and "Federal Trade Commission," in *General Bulletin No. 261* (July 21, 1916). Quotation is from Wilson to Samuel Miles Hastings, July 28, 1916, in Link et al., *The Papers of Woodrow Wilson*, 37:492–93.

24. "Wilson's Stand on Tariff: Opposed to Special Commission for Scientific Legislation," *New York Times*, September 26, 1915, replying to Cox's letter of August 24, 1915. Frank W. Taussig, "Proposal for a Tariff Commission," *North American Review* 203 (May 1916): 194–204. See also David F. Houston, *Eight Years with Wilson's Cabinet, 1913 to 1920*, 2 vols. (reprint, New York: Doubleday, 1970), 1:2, 196–97; 2:187. See also Bernhardt, *The Tariff Commission*, pp. 13–16, and Kenkel, *Progressives and Protection*, pp. 102–4.

25. Houston, *Eight Years*, 1:196–97. Cf. Kenkel, *Progressives and Protection*, pp. 113–15. On Wilson's Progressive support, see Arthur S. Link, *Woodrow Wilson and the Progressive Era, 1910–1917* (New York: Harper and Row, 1954), pp. 239–40. See also Link, *Wilson: Confusions and Crises*, pp. 341–45.

26. Wilson to Kitchin, January 24 and 26, 1916, reprinted in *New York Times*, January 27, 1916, "President Answers Criticism on Tariff." See also *New York Times*, January 26, 1916, "President Asks for Tariff Board." Wilson quotation from "President Expects America to Lead: Predicts That Nation Will Be Thrust Out into Economic Mastery," *New York Times*, February 11, 1916. Second quotation from Wilson to Samuel Miles Hastings, July 28, 1916, in Link et al., *The Papers of Woodrow Wilson*, 37:492–93. Wilson here also cited European dyestuffs dumping as a danger to U.S. postwar trade. Cf. Parrini, *Heir to Empire*, p. 214. Link phrased Wilson's decision as having "gone over to the protectionist principle" (see *Woodrow Wilson and the Progressive Era* [New York: Harper and Row, 1954], p. 229n), whereas Parrini more accurately notes Wilson's shift in the context of a broader bipartisan consensus for "open door tariffs" (chap. 8). As an example of concern over dumping, the administration was considering antidumping and unfair trade practices laws to counter an expected resurgence of the German dyestuffs industry that would threaten the development of the nascent U.S. industry, according to a *New York Times* (September 29, 1915) account of a meeting between Thomas A. Norton, the government dyestuffs and chemicals expert, Redfield, and E. E. Pratt of the BFDC.

27. Kenkel, *Progressives and Protection*, pp. 121–26.

Bibliography

Primary Sources

Personal Papers
Manuscript Division, Library of Congress, Washington, D.C.
    Nelson W. Aldrich Papers.
    Albert J. Beveridge Papers.
    Philander C. Knox Papers.
    Franklin MacVeagh Papers.
    Theodore Roosevelt Papers.
    Elihu Root Papers.
    J. C. Spooner Papers
    William H. Taft Papers.
    David A. Wells Papers.
Nicholas Murray Butler Library, Columbia University, New York
    Frank A. Vanderlip Papers.

Archival Collections of Organizations
Commerce and Labor, U.S. Department of. Record Group 40. General Records
    of the Department of Commerce, 1903–14. U.S. National Archives, Wash-
    ington, D.C.
Merchants Association of New York. Pamphlets in New York Public Library
    Pamphlet Collection.
State, U.S. Department of. Record Group 59. Numerical and Minor Files,
    1906–10; Decimal Files, 1911–12. U.S. National Archives, Washington, D.C.
Tariff Commission, U.S. Record Group 81. Records of the Tariff Board, 1909–
    12. U.S. National Archives, Washington, D.C.

U.S. Public Documents
U.S. Bureau of the Census. *Twelfth Census of the United States, 1900*. Vol. 7,
    Manufactures. Washington, D.C.: GPO, 1902.
U.S. Congress. House. Committee on Investigation of United States Steel Cor-
    poration (Stanley Committee). *Hearings*. Vol. 6, part 2, *Extracts, Minutes of the*

United States Steel Corporation and Subsidiary Companies. Washington, D.C.: GPO, 1913.

——. Committee on Ways and Means. *Customs Administrative Act—Licensing of Custom-House Brokers*. Report of Hearings, February 23–March 2, 1906. 59th Cong., 1st sess. Washington, D.C.: GPO, 1906.

——. *A Permanent Tariff Commission: Hearings before the Speaker of the House of Representatives and the Chairman of the Committee on Ways and Means*. 60th Cong., 1st sess., February 4, 1908. Washington, D.C.: GPO, 1908.

——. *Philippine Tariff, Appendix: Public Hearings in the Philippine Islands before the Secretary of War*. 59th Cong., 1st sess. Washington, D.C.: GPO, 1906.

——. Select Committee on Lobby Investigations, *Charges against Members of the House and Lobby Activities of the National Association of Manufacturers, Hearings*. 4 vols. 63d Cong., 1st sess. Washington, D.C.: GPO, 1913.

——. *Tariff Hearings, 1908–1909; Free List and Miscellaneous*. Vol. 7. Washington, D.C.: GPO, 1909.

U.S. Congress. Senate. Committee on Foreign Relations. *Hearings on Treaty with France*. 56th Cong., 1st sess., Sen. Doc. 225. Washington, D.C.: GPO, 1900.

——. Subcommittee of the Committee on the Judiciary. *Maintenance of a Lobby to Influence Legislation: Appendix. Exhibits Introduced during the Hearings*. 4 vols. 63d Cong., 1st sess. Washington, D.C.: GPO, 1913.

U.S. Department of Commerce and Labor. *Customs Tariff of the German Customs Union*. Tariff Series, no. 7. Washington, D.C.: GPO, 1908.

——. *The International Harvester Company*. Washington, D.C.: GPO, 1913.

——. *Monthly Consular and Trade Reports*. Washington, D.C.: GPO, 1905–7.

——. Bureau of Statistics. *Exports of Manufactures from the United States and Their Distribution by Articles and Countries, 1800–1906*. Washington, D.C.: GPO, 1907.

U.S. Department of State. *Foreign Relations of the United States*. Washington, D.C.: GPO, 1898–1910.

——. Introductions to "Review of the World's Commerce" [by Frederic Emory]. In *Commercial Relations of the United States*. Washington, D.C.: GPO, 1898, 1899, 1900.

——. *Tariff Negotiations between the United States and Foreign Governments*. Washington, D.C.: GPO, 1910.

U.S. Federal Trade Commission. *Cooperation in American Export Trade*. Part 1. Washington, D.C.: GPO, 1916.

——. *Food Investigation, Summary*. Washington D.C.: GPO, 1918.

——. *The Meat-Packing Industry, 1919*. Part 1. Washington, D.C.: GPO, 1919.

U.S. Industrial Commission. *Preliminary Report on Trusts and Industrial Combinations*, Vol. 1. *Testimony*. Washington, D.C.: GPO, 1900.

——. *Report*. Vol. 13. *Report of the Industrial Commission on Trusts and Industrial Combinations*. Washington, D.C.: GPO, 1901.

U.S. Tariff Board. *Cotton Manufactures*. Washington, D.C.: GPO, 1912.
————. *The Pulp and News Print Industry*. Washington, D.C.: GPO, 1911.
————. *Reciprocity with Canada*. 61st Cong., 3d sess., Sen. Doc. 849. Washington, D.C.: GPO, 1911.
————. *Wool and Manufactures of Wool*. 2 vols. Washington, D.C.: GPO, 1912.
U.S. Tariff Commission. *Colonial Tariff Policies*. Washington, D.C.: GPO, 1921.
————. *Handbook of Commercial Treaties*. Washington, D.C.: GPO, 1922.
————. *Reciprocity and Commercial Treaties*. Washington, D.C.: GPO, 1919.

Proceedings, Organization Documents, and Trade Journals
American Industries. Biweekly Newspaper of National Association of Manufacturers. 1902–13.
American Stock Growers Association. *Proceedings*. 1905.
American National Live Stock Association. *Proceedings*. 1906–11.
Annual Reports of the Chamber of Commerce of the State of New York. New York: Chamber of Commerce, 1899–1910.
Farm Machinery. Agricultural Implements Newspaper, Chicago. 1898–1910.
Merchants Association of New York. *Bulletin of the Merchants Association of New York*. 1901–10.
————. *Revision of the Customs Laws: Report of the Committee on Customs Service and the Revenue Laws*. Revised edition. New York: Merchants Association of New York, 1906.
————. *Yearbook*. 1902–4.
National Association of Agricultural Implement and Vehicle Manufacturers. *Annual Convention Proceedings*, in *Farm Machinery*, 1898–1910.
————. *Commercial Reciprocity*. Chicago: National Association of Agricultural Implement and Vehicle Manufacturers, 1901.
————. "Report of the Special Tariff Committee of the National Association of Agricultural Implement and Vehicle Manufacturers to the Executive Committee, 1906." [By H. E. Miles et al.]. Typescript in the Theodore Roosevelt Papers, Library of Congress, Washington, D.C.
National Association of Manufacturers. *Proceedings* of Annual Conventions, 1895–1912.
National Live Stock Association. *Proceedings*, 1899–1906.
National Reciprocity. Journal of the National Reciprocity League, 1902–3.
Proceedings of the National Reciprocity Conference Held under the Auspices of the National Association of Manufacturers of the United States of America. NAM Circular of Information no. 43. Philadelphia: National Association of Manufacturers, 1901.

Books, Articles, Speeches, and Collected Works
Adams, Brooks. "Commercial Future: New Struggle for Life among Nations." *Fortnightly Review* 71 (February 1899): 274–83.

———. "Reciprocity or the Alternative." *Atlantic Monthly* 88 (August 1901): 145–55.

———. "The Spanish War and the Equilibrium of the World." *Forum* 26 (August 1898): 641–51.

Aldrich, Nelson W. "Industrial Ascendancy of the United States." In *Corporations and Public Welfare*, Supplement to *Annals* 15 (May 1900): 155–68.

Arbuthnot, C. C. "The National Tariff Commission Convention." *Journal of Political Economy* 7 (April 1909): 220–27.

Armour, J. Ogden. "The Tariff and Our Foreign Trade in Meats." *Annals* 29 (May 1907): 97–101.

Atkinson, Edward. "British Manufactures and the Policy of Unfettered Commerce." *Engineering Magazine* 21 (April 1901): 1–25.

———. *The Dominion of Coal and Iron.* Prepared for submission at the Meeting of the American Association for the Advancement of Science, June 1900. Baltimore: Manufacturer's Record, 1900.

Austin, O[scar] P[helps]. "Expansion of American Commerce: Past, Present, and Prospective." Address delivered before the American Association for the Advancement of Science, at Pittsburg [*sic*], Pa., July 2, 1902. Washington: AAAS, 1902.

———. "Has the Threatened War against American Manufactures Begun?," *North American Review* 173 (November 1901): 684–93.

———. *Modern Export Trade.* New York: Business Training Corporation, 1916.

———. "Modern Tariff Systems: The Maximum and Minimum, Conventional, and General Tariff Systems of the Principal Countries of the World." In U.S. Department of Commerce and Labor, Bureau of Statistics, *Summary of Commerce and Statistics,* 1902, pp. 3095–99. Washington, D.C.: GPO, 1902.

Beveridge, Albert J. "Revision Necessary—By Commission." *Reader* 10 (November 1907): 618–20; and 11 (December 1907): 73–81.

Conant, Charles A. "The Anatomy of the New Tariff." *Review of Reviews* 16 (July–December 1897): 167–74.

———. "The Economic Basis of Imperialism." *North American Review* 167 (September 1898): 326–40.

———. "The Future of Political Parties." *Atlantic Monthly* 88 (September 1901): 365–73.

Culbertson, William S. "Equality of Treatment among Nations and a Bargaining Tariff." *Annals* 94 (March 1921): 160–75.

———. "The Tariff Board and Wool Legislation." *American Economic Review* 3 (March 1913): 59–84.

Cummings, John. "Cost of Production as a Basis for Tariff Revision." *Journal of Political Economy* 17 (March 1909): 153–57.

Depew, Chauncey M., ed. *One Hundred Years of American Commerce.* New York: D. O. Haynes, 1895.

Dietzel, H[einrich]. "The German Tariff Controversy." *Quarterly Journal of Economics* 17 (May 1903): 365–416.

Downing, Thomas. *Customs Administrative Features of the Aldrich Tariff Bill: A Report to the MANY by Its Committee on Customs Service and Revenue Laws, June 8, 1909.* New York: Merchants Association, 1909.

Emery, Henry C. "The Best Way to Work for Tariff Revision." Speech before the American Economic Association, December 1908, *American Economic Association Quarterly*, 3d ser., 10 (April 1909): 287–99.

———. "Economic Investigation as a Basis for Tariff Legislation." *American Economic Review, Supplement* 2 (March 1912): 19–25.

———. "The Plans of the Tariff Board." *New York Times Annual Financial Review*, January 8, 1911, p. 16.

———. "The Tariff and Foreign Trade." In *Official Report of the National Foreign Trade Convention*, May 27 and 28, 1914, pp. 258–73. New York: National Foreign Trade Council, 1914.

———. *The Tariff Board and Its Work.* Washington, D.C.: GPO, 1910.

Fisk, George M. *Continental Opinion regarding a Proposed Middle European Tariff Union.* Baltimore: Johns Hopkins Press, 1902.

———. "The Payne-Aldrich Tariff." *Political Science Quarterly* 25 (March 1910): 35–68.

Ford, Worthington C. "Commercial Superiority of the United States." *North American Review* 166 (January 1898): 76–84.

———. "The Turning of the Tide." *North American Review* 161 (August 1895): 187–95.

Jenks, Jeremiah W. "The Economic Outlook." Review of *Recent Economic Changes*, by David A. Wells. *Dial* 10 (January 1890): 252–54.

Johnson, Alvin S. "Protection and the Formation of Capital." *Political Science Quarterly* 23 (1908). Reprinted in *Essays in Social Economics*, pp. 120–41. New York: New School, 1952.

Jones, Chester Lloyd. "The American Interpretation of the 'Most Favored Nation' Clause." *Annals* 32 (September 1908): 119–29.

La Follette, Robert M. *La Follette's Autobiography.* Madison, Wis.: Privately printed, 1913.

Laughlin, James Laurence. "The Tariff Commission and Its Problems." *New York Times Annual Financial Review*, January 8, 1911, p. 17.

Laughlin, James Laurence, and H. Parker Willis. *Reciprocity.* New York: Baker and Taylor, 1903.

Leroy-Beaulieu, Paul. "Conditions for American Commercial and Financial Supremacy." *Forum* 20 (December 1895): 385–400.

Miles, H. E. "How the Tariff Affects My Business." *American Industries* 6 (November 15, 1907).

———. "Tariff Revision from the Manufacturer's Standpoint." *Popular Science Monthly* 74 (May 1909): 450–56.

———. "Why Manufacturers Want Tariff Revision." *North American Review* 187 (January 1908): 34–45.

Miller, C. R. "The Next Steps in Tariff Reform." In *Corporations and Public Welfare*, Supplement to *Annals* 15 (May 1900): 187–99.

North, S[imon] N[ewton] D[exter]. *The Need for a Permanent Tariff Commission*. Boston: Rockwell and Churchill, 1902.

———. "The Tariff and the Export Trade of the United States." *Annals* 23 (January 1904): 1–11.

Osborne, John Ball. "Our New Commercial Pact with Germany." *Harper's Weekly* 51 (September 14, 1907): 1338, 1358.

Parry, David M. "Reciprocity and the Middle West." *Annals* 29 (May 1907): 22–25.

Parsons, James G. *Protection's Favors to Foreigners*. New York: Reform Club, 1909. Reprinted, 61st Cong., 1st sess., Sen. Doc. 54. Washington, D.C.: GPO, 1909.

Porter, Robert P. "The Tariff Policy of Our New Possessions." In *Corporations and Public Welfare*, Supplement to *Annals* 15 (May 1900): 171–84.

Powers, H. H. "Expansion and Protection." *Quarterly Journal of Economics* 13 (July 1899): 361–78.

———. "The War as a Suggestion of Manifest Destiny." *Annals* 12 (September 1898): 185–86.

Reinsch, Paul S. *Colonial Administration*. New York: Macmillan, 1905.

———. "The New Conquest of the World." *World's Work* 1 (February 1901): 425–31.

———. *World Politics at the End of the Nineteenth Century*. New York: Macmillan, 1900.

Reynolds, James B. "The Tariff Commission Plan: Its Facts and Fallacies." *North American Review* 203 (June 1916): 852–66.

Richardson, James D., ed. *A Compilation of the Messages and Papers of the Presidents*. Vols. 13–15. New York: Bureau of National Literature, 1917.

Roberts, George E. "The Origin and History of the Iowa Idea." *Iowa Journal of History and Politics* 2 (January 1904): 69–82.

Robinson, E. V. "Tariff Legislation—Discussion." *American Economic Review, Supplement* 2 (March 1912): 37–41.

Root, Elihu. "Development of the Foreign Trade of the United States." *Annals* 29 (May 1907): 1–9.

Schierbrand, Wolf Von. "Our Tariff Differences with Germany." *Review of Reviews* 32 (August 1905): 205–7.

Shaw, Leslie Mortier. *Current Issues*. New York: D. Appleton, 1908.

Springer, William M. *Tariff Reform the Paramount Issue: Speeches and Writings on the Questions Involved in the Presidential Contest of 1892*. New York: C. L. Webster and Co., 1892.

Stone, N. I. "Dual Tariff Systems." *American Economic Association Quarterly*, 3d ser., 10 (April 1909): 301–13.

———. "How the Germans Revised Their Tariff." *Review of Reviews* 32 (December 1905): 719–21.

———. "The International Aspect of Our Tariff Situation." *North American Review* 180 (March 1905): 381–93.

———. "Is a Tariff Commission Necessary?," *American Industries* 6 (December 1, 1907): 29–30.

———. "Most-Favored-Nation Relations between Germany and the United States." *North American Review* 182 (March 1906): 433–45.

———. "The New German Customs Tariff." *North American Review* 181 (September 1905): 392–406.

Taussig, Frank W. "The Report of the Tariff Board on Wools and Woolens." *American Economic Review* 2 (June 1912): 257–68.

———. "The Tariff and the Tariff Commission." *Atlantic Monthly* (December 1910): 721–29.

———. *Tariff History of the United States*. 6th ed. New York: G. P. Putnam's Sons, 1913.

Towne, Henry R. *The Neutral Line*. New York: Merchants Association, 1909.

Towne, Henry R., W. A. Marble, and Charles R. Lamb. "Report of the Merchants Association Delegates to the Reciprocity Convention." *Merchants Association Bulletin* 1 (December 1901): 2–3.

Vanderlip, Frank A. *The American Commercial Invasion of Europe*. New York: National City Bank, 1902.

Weld, L. D. H. "'Costs' and the Tariff Board." *Journal of Political Economy* 20 (May 1912): 492–508.

Wells, David A. "The Creed of Free Trade." *Atlantic Monthly* 36 (August 1874): 204–20.

Willis, H. Parker. "'Costs' and Tariff Revision." *Journal of Political Economy* 19 (May 1911): 361–84.

———. Economic Investigation as a Basis for Tariff Legislation." *American Economic Review, Supplement* 2 (March 1912): 26–36.

———. "Reciprocity with Germany, I." *Journal of Political Economy* 15 (June 1907): 321–44.

———. "Reciprocity with Germany, II." *Journal of Political Economy* 15 (July 1907): 385–97.

Wilson, William L. "The Principle and Method of the New Tariff Bill." *Forum* 16 (January 1894): 544–46.

———. "The Tariff." Speech, in *Congressional Record*, 53d Cong., 2d sess., vol. 26, app. 1, pp. 193–98.

Secondary Sources

Books

Baker, Richard Cleveland. *The Tariff under Roosevelt and Taft*. Hastings, Neb.: Democrat Printing Company, 1941.

Beard, Charles A., and Mary R. Beard. *The Rise of American Civilization*. 2 vols. New York: Macmillan, 1930.

Becker, William H. *The Dynamics of Business-Government Relations: Industry and Exports, 1893–1921*. Chicago: University of Chicago Press, 1982.

Berglund, Abraham, and Philip G. Wright. *The Tariff on Iron and Steel*. Washington, D.C.: Brookings Institution, 1929.

Bernhardt, Joshua. *The Tariff Commission: Its History, Activities, and Organization*. Institute for Government Research Service Monographs, no. 5. New York: D. Appleton, 1922.

Braeman, John. *Albert J. Beveridge: American Nationalist*. Chicago: University of Chicago Press, 1971.

Bray, Thomas James. *The Rebirth of Freedom*. Indianola, Iowa: Record and Tribune Press, 1957.

Brewer, Anthony. *Marxist Theories of Imperialism*. London: Routledge and Kegan Paul, 1980.

Clark, Champ. *My Quarter Century of American Politics*. New York: Scribner's, 1920.

Edminster, Lynn R. *The Cattle Industry and the Tariff*. New York: Macmillan, 1926.

Ellis, L. Ethan. *Reciprocity 1911*. Washington, D.C.: Carnegie Endowment, 1939.

Etherington, Norman. *Theories of Imperialism: War, Conquest, and Capital*. London: Croom Helm, 1984.

Faulkner, Harold U. *American Economic History*. 8th edition. New York: Harper Bros., 1960.

Furner, Mary O. *Advocacy and Objectivity*. Lexington: University of Kentucky Press, 1975.

Gwinn, William Rea. *Uncle Joe Cannon, Archfoe of Insurgency*. N.p.: Bookman Associates, 1957.

Hechler, Kenneth. *Insurgency: Personalities and Politics of the Taft Era*. 1940. Reprint, New York: AMS Press, 1970.

Hessen, Robert. *Steel Titan: The Life of Charles M. Schwab*. New York: Oxford University Press, 1975.

Hoffman, Ross J. S. *Great Britain and the German Trade Rivalry, 1875–1914*. Philadelphia: University of Pennsylvania Press, 1933.

Hogan, William T. *The Economic History of the Iron and Steel Industry in the United States*. 2 vols. Lexington, Mass.: D.C. Heath, 1971.

Johnson, Emory R., T. W. Van Metre, G. G. Huebner, and D. S. Hanchett. *History of the Domestic and Foreign Commerce of the United States*. 2 vols. Washington, D.C.: Carnegie Institute of Washington, 1915.

Kenkel, Joseph F. *Progressives and Protection*. Washington, D.C.: University Press of America, 1983.

LaFeber, Walter. *The New Empire: An Interpretation of American Expansion, 1860–1898*. Ithaca, N.Y.: Cornell University Press, 1963.

Livingston, James. *Origins of the Federal Reserve System: Money, Class, and Corporate Capitalism*. Ithaca, N.Y.: Cornell University Press, 1986.

McCormick, Thomas J. *China Market: America's Quest for Informal Empire, 1893–1901*. Chicago: Quadrangle, 1967.

Parrini, Carl P. *Heir to Empire: United States Economic Diplomacy, 1916–1923*. Pittsburgh: University of Pittsburgh Press, 1969.

Perloff, Harvey S. *Regions, Resources, and Economic Growth*. Baltimore: Johns Hopkins Press, for Resources for the Future, 1960.

Pletcher, David M. *The Awkward Years: American Foreign Relations under Garfield and Arthur*. Columbia: University of Missouri Press, 1962.

Porter, Kirk H., and Donald Bruce Johnson. *National Party Platforms, 1840–1968*. Urbana: University of Illinois Press, 1970.

Pringle, Henry F. *The Life and Times of William Howard Taft*. 2 vols. New York: Farrar and Rinehart, 1939.

Sharkey, Robert P. *Money, Class, and Party: An Economic Study of Civil War and Reconstruction*. Baltimore: Johns Hopkins Paperback Editions, 1967.

Sklar, Martin J. *The Corporate Reconstruction of American Capitalism, 1890–1916: The Market, The Law, and Politics*. New York: Cambridge University Press, 1988.

Stanwood, Edward. *American Tariff Controversies in the Nineteenth Century*. Boston: Houghton Mifflin, 1903.

Steigerwalt, Albert K. *The National Association of Manufacturers, 1895–1914: A Study in Business Leadership*. Ann Arbor: University of Michigan Press, 1964.

Stephenson, Nathaniel. *Nelson W. Aldrich*. New York: Scribner's, 1930.

Stern, Carl W[ilhelm]. *Importing: With Special Attention to Customs Requirements*. New York: Business Training Corporation, 1916.

Stone, N. I. *One Man's Crusade for an Honest Tariff: The Story of H. E. Miles, Father of the Tariff Commission*. Appleton, Wis.: Lawrence College Press, 1952.

Terrill, Tom E. *The Tariff, Politics, and American Foreign Policy, 1874–1901*. Westport, Conn.: Greenwood Press, 1973.

Unger, Irwin. *The Greenback Era: A Social and Political History of American Finance, 1865–1879*. Princeton, N.J.: Princeton University Press, 1964.

Viner, Jacob. *Dumping: A Problem in International Trade*. 1929. Reprint, New York: A. M. Kelly, 1966.

Weinstein, James. *The Corporate Ideal in the Liberal State, 1900–1918*. Boston: Beacon Press, 1968.

Wiebe, Robert H. *Businessmen and Reform: A Study of the Progressive Movement*. Cambridge, Mass.: Harvard University Press, 1962.

Wilkins, Mira. *The Emergence of Multinational Enterprise: American Business Abroad from the Colonial Era to 1914*. Cambridge, Mass.: Harvard University Press, 1970.

Williams, William Appleman. *The Contours of American History*. New York: Quadrangle, 1961.

———. *The Roots of the Modern American Empire: A Study of the Growth and Shaping of Social Consciousness in a Marketplace Society*. New York: Random House, 1969.

———. *The Tragedy of American Diplomacy*. New York: Delta, 1962.

Williamson, Harold F. *Edward Atkinson: Biography of an American Liberal 1827– 1905*. Cambridge, Mass.: Riverside Press, 1934; Arno Press, 1972.

Wills, Henry Tarleton. *Scientific Tariff Making: A History of the Movement to Create a Tariff Commission*. New York: Blanchard Press, 1913.

Yeager, Mary. *Competition and Regulation: The Development of Oligopoly in the Meat Packing Industry*. Greenwich, Conn.: JAI Press, 1981.

Younger, Edward L. *John A. Kasson: Politics and Diplomacy from Lincoln to McKinley*. Iowa City: State Historical Society of Iowa, 1955.

Articles

Burch, Philip H., Jr., "The NAM as an Interest Group." *Politics and Society* 4 (Fall 1973): 97–130.

Burnham, Walter D. "Party Systems and the Political Process." In *The American Party Systems: Stages of Political Development*, ed. W. D. Burnham and W. N. Chambers. New York: Oxford University Press, 1967.

———. "The System of 1896: An Analysis." In *The Evolution of American Electoral Systems*, by Paul Kleppner et al. Westport, Conn.: Greenwood Press, 1981.

Chandler, Alfred D. "The Beginnings of 'Big Business' in American Industry." *Business History Review* 33 (Spring 1959): 1–31.

Claire, Guy Shirk. "Reciprocity as a Trade Policy of the United States." *Annals* 141 (January 1929).

Coben, Stanley. "Northeastern Business and Radical Reconstruction: A Reexamination." *Mississippi Valley Historical Review* 46 (June 1959).

Ferguson, Thomas. "Party Realignment and American Industrial Structure: The Investment Theory of Political Parties in Historical Perspective." *Research in Political Economy* 6 (1983): 1–82.

Gallagher, John, and Ronald Robinson. "The Imperialism of Free Trade." *Economic History Review*, 2d ser., 1 (1953): 1–15.

Hannigan, Robert E. "Reciprocity 1911: Continentalism and American Weltpolitik." *Diplomatic History* 4 (Winter 1980): 1–18.

Kaufman, Burton I. "The Organizational Dimension of United States Economic Foreign Policy, 1900–1920." *Business History Review* 46 (Spring 1972): 17–44.

Kramer, Helen M. "Harvesters and High Finance: Formation of the International Harvester Company." *Business History Review* 38 (Autumn 1964): 283– 301.

Lake, David A. "International Economic Structures and American Foreign Economic Policy, 1887–1934." *World Politics* 35 (July 1983): 517–43.

Milward, Alan. "Tariffs as Constitutions." In *The International Politics of Surplus Capacity*, ed. Susan Strange and Roger Tooze, pp. 57–66. London: George Allen and Unwin, 1981.

Novack, David E., and Matthew Simon. "Commercial Responses to the American Export Invasion, 1871–1914: An Essay in Attitudinal History." *Explorations in Entrepreneurial History*, 2d ser., 3 (Winter 1966): 121–47.

Parrini, Carl P. "Theories of Imperialism." In *Redefining the Past: Essays in Diplomatic History in Honor of William Appleman Williams*, ed. Lloyd C. Gardner. Corvallis: Oregon State University Press, 1986.

Parrini, Carl P., and Martin J. Sklar. "New Thinking about the Market, 1896–1904: Some American Economists on Investment and the Theory of Surplus Capital." *Journal of Economic History* 48 (June 1983): 559–78.

Platt, D. C. M. "Economic Factors in the New Imperialism." *Past and Present* 39 (1968): 120–38.

Rosenberg, Emily S. "Foundations of United States International Financial Power: Gold Standard Diplomacy, 1900–1905." *Business History Review* 59 (Summer 1985): 169–202.

Rothstein, Morton. "America in the International Rivalry for the British Wheat Market, 1860–1914." *Mississippi Valley Historical Review* 47 (December 1960): 401–18.

———. "The International Market for Agricultural Commodities, 1850–1873." In *Economic Change in the Civil War Era*, ed. David T. Gilchrist and W. David Lewis. Greenville, Del.: Eleutherian Mills-Hagley Foundation, 1965.

Scheinberg, Stephen. "Invitation to Empire: Tariffs and American Economic Expansion in Canada." *Business History Review* 47 (Summer 1978): 218–38.

Sklar, Martin J. "The N.A.M. and Foreign Markets on the Eve of the Spanish-American War." *Science and Society* 23 (1959): 133–62.

———. "Periodization and Historiography: The Corporate Reconstruction of American Society, 1896–1914." Paper presented at the annual meeting of the Organization of American Historians, Los Angeles, April 1984.

———. "Woodrow Wilson and the Political Economy of Modern United States Liberalism." *Studies on the Left* 1 (Fall 1960): 17–47.

Solvick, Stanley R. "William Howard Taft and the Payne-Aldrich Tariff." *Mississippi Valley Historical Review* 50 (December 1963): 424–25.

Terrill, Tom E. "David A. Wells, the Democracy and Tariff Reduction, 1877–1894." *Journal of American History* 56 (December 1969): 540–55.

Wehler, Hans-Ulrich. "Bismarck's Imperialism, 1862–1890." *Past and Present* 48 (August 1970): 128–33.

Williams, William Appleman. "Brooks Adams and American Expansion." *New England Quarterly* 25 (June 1952): 217–32.

Williamson, Jeffrey G. "Late Nineteenth Century American Retardation: A Neo-classical Analysis." *Journal of Economic History* 33 (September 1973): 581–607.

Dissertations

Govan, James F. "Union and Strength: The Political Program of the Tariff Reformers, 1903–1913." Ph.D. dissertation, Johns Hopkins University, 1960.

Harvey, Walter Bennett. "Tariffs and International Relations in Europe, 1860–1914." Ph.D. dissertation, University of Chicago, 1938.

Queen, George W. "The United States and the Material Advance in Russia, 1881–1906." Ph.D. dissertation, University of Illinois, 1941.

Index